The Digital Media Handbook

The Digital Media Handbook is an essential guide to the historical and theoretical development of digital media, emphasising cultural continuity alongside technological change, and highlighting the emergence of new forms of communication in contemporary networked culture.

Andrew Dewdney and Peter Ride present detailed critical commentary and descriptive historical accounts, as well as a series of interviews from a range of digital media practitioners, including producers, developers, curators and artists.

The Digital Media Handbook highlights key concerns of today's practitioners, analysing how they develop projects, interact and solve problems within the context of networked communication.

This book is a substantially revised edition of *The New Media Handbook* by the authors, with new content and entirely new case studies, including:

- new chapters on networks and convergent media
- essays on the history and theory of digital media
- essays on contemporary issues and debates
- interviews with digital media professionals
- a glossary of technical acronyms and key terms.

Andrew Dewdney is a Professor of Educational Development at London South Bank University, UK, where he teaches about digital media in network culture and is the Principal Investigator of the Digital Art Gallery Programme. He has a particular research interest in the impact of digital media upon museums, and his recently co-authored book, *Post Critical Museology: Theory and Practice in the Art Museum*, was published by Routledge in 2013.

Peter Ride is Principal Research Fellow at the University of Westminster, UK, where he is Course Leader in the MA Museums, Galleries and Contemporary Culture. He works in the field of digital and visual culture. He is also a digital media and art curator and was previously the Artistic Director of The Digital Arts Development Agency (DA2).

MEDIA PRACTICE

Edited by James Curran, *Goldsmiths College, University of London*

The *Media Practice* handbooks are comprehensive resource books for students of media and journalism, and for anyone planning a career as a media professional. Each handbook combines a clear introduction to understanding how the media work, with practical information about the structure, processes and skills involved in working in today's media industries, providing not only a guide on 'how to do it' but also a critical reflection on contemporary media practice.

The Digital Media Handbook

Second edition

Andrew Dewdney
and Peter Ride

Routledge
Taylor & Francis Group

LONDON AND NEW YORK

Second edition published 2014
by Routledge
2 Park Square, Milton Park, Abingdon, Oxon OX14 4RN

and by Routledge
711 Third Avenue, New York, NY 10017

Routledge is an imprint of the Taylor & Francis Group, an informa business

© 2006, 2014 Andrew Dewdney and Peter Ride

First edition, *The New Media Handbook*, published by Routledge 2006.

British Library Cataloguing in Publication Data
A catalogue record for this book is available from the British Library

Library of Congress Cataloging in Publication Data
An application for CIP data has been submitted to the Library of Congress

ISBN: 978-0-415-69989-1 (hbk)
ISBN: 978-0-415-69991-4 (pbk)
ISBN: 978-0-203-06694-2 (ebk)

Typeset in Helvetica Neue and Avant Garde
by Florence Production Ltd, Stoodleigh, Devon, UK

MIX
Paper from
responsible sources
FSC® C013056
www.fsc.org

Printed and bound in Great Britain by
TJ International Ltd, Padstow, Cornwall

Contents

Illustrations

CHAPTER CASE STUDIES

ILLUSTRATED CASE STUDIES

1 Social networks and geopolitics: Jon Thomson and Alison Craighead, *October*

2 Augmented reality: Pure Land: using augmented reality for museums and heritage

3 Data tagging: *Tales of Things*

4 Visualising data: Maurice Benayoun, *Mechanics of Emotions*

5 3-D modelling as portraiture: *Susan Sloan, Studies in Stillness: Motion Capture Portraits*

6 Crowdsourcing and the London 2012 Olympic Games

TABLES

Interviewees

Matt Adams, Blast Theory, artist group
www.blasttheory.co.uk

Frank Boyd, Director of the Creative Industries Knowledge Transfer Network UK
connect.innovateuk.org/web/creativektn

Andrew Chetty, Production Director of ditto communications agency and consultancy
www.ditto.tv

Jane Finnis, Chief Executive of Culture24, culture sector networking organisation
www.culture24.org.uk

Matt Locke, Director of Storythings, consultancy and creative production company
www.storythings.com

Jane Prophet, artist and co-producer of *TechnoSphere*
www.janeprophet.com

Richard Sedley, Director of Design of Seren, customer experience consultancy
www.seren.com

Katrina Sluis, Curator of the Digital Programme at The Photographers' Gallery, London
www.thephotographersgallery.org.uk

John Stack, Head of Tate Online at Tate, art museum
www.tate.org.uk

Maria Stukoff, Head of Academic Game Development for Sony Computer Entertainment Europe
www.ukplaystation.com

Rainer Usselmann, Director of Happyfinish, creative production and post-production agency
www.happyfinish.co.uk

Acknowledgements

We would like to acknowledge the help and support of the following people, without whom this project would have been even harder than it was to keep on track.

PETER

I would like to thank the all interviewees for their significant participation and advice on this project, my colleagues at the University of Westminster and my partner Ian Iqbal Rashid for his constant support and enthusiasm.

ANDREW

I would like to thank my undergraduate students at London South Bank who have engaged so positively and with healthy scepticism to the two courses I teach, New Media and Digital Arts and Critical Cultures. I would also like to acknowledge my indebtedness to Katrina Sluis and Daniel Rubinstein, who shared the office next to mine in Borough Road and without whose sustained, critical and scholarly conversation about all things digital my task would have been immeasurably less interesting. My gratitude to Catherine as always, to Alice and Max, who provide a compelling motivation for life, and now to their children, Oscar, Thea and Astrid, who have given me a new event horizon.

CHAPTER 1

Introduction

WHAT KIND OF BOOK IS THIS?

This is one of a number of books in a series of handbooks produced by Routledge for students of the arts, media, cultural studies and social sciences and for anyone wanting to work professionally in media. The series, started in the 1990s, has its roots in the expansion of media courses in schools, colleges and universities, which were reflecting the growing importance of media in culture and society. Some of the original titles in the series have run to several editions, while new titles are still being added as the professional and intellectual world of **digital** media continues to expand. Existing handbook titles reflect an historical organisation of mainstream media, such as newspapers, radio, advertising, television, photography, magazines and public relations. *The Cyberspace Handbook*, published in 2004, indicates the way things were moving and *The Social Media Handbook* (2013), reflects the most recent developments.

This is a new edition of what started its published life in 2006 as *The New Media Handbook*, and the change of title to *The Digital Media Handbook* is an indication of how the practices of professional media production continue to change and the need to update the account. The book contains a completely new set of interviews and discussions with ten professionals reflecting upon their practices and illustrated case studies of creative projects, together with a series of new and revised essays discussing the historic, theoretical and current state of the field.

Digital media is highly susceptible to fashionable preoccupations with the latest technological innovation, and the past decade is no exception. Attention has shifted from wireless and streaming to cloud computing and crowd sourcing as the new and latest developments that characterise the medium. Critical commentary has also shifted gear, from seeing the Internet as a new dawn of creative freedom, to seeing the Internet as a system of exploitation and control. This book discusses both of these shifts, and it does this because it takes a wider view of what constitutes digital media and emphasises the longer history of technological change in media. The case studies in this book will give the reader a vivid picture of contemporary concerns of professionals at the forefront of their field, while the essay chapters provide a broad framework for considering the continuing development of the study of digital media.

The style and approach across the series is different, with no imposed house style, but the books have a common aim, which is to articulate what is involved in the professional practice of contemporary media. To paraphrase the series editor, James Curran, the aim of the series is to provide comprehensive resource books that are something between a 'how-to-do-it' manual and a critical reflection of contemporary media. In the case of digital media this is no easy task because, as the reader will soon discover, digital media is, by its very nature, a hybrid practice involving a wide range of practical skills and intellectual resources as well as numerous competing critical commentaries. We have chosen to grapple with the essential diversity of our subject by combining critical commentary, descriptive and historical accounts with a series of case studies of professional digital media practitioners operating in the convergent media environment. In doing this we hope that we provide a sufficiently broad selection of material to construct a kind of provisional and updated 'map' of some of the established and emergent 'territories' of convergent media practice.

The change of title from *The New Media Handbook* to *The Digital Media Handbook* has been made in consultation with the publishers, as part of revising the book. The interesting and exciting aspect of this process has been in striking a balance between the old and new account in deciding what to retain, what to reject and what to add. It is clear to us in surveying the current landscape that certain kinds of digital media have persisted and been built upon, while newer practices, very much associated with networked and converging media, have emerged. As far as titles go, the term 'new media' still has currency, but as we said in the first edition, there is a problem with just how long something can be 'new', and the past seven years have shown the degree to which all media production now operates in the converged digital environment of computing. We still think there is a degree of interchangeability as well as distinction between the terms **new media** and **digital media**, which is discussed further on in this introductory section. The important point to bear in mind is that the organising approach and distinct contribution of this volume is to discuss digital media from the perspective and needs of professional practitioners and, above all, to remember that the current period of **hybridity** and **convergence** inevitably characterises a set of practices that continue to evolve under fluid conditions. There is no reason to suppose that the enormous changes of even the last decade will be followed by any fewer over the next decade.

Currently, 'networked media', 'online media', and 'social media' have come to the fore as specific extensions of digital media. The naming of these areas of media practice is both a practically informative matter as well as being culturally coded. The aspirational language associated with the early development of the Internet, which spoke of 'uncharted space' and 'new frontiers', has given way to both a new pragmatism about the Internet, on the one hand, – yes, the Internet is a real network of connections between computers – and, on the other hand, the term network is now used to signal the idea of social connectedness. Being networked and being online carries a sense of presentness and connectedness through the metaphor of spatial extension. The retention of a spatial or geometric metaphor in defining media as a network shows just how hard it is to think about the network of computers as a list of files or a mathematical equation, for example. The intangibility of data, stored and transmitted electronically through microchip technology, is harder to grasp than the spatial conjuring of networks. The metaphoric account of digital media helps us to understand what we think about our media and how we imagine its shape and future direction. In uncovering the roots and sources for the spatialisation of human computer interaction, the book draws upon a number of academic disciplines, most notably cultural and media studies.

Handbooks and guides have to be useful. The comparison with travel guides springs to mind here. Imagine that you are on a journey in a place unknown to you and you need to orientate yourself to the people, place and culture. In this place you need to get your bearings and find somewhere to stay. There are many ways in which you could set about doing these things, but a guidebook is a good starting point. It is a feature of the moment we are in, and one we examine throughout this book, that more and more people are travelling both in the real world and in cyberspace and with this using the Internet rather than guide books to plan travel in the real world. The exponential expansion of the use of the Internet is not, however, making the printed book redundant, only changing the way we use books. This book is designed to help you find your way around an emergent subject and a set of complex, convergent digital media practices. It will, we hope, show the main contours of the subject, locate the main centres of interest and even chart many of the routes and connections between them. Like all guides and maps, it is important to recognise that this book constructs an order upon its landscape, which is inescapably partial and selective. The guide comes with its own built-in perspective. Inevitably it has its omissions and in relationship to the emerging field, it will have uncharted territories. This is only to be expected in a period of unfolding technological development and continuous extensions in media practice. The mapping task is like trying to represent something that is in a state of flux, possibly like attempting to map the surface of the sea, for which, interestingly enough, computer architectures are good at simulating. The map provided in this book contains conceptual definitions, accounts of technologies and a selection of cultural practices based upon digital media. The book is thankfully not the first attempt to do this, since digital media is already being studied from a variety of different viewpoints and disciplines. We start the book by identifying some of the different ways in which digital media has been charted by media professionals and academics over the last decade.

Any book with the words digital and media in its title runs the risk of being thought of primarily as either as a book about technology, or a book about commerce and industry. While the book touches upon and discusses both technology and the industries of media it is in essence about neither of these things, but rather about what people do with technologies in creative environments and is therefore about the possibilities for and realisation of human thinking, feeling and communication in the still emerging medium of computing. The significance of the digital for us here lies in identifying ideas, feelings and experiences that are and can be grasped and understood through the new digital medium in different and challenging ways. In this process individual or social communication is bound to occur, such that new insights and discoveries about ourselves and the world take place. This is a definition of the digital media that emphasises the creative, social and cultural significance of change, a process that can also be defined as a **paradigm** shift in modes of thinking.

In adopting this view we have found that we also need to provide an understanding of the historical and theoretical development of digital media that emphasises the complex continuities in the technological developments associated with particular cultural uses of media, rather than understanding digital media as replacing what has gone before. The book is organised around a set of creative practices in digital media as a direct consequence of attempting to understand digital media as embedded in concrete cultural developments.

The invention of the printing press in Europe from the 1450s led to the rapid and widespread development of print culture. The spread of print media was the basis of new forms of reading and writing and the general diffusion of knowledge in a continuous process over the next 500 years. In the twenty-first century, long after print media could be considered in any way new, it continues to be a major means for the communication of thought, feeling and experience. While this book was produced with the use of computers, researched, written, edited, designed and laid-out on screen, its form is still words printed in black ink on bleached paper on pages in a fixed order and bound together with glue. Academic publishers still make their living from selling books, although increasingly also by selling their electronic ebook equivalent. Reading from screens in addition to pages of printed books has increased dramatically over the last decade as smaller and lighter portable computers with longer battery time have been designed specifically for downloading text, such as the Kindle, or for downloading image and text, with the Apple iPad and other PC tablets. Academics and teachers know that today's busy, cash strapped students do not want to have to buy large quantities of course books nor spend long uninterrupted periods of time reading. Given an A-Level or undergraduate assessment essay on the topic of digital media, the majority of students will use online sources for their writing. The old medium of the printed book now continues in a world in which more and more knowledge is stored as data, transferred and accessed electronically. In this world the book remains an important organising tool for thinking, while not for storage or transmission. Culturally, reading and writing cross and re-cross the old and new forms of printed page and screen. This crossing of boundaries and the convergence of forms is the territory we explore.

OUR APPROACH

Within the approach outlined above, we can identify three things that mark this book out from the growing literature on the subject of digital media. First, it looks at digital media from the point of view of the practitioner. By this we mean that the book is organised around digital media artefacts, their producers and production. It aims to stay close to the many issues that beset the digital media producer, half of which are about making machines do what you want them to do and the other half about wondering why you are trying to do it in the first place. Digital media practitioners worry away, alternately, about getting the technical detail right or whether they should be spending half their life in front of a computer screen. This is why so many digital media art projects in particular have had technology written into their content.

Second, the book looks at the practitioner as primarily a creative, rather than technical person. We are not writing a computer or software manual and this is not a 'how to do it', but more a 'how to think it' guide. The book's interest in hardware and software is from the point of view of how they are used creatively. This means looking at what people are doing with technologies as well as how they understand what they are doing. In this respect the case studies and examples often privilege the position of the creative producer working in specific cultural and institution contexts. The case studies and examples are equally drawn from people working outside of the corporate mainstream of digital media commerce and within it. We focus upon a range of independent practitioners because they illustrate many of the wider understandings and problems we discuss about what is characteristic about digital media practice. The fact that we have often chosen to examine the work of people based in contemporary cultural contexts, rather than in science or commerce, is again because we consider that their projects illustrate the links between ideas, forms and audiences. Many of our cases studies point up the collaborative nature of the practice of digital media and interestingly points to the fact that people collaborate across different specialisations.

EDUCATION AND TRAINING

Because of this particular approach to digital media practice the book discusses at many points the meaning of that much used and abused term creativity and its relationship to intellectual and craft skills. Traditionally, the training of media arts practitioners was carried out 'on-the-job', so to speak, which involved a lot of watching and copying what other trained people did. This watching and copying was the way in which knowledge, skills and techniques necessary to production were acquired, in the process of doing, rather than being formally taught. At the height of analogue broadcast and print media, up until the end of the 1970s, media training was organised under a system of apprenticeships. Apprenticeships had a much longer history as a system of craft and industrial training in which the necessary knowledge and skills of a practice were passed-on. Such training was done as an inseparable part of the process of production. Today the widespread formal apprenticeship system has gone and has been replaced by education and training programmes, which take place at a distance from the production process, mostly in colleges. The apprentice, working alongside the 'craftsman' or skilled operator in the production process, learned by copying and doing. The apprentice would know that something had been done the right way and was of a high standard, as the artefact was produced and approved by those who were already trained. On-the-job training still takes place, but in more casual and, importantly, more short-term ways. Changes in the social organisation of industrial and commercial training reflect the global restructuring of industrial production. Today products are no longer produced all in one place (the vertical factory system); they require shorter and shorter turn-around-time in consumer markets, and involve ever greater levels of automation brought about by the introduction of new technologies.

When considering the training and education of a digital media practitioner, we still have to take into account a differentiation of knowledge and skills in the production process itself. One of the biggest distinctions in conventional media production is that between so-called 'creatives' and technicians. The production of media is still organised under a system in which labour is divided into separate specialist tasks. The system of media training reflects this division of labour in different ways. There is first and foremost a primary distinction between those who develop and define the content of programming and those who put programmes together. The first group (content providers) including writers, producers and directors, are deemed to be the creatives, and the second group, the film and studio crews who operate the equipment of production and post-production, are deemed to be technicians. Within each of these groups production is refined into further specialisations that reflect either the degree of technical or creative complexity, the differences between front-end and back-end programming for instance.

In contrast to the divisions of labour that operate in the industrial and commercial production of media, the production of art is conceived of as a holistic process under the direction and control of the artist. Novels, poetry, plays, music and works of visual art are still largely the products of individual creators, even if groups are then needed to technically produce or perform them. In most of these art forms it is assumed that the artist both conceives of the work and has the personal skills to produce the artefact itself. Even when an art form requires technical assistance – for example, the large scale public sculpture that needs industrial production techniques and is factory produced – the resulting work is valued and understood as that of the artist, rather than the result of a team of people.

How these different traditions and divisions of production relate to digital media is a question this book continually considers, partly because digital media practice is continuous with existing art and media practices and partly because at points it has a new and challenging organisation. What is clear is that digital media represents a convergence of previously distinct communication forms in which skills and practices overlap and boundaries between previously distinct operations of production blur. This convergence leads to greater team working and collaborative approaches, which require a creative **synergy** between people working together.

CREATIVITY

The other issue arising from our discussion of creativity relates to the conceptual and imaginative dimension of the production process. Where do creative ideas come from would be a practical question here. For the new student of digital media to be told something they have done is, or is not, a creative solution, can be a complete mystery. What is considered creative in practice at any one time can follow fashion as much as it can a more enduring set of rules. Creativity can also be as much about breaking rules as it can be about following them. The approach we explore in this book is to think of creativity not as an inherent property of either an object/artefact, nor as an exclusive quality of the producer/artist. Instead we define creativity as a given set of common values in a process of communication, which involves not only the artist and their product, but also those who listen, see, read and appreciate what has been made. We go on to say that it is important to consider what creativity in digital media entails and where the prevailing models of creativity and imaginative practice come from. Developing your creative process requires both research and a **method**, which is why *research methods* are one of the most significant components of structured education programmes.

Third, the book looks at digital media in context. The books adopts the view that the artefacts of digital media are not simply the outcomes of the creative use of new machines, but are also shaped by the cultural, institutional and financial conditions in which the people who make digital media artefacts work. In fact, in many instances of digital media projects, there is no artefact as such, not in the obvious cultural sense of permanent works, but rather a record of a temporary process of communication. By keeping the creative practitioner and their projects at the centre of the book we hope to provide a closer, more textual definition of the relationship between technology, media practices and our contemporary culture, bearing in mind that these are changing relationships.

THEORY AND PRACTICE

The book is written from a producer or practitioner point of view, while at the same time continually 'signposting' the relevance of theory to practice. Theory is another one of those thorny terms we need to be clear about, since it has different meanings for different groups and in different contexts. Theory can mean either the direct explanation of how things work, what we might call **applied theory**, or an explanation about why and how a thing exists at all, which we might call **abstract theory**. Certainly all theory is an abstraction from concrete objects in the world and the difference between applied and abstract theory is a matter of degree, rather than a matter of kind. However, in English language culture, the distinction between abstract and applied theory is perceived and lived as marking a hard-walled separation between the speculation about and the application of knowledge in 'the real world'. The real world here is that of business and production where there is literally little or no time for speculation or reflection upon practice. Speculation on causes, purposes and meanings can and often does appear as an idle or unprofitable waste of time measured against the urgent process of getting the job done. The more theory questions the meanings and purposes of a practice the more likely it will be perceived as not belonging to 'the real world'. Operational knowledge, on the other hand, is experienced as contingent and necessary and unquestioningly belonging to the real world. The problem with this distinction is that operational knowledge (what we might call, know-how as opposed to know-why) always has embedded within it assumptions and precepts derived, at some point, from abstract theory (know why). This is what we mean by saying the two are not distinct but continuous. But in the real world theory and practice are separated and organised so that some people are involved as theorists in the institution of the academy, while practitioners belong to the world of commerce and industry. This is fine as far as it goes, in fact it is the way our society organises and naturalises the separation. Operational knowledge is a kind of theoretical shorthand, since it is not necessary to rehearse first causes and principles in order to get on with the job. The primary difficulty with theory for practitioners is that while applied theory appears immediately relevant to understanding how something 'works', abstract theory appears to overly question or even negate the value of practice. Of course, reaching a point where theory replaces the practice, rather than illuminates it, is an extreme, but it has been said many times in our experience, as teachers and producers, that 'too much' theory, or the 'wrong' theory, or theory badly explained does little to enhance either the cause of theory or improve practice. The counter to a kind of indiscriminate theoretical overload is not to reject all theory and theory teaching, but to require theory to be made clear, accessible and relevant to the pressing issues of practice. While much of mainstream media practice is conducted every day at a distance from conceptual-based theorising, innovative or progressive work is often much closer to ideas, debates and issues that are also being analysed at the theoretical level. The book deals with the theory–practice relationship in a number of ways. First, in the body text where accounts of key concepts and ideas are explained, second, in the course of the edited interviews and, third, in the summaries that accompany the case studies.

WHAT IS DIGITAL MEDIA?

As we discuss throughout this book, the question of what is and is not digital media remains open and ongoing. Some definitions of digital media focus exclusively upon computer technologies while others stress the cultural forms and contexts in which technologies are used – for example, art, film, commerce, science and above all the Internet. For us there is a third term in the digital media equation after technologies and cultural forms, that of cultural concepts. Cultural conception refers to an active and shaping set of ideas and the underlying theories or wider discourses to which they belong that informs what the practitioner does. The active 'ideas' that are worked upon in practice arise from both the technology, the cultural context and the cultural concepts and, as our case studies and examples show, carry cultural concepts from one context into another. We also argue throughout this book that our understandings of technology are themselves a product of a given set of received ideas, which means that we can't easily separate our general ideas of technology, as socially good, bad or indifferent, from machines designed for particular uses. The motor car is a good example of a conflictual relationship with technology because we like the convenience and reliability of motor travel, but not its environmental impact. As with all of our attempts in this book at defining digital media, they remain necessarily fluid by virtue of its developing and evolving character; however, our underlying formula of technology, plus concepts, plus contexts, will serve as a guide.

WHO ARE THE DIGITAL MEDIA PRACTITIONERS?

One of the recurring observations to be made about people working in digital media is how varied their backgrounds are. No two people, it would appear, share the same set of skills, aptitudes, knowledge or skills. In part this is to be expected of a relatively new discipline with relatively new formal training routes and where, instead, people seem to have an existing practice from which they develop an evolving interest in the current possibilities presented by social networking, interfaces, motion graphics or interactivity. The case studies are all demonstrations of this principle that practitioners, in general, migrate from one set of practices into another, often retaining elements of previous practices. This is an example of the hybrid nature of digital media in which the skills of, say, the writer or film-maker are configured and developed in a different technological and organisational context. The hybrid and fluid migration across subjects, jobs and practices makes it difficult, but not impossible, to describe at a general level what skills and training are needed to work in digital media. In fact there is no one set of skills, or established bodies of knowledge, that will fit a person to work in the area. Thinking in terms of fixed skills or progression routes goes against the grain of the fast moving, convergent, fluid and still-evolving nature of digital media practice.

Also, we have demonstrated that digital media practices are largely made up from the established media practices of, for example, scriptwriting, image making, graphics, editing, composing and so on. Each of the case studies explores a different configuration of established and emerging skills. They show how a combination of grounded knowledge of a media discipline together with an operational familiarity with computer systems and software is in evidence in practice. But how this combinatory set of knowledge and skills is achieved varies widely, depending upon the context in which someone is working in and the models of practice adopted. Models of practice inform how media is produced and how individual roles are understood. Models of practice become established over time and serve to set out the rules and procedures of how things gets done and who does what. The production of novels, paintings or films each contains work for many more people than an author, artist or director. Art and media products entail a pre-production stage involving, in different ways, the initial expression of an idea, its development within a particular form, the commissioning and financing of a work.

There is, of course, great variation in the control over pre-production, which takes us back to different models of practice. Work produced for an established client and market will conform tightly to the boundaries of what is agreed financially and contractually. In contrast, work produced speculatively, by an individual working on their own will operate in a context specified only by the implicit discipline of the practitioner. This is not to say, however, that the model of practice of the individual working for themselves is any more or less unencumbered or 'free', than that of a practitioner working in a group, or for a client. The model of practice that privileges the unconstrained context of the individual, operating within exclusively self-regulating boundaries set by themselves, belongs, of course, to the European Romantic tradition (see the discussion on creativity). Models of practice remain largely implicit to the contexts of practice, rather like trade secrets, and are understood through practice – acquired, that is, on the job. The purpose of reflecting upon models of practice in digital media is to demonstrate the range of practice strategies in operation and to identify what a number of them have in common.

GENERIC SKILL SETS

Creativity is essentially the process of generating and developing ideas or, more properly, beginning to articulate your ideas through research and method. Ideas that can be turned into successful media objects have to go through a *proposal stage* and proposals are a first articulation of how an idea might be realised. Development is the process of beginning to turn abstract possibilities, the vision and idea, into concrete realities and is a process of engaging others through the proposal in ideas. The development of ideas is an open process in which a proposal would go through changes as it is engaged and related to the *resources* and *support* needed to realise the idea. Ideas can and most often do change in subtle or drastic ways during the developmental stages as they are tested out in the context of possible realisation. Research is a generic skill that happens at all stages of production and post-production. At very early stages of visioning development research is focused upon the content and intellectual coherence of ideas, whereas at later stages research might focus upon resources and responses. **Networking** has become a contemporary generic skill in many occupations and in media has always been a strong aspect of how opportunities are seized and work commissioned. Networking, as distinct from nepotism, is not only about who you know, but about good communication and awareness of the field of opportunities at any one time. Networking is about establishing connections between people and their roles in order to maximise the possibilities of realisation. **Collaboration** is again a common skill in media and extends naturally to digital media, since by nature digital media is a group and collaborative activity. Collaboration can of course take many forms from jointly authored and produced work, working with people from different disciplines, or working within an agreed division of labour within a set production. Production will take many forms depending on the particular expertise of the practitioner. It will encompass organisational, managerial and communication roles, through specific skills in the cultural forms of writing, programming and design, through to marketing and promotional. Any and all of the aspects of realising a digital media work for a given or new audience is included in the production process.

While it might be said that such skills or qualities relate to a wide spectrum of human activities, we argue that it is the combination of all of these activities that marks out digital media at this point in time. All of these attributes are given their specific meaning in definite contexts, which will mark out their significance to a particular activity. In digital media contexts each of these 'roles', as we are calling them, take on specific characteristics.

The actual roles of the practitioners in our case studies are of course more known and conventional. The case studies encompass the roles of the strategist, producer, curator, web manager and artist, working with, in, and on digital media. The creative identity of individuals highlighted in the case studies indicates that at present it is the established rather than the emergent cultural role that is retained. The role of the artist is a case in point since it provides an obvious identity and role in relation to certain kinds of production. But the case studies reveal people who combine distinct knowledge and skills from different practices in the hybrid mixture that is digital media.

THE CASE STUDIES – CONTEXTS OF PRACTICE

Our discussion of the generic roles of the digital media practitioner are to be understood in relationship to the contexts of digital media practice. Context can and does mean many things, from your place of work right through to the accumulation of your life experiences. Context is therefore practical, social and intellectual, and it should be born in mind that at its widest all of these dimensions of our context set and shape a given set of possibilities. This is not to say that we have no control over what immediate context we choose to work in, nor that we are incapable of changing our context and ourselves in the process. However, the recognition of and reflection upon the dimensions of our full context – our historical, social, cultural and economic formation – does allow us to understand the conditions in which we operate. The value of this point is to focus attention on the need for and process of gaining insight into our context as one measure of gaining control over how we approach our own productions within any given set of circumstances. Context remains a crucial aspect of how practices are organised and institutionalised in the production process. Context is also central to the ways in which the products of practice are received. The context of the reception of work will in large part determine how work is interpreted, appreciated and valued. The context of reception will also determine who gets to value and use work because it establishes the audience and their expectations. Understanding both the production and reception contexts of work as a practitioner of digital media is important precisely because the designation of cultural value is not yet established or settled. What, after all, is the context of Net Art, which, unlike its object counter-part in an art gallery, has an institutional context that gives the object status and provenance. The work in the gallery carries with it the approval of the institution, whereas a website, which is a work of art, remains undifferentiated within the horizontal plane of TPC addresses. The web is a differentiated but non-hierarchical organisation of cultural material in which the good jostles with the bad, or worse. As a context it has been embraced by a generation of artists and digital media practitioners who precisely value what they take to be its democratic and accessible characteristic over that of what is perceived as the hierarchical and exclusive character of national and international cultural organisations. Whatever the merits of the argument in this particular case, it is a demonstration that the context in which work is produced or in which it is received is significant and shapes the limits and possibilities of practitioner roles.

GENERIC INSTITUTIONAL CONTEXTS OF DIGITAL MEDIA

What then, in more detail, are the contexts for the production of digital media? From our case studies we get a generic picture of the institutional contexts of production and consumption of digital media. There is the obvious context of business and commerce built around the dot.com industry that emerged in the 1990s, which is increasingly based around creative and advertising agencies as well as the digital media end of established media production. Then there is the context of cultural institutions, mostly in the public sector, but including private charities and trusts, operating at international, national and regional levels. These could include museums, galleries, dance companies, orchestras, arts centres, arts projects and arts organisations. In the UK, for example, there are a small number of Arts Council supported digital media organisations. Mainstream media institutions in film and animation production, television production and broadcasting, graphic and architectural design studios, print journalism and music companies all have some relationship to digital media either because they have digital media offshoots, mostly related websites, or because aspects of their production processes are based in digital technologies. Finally, we should consider that educational institutions provide a serious institutional context for digital media development and practice in the form of teaching, research and training. Schools, colleges and universities have all had considerable government investment in information technologies, which are used by teachers, pupils, lecturers and students alike. Universities are also able to invest in up-to-date hardware for research purposes in a variety of subject disciplines from the obvious context of computer science and engineering, through to media production, art and design and on to the social sciences and health. In all of these educational contexts the possibility of using digital technologies for cross disciplinary and collaborative projects is present.

The commercial, media, cultural and educational dimensions combine to form the broad operating context of digital media. In each case they provide the resources and funding, the plant and hardware for work to be undertaken; they provide employment and fees for work to be produced in both profit and not-for-profit organisations. We recognise that not all digital media practice can be neatly fitted into this scheme, but we consider that the great majority will have some relationship to this pattern. One exception to our scheme, where work is produced outside of these major institutional and productive work contexts, is that of freelance artist/producer. With the miniaturisation of computer memory and the lowering of costs of originating digital capture, many more practitioners can work independently, often using the physical space of home or a small studio. For the freelance producer, this amounts to a form of 'cottage industry' where it is unnecessary to attend a 'factory' or the modern office, because the productive workstations are personally owned and access to the network can be from anywhere. But the fact that many freelance digital media practitioners can work from home is not the same as saying that their production has no relationship with the main institutional contexts, which we have indicated. In fact 'outsourcing' and 'subcontracting' have been familiar modes of the organisation of media labour for the last two decades, and in some cases, photography for instance, they are the dominant historical model.

The significance of the major institutional contexts here is that they play a large part in defining the parameters of what is produced. The corporate world has over the past decade, begun to dominate and shape the current possibilities of the nternet, with more defined and stable patterns of production and distribution of content and services, with a much more formal division of markets and labour. The most obvious areas being advertising, web browsing and content providers, while the computer hardware market has been driven by mobile devices. Markets and their division of labour differentiate digital media practice in the cultural sector of museums and galleries to a lesser extent, because it is not 'driven' primarily by the commercial imperatives of profit and loss. A consequence of the public sector's 'not-for-profit' financial standing is that 'start-up' capital is wholly dependent upon public funding or private donation, and the whole economy of the public cultural sector, in the UK and Europe in particular, is a tiny fraction in comparison to the major economies of dot.com or online entertainment. This is also true of the education sector, although in comparison to the cultural sector there has, over the last decade, been a marked increase in funding for research and teaching in digital media areas. The paradigm case for research development of digital media in an educational context remains that of the Massachusetts Institute of Technology (MIT). In Europe and the UK, such levels of government funding are more specifically targeted at the hard, scientific, rather than soft, cultural end of technological research, and the corporate investment in UK universities for digital media research is on a much smaller scale. It should also be remembered that the last decade has seen development on a global scale with the 'developing' economies, particularly China, becoming 'big players' in the dot.com world.

GENERIC INTELLECTUAL CONTEXTS OF DIGITAL MEDIA

The institutional and industrial organisation of digital media, define the mainstream practical context of production, but what of the more nebulous cultural and intellectual contexts of the margins, how are we to define what this looks like organisationally? The margins of digital media refer here to the realm of what might be the as-yet-untested and experimental fringes of what is possible. Defining how the experimental fringe works and organising for its growth in education and training is a much harder thing to achieve than training for existing needs using tested approaches. What we are calling the margins includes the realm of your own biographical experience and how that has shaped interests, formed obsessions and establishes a potential for creative development. There is no doubt that each one of us does carry and embody a unique set of experiences and understanding. At the same time that unique body of experience has been acquired in a given historical, social, psychological and cultural context. Common accounts, versions and understandings of human experience are carried and recounted in part by the same practical institutions and organisations of education and media, which we have already identified. Any one such institution, let alone the total, contains a richness and diversity of intellectual and cultural knowledge and experience, which as individuals we actively engage with. We might say that each individual has a unique pathway through a common and available cultural stock. Further than this in any one historical context or period, there exist common preoccupations and focuses of attention, what we elsewhere have also referred to as discourses or narratives. Such discourses are another dimension of context, which set the parameters or frameworks of our ideas and questions. In our case studies the reader will see some of these at work.

There are a number of related intellectual frameworks and debates in digital media, which are currently being worked through, in the different institutional contexts of commerce, culture, education, and training. We characterise three main inter-related discourses as (a) the human–machine relationship, (b) access and control of networked communication and (c) representational–non-representational systems. These discourses, or debates, form the wider theoretical context within which more particular practical interests, in non-linearity, authorship, montage, immersion or emergence, for example, fit. The intellectual frameworks, or discourses, are also historically traceable in the formation of digital media from the intellectual disciplines of European philosophy, science and literature.

WRITERS' CONTEXT

Our own historical and intellectual context as writers also informs the approach of this book. Everyone has a context and our current one, the one that impinges upon this book, is foremost fashioned by working in higher education involved in teaching and research. Beyond this immediate context is a much longer shared history of working in the independent and community arts sector media during the 1970s and 1980s, which has shaped our perspectives on digital media. The paths of our working lives crossed at numerous points prior to coming together to write this book. Peter, for instance, was the Director of Photography at the Watershed Media Centre in Bristol in the late 1980s, 18 months before Andrew took up the same post. Between 1993 and 1997, Andrew was associated with Artec, a London based digital media training agency funded by the Arts Council of Great Britain and the European Social Fund, working on an early and pioneering digital media project *Silver to Silicon*. Subsequently, Peter went to work at Artec after leaving Cambridge Darkrooms. We came together again in 1999, with the establishment of the Digital Arts Development Agency, in which Peter was the Artistic Director and Andrew was the Chair of the Board of Directors. The Watershed Media Centre in Bristol was Britain's first dedicated Media Centre, largely funded by the British Film Institute, and later by major project funding from the Arts Council's Photography Panel. Cambridge Darkrooms was, for a time, also supported by the Arts Council, as was Watershed, to be centres for the educational development of photography by providing darkroom production and exhibition facilities. They were just two of a network of regional centres in the UK, which supported the exhibition of contem-porary independent media projects at that time. Both of us took up positions in universities in the late 1990s, Andrew as Head of Film and Photography at Newport School of Art and Design and later Head of Arts and Media at London South Bank University, and Peter at the University of Westminster, where we have kept in contact through shared projects in our professional field of new media curation and exhibition. The importance of these shared points leading to the project of this book lies in the fact that this network was committed to the critical exploration of contemporary media and the development of greater opportunities for practitioners working outside of the mainstream of publishing, broadcasting and national museums and galleries. The aim of this media network was to provide a resource that was relevant to local and regional cultures of place and identity and to bringing the means of media production to a wider and more diverse group of practitioners. Today, some of these same centres are at the forefront of the exploration of digital media along with newer organisations, which have sprung up in less than a decade. The history of independent practice in film and photography in the UK and the cultural politics of that tradition connect, in important ways, with the project of this book both through the case studies, often examples of independent producers, but also in the perspective on the importance of focusing upon practice itself.

ORGANISATION OF THE BOOK

The book is divided into five parts: Networks, Convergent Media, Creative Industries, Digital Media, and Histories and Theories. The first provides a discussion of contemporary digital media in terms of its material and cultural operating networks and the convergence of media in digital **code**. Part II looks at newer forms of convergence in a discussion with three digital media strategists, Frank Boyd, Matt Locke and Richard Sedley. Part III looks at emerging practices of gaming and play in a discussion with Maria Stukoff, Matt Adams and Jane Prophet. Part IV outlines the foundational terms and character of computational media – which are code, information, interface and interactivity – and discusses how a curator, Katrina Sluis, and company director, Rainer Usselmann, professionally engage with the computer-generated and networked image. The final part outlines elements of a history of digital media and the key theoretical ideas.

THE ORGANISATION OF THE CASE STUDIES

The material is organised so that the case studies and examples are related to the general explanations of concepts and ideas. The case studies and key examples comprise over a third of the book and contain a wide variety of discussion on nearly all aspects of digital media practice. They include how people became involved in digital media, how they organised and funded projects, how they set up companies or worked in existing institutions. They also include the process of project development, from ideas to realisation, and how people collaborate and network. Finally, they include accounts of completed works and how they have been received and what happens to them afterwards. In the second and third sections of the book the interviews focus upon the wider discussion of issues effecting digital media practices of the future. The case studies were produced from research interviews and are edited to be relevant to the specific sections of the book and the ideas they discuss.

At the beginning of each case study there is a statement that locates the discussion within the broader concepts of the book, plus a short overview of an individual's practice and their operational role. At the end of each case study there is a section cross-referencing issues and raising further questions. The case studies have been carefully edited and synthesised from much larger interviews and email correspondence in order to make them relevant to the issues discussed in each section of the book. In this way it is hoped that the reader will be able to move between the direct reflections of practice to the wider discussion of concepts and ideas. There is a common set of 'generic skills' that we have identified across the practitioner accounts. The skill set we are identifying encompasses technical skills, conceptual skills and social skills and can be defined around the following terms, visioning, development, research, networking, collaboration and production.

The material within each section is structured by a set of underlying questions that students, producers and users of digital media might reasonably want to ask, like, what is digital media and how is it being used; what are the key concepts and issues in digital media; and what are the emergent forms and skills of digital media?

PART I: NETWORKS

This section of the book provides an account of networked computing, starting with a consideration of the concept of a network and asking why 'network' is such a powerful and all-embracing contemporary term for people working in the arts and media. It follows this discussion with a descriptive account of computer networks and the practical and organisational make-up of the Internet and the World Wide Web. The discussion of networks moves between an understanding of their organisation in computing and their social and cultural meaning. Convergence is a key concept within the book as a means of accounting for digital media. The section includes a discussion of what media is, what it does and how it relates to the general processes of human communication. It includes two case studies. The first is with John Stack, who is the Head of Tate Online, discussing the implementation of the second iteration of Tate's website and digital networked strategy. The second case study is with Andrew Chetty, the Production Director of ditto, a communications agency and consultancy practice operating in the media sector, which looks at networking from a commercial point of view.

PART II: CONVERGENT MEDIA

Part two discusses the convergence of media forms in digital computing and how this has led to the present practices of networked media. It looks at the basis of convergence in digital code, providing an account of how computer coding relates to the cultural code of communication through language. The case studies of Part two, with Frank Boyd, Matt Locke and Richard Sedley, all, in one way or another, expand upon how the operating environment of digital media is currently configured and how it is likely to change with changing user and consumer habits.

PART III: CREATIVE INDUSTRIES

This section is taken up with a more detailed discussion of the contexts of practice and the kinds of practices involved in contemporary digital media. It contains three important case studies of practitioners who exemplify emergent and convergent practices of engaging with data in forms of gaming and play.

PART IV: DIGITAL MEDIA

This section focuses specifically upon three key concepts in digital media: interface, interactivity and digital code. The digital is explained in relationship to a discussion of the differences it has compared with analogue technologies and mediums, as well as containing a discussion of the importance of understanding the concept of code. Interface considers both the physical apparatus by which we communicate through and with a computer as well as the conceptual, metaphorical and practical designs of graphical user interfaces. Interactivity rehearses the arguments for and against interactivity, being the defining feature of digital media as a radically new cultural form. It discusses the importance to digital media of two further key concepts, **convergence** and **information**, and relates them to the question of whether digital media has a distinct digital aesthetic and what that might consist of and in.

This section also considers whether digital media can be thought of as a single new medium, a new paradigm, with the database as its essential form, or whether we should think about digital media as the umbrella term under which a range of continuing media practices and cross disciplinary interests intersect. In discussing the character of digital media we address the question of how digital media is changing aesthetic responses to existing analogue media forms. Convergence is explained not only as a technical feature of digital systems and code, but also in terms of the social and economic convergence of communication systems. Possibly the most overused, yet least understood term in digital media and digital technologies is that of 'information'. Most of us are familiar with the linguistic currency of living in an 'information age' or that there has been an 'information revolution', phrases that are most often used to signal the greater importance of computers in work practices and the phenomenal rise of networked computers. But what is information and how has the computer database come to be the repository of so much information? In our discussion we attempt to distinguish the difference ways in which knowledge, experience and cultural texts are considered as information and data. The discussion of convergence, data and information is important for the ways in which we go on to discuss the question of a digital aesthetic, which we consider in three ways, digital media as an extension of existing media, digital media as a break with existing media and digital media as a crisis in culture. In each of these terms we consider the rules of representation, breaking the rules and the constitution of a new system.

PART V: MEDIA HISTORIES AND THEORIES

This section puts together an outline for a history of digital media, a discussion of cultural contexts and intellectual frameworks, concluding with a discussion of networked computing provoking a crisis in the established European tradition of representation. Digital media histories acknowledge the different strands of media and cultural development that have contributed to the shaping of digital media. These include what on the face of it is a disparate collection, including circus, theatre and children's games, along with the more obvious contenders of photography, film, radio and television. The list serves to make the point that any history of digital media has to take account of how analogue media technologies as well as cultural forms have *converged* and been *remediated* by computing. Having outlined the historical strands that make up a provisional history of digital media the section moves to discuss the cultural contexts of digital media, distinguishing between different commercial, industrial and cultural practices. It touches upon film, photography, digital sound, games and social media as some of the primary contexts for the application of digital media. The context of practice also includes the intellectual framing of digital media, in academia and serious journalism, as well as in professional strategy and policy discussions. Having outlined an intellectual framework within which contemporary debate is taking place, the section extends the discussion to consider the idea that computing is bringing about a crisis in previous representational systems and discusses this in terms of *simulation*, the *synthetic image* and the *post-human*.

CHAPTER 2

Digital media as a subject

Throughout writing this book we have been conscious that we are adding one more volume to the growing literature on a subject that is still uncertain of itself and its titles because of its very hybridity. Digital media is a fluid term, which migrates across many subject boundaries and is co-opted by them – digital humanities, being one of the more recent examples. There is already a sense that we are now in a post-digital moment, precisely because the digital has become part of everything and therefore no longer distinguishes anything specific. As current academic fashions go, there has been a wholesale shift from 'the digital' to 'the networked', which is charted at a number of key points across the book. This chapter discusses the subject of digital media as it is shaped by and met in education. Understanding digital media involves thinking about how it has been framed for study, which is not at all the same thing as how digital media practice takes place in the rest of the world. Students of digital media will have different interests, perspectives and ambitions and will take different things from this book. It is in this knowledge that the discussion of digital media as a subject can be framed in a number of distinct ways, which are laid out in what follows.

NEW MEDIA AND DIGITAL MEDIA?

There are a growing number of digital media titles on the bookshelves and in some important respects there is an overlap between work being described as new media and that defined as digital media. The main problem with the term digital media is that it has a tendency to privilege technology itself as the defining aspect of a medium, as if all digital media practice will be first and foremost about, or reflect the character of, digital technology. However, continued technical convergence in media production alongside of the growth of social media now questions the emphasis upon both sets of terms. New media, for example is now very much the established basis of most online user practices and digital media is entailed in most media production, leaving us with the question: what does either term distinguish?

The term new media still signals more about the dimension of the contemporary cultural concepts and contexts of media practices than it does about simply an integrated set of technologies. It is important and absolutely central to the approach of this book that the technological means and cultural and expressive practices are thought of as inseparable parts of the term digital media. The relationship between technologies and cultural and media practices needs to be understood as linked at every stage, from strategy, research and development to use. While this book has now adopted the term digital media over that of new media, this is in part because of the recognition that new media builds in its own redundancy. It takes little mental effort to reflect that all media must have been new at some point in their history and the question is then quickly begged, when will new media stop being new and become old or just media? The general answer is of course that new media will become old media when something else comes along that is significantly different. Superficially, the term new media suggests that at the core of its meaning it is its 'newness', or novelty that interests and excites. But novelty is by nature ephemeral and the excitement of the new quickly wears thin. The new, by definition, has not stood the test of time, but historically we are aware that the new can also indicate a set of more radical and fundamental shifts and changes in the ways in which human affairs are conducted. Hindsight has taught us that the twentieth century contains a catalogue of 'the new' in many areas of everyday life as well as in extraordinary scientific and cultural achievement. Indeed, the twentieth century was established on the legacy of progress bequeathed by the industrial revolution. Ideas about the newness of new media and its technological base are deeply rooted in the historical notion of social and scientific progress.

NEW MEDIA

In 2000, the term 'new media' emerged as a preferred term for a range of media practices that employed computer-based digital technologies. New media also emerged as a key institutional term in education and cultural policy and led to degree titles, research centres and independent organisations. This made new media an academic and intellectual subject as well as a practice. This was most evident in four key books of the time, which represented an emerging field of interest around which a history and theory of the subject and its objects and practices in the wider world was constructed.

BOOK ONE

M. Lister, J. Dovey, S. Giddings, I. Grant, and K. Kelly (2003) *New Media: A Critical Introduction*. London: Routledge.

This book does the difficult job a locating and tracing the underlying strands of argument that in one sense make up the academic study of new media. The book has a cultural constructivist framework, which seeks explanations of technology in what people do with technology rather than in the technology itself. The book consistently takes to task technological determinism in all its forms, resisting an account of new media as so many (determined) effects of a technologically based medium. In an important section the book re-looks at the debates generated by the very different work of Marshall McLuhan and Raymond Williams writing in the 1960s and 1970s in relationship to television. Overall this book adopts the approach of showing how new media can be thought of as part of a continuously evolving pattern of media codes and conventions.

BOOK TWO

L. Manovich (2001) *The Language of New Media*. Cambridge, MA: MIT.

In contrast, Manovich encompasses both continuity and radical rupture in his account of new media in which he outlines what he takes to be the principles of a distinct medium. His argument for continuity is that the cultural language of new media is derived from ways of seeing and communicating located in the predominance of film and cinema over the twentieth century. He argues that the digital basis of new media, rather than the analogue medium of film, requires us to develop a new language of computer code. Manovich essentially argues that numerical representation, modularity, variability and transcoding radically change what can be done, expressed, thought and communicated with a medium and that we need to develop a new software theory, rather than cultural theory, to account for new media objects.

BOOK THREE

J. Bolter and R. Gruisin (1999) *Remediation*. Cambridge, MA: MIT.

This book offers a further and distinct framework for understanding new media. The authors also provide a historical contextualisation of new media, which articulates two distinct, if not binary opposite, traditions within cultural media. These they define as hypermediacy, our human interest in multiple, mediating processes, and immediacy, our desire for the eradication of all traces of mediation and to have absolute transparency. These twin tendencies, previously separated in cultural representations as different from each other as medieval churches – hyper-mediated environments – and photography – the transparent window on the world – now battle it out on the computer screen. For Bolter and Gruisin the presence of immediacy and hypermediacy in new media is the re-mediation of all previous media. They point to television as the current battleground between two cultural forms and technologies and conclude that the computer will remediate television.

BOOK FOUR

N. Wardrip-Fruin and N. Montfort (2003) *The New Media Reader*. Cambridge, MA: MIT.

This book sets out to provide us with the seminal historical texts of the computer, not as an advanced calculator, but as an a new 'poetic' medium. The book carries two positioning introductions by Janet H. Murray and Lev Manovich, both of which argue for a conception of computing as a new medium of expression, which has taken over 60 years to emerge in its own right. *The New Media Reader* selects and assembles published articles and papers from computer scientists, engineers, artists and philosophers over six decades (1941–94). It does this in order to create a new canon, or intellectual context, for contemporary practice.

These four books were defining of new media at the turn of the century and now represent important parts of the expanding theoretical field of how digital media might be understood. All four books provide historical contexts that differ but overlap. At the core of all the debates is the struggle to understand the relationship between the cultural language of new media and the scientific and technical apparatuses and systems upon which it is based. The complex relationship between culture and technology lies at the heart of understanding and practising new media. The histories provided in these four works share a common framework in the development of computing. They differ in the degree to which they include histories of representational media as essentially part of the history of new media.

The shift of focus within digital media to networked practices and greater use of mobile technologies has led to new preoccupations among academics, scholars and commentators, which is reflected in more recent publishing. Of more recent titles, we would recommend the following as signalling some of the new preoccupations with convergence and networks.

NEW BOOKS

Kitchin, R. & Dodge, M. (2011) *Code/Space: Software and Everyday Life*. Cambridge, MA: MIT.

This book is part of a series whose editors include Lev Manovich, Mathew Fuller and Noah Wardrip-Fruin, and it represents a growing field of studies into the expanding and profound influence of software on the world through transduction and automated management of data. It examines in detail the part played by software code in the shaping of the cultural and social possibilities of networked culture.

DIGITAL MEDIA AND ELECTRONIC MEDIA

Electronic media also has a bearing upon our use of the term digital media. Electronic media privileges the power source of a group of related technologies as its defining feature. Electronic media groups together all those media that are dependent upon and structured through the science and technology of electrical transmission. At this general level electronic media is also an historical term for grouping together a characteristic element of electronic communication, which developed from the late nineteenth century and includes the media of telegraphy, telephone, radio, television and computing. Electronic media can be considered as a transparent transmission system for the content of previous human communication media, the medium itself being considered a neutral carrying system for sound and image. Conversely, electronic media can also be considered to shape its content profoundly, so that, for example, radio represents the one-way transmission of a disembodied human voice, whereas speech could be considered embodied in a two-way human interaction. Marshall McLuhan generalises this understanding to the idea that the content of any medium is always another medium, that is to say that the content of writing was speech and that speech was the content of telegraphy (McLuhan, cited in Wardrip-Fruin and Montfort 2003:203). The term electronic media also connotes many things about the characteristic of the communications that are electronically based. McLuhan also articulated that since the content of any medium is always another medium then the medium is also, always, the message. From this thinking it is possible to say that the content of electronic media is electricity. An example here would be electronic music. We all know and accept, as a matter of course, that the majority of music we listen to is recorded and transmitted using electronic and increasingly digital technologies. The listener still demands a high degree of fidelity to an original source of sound in their music technology. At the same time we also accept that there is a category or genre of music that we distinguish by the overall organisation of sound as electronic. We also know that electronic music is something quite different from acoustic instruments that have been electrified and amplified. We long ago accepted that electronic amplification of instruments and the human voice changed – mediated – the sound we heard. But in listening to electronic music we expect to hear sounds that have been made by a specifically electronic instrument, namely that range of music technologies that comes under the banner of synthesisers.

Electronic media is a useful term for categorising those cultural media forms that have emerged as a subset or genre within a larger practice, art or music on the one hand, printing on the other. The use of language to create new terms, by which we can mark out significant changes in our experience of cultural products, does tell us something about how we are thinking about those changes. For example, is it interesting that while we are happy to think of electronic music, art or print journals, we don't think of electronic film or electronic photography. So at one level the term electronic media distinguishes little other than telling us that electricity is the basis for the medium, in the literal sense of the materials and machines that drive that given cultural media – the daily newspaper for instance, has an electronic version. Like digital media, electronic media foregrounds the technological means as the defining feature of our experience of a medium.

CYBERSTUDIES

Digital media also has an overlap with cyberculture and its academic counterpart cyberstudies, which refer to those writings dedicated to the discussion and description of how people are using the Internet and the World Wide Web. There are several strands to the **discourse** of cyberspace. Technically cyberspace can be defined simply as a computer network consisting of a worldwide network of computer networks that use the TCP/IP protocols to facilitate data transmission and exchange. Culturally and in terms of the popular imagination, William Gibson's fictional definition of cyberspace as, 'a consensual hallucination experienced daily by billions of legitimate operators' (Gibson 1984:51), extends the idea of cyberspace to the social and psychological meanings of the operations and exchanges between users of the network of computers. In addition we would also have to include cybernetics, as a branch of learning that brings together theories and studies on communication and control as a part of cyberstudies. The term cybernetics gained currency in its use by Norbert Wiener to define studies in the interaction of goals, predictions, actions, feedback and response in human and machine systems. Cyberspace encompasses interests in the human–machine interaction and in the human presence within computer data systems. Studies of the current cultural practices focus upon screen-based textual or graphic interaction and communication in online multi-user communications, email or gaming. However, research, sponsored by governmental or commercial agencies for military or civic purposes, is interested in the development of human–machine interaction and human presence within computer data systems in more far-reaching ways. Research in artificial intelligence (AI) and intelligent software agents (IA), together with advanced robotics, moves along the lines of the creation of cyborgs as various kinds of hybrids between humans and machines. Research in the human presence and interaction within computer data systems takes a number of current forms through the development of more complex simulators, which can create highly immersive virtual or simulated 'real' environments. In addition current research is focusing upon the augmentation of reality (AR) through the use computer data systems and wireless receiving systems to deliver new levels of spatially specific information. From the perspective of digital media practice, cyborgs, robots and virtual reality largely remain the province of advanced research, while the concepts and indeed the language have a level of cultural currency at the level of the techno-imaginary.

DIGITAL MEDIA AND CYBERSPACE

Clearly what happens in cyberspace is directly related to digital media, which, as you will remember, is defined here more widely as the media and cultural practices of working with computers. We have included key case studies of art projects based upon the Internet and therefore at one level can be considered projects in cyberspace. Cyber-theory and cyber-cultural studies have rapidly developed analyses and descriptions of online communication as a parallel virtual world. Bell and Kennedy (2000:1) offer a broad definition of cyberstudies as consisting of, 'domains of digital communication and information technologies', which include, 'the Internet, email, chat rooms, MUDs, digital imaging systems, virtual reality, new biomedical technologies, artificial life and interactive digital entertainment systems'. Such an inclusive definition unites around technological systems and our interaction with them. Bell is quick to point out that, in his terms, these are all 'technocultural constructions' in which the place of human imagination and presentation remain central. Bell's emphasis is squarely upon the cultural use and value of technological systems and the inclusive definition of cyberstudies offered by him above places cyberstudies as an extension of the established academic arena of cultural studies. In a similar way, digital media is to media studies what cyberstudies is to cultural studies. Put another way, the current need to understand the impact of new digital technologies upon established cultural and media practices and organisations is also changing cultural and media studies as a subject.

THE DIFFERENCE BETWEEN CULTURAL AND MEDIA STUDIES APPROACHES TO DIGITAL MEDIA

While media and cultural studies are closely related, they are also historically distinct in their focus of attention as well as in their methods. Traditionally media studies focused upon five key aspects of the production and consumption of broadcast and print media, the institutions, industries, medium, texts and audiences. Within this framework media studies developed specific studies of radio, television, newspapers, magazines and cinema, although cinema has had another academic context in film studies. This division of media into production and consumption and into discrete stages and specific forms also produced two distinct types of analysis. The first type of analysis consisted of empirical studies, largely drawing upon the research methodologies of social science, which sought to find out (a) the effects of media upon individuals and groups, and (b) the ways in which ownership, regulatory legislation and industrial production shaped media products. The second type of analysis drew upon distinctly different traditions in linguistics, literature and philosophy in order to analyse the media object itself. Such analysis separated out the media 'text' from its immediate context of production and consumption in order to look in detail at how meaning was constructed. We could simplify these traditions and say that media studies in Europe and North America has for the last 20 years primarily focused upon two things, the economic and social organisation of public media and media products as textual representations. The introduction of new technologies in mainstream media production, initially in the print industry, then in music production and later in broadcasting, required media studies to reconsider questions of technology. The rapid development of the Internet and the World Wide Web from the mid-1990s required media studies to consider a wholly new medium. It is not surprising that media studies initially approached the study of cyberspace primarily as a new, global form of communication based upon the network of networked computers. Media studies as an academic discipline is continuing to adapt to the convergence of media in digital forms as well as extensions of digital media and, not unnaturally, it is building upon its existing frameworks of study, types of analysis, theories and concepts. A good example of how North American academics are adjusting media studies to new media studies can be found in Everett and Caldwell (2003).

CULTURAL STUDIES AND CYBERSPACE

Cultural studies clearly overlaps with media studies, since media plays a large part in everyday life, which was the founding object of cultural studies. Cultural studies focused specifically upon the experience of everyday life and of the shared traditions, First published in 1961, Raymond Williams's book *Culture and Society* argued for an enlarged definition of culture as 'a whole way of life', which broadened the academic study of culture from a narrow concentration on a selective tradition of literature, science and arts to include studies of popular and everyday culture. Williams's expanded version of culture paved the way for the development of British cultural studies, which certainly shared a broad tradition of social science research methods and empirical study with parallel developments in media studies. It also developed forms of textual analysis to account for specific cultural practices, dress and fashion and popular music, for instance, as well as more theoretical models of culture and the role of culture in social reproduction. Unlike media studies, cultural studies has been more pronounced in focusing upon subordinate and marginal cultures and through this has focused more fully upon resistance and transgression in the face of dominant and official cultures of communication. While cultural studies, reflects its sociological roots in examining the social organisation and reproduction of culture, it also allowed for the ethnographic exploration of the cultural experience of the individual within the group. This interest in the local and specific experiences of individuals and sub-groupings defines one of the ways in which cultural studies have sought to define cyberstudies. It is not surprising therefore to find debates about sexuality, the body and subjectivity in the forefront of interest in what is happening in cyberspace. Cyberculture has been defined as an alternative to actual social and spatial cultures and online identities have been described as offering the individual freedoms, not otherwise available in real space (Turkle 1995:25). But from the perspective of digital media practice, cyberstudies is, at its best, a necessary extended research project, drawing upon a number of empirically and theoretically based forms of analysis, attempting to understand and define what we are doing when we are online, or engaged in certain interactions with a computer program and a screen.

DIGITAL MEDIA AND VISUAL CULTURE

Before leaving academic approaches to the study of digital media we need, briefly, to make reference to visual culture. Visual cultural studies have a claim to be an emergent field of study, if not a discipline (Mirzoeff 1999:7), which holds some explanatory power in relationship to digital media. The basic argument of visual cultural studies is that human culture has become more and more reliant upon the visual dimension of human sense perception in communication. The development of large-scale media technologies throughout the twentieth century is pointed to as evidence of the growing emphasis and social reliance upon visual communication.

Photography, film, television and photo-print create a visual environment, which have moved a culture dominated by the word to a culture dominated by the image. It follows, in this argument, that academic study needs to take on the full significance of this fact and to bring together what have previously been separate objects of attention, with their own distinct modes of study. Visual cultural studies constructs a new genealogy in which the study of visual and plastic arts are the precursors of the study of photography, film and television. Visual cultural studies conceptualises the rise of the visual in communication in two ways. It does this first, by arguing that vision is a cultural practice, which has changed over time, rather than a biologically fixed function of the human eye and brain, and, second, by redefining the autographic and later mechanical modes of visual reproduction as visual technologies. The first argument leads visual cultural studies to place visuality at the centre of communication, requiring a renewed interest in the science of vision and perception and in how and what can be represented. In bringing autographic reproduction in painting and printing and mechanical reproduction in photography film and later video together as visual technologies, a renewed emphasis is placed upon the role of the medium in defining the message. The study of visual culture includes then the production and consumption of vision, or the operations and modes of vision in a given cultural and historical context. Within the study of visual culture the development and application of new digital technologies in image technologies enlarges and quickens the argument for the centrality of the study of visuality as defining of contemporary cultural experience. The argument is supported by the convergence of the telephone, television and computer in new screen-based interactive systems that are increasingly centred on the potential realisation of full screen, real time, video streaming, as the most desired and popular form of interface. The characteristics of such future screen-based visual interfaces, their aesthetics and effects, have been considered to be either that of the highly immersive, which moves the argument from visuality to virtuality, or that of the depth-less surface of the hypermediated screen.

DIGITAL MEDIA, ELECTRONIC AND NET ART

Digital media also has increasing currency as a distinct category of twenty-first-century art. The current moment is one in which a range of digital media practices is being (re)contextualised within art historical and contemporary curatorial fields and institutions (Graham and Cook 2010). This is taking place through art institutions commissioning installation or networked projects, creating archives and in constructing a canon of works and a historical narrative of their development. The main argument being advanced is that digital media art practice is a new avant-garde, an art practice of the future, ahead of its time and as yet not fully capable of being recognised or accepted (Rush 1999:217). In defining digital media practice as the latest avant-garde within the European modernist art movement, whose values and interests is part of an established tradition. In such a context digital media practice takes on the mantle of the modernist/post-modernist goal of pushing the boundaries of the medium of art itself. Paul (2003:9) distinguishes two categories of digital art, one that uses digital technologies as a tool for the creation of traditional art objects and the other, 'that employs digital technologies as its very own medium, being produced stored and presented exclusively in the digital form and making use of its interactive or participatory features'. Paul acknowledges the difficulties of categorisation in a period in which digital media practice is evolving and changing, nevertheless, her categories distinguish between 'tradition' and 'digital media', and like Rush sees the medium specific definition as forward looking.

DIGITAL MEDIA STUDIES RESHAPING THE MEDIA STUDIES AGENDA

Established media studies tends to divide the media field into a number of areas of discrete study, each of which is intended to denote sections of the overall process of media production and consumption. Media studies is still thought about and taught in terms of the categories of institutions, industries, audiences, forms and languages. Such categories had explanatory currency with a post-war period of relative stability within the major, nationally organised media organisations. But with the internationalisation of media ownership and deregulation of public broadcasting the idea of a unified 'mass media' became increasingly challenged. The expansion of satellite transmission and reception and the rise of the Internet have created a much more diversified pattern of media production and consumption. As media studies as a discipline begins to account for the introduction of digital media technologies and practices in the established media landscape as well as account for the emergence of distinct digital media forms its explanatory paradigms will be tested and modified.

NETWORKED AND CONVERGENT MEDIA

In higher education network media and convergent media are the newly emerging terms around which courses and research are being organised. At the present time they remain little represented in existing titles, although it is possible to see much more reference to their growing importance in course descriptions. We have no doubt that existing programmes in digital and new media will migrate towards a much greater emphasis upon network and convergence.

SOFTWARE STUDIES

Software studies is an interdisciplinary approach to digital media, which focuses upon what software does in shaping or determining use and meaning. It takes software as its object, rather than what is done with software in the interface. It is concerned with the ways in which programming and source code operate in 'language like ways' and in many respects emerged from the emphasis originally made by Manovich and which can be traced back to Marshall McLuhan's work on 'the media as the message'. It seeks to analyse the 'invisible' effects of software upon meaning and use and is different in emphasis from new media studies, which focused upon interfaces and observable effects of online and digitally based communication media. Methodologically, software studies attempts to straddle or synthesise approaches from the humanities and aspects of the computational sciences, although it is distinct from software engineering. Software studies seeks an account of software as a humanly constructed object that operates codes of cultural meaning at one remove.

RETURNING TO THE MAPPING METAPHOR

Mapping is probably the strongest metaphor and ordering concept of the book. It is a mapping exercise. But unlike a map of the Earth's surface, our subject is not already unified, it is not already one thing, but rather has a number of different layers and surfaces that are not simply visible or exposed. To extend the metaphor, we cannot spatialise all the dimensions of the subject on one plane. Digital media is a complex and layered subject, which includes both technical, historical, practical and theoretical knowledge. Digital media is characterised by its hybridity, or by the convergence or overlap of previously distinct media operations, skills and techniques. It follows therefore that it will contain different orders of knowledge and understanding.

ACADEMIC BOOKS ON DIGITAL MEDIA

There are a growing number of excellent books that offer the student of digital media a range of perspectives on the subject. It should be remembered that all accounts of digital media will be partial and will be written from a certain perspective or position, whether such positions are made explicit or not. The best books will be able to critically reflect on their own position and may well engage in debate with other views and positions.

Many of the ideas and points raised in the above summaries are expanded upon in greater depth in Part II in the discussion of new media languages and in Part III, which looks at the key debates. There are, of course, of many more valuable books that appear on book lists and bibliographies, which the student of new media would need to read and make reference over sustained study. The four we have singled out are important because they are all recent attempts to provide a specific framework for new media, as opposed to discussion new technologies within different disciplinary boundaries.

THE LANGUAGES OF DIGITAL MEDIA

Digital media arts practices and their corresponding educational study are talked and written about in a particular way, which we could call a parlance or linguistic subset. We could also call it jargon or rhetoric, although that has the pejorative overtone of a use of language that is unnecessarily complex or exclusive. There is still a strong belief that if something is worth saying then it can be said simply. There is great merit in this tradition of plain speaking, but the communication of new thoughts and meanings is itself a hard task. In countering the emphasis in everyday life towards excessive simplicity, it should also be recognised that language is itself a means of discovering meaning, and that our ideas and experience change – that is, we have new experiences, which we struggle, through language, to communicate. It is in this later respect that we should see digital media language as the attempt to grasp the significance of digital media and to assess the possibilities of computer mediated communications.

The typical ways in which digital media products and systems are discussed among the community of producers and critical reviewers will include specialist technical terms and abstract concepts. This is what we will call the conversational language of digital media and we discuss it in the following two sections. First, we deal with key concepts in digital media and then discuss the ways in which they are entailed in discourses about technology.

For our purposes here we can define the two most prominent forms of digital media language as the technical and the conceptual, both of which share buzz words, abbreviations and acronyms, which, to the uninitiated, make little sense. Cookies, blogs and Bluetooth, have the ring of an animated cartoon rather than the technical description of email protocols or wireless computer systems, while technical acronyms such as RAM and ROM, JAVA, HTML, HCI and GUI, to mention but a few, remain, impenetrable. Conceptual terms such as convergence, connectivity and conviviality or immersive, immediacy and immanence, come from a language used to describe human social exchange rather than a relationship to a machine. This combination of technical and conceptual terms creates a differentiated, but shared cultural language of knowledge and interest as well as assumed aims and purposes. Take for example this review of an Olympus digital camera on the wired.co.uk website:

> Both RAW and JPEG images can fly into the E-M5 at a 9fps burst rate with awfully impressive results up to ISO 6,400. Olympus' default algorithms tend to over-sharpen JPEGs (this can be dialled down in-camera), but they are still on par with the tops in the mirrorless realm. RAW images are equally pleasing, with lots of highlight and shadow latitude for creative control once they're downloaded.
>
> (Lynch 2012)

Such technical writing and its language is, of course, typical and widespread in the marketing of high-tech consumer products. We are all familiar with the hobbyist, some might say 'nerdy', fascination with technical specifications, manuals and gizmos. There is nothing culturally new in this and it can and should be viewed as an extension of an existing popular fascination with machines. When thinking about the use of technologies in the production of digital media we should note that the technical language of functionality is also a language of purpose. When a technical review talks about a mobile being more or less friendly a strong value judgement is being made about what we want to do with wireless technology. Here 'friendly' becomes synonymous with 'simple to use'. However, the more simple a powerful computer processor/and wireless receiver and transmitter (a mobile phone) becomes, the less we understand of its potential, the technology and its programming language becomes invisible in order that we can use it simply. There is, potentially, a large 'cost' in this trade-off between technology and simple use, which the other difficult, theoretical part of the language struggles to make visible.

Describing what a computer can do, the technical specifications of RAM and ROM, for instance, is not only descriptive of what a computer hard drive does, it also contains implicit cultural ideas about what we want a computer to be and how we want to relate to it. Why do we want/need faster and faster processors and greater and greater memory? The many answers to this question have to be sought in looking at the located purposes, for which computers are used. The instances are many, from highly secretive military research contracts for intelligence gathering and weapons systems, through civil administrative record keeping and surveillance, to the use of computers in health and education, and in many forms of media communications.

TECHNICAL LANGUAGE

The language of computer functionality is most obviously part of a technical language which has most agency in computing science and engineering and is evident in technical specifications and technical coding and hardware manuals. Software manuals are interesting in that they straddle the world of coded functionality and the end user.

Software manuals

Software manuals are typically clearly written and contain copious diagrams alongside the text and are designed to be read in conjunction with using software programs. Such manuals use the time-honoured training technique of, here is how you do it, now you try. The manuals are hierarchical and linear in structure, starting with simple instructions and working up to more complex operations. Unproblematic and boring we might say. Boring because until you have memorised the commands and functions sufficiently, you have to keep referring to the manual for the next step and unproblematic because they simply tell the user the functions of the program so that they can use it in whatever way s/he wants. Software manuals are written as a language of instruction, rather like a knitting pattern, recipe, or the assembly instructions for model kits. This, for example, taken from Macromedia's Flash manual:

> Click the paint bucket's hot spot (the tip of the drip of paint) somewhere inside the outline shape or within the existing fill. The shape fills with the gradient currently selected in the Fill Focus color chip.

Such an instruction would make perfect sense to those familiar with the PC or Mac operating environment and authoring interface. We know what 'click' means, without having to explain the function of the mouse and cursor, we know that the paint bucket is a graphic icon which operates as a functional command and so on. As we acquire familiarity with the practice of using computers and their software, so we become familiar with the uses of the language in which is it described. Equally as competence in the use of software develops, including all the short-cuts and personalised uses of tools and commands, it becomes unnecessary to verbalise how we achieved a particular operation, it becomes what we have previously called, know-how.

The technical language of software, like the technical language of hardware, also contains implicit linguistic pointers to assumed purposes as well as functions. Take, for instance, the following passage from the Macromedia Flash manual:

> Flash 4. Sports an updated interface that brings Flash closer in look and feel to other Macromedia products. Some of the most exciting additions to Flash 4 are beyond the scope of this book but may spur you to learn the basics so that you can later soar with the full flexibility of Flash.

Paraphrasing somewhat we can see that an aspiration to be as flexible as possible is being marked out so that the user might achieve something like the experience of soaring – that is, the imagined freedom of the human body in flight, the experience of speed, apparent weightlessness and uninterrupted vision. This is a conventional cultural metaphor for a certain kind of immediate bodily freedom and in the case of Flash 4 it is being promised through the redesign of the 'look and feel of the interface'. In reality, of course, the user is physically confined by the keyboard and screen in the human computer interface. This is just one small example of how wider purposes and aspirations become encoded in the technical language of computer hardware and software.

CONCEPTUAL LANGUAGE

The implicit and unproblematic references to the aims, aspirations and purposes of computer use in the technical vocabulary – that is, the metaphorical allusions such as soaring or navigating, become the starting point for a conceptual language of digital media developed within the context of education and academia (precisely the context of the production and consumption of this book). It is important to stress that the academic vocabulary of digital media is not unitary or indeed homogenous. We should say that there are a number of different conceptual vocabularies, reflecting different academic subjects, each containing their own historical direction and concerns, in short, their own 'take' on digital media. While the conceptual lexicon reflects different disciplines there are, nevertheless, a number of key conceptual terms that are now established as essential aspects of the practices and concerns of digital media. Terms such as the digital, digitality, digitextuality, cyberspace and cyberbodies now define essential characteristics and dimensions of the new computer environment. Interface, interactivity, hypermediacy, **navigation** and networks are key terms for discussing human computer/machine exchange. Virtual worlds, identities and realities, characterised alternatively as rich, immersive or augmented are key to the discussion of the qualitative and subject experience of computer-based technologies that extend human sense perceptions. Smart architecture and conscious networks and distributed data systems are most often the conceptual signposts for the aspirations of artificial (machine) intelligence. These key terms, among others provide the conceptual landscape in which current digital media practices and future aspirations are grasped. On inspection the conceptual vocabulary combines the cultural discussion of human purpose and intention with the technological discussion of applications. This distinction has been elaborated as the essential difference between the project of the engineers and that of the humanist scholars. The engineers have embraced a technological project in which instruments and machines (computers) organise not only our outer world but consciousness itself, while the humanist scholars recognise this world of technology as problematic and seek to focus on the manifest lack of clarity about our relationship to what we have brought into existence (Murray 1997:9). While it is true that this distinction points us to two distinct discourses, in our terms, languages of digital media, which primarily inform the technical on the one hand and the conceptual on the other, it is by no means a neat divide. As Murray points out the engineers are not in a culturally and philosophically 'value free' technological world of instruments, and the humanist scholars are not without dreams of what machines can do. We would also add that these are two somewhat abstract groupings that do not translate neatly in the more messy social and cultural fabric of everyday and institutional life. Gaining an overview of digital media and its development will involve a much more complex grasp of the material organisation and institutional systems (the apparatuses) in which all of the different, sectional interests in digital media are maintained.

In setting out the terrain of technical and conceptual terms that define current electronic machines and how we are using them, we prefer to think in terms of discourses/historical narratives (tropes) through which technology is and its relationship to culture and society and communication and representation is understood. While we discuss technological discourses in Part II, it is worth noting here that many of the 'buzz' words and phrases belong to these more extended accounts and narratives. Digital media studies, as much as old media studies, accepts that the communication and representation of human knowledge and experience necessarily involves language and technological systems; 500 years of print culture for instance; or, 150 years of photography and 100 years of film. One of the crucial starting points for understanding the languages of digital media is, therefore, to define how digital media, as distinct from old media, requires us to rethink the intercession of media technologies in human experience.

This task of rethinking how media practices work in society and for individuals, how digital media is changing existing patterns of communication and evolving new ones, is the larger task of the whole discipline of media studies. The question of the languages of digital media becomes central to this task since there is an enormous continuity between, as well as transformation of, media practices. The production of newspapers and television has been technically transformed by the introduction of technologies, which have, over two decades, transformed industrial working practices. Yet at the same time we continue to think of the newspaper and broadcast television as continuous with what has gone before, and in many ways discussed in the same ways using the same terms.

It must now be obvious from what we have said so far that in looking at the languages of digital media it is necessary to have more than simple 'dictionary' definitions of the vocabulary of digital media, instead we need a map that shows the various levels of connections and disconnections, within and across the technical and conceptual terminologies.

How we communicate using computers as a medium is an important question and since human communication has always involved the development and use of language structures, we need to consider how computer-based forms of communication relate to a complex of instructions, manuals, lists, formulas, procedures and tools, coded numerically, linguistically and graphically. There are three related senses in which a language of digital media can be discussed:

Definition 1:	existing cultural languages	image/text/sound
Definition 2:	medium specificity	modularity/variability automaticity/interactivity
Definition 3:	computing practices	socio-technical construction.

First, can we consider whether the distinctive features of computer communication, the digitisation and storage of networked data, programming and software use operate in any way like existing cultural languages. The graphical interface of end-user computer communication remains, for the time being at least, image and text based, and while this is continuous with analogue visual and textual communication the computer loads image and text in active windows that can be endlessly replaced and modified. Looking at how digital media operates using a variety of language elements builds upon established ways of accounting for how meaning is achieved in other media forms such as literature, graphics, film or photography. The communication of meaning in film, for example, is achieved through a combination of the technical apparatus for creating moving images and synchronised sound and the cultural forms, or the rules and conventions of actions, events and scenes within the filmic image. Currently film and photographic theory are having to reconsider how the introduction of digital technology is changing the ways in which we have come to understand the production and use of certain kinds of images in media forms such as Hollywood movies and photojournalism (Mitchel 1994; Manovich 2001) The graphical computer interface is therefore able to be discussed and analysed in the same terms as existing media – that is, as representational systems.

The second sense of a language of digital media is that discussed by Manovich in which he conceptualises the characteristic principles of the visualisation of data. These have been discussed elsewhere as, numerical representation, modularity, automation and variability. His fifth category, transcoding, refers to all those aspects of cultural translation that take place in software and operating system design that sustain the graphical interface. Transcoding is similar to Bolter and Gruisin's understanding of technical remediation. The importance of Manovich's characterisation is that it defines a medium specificity and his principles might be considered to define something of the digital aesthetic. The other dimension of medium specificity is Interactivity, which in this account is given more prominence and distinction than in Manovich's account. For Manovich interactivity is a feature of automation, but in our account interactivity is both a defining feature of the technical interface *and* a culturally coded mental procedure, which can't be limited to automation. We have discussed elsewhere that design for interactivity is a significant feature of the hierarchies of information search and find. The discussion of the principle of interactivity in computing has acted-back upon our thinking about all previous cultural medium's as essentially interactive, which has been an important counter to the idea that analogue media in particular were one-way messages, or non-interactive.

The third understanding of digital media language as socio-technical construction is more complex and refers to (i) the technical conception, design and construction of computers and networks, (ii) the implicit assumptions about the purposes and applications of computing and operations and practices of computer scientist and (iii) the even more complex arena in which the entire technical system of computing is taken up, routinised and operationalised. The socio-technical construction might metaphorically be seen as a network itself, and certainly Actor Network Theory (ANT), which we've referenced elsewhere, is a means of spotting the links in a chain, or tracing associations between social and technical operations. Socio-technical construction involves scientists, engineers, technicians, producers and designers, and all end users, whether in the routine procedures of work which involve millions of people, the innovative practices of creative practitioners or even the critically reflexive practice of those who study and conceptualise digital media.

THE LANGUAGES OF ESTABLISHED MEDIA AND COMMUNICATION

As we have noted, the language of digital media can be understood by a comparison with those of highly developed media communications. The ways in which film, photography, television, print culture, musical forms, drama, theatre, dance and the visual arts communicate constitutes an historical archive upon which computer mediation communication is being established.

Media communication is not the same thing as a specific media language, as the large volume of academic writing on the subject makes plain. Most critics would agree that media forms operate like a language, rather than strictly obeying the rules of human spoken and written languages. This is evident when we consider visual language for instance. Paintings are not composed out of regulated, systematised linguistic elements because colour, shape and texture do not operate like letters, words and sentences, yet culturally we are able to talk of 'reading' as much as viewing or contemplating a painting. Whether the discussion is of painting, photography, film or television as a language, strictly speaking, an analogy with speech and writing is being made. Language is a mode of communication-based upon a code – that is, letters, words and sentences governed by a set of grammatical rules. In practice none of our list of developed cultural and media forms of expression and communication can be strictly called a language, because we are unable to break them down totally to a rule-based code. Nevertheless, the 'language-like' nature of modern media has been extremely important in understanding how complex meanings, much of which go beyond the obvious or literal message, are encoded and decoded. Digital media language borrows, adapts and transforms elements of existing and established encoding methods of communication. How it does this is the subject of this section.

Over the past two decades the academic discipline of media studies has consistently attempted to analysis media forms in terms of their language-like properties. Television, film and photography have all been treated to systematic theoretical and empirical analysis in attempts to discover their underlying, or structural organisation. The common core of this endeavour has been to identify the constituent parts of a media message, whether that is a single photographic image, or a discrete television programme, or a sequence of edited film. In breaking down the media message into its smallest units of meaning, media forms are being treated as if they were a formal language in the same way that words and sentences obey a set of grammatical rules. Of course the study of media forms as languages does not represent the whole of the discipline of media studies, which is also interested in the social, political and economic organisation and regulation of media, as well as its reception by audiences. Nor does the specific tradition of analysis that flows from studying media texts as linguistic structures represent the only position on the analysis of the media text. However, it does remain a powerful general way of thinking about media messages that has been shaped by structuralist and semiotic theory. If there is a current consensus on how the communicative structures of photography, film and television work, it is one that recognises a multiplicity of ways in which they can be analysed and the attempt to develop a single scientific method for analysis has been largely abandoned. But, with the advent of digital media the question arises again about structure and language because the emergent digital media forms all have a common technical code, and they are re-purposing, or hybridising all existing and highly developed media forms of communication. A very good example of how a language developed to account for an analogue media has continued into digital media is film.

FILM, LANGUAGE AND DIGITAL MEDIA

Film as a medium of expression and communication consists of both a particular set of related apparatuses, cameras, lighting systems, sound recording equipment and editing, as well as a body of shared cultural knowledge about how to construct images and sounds and put them together in ways that make sense in particular cultural contexts. The knowledge about film apparatus and how to use them to make meaning is reproduced in a variety of contexts, through publishing, education and the production companies that train and pass on the know-how of film-making. Film has developed a range of distinct forms each with their own rules or conventions that vary from culture to culture. For example, contemporary Indian cinema – 'Bollywood' – happily mixes Hollywood naturalistic continuity editing with anti-illusionist traditions of Hindu mythology. The question of whether film is an exact language, or whether it functions like a language is the subject of film theory, which has, over the last 50 years, generated a number of distinct conceptual approaches to the analysis of different film forms. It is useful to briefly characterise the key approaches to film analysis since they have a bearing on one of the primary ways in which digital media, is being discussed in terms of the re-mediation or re-purposing of old media.

How film 'works' to create meaning has been generally understood and studied in relationship to the various stages of film production and consumption. Different theoretical and analytical traditions have established themselves to account for how films get made and how they are valued and interpreted. The emphasis upon film as a language is most associated with forms of analysis that treat the film as a 'closed text', such analysis 'brackets out', or suspends attention to all those factors of the social and economic production and consumption of film other than the specific combination of image and sound that make up a discrete and completed object. Analysing film as a text, is based upon the assumption that over time, film apparatuses and the cultural conventions that govern actions, objects and events within the film frame, have combined to create a structure in which there is something like a film grammar, syntax and vocabulary. Such film language involves the combination of the distinct technical practices of cinematography, acting, scripting and editing, which have coalesced over time and in different cultural contexts to form the distinctive 'rules' of specific cinemas.

Film theory has striven to reveal the underlying rules, both cultural and technical, of film language and meaning. In this endeavour film theory has produced a number of distinct analytical positions that highlight key different perspectives of the cultural experience of cinema. Film theory focuses upon four interrelated but distinct aspects of the development and use of film as a medium from the producer to the receiver. These fours aspects can be defined as; intentions and role of the film maker (auteur theory); types and styles of film (realism, genre, textual and structuralist theory); the cultural context in which film is produced and received (intertextuality, post-colonialism, feminist and queer theory); and the ways in which an individual is socio-psychologically positioned to experience the film (spectator theory, psycho-analysis, post-structuralist, post-modernist theory). Of course any one of these positions within film theory is attempting to account, not simply for a part of the process, but the overall meaning of film in culture. It is always a case of stressing the centrality of one of the four dimensions in (over)determining the others. Most recently there has been a recognition within film studies (Stam 2000: 8) that it is unlikely that we will ever produce one overarching or totalising account of how film generates meaning and that it is more fruitful to see various theoretical accounts forming a grid which, when applied to concrete examples of film, illuminates their different aspects.

It would be quite possible to apply any of the perspectives on and principals of film theory to digital media artefacts and yet very little detailed analysis of digital media artefacts and their user modes of engagement has, so far, been undertaken or published. By their nature (interactive) digital media artefacts present a different set of difficulties for the researcher or critic, since by nature they do not present or represent themselves, whether on- or offline as unitary and finite texts. In addition interactive media embraces, if not celebrates the idea that it is the user, not the producer, who is the author of the 'work' by virtue of the user's choice and navigational path through a programmed data-set. No two users, it is argued, will have the same experience of what constituted the work. Of course no two people will experience a film in the same way, yet the film as cultural object is the same object for both, while the interactive media artefact is different for each viewer. But the close scrutiny and analysis of interactive media artefacts has to start somewhere, and we would argue, it is possible to set about analysing or critiquing interactive media artefacts using a range of theoretical tools derived in part from the analysis of film.

The application of digital technologies, in compositing and editing moving images, also means that part of the emerging language in which digital media is being understood and framed also now relates to new ways of understanding film and hence is included in film studies. This is part of the phenomena of media convergence in which the application of digital technologies to analogue film is changing first and foremost the distribution forms of film. One of the noticeable effects of digital distribution is that cinema is less separated from other media platforms. The installation of digital television and the scaling up of the domestic screen will make 'home cinema' an established cultural experience. Further technical developments in broadband signalling will shortly complete the convergence of the computer and television as a new platform for home entertainment in which subscription or pay-as-you-go based film-on-demand services will be the norm. The projection of 35mm or 70mm film in cinemas is also challenged by digital technologies increasing ability to simulate the resolution of the projected chemical film image. More cinemas now use digital projection than 35mm film projection.

Digital technology has shifted the boundary between film and television at the level of distribution and reception of the product of film as well as changed the nature of film production. The digital recording of the moving image can simulate most of the technical and aesthetic qualities of film. At this stage, rather as we have already seen with digital photography, the major film industries are adopting digital recording equipment and formats as standard. Digital technology has been used in the offline editing of film for a long time now and the shooting and editing in digital format makes the entire process seamless. The other major and more visible effect of digital technology in film post-production is in special effects (SFX). Special effects consists of enhancing exceptional effects of the behaviour of objects in time and space, which normally cannot be seen or witnessed, such as explosions, earth quakes, death defying leaps, etc. Such effects can be staged as live-action in front of the camera, or by treating the film after it has been shot in post-production, through montage and animation of other filmed material. Digital technology provides for the seamless layering and compositing of live action and animation in ways that produce a new photo-realist hybrid. Directors can now render a unified and credible moving image of any imagined world conjured-up by writers. Another way of putting this is to say that computer generated image (CGI) software programs merge material generated from external sources with animated material produced by computer algorithms.

The use of CGI in post-production film-making has had effects on the product of mainstream Hollywood film, which has been noted in film studies as another way in which film is becoming less distinct from digital media. Digital media's capacity to incorporate, or remediate, all previous media suggests that film will develop new and as yet unlooked for outcomes in online, interactive or immersive media. Computer and video games already constitute a form of interactive digital film for game players.

Computer modelling and rendering of objects and spaces that can be given photo-realistic behaviours and properties also changes/extends the established language of film making that evolved from the codes and conventions of the movement of the film camera and its implied point-of-view. In the virtual space created by vectoral graphics the space and objects can be 'seen' from any position, defying the laws of physics that apply to the movement of objects in the real world or the positions and movements of the human body. In film, science fiction and cartoons have previously exploited and deployed special effects that allow characters in film to defy gravity or travel across time. But CGI also brings forward the possibility of endlessly changing the position of the audience in relationship to space, objects and actions within space, by putting them in an all-seeing point-of-view relative to the position of the virtual camera. It is a computer algorithm that determines the position and angle of view, rather than the lens and frame of a real camera located in real space. The same is true of virtual lighting in CGI. The filmic image is produced by reflected light from either the sun or artificial lights or both. Lighting is part of the language of film, producing particular effects of place and space related to the natural world and of mental states. Lighting objects in a computer rendered world follows the logic of lighting codes derived from previous film convention if it wishes to reproduce a given aesthetic style or look, but it can also assign different light values to different objects within the same scenes as well as lighting a scene from virtual positions.

Part I

Networks

CHAPTER 3

Networks

THE NEW EMPHASIS ON NETWORKED CULTURE

Appreciating the significance of the new emphasis upon networks for digital media practice requires an understanding of what a network is. Networks involve and rely upon technical, social and cultural systems, which order and replicate the elements required for communication. The effort to grasp the complexity of networks, or to at least have an overview of what is involved, is central to the practices of creative digital media. While the student of computer engineering primarily needs to understand technical networks and conversely the student of sociology studying networks focuses upon human behaviour, the creative media practitioner needs to grasp the importance of network as threefold; technical, social and medial. This is of course another way of pointing to the **hybridity** of digital media whose central feature is that of **convergence**, and it is because of this that digital media practitioners need a hybrid set of knowledge and skills in order to practice with any degree of understanding about what they are doing. What follows is a discussion of networks in the three related 'registers' of the social, medial and technical.

Networks depend upon codes and conventions, which can be understood simply as the 'rules' of exchange and use. Such rules are not fixed, nor even written down, but they are nevertheless the basis upon which 'common agreement' and 'shared practice' on how things take place. In practice the rules are never fixed, but continuously extended, modified, and even broken as a new rule is established. Another way of putting this is to say that networks entail technical and cultural protocols within their operations. The relationships between; the technical protocols in the ordering of computer code; the social codes of human communication; and the cultural code through which communication is made possible are complexly entwined. Creative new media practitioners need to be constantly alert to such complexities, because, on the one hand, the software applications limit as well as facilitate the possibilities of their use, while on the other hand, the social uses of computing are not simply governed by computer systems. The cultural coding of network communication, what we are calling here the medial dimension is the most important to the digital media practitioner's sphere of operation. The cultural, or medial, stands between technical coding and social use.

WHAT IS A NETWORK?

The expansion of personalised computing and the 'gold rush' days of Internet start-up companies began in earnest from the 1990s, followed by Web 2.0 development after 2004 and has continued to expand ever since. Much has happened in the past ten years in the ways in which individuals and organisations increasingly rely upon computers to manage their affairs and automate functions, from the most local and ordinary of activities of organising everyday life through to the most complex and overarching social, military, economic and scientific organisation. We now use computers in performing the most ordinary of acts, such as communicating with friends, the organisation of work and leisure time, the new ways in which we shop, or deciding what media to watch or music listen to. Conversely, some of the most collective and complex of transactions, such as banking, the production and distribution of the things we consume, predicting changes in the world's climate, or treating cancer, can no longer be accomplished without the aid of computers. Grasping the speed and scale of our increasing reliance upon and interaction with computers is proving hard to keep up with and contemporary discussion reflects our unease and uncertainty about our relationship with computers and how computing is changing life.

The experience of 'living with computers' raises a number of fundamental questions about the long history of technological advances, which have led to what now we generally take to be the 'Information Era'. Are we in the common way of thinking about progress improving our lives through advancements in the deployment of 'clever' machines, or are we, as an increasing number of commentators are suggesting, making life harder for ourselves? Do computers work for us, or do we, strange as it might sound, work for computers? While this may seem a very big question, almost in the realm of science fiction, the statistical evidence points to the fact that where people have a connection to a computer network, they are spending more and more of their waking hours in front of a screen, connected to the Internet. Humans have developed machines for known purposes as well as discovering new purposes and pleasures in using machines. In the industrial and post-industrial centres of the world there is very little organised work that does not involve continuous interactions with computers and those computers are networked.

Over the last two decades the central characteristic of this new landscape of computing has been the growth and further developing of computer networks. We no longer use computers as the standalone machines of their historical origins, each one performing as a separate entity and containing the data and operating system needed for the job in hand. The central feature of computing in the twenty-first century is that computers are connected to one another in a network. So important has the network of computers become that the idea of the network has been extended to think about society and culture as a whole, such that the idea of the network is one of the most powerful organising ideas of the present. It is now common to think of our associations and affinities with others as a social network and society itself is now reflected as a network. No other term, idea and concept so marks the current period as that of network and precisely because of this it is crucially important to understand what is meant by a network and to distinguish some of its uses and applications.

THE CONCEPT OF NETWORK

The term network can refer to many kinds of arrangements, groupings, intersections and exchanges between very different kinds of things. The most obvious and easy to understand use of the term network, though still complex in organisation, refers to physical connections in a system. So for example road networks express an organisation of motorways, major and minor roads, criss-crossing the country and joining up places. The rail network likewise is an organisation of railway lines, signalling systems, trains, stations and timetables. Not all networks are so obviously visible – for example, organised communication systems such as television involve a complex network by which programmes are made as well as depending upon a network of broadcasting stations across the country, which simultaneously relay programmes in real time. Such material networks can be schematised and given diagrammatic or even topographic form in which the connections between their points, or nodes, stations and tracks, in the example of a rail network, can be represented by intersecting straight lines. The spider's web is a common visual example of a complex network of several different kinds of thread, and it is not for nothing the Internet is imagined and indeed uses a web of connections, in the form of the World Wide Web. Yet other kinds of networks contain no obvious or visible signs of their connecting threads, such as a support network of either professionals or friends. In such an example the invisible threads of relationships are performed by groups of people in time and space and even though a support network might also entail many material signs of the operations of membership – such as meetings, lists of members – the presence of the network, especially in informal networks, is only made present by the continuous actions of those involved. Networks abound and are interwoven through working and social life, such that it is common to refer to much of what people do as networking. All of these uses of the term network, whether abstractly conceived or physically present, have the common characteristic of a structured set of connections between distinct entities, be that the tarmac of roads, the copper wire and circuits along which electrical impulses travel, the organisation of airwaves, or individuals who meet and share interests and concerns.

WHEN IS A NETWORK NOT A NETWORK?

Both the idea and the technologies of networks are an increasingly defining feature of contemporary human organisation and thinking, and this presents new problems of distinguishing between different types and uses of the term network. If the term network is to be used, as an overarching and defining feature of most human association and organisation, then the term is in danger of losing much of its usefulness. In some recent cultural writings the idea of a network has been expanded to embrace society or culture itself, so that society is considered as a category of network, or that we are living in a networked culture. These are important new emphases in the effort to understand change on a variety of scales, from the global to the local. An all-embracing idea of network is then not necessarily helpful when attempting to distinguish what is happening in the relationship between distinctly human and computer networks. The idea of network is an important new emphasis in an understanding of current human communication systems, and more specifically to the environment, or ecology in which digital media operate. Equally the term network has become a fashionable general term, used as a substitute for a variety of existing concepts and ideas about connections between people, objects and events.

The value of characterising current forms of society as networked cultures is because a new organisation of culture can be detected, which in important and structural ways differs from either a previous organisation of culture, which was not networked, or other cultures that are not networked. The point of emphasis being what has changed, or is new, in either or both the organisation of culture itself or in our thinking about culture – that is, culture has previously had networks, but they were not given sufficient importance as their defining feature. Currently there is a very real confusion between, on the one hand, identifying and describing the recent emergence of a distinct socio-technical network in networked computing, and, on the other hand, revising ideas about human culture and society in terms of computer networks. Now the relationship between these two formulations of the rise of computer networks in society and human life thought of in terms of computer networks, is very complex precisely because in the developed world networked computers have become more and more integrated with humans affairs.

THE POLITICS OF THE NETWORK

Some discussion of what is meant by the 'politics of the Internet' and why it is a crucial context for understanding online digital media practices, needs to be had.

By politics we mean all those aspects of our lives that involve direct and indirect consequences for others of our actions in pursuit of self-interest, whether individually, as a group or, more abstractly, in social ways. Such a broad definition of course threatens to make everything we do political, since there is very little in our lives that does not have effects upon the world, and this is precisely the point. Politics in the sense intended here is more than our allegiances to political parties, our voting intentions, or the causes we believe in. Politics in this wider sense involves the way in which we live, recognising that the conditions of our lives are not within our own choosing. What can be seen is that politics is an organisational set of arrangements, which differentiates individuals and groups and regulates the distribution of knowledge and resources, within which everyday life takes place. Basic as it is, the most glaringly noticeable feature of current human organisation is the asymmetrical or unequal distribution of resources on a local as well as global scale, and it this that drives and gives rise to organised political activity. But it is not hard on this definition to make the leap between the politics of the regulation of resources in human activity and the competing interests represented within the Internet. There is a politics attached to the ways in which the Internet creates selective access and distribution to its resources.

Because of the participatory nature of the Internet its history is important to the communities that helped shape the Internet. Castells (2001), as noted elsewhere, has examined the social shaping of the Internet over the past four decades and delineates between those who saw the Internet as a new free and open system of communication and those who saw its potential as an extension of commercial and profitable business activity. The tension and conflict between these tendencies is one way of understanding the political context of the Internet, and currently they have reached what many commentators see as a crucial stage. Curran *et al.* (2012:7) sum the situation up by recognising that the Internet has had a decisive impact upon the world, but that many of the predictions made over the past decade about how it was radically restructuring the world economy and creating a more level playing field for the creation and distribution of resources have not materialised. They point out that while the Internet has modified what they call the 'nervous system' of the economy, through data suppliers, configuration of markets, volume and velocity of global financial transactions, these are more continuous institutionally with the previous organisation and control of markets. The Internet has not led to a great cascading of wealth down to 'investors', nor created the level playing field between large corporations and small businesses. Instead, they point out that the Internet has been reorganised along the lines of a few very powerful corporate players controlling the circulation of data and making huge profits. This is a line of argument extended by Lovink (2012:6) when he points out that Web 2.0, far from extending a user democracy through greater participation and sharing, has done the opposite. Lovink argues that the 'social media' revolution of Web 2.0 created the conditions in which data mining of user profiles has led to users' demographic details being sold on to third parties through the control of distribution channels. In a curious reversal of the idea of the freedom to communicate and share, critical commentators demonstrate that this is a form of free labour, a new form of 'communicative capitalism' (Dean 2009), which is being monetised by Apple, Amazon, eBay, and Google, to name the most obvious. The analysis of the politics of the organisation of the Internet is then a crucial context of digital media practice that participates in online culture. While the corporatisation of the Internet characterises the most recent and powerful development, the Internet continues to surprise us, against such corporatising trends, in its capacity for people to explore collective values. This is something that will be discussed further in considering the intellectual framing of debates.

COMPUTER NETWORKS

The Internet and World Wide Web are the current developed forms of human–computer interaction, configured by hard and software and by graphical user interfaces. Conceptually it is necessary to grasp this nexus of social and technical systems as both specifically human, which is to say social and cultural as well as machinic and corresponding to the technical codes and operations of computing. In an older distinction, the Internet and World Wide Web are scientific and artistic achievements in equal measure. For this reason it is important to understand what is also referred to as online networked media as consisting of both a cultural structure and a machinic culture, the first still based in the semiotics of

Cultural Layer	*Representational systems:* image, text, sound
	Cultural conventions: narrative, perspective, composition, story, encyclopedia, etc.
Computer Culture	*Digital Media:* transcoding/compositioning
Computer Layer	*Physical structure:* by which electromagnetic impulses are organised to transmit codified data
	Data structures/machine readable packets of information bits/bytes

FIGURE 3.1
The three layers of network media

communication, while the second based in mathematics. One way of representing this is to see the operations of network media as having two basic layers, with digital media as an interface between them. The cultural layer sits, metaphorically speaking, on top of the computer layer, and consists of applications and software that convert operations and command code into the textual, visual and auditory interface. The computer layer is the technical layer, consisting of the physical structures of the technologies. Between these two layers lies the emergence of a new set of practices and knowledge based upon the transcoding of digital information, which operates as an intermediary layer. In describing computer networks it will be necessary to move between different understandings of the cultural and computer layers.

Local area networks (LANs)

A computer network can be as simple as two computers physically linked by cable or wireless device in order that information can be passed from one to the other and with the addition of peripheral digital devices information stored on computers can be exported to printers or new information imported as new data files. Groups of computers, such as those used in schools, universities and businesses are also networked in what is termed a local area network, or LAN, which refers to the technical ways in which the computers are connected and by which information is routed. LANs have different technical 'topologies', or maps, of how the computers are linked.

Local area networks allow groups of computers to share information through a hierarchy of physical structures, which control access and route information. Groups of computers organised in a local area network also structure connections to other related LANs and to the Internet, which is a network of network computers, which accesses and distributes the information of the World Wide Web. If all of this seems complex and confusing, it is, and some form of simplified model of the different kinds of networks and their structures will help in grasping the extent of and hence importance of the spread of networked computers. While LANs are the simplest models of network, there are bigger networks such as wide area networks (WANs) or metropolitan area networks (MANs).

Open systems interconnection (OSI)

Computer networks have a physical structure organised in a hierarchy of information functions and operations.

The layers of the OSI make networking possible between computers and indicate the function being performed or carried by the coding that is organising the flow of electrical binary signals. The physical computing network is of primary interest to computer engineers and programmers, who build, develop and maintain the physical network. The OSI developed over time into an industry standard set of

Layer	Data Unit	Function
1. Application	Data	Network process to application
2. Presentation		Encryption/decryption
3. Session		Managing application sessions
4. Transport	Segments	End-to-end connection/reliability
5. Network	Packets	Path determination/logical address
6. Data link	Frame	Physical addressing
7. Physical	Bit	Signal and binary transmission

FIGURE 3.2
Structure of computer network (seven-layer model of open systems interconnection, OSI)

protocols. The diagram above shows seven layers within the computer layer, or physical computing.

The OSI has developed as a means of standardising computer networks in order that they can interface with each other and function to flow data between networked machines without error. In the diagram of the seven layers that make up an operating network, each layer will only communicate with its peer level and is unaware of the activities of all the other layers, but each layer provides a service to the layer above and receives services from the layer below, each layer has its own method of data organisation as it passes the data to the layer below. The function of the bottom, or physical, layer is to move data in the form of electromagnetic signals across a transmission medium. The physical layer defines electrical and physical specifications for devices. The data link layer is responsible for moving a selection, or frame, of manageable bits of information and provides the functional and procedural means to transfer data between network entities and to detect and possibly correct errors that may occur in the physical layer. The network later delivers the individual packets of bits from the source host to the destination host, providing a procedural means of transferring data of variable sequences.

The transport layer delivers a message from one process to another providing transparent transfer of data between end users, providing reliable data transfer services to the upper layers. The *Transmission Control Protocol (TCP)* and the

User Datagram Protocol of the Internet Protocol suite are categorised as layer four protocols within the OSI. The session layer is responsible for control and synchronisation of data and the presentational layer functions to translate, compress and encrypt data. The final 'upper level' of the application layer controls the operations of file transfer, access and management, mail and directory services.

Open source

The OSI relies upon a *source code*, and one form of such code is open source, which is freely available and which can be modified from its original design. Open source developed within the technical computer community as a response to proprietary software owned by corporations. The open source 'movement' has its origins in the belief that the Internet should be developed as an open and free form of human communication and therefore the means of communication should not be owned or controlled. Currently the use of open source code is more a pragmatic matter of continuing collaborations and peer productions in improving and sharing code for redistribution within the community of users.

Corporate expansion and control

In contrast to the open source 'movement' within the technological community, the Internet continues to develop along corporate and commercial lines in which software for computer communication is developed as products to be sold, managed and licensed. Microsoft is a multinational company that dominates the global software market with its integrated operating system, while Google's search engine dominates the Internet. The integration of the web browser Internet Explorer with a new version of Microsoft's Windows operating system led to a celebrated and historic court case in 1998 in which the United States Department of Justice filed a series of civil actions to stop Microsoft integrating and selling the Internet Explorer as part of Windows of the basis that it constituted a monopolistic practice, breaching fair practice and giving Microsoft and unfair advantage over other companies including Apple, Java, Netscape and Linux among others. The judgement found that Microsoft had deliberately taken actions to protect its monopoly; however, in a series of appeals Microsoft managed to deflect being broken up as a company as well as developing a version of Windows that included Explorer. It further managed to avoid the consequences of a judgement that ordered Microsoft to make its source code freely available, by only releasing limited versions. What is important about the case is that while Microsoft has continued as a large multinational corporation, which still dominates the PC market and remains undaunted by the case, the Internet community has become wary of corporate and monopolistic practices. The irony of course is that there is inherent computer logic in providing an integration of operating systems and web browsers in an interface on the basis that it makes access and use more seamless and apparently universal.

The extension of corporate interests in the Internet are not only reflected in the computer layer in terms of the sale of hardware and software, but now, with the expansion of social networking, also focus upon business development within the cultural layer. There has been a major shift from Web 1.0 and Web 2.0 towards distribution platforms and the software applications that can deliver content. The presence of corporate interests within social networking reflects new and powerful ways of reaching potential consumers. Companies and corporations are using social networking to develop brand awareness and loyalty through strategies of long-term 'community development'. This is a relatively new development in using the Internet as a sales channel and traffic lever and is a growing area of out sourced employment to companies, which manage the presence of businesses within social networking through the production of directed content.

The Internet

The physical network of computers and their technical operating systems are the basis upon which the Internet is built and is a distributed and non-linear network of networked computers. At its simplest the Internet can be thought of as a global postal system, enabling computers to transmit and receive small packets of digital media. The network of network computers consists of millions of different kinds of computers whether mobile or desktop, hardwired or WiFi, personal or business, which are all randomly connected by high-speed fibre optic cables, regular network cables, wireless transmitters, and satellite connections. As a 'postal' communication system between networked computers the Internet needs a system of addressing packages of information (bits) and needs a common Internet protocol (IP), which is a numerical number label assigned to each device in the network in order that files can be transmitted. The Transmission Control Protocol (TCP) complements the IP, and it is commonly referred to as TCP/IP, which is used by the World Wide Web. The cultural significance of these protocols is its ability to allow disparate computers to talk to one another.

As the Internet has expanded its network of network computers it has done so in an increasingly hierarchical structure so that the Internet can now be thought of as having a 'backbone' in the form of high-capacity network access points (NAPs), which are located in key regions of the world and who put in place the high speed connections that link together larger networks and nodes from around the globe upon which the Internet relies. It is in the interests of the owners and providers of NAPs to make agreements on the connectivity of their services to Internet users. The Internet today is best understood as a series of levels of networked computing in which the top level network access points are large corporate providers, mostly in the United States, which provide management and hosting services, such as cloud computing. Such corporations as Savvis, Global Crossing and Qwest Communication International started in the mid-1990s and have grown into the 'backbone' of the Internet. Level two networks such as British Telecom, Deutsche Telekom and France Telecom pay the level-one providers for IP access, which they

Internet refers to the global information system that:

(i)   is logically linked together by a globally unique address space based on the Internet Protocol (IP) or its subsequent extensions/follow-ons;

(ii) is able to support communications using the Transmission Control Protocol/Internet Protocol (TCP/IP) suite or its subsequent extensions/follow-ons, and/or other IP-compatible protocols; and

(iii) provides, uses or makes accessible, either publicly or privately, high level services layered on the communications and related infrastructure described herein.

(Federal Networking Council 1995)

then sell on to individual and group users. The development of the Internet by computer scientists working in academic and research establishments have formed various national and international organisations over time in order to develop the common protocols, regulate networks and discuss the future of the Internet. In October 2012 a treaty on the management of the Internet discussed at a United Nations summit was rejected by most Western democracies on the basis that the Internet had developed without regulation over the past 25 years. In the United States, the Science and Technology Council chartered The Federal Networking Council, which in 1995 passed a resolution that defined the Internet as follows.

Computing power

As the network of network computers grows on a global scale, which currently sees no slacking off nor end in sight, first level Internet providers need ever larger amounts of computing power, provided by data centres, which in turn need greater amounts of energy to maintain them. The driver of the new giant server centres is the second dot.com business model of software as service, represented in cloud computing by Google and Facebook.

The World Wide Web

Generally the terms Internet and World Wide Web (or abbreviated to the web, WWW, or W3) are used interchangeably, but although closely affiliated they are not the same thing. The Internet refers to the network of networked computers, made up of the high-speed connectors, transmission services and the management and storage of large-scale data described above. The World Wide Web refers to a system of hyperlinking documents accessed through a web-browser and distributed via the Internet. The WWW might be thought of as an archive, or even a library, of documents, electronically stored files, which can contain any permutation of texts, moving and still images and graphic for which there is a software program to encode them. The documents of the WWW are accessed by a *web browser*, which is a software application or program written to enable document presentation, transmission and retrieval, through a protocol code, linking computer files. The first web browser was developed by Tim Berners-Lee in 1990 and hence it can be said that he was primarily responsible, working with others, for the creation of the WWW, although many other scientists and technologists had conceived of a cross-indexing or non-linear system for accessing computer documents. Other innovative web browsers were soon to follow, such as Mosaic, later renamed Netscape, developed by Marc Andreessen in 1993. Web browsers allow users to link documents by an agreed system of naming documents in order that they can be located. Web browsers have been continuously developed commercially by computer corporations such as Apple, Microsoft and Google, integrated with their own operating systems and/or applications, as preferential portals for users to navigate the web. Apple's Safari, Microsoft's Internet Explorer, Google's Chrome have become the most prominent forms of proprietary web browser software applications in the computer market. Today the WWW is a networked set of documents, estimates of its size vary, but it is generally agreed to be in the order of tens of billions, which continue to be culturally ordered by a technical system of interrelated hyperlinks, allowing producers and users to create links and to be able to 'jump' from one link to another. Technically, hyperlinks rely upon a coded system of identification of each document, which gives it a unique address, known as uniform resource identifiers (URI), which locate documents within databases, services and servers.

Hyperlink

Hyperlinking is a v. :y clear way of thinking of the WWW as a collection of documents, stored electronically, which can be accessed simultaneously from a networked computer interface. A hyperlink is a means of locating, either a whole document, or an embedded element within a document, and hence can be thought of as a key element of an indexing system. In the history and theory of digital media, hyperlinking is seen as a computer **remediation** of previous **analogue** document indexing systems, for example the card system used in libraries to locate and cross reference material in the stock of books. A hyperlink contains the address to a document located on another server on the Internet. The WWW is based upon hyperlinking using the hypertext transfer protocol (HTTP), which is a computer protocol. Hypertext mark-up language (HTML) is the agreed coding system allowing users to navigate around the Web's 40 billion public web pages.

Wikipedia is an example of a *hypertext* in which words and phrases in the text are referenced by a hyperlink to other terms and definitions. A Google search is a further example of hyperlinking in which typing in a search term brings up a page of URLs, which a web browser initiates a series of codes in order to fetch and display the web page.

Web 2.0 and social networks

Continuous technical developments of the Internet and the World Wide Web are paralleled by and inseparable from the uses for which they were designed and the uses to which they are put. The Internet did not come into the world as a perfect design, perfectly executed, but rather developed haphazardly and organically, because of its non-centralised network structure. While the WWW was deliberately being developed for the sharing of information among different communities of users, no one clearly foresaw that the Internet would become as important as it has for social sharing. The emergence of social networking as a major use of the Internet from the late 1990s is identified with cumulative changes in software development that allowed end users to do more than access static pages on the WWW, but allowed users to interact directly with other users. The term 'Web 2.0' registered a profound set of changes in which websites included software that gave users the ability and opportunity to generate their own content and to share that within designated online communities. Web 2.0 and beyond was made possible by a grand combination of more sophisticated, but simpler to use and cheaper digital technologies for the production of media, combined with graphical hyperlinking software applications and greater storage and distribution capacity in the computer layer. Social networking and file sharing sites represent one powerful and largely unforeseen outcome of such developments, while at the same time being prefigured by the network itself and reflected in part by deliberate attempts to develop the **interactive** possibilities of software. Facebook is a prime example of a project that had a local origin in American college life, conceived initially as a website for a closed group of Harvard students to post images and texts to each other. Facebook was launched by Marc Zuckerberg and associates in 2004 and by 2012 had over 1 billion active users worldwide and with over 40 per cent of the US population having a Facebook account. However, while Facebook remains the most spectacular example of the rapid growth of social networking, there has been a parallel development of other major sites, include YouTube, Twitter, Pinterest, Tagged, Google+, LinkedIn, Instagram and Tumblr.

THE POLITICS OF SOCIAL NETWORKING

In describing the growth of computer networks in terms of the combination of the technical, social and medial it is crucial to recognise that questions of the ownership and control of the network are written into its very architecture and the uses to which it is put. Debates over the ownership and control of the Internet represent one important aspect of the complexity of network culture and are something, which crosses all level of practice and concern. Much has been written on the history of the social shaping of the Internet as well as there being much contemporary commentary upon matters of privacy versus openness and security versus freedom. Manuel Castells' account shows how different and competing interests have been at work since the Internet's inception. Castells describes the formative develop-ment of the Internet as a series of tensions, oppositions and alliances reflecting scientific cultural and commercial interests and beliefs of academic scientists, computer programmers and early users. Within these groups he distinguishes the tendency towards developing a free and open new system of communication in opposition to the controlling and commercial interests of established media from an entrepreneurial tendency who saw in the Internet an extension of commercial media interests. Both of these tendencies have exerted a profound influence upon the direction and character of the Internet and their joint presence as shaping forces and interests account and continue to shape debate as well as practice.

PUBLIC vs PRIVATE

Traditional media publishing has long been the subject of law governing what can and cannot be said in public and what can and cannot be published about individuals or organisations without their consent. Legal frameworks continue to be pushed to their limits, challenged or reinforced in the courts by publishers and authors. The Internet as a major new form of publishing is now deeply caught up in these self-same matters of copyright and privacy. Internet privacy concerns all information, whether directly or indirectly personally identifying, which is stored and distributed on a computer, related to individual users. The question of privacy on the Internet raises a central question of whether indeed privacy is possible in such a public medium, since broadcasting personal information is an express purpose of online services, conversely users need mechanisms to protect them from equally calculated abuses by those who have the position to extract and use personally related information.

Many legal issues arise from the fact that the Internet is now the foremost means of both personal and public communication, ranging from: users making unintended disclosures by virtue of not understanding software protocols; users revealing information about a third party using the anonymity of the Internet; user information being unlawfully accessed for criminal purposes; and user information being accessed for surveillance purposes. Such issues have led to the development of specialist knowledge deployed to counter such threats to both the functionality and openness of the Internet. The Internet has become a fourth dimension in human life and **cyberspace**, like 'real life' is inhabited by spies and criminals; intelligence operations and counter intelligence; by the innocent and guilty. Human life has not only been extended and changed by the deployment of computers, but also replicated in cyberspace. In many of its forms, 'cybercrime' is clear-cut and no different from crime in the real world, where fraud or stealing has a clear criminal intent, using corrupted software, or malware, to gain illegal access to information. However, there is a large arena of Internet activity in which information is acquired under circumstances and in ways, which are much less clear-cut. Information stored on networked computers poses the constant risk of access and those risks can include the loss of network resources and confidential information, related to state security, banking and ecommerce. While the technical means of by-passing encrypted code to gain access to information stored on networked computers poses problems of security as well as disclosure, the motives for such access reflect a spectrum of social interest from the ethical to criminal. The growing industry for greater systems of information security to protect individuals and companies from data theft is paralleled by the equal industry for 'data mining', in which the legitimacy of data gathering on the behaviour of citizens using the Internet constitutes an equal threat of intentional and unintentional surveillance. 'Data analytics' is a commercially legitimate and growing sphere of business for analysing behaviours in order to predict trends in user behaviour, most obviously in respect of consumer spending. Companies can target their products and services more specifically both online and in related offline marketing and advertising campaigns, and hence more effectively, if they have reliable information on data sets, which show, for example, that people who like watching the genre of thriller movies are more likely to order a take-away meal than those who don't. Amazon is an example of an online retailer that deploys analytics on user behaviour as a standard method. If you bought this, you might also but this; if you bought these books, you might also like these others and so on. Google Analytics is a software product service that offers continuing monitoring and reporting upon web traffic using its own data gathering on users, which can be customised to user interest.

GOOGLE ANALYTICS

Overview

Google Analytics' Intelligence reports automatically monitor your website's traffic and highlight any significant changes, making you smarter and your work easier. At any time, you can look in your Intelligence reports or create a Custom Alert to become aware of any sudden or unexpected changes in your site metrics. This groundbreaking detection technology in Google Analytics is smart enough to highlight what you should know, while being easy to use.

With Analytics Intelligence, you'll discover things that you might otherwise miss and focus more on taking action instead of sifting through data. Just take a look – it's working right now. Dig less.

(Google Analytics n.d.)

SURVEILLANCE

A video obtained by the Guardian reveals how an 'extreme-scale analytics' system created by Raytheon, the world's fifth largest defense contractor, can gather vast amounts of information about people from websites including Facebook, Twitter and Foursquare.

Raytheon says it has not sold the software – named Riot, or Rapid Information Overlay Technology – to any clients.

But the Massachusetts-based company has acknowledged the technology was shared with US government and industry as part of a joint research and development effort, in 2010, to help build a national security system capable of analysing 'trillions of entities' from cyberspace.

The power of Riot to harness popular websites for surveillance offers a rare insight into controversial techniques that have attracted interest from intelligence and national security agencies, at the same time prompting civil liberties and online privacy concerns.

The sophisticated technology demonstrates how the same social networks that helped propel the Arab Spring revolutions can be transformed into a 'Google for spies' and tapped as a means of monitoring and control.

(Gallagher 2013)

The field of data analytics is of enormous importance to the future shaping of networks precisely because of the competing and in some cases conflicting purposes for its uses. Currently there is a fundamental lack of understanding on the part of users about how information they willingly 'give' to the computer, both in terms of what files they upload, but also the 'signature' of their Internet behaviour relating to when and where they log in and who and what they link with, is being used by the companies they supply it to as well as the others who are able to track such information. One startling recent example will serve here to underline the current state of surveillance.

THE SCOPE OF MEDIA WITHIN NETWORKS

This chapter has described the growth of computer networks with an emphasis upon the importance of understanding the relationship between technical systems and human purposes and behaviours. A crucial pivot in these relationships is the human computer interface (HCI) and how it is structured. In describing the operations of the Internet this we have seen how the network of network computers is both a technical network based upon the computer layer as well as a cultural layer, made up the behaviours, interests, motives and purposes of users, whether individually, or collectively. The relationship between data and human purposes is made intelligible in the cultural layer, imagined as 'sitting on top' of the numerical code by which computers 'talk to each other'. While we know that there is a deeper layer of causality and effect between the material organisation of network computers, the mathematical abstract of computer code and the humanly readable interface, much more research will is needed to fully understand this complexity. For the purposes of considering the cultural layer, we can now turn to an account of the mediation of the human computer interface, or in other words, how media and its codes and conventions have been repurposed, or **remediated**, by digital code.

C@SE STUDY

ILLUSTRATED CASE STUDY 1: SOCIAL NETWORKS AND GEOPOLITICS

Jon Thomson and Alison Craighead, *October*

Mobile networks have enabled people to communicate instantaneously, but this also means that social activity is aggregated by individuals or groups connecting with each other. In particular, major political events in the last decade have shown how small-scale and local activities can be linked together as part of a national or international movement.

Artists John Thomson and Alison Craighead illustrate this in their project *October*, which looks at the Occupy movement of 2011 in 2012 that responded to the world economic crisis. Their project, which is designed to be shown in galleries, uses films that were posted to YouTube and Internet sites by people taking part in the global Occupy movement. The movement emerged primarily from Occupy Wall Street in New York, and a global day of action on 15 October 2011 signalled a massive propagation of the Occupy movement from Wall Street around the world to over 800 international locations. The spread of information about Occupy largely took place through social networks.

October shows how the participants in the Occupy movement documented their protests by using social networking to a live international audience. But it also shows how important social networking has become as a platform that provided an alternative form of information distribution, to publicise and advocate what protesters were trying to achieve, to spread tools and techniques of protest – and record how to police and other authorities were responded to them in the clampdowns that followed.

C@SE STUDY

FIGURE 1
Stills from *October* showing images from video clips uploaded to YouTube

FIGURE 2
Stills from *October* showing images from video clips uploaded to YouTube

FIGURE 3
Stills from *October* showing images from video clips uploaded to YouTube

FIGURE 4
Stills from *October* showing images from video clips uploaded to YouTube

C@SE STUDY

FIGURE 5
Stills from *October* showing images from video clips uploaded to YouTube

FIGURE 6
Stills from *October* showing images from video clips uploaded to YouTube

C@SE STUDY

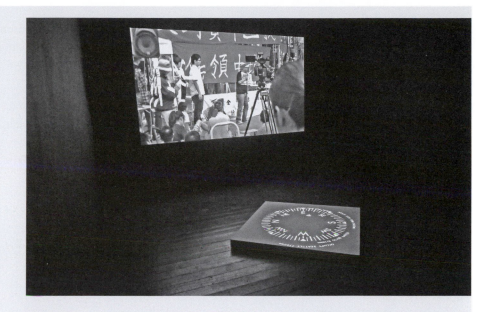

FIGURE 7
Installation of *October* showing the projected compass and projection screen (2012)

The artists explain:

> we wanted the viewers to consider what it means to witness
> something that can only be apprehended, represented and
> documented through the mediated space of the Internet. We wanted
> to do this by going back to the networks that spawned Occupy as a
> global phenomenon in the first place.

An important aspect of this form of self-documentation, which is
emphasised by this art project, is that the Occupy movement was not
hierarchal and had no central organisation. Therefore social networks and
search engines allowed people to access information and material from
contributors whether they were single people operating alone or part of
well-organised groups.

The gallery installation places the viewer in front of a stream of video
footage. A projected image of a compass on the floor interacts with the
montage by using metadata to show where each clip originated, and
where that place is in relation to the geographical location of the gallery
where it was being shown. By presenting the work this way, the artists

C@SE STUDY

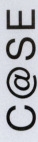

argue, 'we wanted to place the viewers in the centre of the information, so that they had a clear idea of where it was coming from in relation to them. By implication it is asking them to consider and make what they will of this information'.

October was exhibited at the Brighton Photobiennial 2012, Brighton, UK. Commissioned by Photoworks. Software development by Matthew Jarvis, sound design by John Cobban and script development by Alison Craighead and Jon Thomson. Graphic design by Cavan Convery.

CHAPTER 4

Case study

Professional networks

Interview with Jane Finnis

How can professional communities use digital networks to expand on what they do, extend their relationships and maximise their impact? This case study looks at the cultural industries and shows how networking allows them to increase their effectiveness as organisations and how it enables them to pool and aggregate their data through powerful media distributors. However, the interview also shows that to have an effective online presence, organisations need to tailor their content to their audience's needs and interests and this requires rigorous analytical research into user traffic and detailed qualitative research.

Culture24 is an online organisation that exists to support the cultural sector in the UK. It runs a website, www.culture24.org.uk. It also collects, curates and shares cultural information from a network of almost 6,000 venues, creating conversations and circulating research into the issues and opportunities digital technology brings to the arts and heritage sector. 'Everything we do is concerned with the ways in which new and emerging digital technologies can act as powerful tools to reach different audiences – culture lovers, families, communities, enthusiasts, teachers, learners and children' (Culture24).

Jane Finnis says of herself:

> I am the Chief Executive of Culture24. I am responsible for the overall leadership, development and direction of Culture24. I spend a lot of my time dealing with policy and strategy issues both for the cultural sector as a whole and Culture24 as a business. I lead our research work about online evaluation and the Museums at Night campaign and I also work internationally with other partners similar to Culture24. I have a cross-disciplinary degree and studied art, film, video and

music. I try and keep track of what is happening in the online world – commercially and creatively and I get inspired by things that make me think differently, feel more connected or make me laugh. I seem to be continuously interested in the gaps and overlaps between different areas of practice and the ways in which technology can completely change the way we think, play or do things.

Culture24 has been in operation for over a decade and over this time has developed a flexible, intelligent and sophisticated digital infrastructure which is able to provide for the creation and distribution of data about culture. Culture24 is at the heart of a cultural movement in which digital platforms have evolved as one of the most effective channels for the sector to communicate, connect and engage with its key audiences.

THE ROLE OF A PROFESSIONAL NETWORK

PETER: How would you sum up what Culture24 says to the world and why it exists?

JANE FINNIS: Our site is saying culture is fantastic – and you can engage with it through digital means. And this may ultimately mean that this changes the way you – the audience member – will engage with culture. But, conversely, it may also mean that even though you engage with something via a digital platform the experience is no different from what you would have if you walk into a room. We tell the cultural and heritage sector that, nowadays, most people experience the world through some sort of digital platform so that if they are not exhibiting themselves through that platform they are not present for that audience.

PETER: How does Culture24 contribute something that the sector does not have already?

JANE FINNIS: We try to place ourselves in the middle between institutions and people and find different ways to engage people on digital platforms. We publish a website which is well written and accessible. It's designed to appeal to people who like culture, but fundamentally it sits on top of a database which has very comprehensive information about the whole country. People can cross search to retrieve information on any one subject, or it can be used to tell people what's on in any particular area.

These are obvious ways that a website can be used, but a less obvious way is to pair it with an event, such as the campaign we run 'Museums at Night'. This is a weekend of late night openings and the purpose of the campaign is to get institutions to think differently about their offer to the public. So the actual events take place in venues and it is a very simple audience development idea by using our digital network, digital marketing and our digital network, that sits over thousands of venues within the UK, to coordinate the campaign.

AGGREGATING DATA AND WORKING WITH THIRD-PARTY WEBSITES

PETER: Although this is not a digital campaign it is something that could not take place without the network, or without the way that connections are being made and a critical mass is formed through aggregated online activity. Would you say that on one hand what Culture24 is doing is using the traditional format of the listings magazine to gather information but also by facilitating a network for professionals and by operating on a digital platform you maximise the opportunities for the cultural community?

JANE FINNIS: The most powerful thing is to sustain the network. We operate as a hub or as an interface so that institutions can see us as a way to grow themselves and to reach audiences. But we can also communicate on behalf of the sector to reach audiences on digital platforms by taking the data that we collect and we publish on our own website, and give it to someone else to publish on a third-party website. We operate with a small team and we are limited by a minimal marketing budget, but we work in a partnership to give the listings information and the key content to a third party like the BBC website, which has a reach that a website like ours can only dream of. This process is invisible but it is a more sophisticated use of the network because we can only ever do on our website what our resources allow us to do.

PETER: Therefore by enabling the BBC to access your listings information on its own website you are in effect extending your network into a greatly more powerful arena. You are not promoting your website but you are promoting the knowledge that comes from your sector and that is in their interests.

JANE FINNIS: We call this curating data. The BBC want content that supports their broadcast programme and we can provide information that is non-commercial and is an activity within the cultural sector. The BBC funds two staff members of Culture24 to moderate data for their website. They are drawing on our network which is paid for out of funding from the public sector but they are adding value to it by supporting it and amplifying the information they get from us. The large number of organisations who work with us can then have their activities promoted by the BBC within their listings. We are also now in a stage of promoting the use of the data to commercial online organisations that might not otherwise have cultural information but have sites which list all sorts of activities events and entertainment.

PETER: In this way the information gains cultural value as it goes on and is used across networks of greater and greater influence. You take information from small or regional museums that may have a lot of connections within their local community but which possibly have limited means to get information out. But if you pass on this information the beneficiaries will still include the local community, but because you are using the information more effectively within your network and by extending it to other networks everyone gains from the magnifying effect.

JANE FINNIS: The important thing to consider is that we are in a two-way relationship with the sector, we are not just an aggregator. We help them craft the information they give us, optimising it for search engine query. As a result they learn to call their events by terms which are easily found by users and that have clear meaning. So this is not just about communication of information it also results in organisations discovering how putting on different sorts of activities can create better results. They then learn how to describe those activities, and how they can make relationships with other organisations, or companies, which will enable them to cross promote.

COMPETITION FOR ONLINE AUDIENCES

PETER: Do you think that there are lessons in here for the cultural sector as a whole?

JANE FINNIS: The biggest problem I think the cultural sector has is attention share online – we just don't have it as a sector! People are not spending their time looking at cultural material online. They are spending huge amounts of time with YouTube or accessing music, but they're not going in any big numbers to museum, gallery or theatre websites. The numbers are tiny. The cultural institution is slipping off the agenda on the web.

PETER: Do you think organisations in the cultural sector have a good enough understanding what the online audience attention means?

JANE FINNIS: Culture24 has run an action research project around ways to measure success which looked at web stats, Google Analytics, social media traffic and mobile traffic. There are lots of examples where individual institutions were doing fascinating projects with Facebook groups, through their Twitter following and are selling tickets, but in the grand scheme of things the audience take-up is minuscule compared to the amount of time people spend on the web. People are spending more and more time online but, while the traffic to institutional websites is certainly growing, it is not growing in proportion to the amount of time that people are spending online. As a result when organisations look at their web stats they see an upward trend but in relation to overall web trends it is actually going down.

RELATING DIGITAL CONTENT ONLINE TO ORGANISATIONAL GOALS

PETER: Obviously this matters if an important target is to increase the take-up of material on digital platforms. And there are lots of reasons to support a quantitative argument that bigger audiences – or increased use – is good, so a slow rate of interest is therefore bad. However, there is a counter argument based around quality that scale doesn't necessarily produce good results.

JANE FINNIS: In the balance between big-scale and small-scale activities, certainly some people are doing small-scale very well. From our research however, that nobody in the sector is doing big-scale well and that to do big-scale requires the resources and services that only a major player like the BBC can offer. This means that organisations can achieve results on a big scale but only if they partner with a major provider. But organisations can do 'small' very well but to do this they have to redefine what success means and to be realistic about the values involved in being deep and engaging.

PETER: This would have to be in relation to what they have invested in and what their main goals are as an organisation.

JANE FINNIS: It doesn't have to be a digital activity but it has to mean that they are engaging people through an online platform. They could be a gallery with an artist in residence online, or they could be a theatre aiming to sell tickets. They have to define their own definition of success. If the organisation is a museum that has invested millions in digitising their collection they may want people to come and spend at least six minutes looking at a number of objects in the online collection and to download something. That could be their definition of an engaged audience. Or they might need to sell a number of tickets or deal with membership enquiries, and do these things all the way through to the end and finish.

PETER: We could generalise about cultural organisations and say they often have three online audiences. We could extrapolate from this and say that these are applicable to many companies and businesses online too, but cultural organisations often have a degree of conformity. One is the audience that thinks of the institution as a venue they may go to and therefore they are accessing it to get information about visiting or about what they might find when they visit. For this group the criteria for success is that they gain the information, use a service or more generally become interested in something on offer. Second, there is the audience that is uses the website as an intellectual or knowledge resource, and for them the criteria for success is that they are accessing an authoritative resource on a special subject, which might mean downloading images from their collection or using the archives for reference material. But third, there is an online community that does not have any concern about the venue and what it offers or the intellectual content but are interested in being part of a dialogue or a community, their success criteria is social engagement and networking. Obviously different organisations will place a different weight on those options or have different priorities.

JANE FINNIS: All organisations need to define their priorities and invest in them. However, this is made more complicated because what our research shows is few of them approach their activity with a focused definition of what success is. Typically they are driven by the need to take their existing services and activities and put them online, whether it's an online collection, an online ticket service, to have a Facebook page or a Twitter account. But in doing so they are not segmenting their audience, developing their product accordingly and evaluating it based on their definition of success to see if it's working at any detailed level.

KNOWING AND TARGETING THE AUDIENCE

PETER: Do you think this is a problem of organisations not knowing how to appeal to people beyond their obvious catchment population, continuing to attract the sorts of audiences they have always had but not being able to make a leap to reach substantially different audiences?

JANE FINNIS: Organisations often think that audiences want to know about them first of all and what they do. They don't realise they have to talk about something that the audiences are interested in first of all to engage them, and then at the end of the chain there is an event that they can go and see. Often the people who are in the institutions are so immersed in the institutional view of the universe that they can't perceive this with outside eyes. The web was sold to a lot of people, not just in the cultural sector, as a way to reach everybody, as a big democratising moment, but the reality has turned out to me much more complex than that.

PETER: This means that organisations that have a clear sense of why they are developing activities online or digital platforms are more likely to be able to evaluate the results they get. The targets they have for their 'real world' activities might be very different from their targets for their online activities.

JANE FINNIS: In the real world targets are usually specific. When an organisation is planning an exhibition or designing a production they would be unlikely to start by saying 'we're going to make a piece of art or theatre production for everybody and about everything'. They would define a specific subject matter, and targeted a particular age group, or one audience demographic. But in the online world it's hardly ever like that. Instead institutions have evolved their online presence from saying 'this is who we are, this is our website and our social networking and these tell you all about us'. However, there have been good examples of online engagement in the cultural sector in the form of micro-sites where institutions have created a website or social media channel based on an exhibition or other event which are highly targeted.

TRACKING USERS WITH WEB STATS AND QUALITATIVE RESEARCH

PETER: What this implies is that there are different approaches depending on whether there has been a clear set of targets on not. And that the difference is often between specifically designed activities or project sites and more generalised sites that present the institutions brand or offer.

JANE FINNIS: The most interesting examples are when an organisation develops a micro site having set their criteria in advance and then build the site so that way they can monitor the site and track the online usage, including the routes through it and its integration with their social media. This provides an integrated approach combining their observations with user surveys and web stats. As a result they can examine how it operates and identify what has been successful.

PETER: Therefore are you advocating an approach that combines quantitative and qualitative research to get a real picture of users?

JANE FINNIS: Ultimately of course you can gather as much data as you want through analytics so it's important to set priorities in deciding what will be useful in matching your targets. That way you can see how it will manifest itself in a quantitative way. Then you need to go a step further to make qualitative judgments about the data. However, you don't produce qualitative data from Google Analytics so you have to intervene and ask questions directly, to test or back up your assumptions. Social media channels can be assessed for qualitative data if the right critical framework is applied but it can be very time-consuming.

PETER: Sometimes this might lead to relatively easy and measurable outcomes but sometimes they might be more elusive about the value of culture, especially if an organisation is in the public sector supported through public funds. Applying targets around the nature of the online experience can lead to questions that all cultural organisations need to ask their audiences. Sometimes these are as hard to ask as they are to answer because they are asking about the value of culture in society. They need to ask where is 'meaning', and where does 'value' lie?

JANE FINNIS: And organisations may say that it lies in the audience's interaction with the artwork. In which case then they have to decide what makes this valuable. This is why the combination of qualitative and quantitative approaches is necessary. Discovering that 3,000 people viewed a site isn't necessarily useful, or measuring how many seconds people spent looking at a single item, because this doesn't say anything about the way in which people are engaging or gain understanding.

SKILLS AND PARTNERSHIPS

PETER: Do you think it is easy for cultural organisation to develop the skills they need to operate this way with digital platforms? What skills do you think they need to prioritise?

JANE FINNIS: This is not easy for organisations as there are so many skills needed. I think organisations need to decide how much investment and resources they are able to put into digital platforms and how important it is to them. Lots of organisations do not have adequate finances, staff, technical ability or web skills. For them the answer has to be partnerships with other people such as other local networks or marketing organisations to promote what they are doing. This is particularly the case now because, in times of financial caution, companies of all sorts resort to cutting their digital posts and marketing in an effort to secure their core functions. In a risk adverse situation for lots of organisations the main issue is survival and that may mean walking away from things that are harder to quantify and therefore justify.

PETER: One of the underlying causes of this approach is that digital activities have been developed as expansion activities not core activities.

JANE FINNIS: The other side of that is that if they really want to survive and grow they have to do the opposite. Which is to take the risks to get into the digital world, because if they get their content right with the right kind of appeal they can reach lots of people. In our research we looked at the relationship between spend and popularity and between spend and engagement. We found that organisations that spend the most money on their websites and online activities had the most popularity, and as a result they had the greatest web stats, the most likes, and the most brand awareness. Of course this is directly due to the effect of marketing. But you don't necessarily get engagement. If you want engagement it requires that you have the right content in the right place for the right people. Organisations who have niche content get better engagement because they attract a committed and interested audience.

FAILURE AND RISK

PETER: There is an issue for many organisations in taking risk and there are risks involved in investing in digital platforms. This may be why many organisations perpetuate what they are used to doing with their online presence. There is less chance of failure in doing what you have done before, or in promoting yourself as a brand in the way you have traditionally done.

JANE FINNIS: The failure is to not recognise that there are failures, for example that the website doesn't work and that people don't respond to it. Organisations need a balanced approach where they can say that they are failing in one area but they are doing other things quite well. Again, to do this you need to have a clear sense of what your targets are.

PETER: In these cases you are describing, you can't have innovative projects without having risk and you can't have risk without the potential for failure. So the issue is how you construct the notion of failure and if you put shame on failure it becomes a problem.

JANE FINNIS: But there is a difference between mismanagement neglect and irresponsibility and project failure. My advice is often don't just give up and shut something down and start again because it isn't working. Instead, examine why it isn't working.

PETER: It's also necessary to recognise that a project should be seen as part of an ongoing development not as a standalone thing in itself. These issues, and the ability to deal with risk and failure, are about professional perception and aptitude rather than about having acquired skills and knowledge. What do you think are aptitudes that you think are needed by people who want to work in the cultural sector?

JANE FINNIS: Organisations need people who are able to see how their role fits into a bigger picture. One of the hardest things, even in an integrated organisation, is in getting people to see how they are role is part of a bigger picture. I think organisations often fail because they're not able to bring people together. I endlessly have to bang people's heads together to get them to tell each other what they are doing. So I am always interested in people who can see beyond their expertise.

CHAPTER 5

Case study

Communication and marketing networks

Interview with Andrew Chetty

How has the advent of digital networks had an impact on the way that communication agencies operate and companies do business with each other? This study discusses how communications and marketing agencies are using new approaches for business-to-business communications in the light of networked communication. This conversation with a producer for a communications agency and consultancy addresses what it means to work as a producer in a specialist area, creating media products for the financial sector.

ditto is an award winning communications agency and consultancy practice dedicated to the technology, finance and media sectors. Andrew Chetty is the Production Director. Andrew has a background as an arts and media producer having run arts festivals, digital technology programmes at cultural organisations and produced large-scale arts and technology events.

Andrew Chetty says of himself:

> I am the Production Director of ditto, which means that I look after all the output that our studio has coming into it in terms of client and culturally-facing work. I make sure that all the teams who are working on a project operate to plan, to budget and to timetable. I am responsible for ensuring that things happen as contractually agreed.

> Customers want to have a meaningful and on-going dialogue with their service providers. They want to be treated as part of a professional, empowered market community, to be part of the conversation, to be listened to and be valued. They want to have a voice in shaping the solutions that are being provided to them. There is no better testimonial or endorsement than an account becoming

a public facing member of your professional market community, collaborating, sharing problems and experiences. This isn't about social media. This is about direct conversations of value. Our customers are creating specific, targeted communities that have depth and purpose; an exclusive club providing members with insights, intelligence and market knowledge. The findings are compelling. Own the account, own the conversation and thereby own the market. If you don't your competition will. This is about getting there first, building on a strong foundation and putting in place the long-term relationship infrastructure for your business.

THE ROLE OF AN AGENCY AND THE SKILLS REQUIRED IN PRODUCTION

PETER: What is your background and what skills are required for your work as part of ditto?

ANDREW CHETTY: My background is being a producer in the music and cultural sector so it's a natural marriage in terms of the planning and scheduling side of things which is where my skills lie. My job is very pragmatic. I'm not responsible for finding creative solutions, I am responsible for managing them, which is the main difference between my job and previous production work I have had in the cultural sector.

PETER: What are the things that make ditto distinctive?

ANDREW CHETTY: A lot of the work that we do at ditto could be described as management consultancy. We specialise in the finance, technology and media sectors. This means our business has a very particular focus. Our clients come to us to help them in communicating business-to-business (B2B), allowing them to run campaigns, sell or launch new products or new services to their sector.

PETER: What is the distinction between B2B communication and most of the online marketing campaigns that we experience? And how does this shape the work you do?

ANDREW CHETTY: B2B is not the same as a business-to-consumer form of communication, as you would see with a company like Coca-Cola or Nike. Typically, a client that is within the finance or the banking sector may want to sell a new product, or existing product, to other banks. They will come to us to help them organise this operation. We work with the clients to build the assets they need to actualise their campaign. Nine times out of ten they are so close to their product that they need outside eyes to help them sort it out. Sorting it out comes in many shapes. Sometimes it is to help them sort out the business plan that is associated with the new service, setting it up and making it operational, and it can also involve looking at how their sales teams and how they engage with their customer base and how they go about selling things.

THE NEW AGENCY MODEL AND THE 'FREEMIUM' MEDIA ECONOMY

PETER: Is this typical of an approach that an agency takes?

ANDREW CHETTY: We take what is called a 'new agency model' approach. Under the old agency model you would typically find advertising companies, and sometimes new media and design companies. With the old model a company that was developing a marketing strategy to promote a product would have a contract with a 'top agency'. The top agency would be the main contact but wouldn't actually do the work, instead it would sub contract out work to other 'sub agencies' that would usually specialise in one specific thing, like putting on an event. That would carry on down creating a chain of agencies.

PETER: And therefore this would result in a financial chain from the client to the sub agencies. How does the new agency model differ?

ANDREW CHETTY: Financially the old agency was built on media 'buy in', where a company would buy media for their clients and they would take a percentage cut, and then the agency would dedicate a team to that client using the profit. When you are looking at old media like TV ads, newspapers or magazine ads that is a huge amount of money because those were very expensive platforms for promotion. But in the media shattered sector that we are now in 'freemium' is the norm – in other words so many media outlets are free. Primarily social media has become such an important channel, and access to it is free, so the media buying business model has suddenly fallen apart, and this has placed a huge pressure on agencies who are now having to re-address how they do things.

PETER: What is ditto's approach to working in a freemium media economy?

ANDREW CHETTY: Agencies like ditto have managed to circumvent this problem by operating in a more multi-strand way. Clients come to us and have one conversation. We define the strategic management of their project as part of this conversation and then we open it to our departments which will build all the assets they need for their campaign. This means that they will be directly in contact to the creatives so they can be as close as they want to be to the creation of the assets which we will then activate.

CREATING AN APP TO ENABLE COMMUNICATION AND NETWORKING

PETER: If your main business is to enable business-to-business promotion and the communication between corporations and their business clients, do you involve yourself in the development of the product itself? Is there always a product in the traditional way or are there times that the product you are promoting is the communication itself rather than a conventional asset?

ANDREW CHETTY: With social networking for business communications it can be both. Recently we worked with a major bank and one of the activities that they wanted to develop was a very particular line of communications with journalists and analysts. One of the roles of the bank is to present financial forecasts. The bank wanted to be able to communicate in a better way to journalists and analysts in order to enable a conversation to take place rather than just disseminating the content of the speeches. We came up with a number of options and built an app that could function as a broadcasting and publishing channel to enable them to publicise the sentiments behind the speech. This created a framework that could then be repeated in any campaign over a period of time. This is an example of the way we get involved in the creation of the final product. But it needs to be said that the bank did not know what the final product would be until we sat down with them and devised it so the product comes out of the process.

PETER: What is the typical scenario when a company comes to you having already defined the product or type of product they want to launch? Do they often have a clear sense of the community or influential members within the sector that they needed to target?

ANDREW CHETTY: This is often the case and we then aim to develop a strategy that may enable them to think about what they're trying to sell in a different way from the approach that they may have used before. This may offer them better way to reach a wider number of people or make their product resonate more effectively. Our principal goal is to shorten the sales cycle. Whereas the typical sales cycle from initial prospect to finish may take 12 months we help them make the process more efficient by giving them better collateral. This gives them more insight and gives them a better approach to allow them to communicate faster.

PETER: Do you bring a different approach based upon a different understanding of what media and networked communications can offer?

ANDREW CHETTY: Frequently those companies are not 'joined up' in the way they go about selling their products, by which I mean they're not thinking about the way the physical sits alongside the digital but instead they are narrowly focused on the way they are accustomed to using a particular channel, for example they are in the habit of doing email campaigns or going to networking meetings where they make PowerPoint presentations. But they need to understand that if they can make their output sit among the suite of assets, and employ a certain kind of script that we would produce for them, then they will engage in a better way, and can use multiple channels simultaneously, and they will sell the product ultimately faster than they are currently doing.

WORKING WITH ASSETS AND CREATING ONLINE COMMUNITIES

PETER: When you talk about 'assets' do you mean the key product itself that clients want to sell?

ANDREW CHETTY: By assets I mean the items that are used by the sales team, the marketing team or the company in general to go out and sell their product to the business sector. Assets can be a range of things.

PETER: Can assets be notional?

ANDREW CHETTY: A lot of the work that we do is creating 'thought leadership' within companies. So what does that mean? There are different ways to sell products, for example you can market them or build collateral and sell it on. But another, and what we tend to do, is to help companies to present themselves as leaders in that field. So we allow them to create 'thought leadership' within their sector. Currently we're working with an international company that specialises in making the software that is used by companies whose business is the management of buildings, from amenities management to the construction, and the software helps them manage those processes. The company is well established in the US and they want to break into the UK. So part of our work at the moment is to take that expertise, package it and place it back into the market and show their peers and their potential client base what they are doing. So we are enabling them to create communities that are driven by their leadership. They can stimulate the discussions that take place in these communities by the presentation of their knowledge and expertise, what we often call presenting 'white papers' and this helps give them an authority as leaders in the sector or 'thought leadership'.

PETER: When you are talking about communities do you mean specifically online communities?

ANDREW CHETTY: This is distinctly different from available social media platforms like Twitter channels. We may use them but they are only a means to an end. These communities are usually invite-only.

TAKING CONTROL OF THE PLATFORM AND CREATING COMMUNITIES OF INTEREST

PETER: What you are describing sounds as though it is a parallel to the way that, in a traditional model, people develop a new product, which could be music, an invention or academic research. They pitch what they have developed within a given sector so that it is familiar and gains significance. They might do this through publishing peer reviewed articles or papers in journals, attending conferences and festivals or taking part in media events. But in your model, instead of always contributing their effort and labour to someone else's platform, the producer controls the platform. And they create communities with a common interest.

ANDREW CHETTY: Absolutely, and when you set up a platform and invite people in, you get them contributing so it is a collaboration. But you also take their insight and you are able to re-purpose this back under the umbrella that you have created.

PETER: From your description it seems that this requires a complex set of skills. First, there is the skill to work with clients and communicate with them at their level and understanding. This means you need to understand the specifics of the language in their sector. Second, you've got to be able to devise and set up the right platform which is a technical aspect. Third, to make that platform work means you have to have the authority to get the right people in and have the right level of credibility in the sector. So it appears that production requires a social and business skill as well as a technological one.

ANDREW CHETTY: We are responsible for understanding the context, to be able to give them the assets to allow them to go and sell better. The complexity comes from the fact that the main thing that drives all our clients is that there is a bottom line. No matter where we start we're always having to understand what it is they're trying to achieve. And usually they want sales – they want to see an X per cent uptake in sales over the year using this approach. If they will invest money they expect to see a return of investment at a certain per cent over a given time period. Therefore there is an underlying pressure from the business model. They are not doing it for any other reason.

PETER: However, you are not responsible for the sales. You are responsible for creating the environment from which they are responsible for the sales. What would be a typical approach to assist a company to engage with their clients?

ANDREW CHETTY: One of the things we do is create what we call 'concept labs' so rather than going out and broadcasting one-to-many, through traditional marketing, or one to a few, we identify people in the business that our businesses want to go to and direct the marketing to them. The next step is to invite them to concept labs to 'solution out' some of the issues. Through this process we help them find answers to their problem using the structure which may include bringing in a number of teams and using software development models.

PETER: What is the typical kind of thing that a business in the finance industry would want to develop?

ANDREW CHETTY: Under the old model it used to be a brochure or a video or a new promotions tool. Now it's an app or one of the platforms I have been describing. They want to have something new to be able to engage with their client base. What a salesperson wants to do is to start a conversation or to continue a conversation. Collateral assets are exactly what they want.

THE EFFECT OF CONNECTEDNESS AND STICKINESS ON BUSINESS

PETER: Is this an example of commercial business in the era of 'sticky attention'?

ANDREW CHETTY: Exactly. Content is king, but stickiness is absolutely the important thing. Stickiness is one of the most important things because once you've got the asset you need to create a stickiness to keep the clients there and to keep them coming back. Hence the reason why we build communities. And our communities aren't about high numbers, our communities are about quality.

PETER: It can be said that networked media has created a shift in the way that people expect to have contact with who they buy services from. The model used to be for a business to develop a good product and to prove it offered a good service. Now it is all those things, but it is also necessary for a business to be 'connected' – to keep in contact with their sector, giving and receiving feedback. Now, a question asked of businesses is do they have an active relationship with their community and do they reinforce it? In short do they have a relationship? These are all the things that we've come to expect through social networking.

ANDREW CHETTY: But in addition to that, the underlying thing that is really important is that there is a business transaction expected from every conversation. So clients like this are not developing projects for brand awareness or to boost their profile. They are doing it to create a business transaction or to lead to a series of outcomes that will result in a business transaction. That is the incentive and if a program doesn't work they will shut it down.

PETER: Are there ways in which a company can increase its value by implementing a campaign to present itself as a 'knowledge leader' or to use communities of common interest to make it more competitive in the marketplace?

ANDREW CHETTY: One of our clients was a company that provided middleware for foreign exchanges. They were interested in raising their corporate value. We put together a campaign that involved editorial and trade press, micro sites, corporate videos, white papers and schedules for where they would be published. In doing so they raised their profile but more significantly they increased their market value. A year later they were very advantageously bought by a major corporation. We weren't responsible for them being bought but corporate action was the intended endgame. To do that they needed to be able to tell potential investors the story, and get them to engage with that story.

PETER: Recently ditto worked with a company called Renew, which secured a contract to create recycling bins for the City of London, in the heart of the financial business district. Renew's innovative proposal was to use these as 'communication pods' by building real-time information screens into the sides of the bomb-proof recycling bins that could carry live data and provide city workers with up-to-date information ranging from weather reports to the latest stock market results. This produced a digital alternative to visual information, which was all the more significant because this was an area of London where advertising was not allowed under city regulations. What was ditto's role in the Renew project?

ANDREW CHETTY: Renew came to us because they had developed something unique. Their recycling pods were designed with video screens in either end and so what the company had effectively created was a broadcast channel for screening content into the streets of London. And most significantly, these were positioned in an area that no advertiser or broadcaster had access to, and being located in the heart of the financial district of London this product therefore offered something unique as it reached one of the most valuable demographics in the world. The company approached us because they had collateral, in the form of airtime, that they could sell. But rather than use a model of selling advertising or seeking sponsorship they wanted to develop a different approach and to sell the concept of the pods as a broadcast point to investors for the project and potential clients. To do this meant building relationships with their target community and this required a sophisticated campaign across multiple platforms so that they could not only promote this unique offer but create a conversation around its advantages and what it could offer. We created a series of websites, mobile apps, video and presentations that would allow them to do that. As a result they achieved their goals in terms of gaining commercial content. The company has now also developed an international profile and the recycling pods with broadcast screens are now in Wall Street and Singapore.

RUNNING THE BUSINESS: THE SKILLS AND EXPERTISE REQUIRED TO WORK IN AN AGENCY

PETER: Who makes up the team at ditto and what sort of professional roles are required to make a project with a client happen?

ANDREW CHETTY: As a company we have a very clear process. It all starts with our editorial team. This team includes people working on brand concepts, copywriting and topline messaging. From the topline all the assets will follow, and this will require content in the form of videos, white papers, themes, websites or micro sites. To create these we have graphic and digital design teams, tech teams for mobile apps, video teams, infographics and lastly a team for events.

PETER: How much of this work is done by members of the company and how much by freelancers?

ANDREW CHETTY: Nearly all is done within the company, unless we have to have highly specialised skills. The strategy of the new agency model means that everyone you need to speak to will be sitting within the studio. And unlike other agencies we don't work on a retainer basis with clients we work on a project-by-project basis. So clients work with us on a specific piece of work.

PETER: How does this compare to the work that you used to do within the arts and music sector as a digital media producer.

ANDREW CHETTY: There's no comparison – it's a world apart. Certainly in both areas I've been responsible for complex projects that required managing multiple levels of operation that happening simultaneously. Sometimes arts projects have had budgets that have been over a million pounds. But the difference between the arts sector and the financial sector is the approach to thinking about the goals and how to reach them. You have to approach financial projects on a completely different level in this sector because at the end of the day there is an empirical measure of the financial transaction.

PETER: Do you think that the approach you have is partly the result of the fact that you came from the cultural sector and developed many of your skills there? So you are, in effect, operating with a convergence of skillsets?

ANDREW CHETTY: Yes, and a significant number of the people who started up ditto came from the cultural sector so it is not an accident. Having a combination of different sorts of expertise can be very important as it gives you different ways of seeing the world.

PETER: Do you find that working in the finance sector gives you the space and impetus to be creative because it is a highly competitive environment?

ANDREW CHETTY: Yes and as a result I think we can innovate more than we could within the cultural sector. One of the things we found at the very beginning when ditto was established was that we would have similar conversations going in parallel. One would be with a client in the cultural sector and one with the client from the financial sector. And our cultural client often had very clear ideas about their preferred way of working, whereas our finance sector client was willing to take the risk with innovation because the reward was potentially great. And that was one of the things that tipped the balance and confirmed to us that we could create a successful and challenging business out of devising multiplatform events and projects in this sector.

CHAPTER 6

Case study

Networking the art museum

Interview with John Stack

How does an institution build on its online presence to stimulate change through-out the organisation? This discussion looks at the digital and online activities of Tate, one of the most influential art museums in the world, with one of the most successful websites. How can an organisation learn lessons from having transforming its website and examining what it can achieve online, and apply that thinking to develop a new digital strategy for the organisation? This discussion also demonstrates how thinking digitally requires organisations to change the way they have traditionally operated, but that as a result it raises issues about the way they communicate their brand and identity, provide authored content and present a space for public opinions.

Tate is one of Britain's leading art institutions, with a mission to 'promote the public understanding and enjoyment of British, modern and contemporary art'. Tate houses the UK's collection of British art from 1500 to the present day and of international modern and contemporary art: almost 70,000 artworks in total, some of which are displayed at four galleries in the UK. Tate's website plays a crucial part in the delivery of its ambitions. It is a world leader among the websites of arts organisations, and one of the most visited cultural sites in the UK, attracting close to 2 million visitors each month. It contains the art collection of Tate as an online resource, research and documentation, marketing and sales material. Tate sees its website as a place for conversation and dialogue, as well as a place to access information. It has a consistently strong following with international visitors and almost 40 per cent of Tate's online audiences are from outside the UK. It employs over 1,000 staff members.

John Stack says of himself:

> I'm Head of Tate Online. My job description says I am responsible for the online content strategy and the online platform. I am responsible for presenting the content, no matter where it comes from, and making sense of it through the technology and the design. So the three areas in which I work are content, technology and design.

DEVELOPING A STRATEGY

PETER: Tate re-launched its website 12 months ago, which substantially changed the way that the website functioned and how it gave access to the institution. Does this mean that you have identified how you want to operate for the foreseeable future?

JOHN STACK: Not at all – we are in transition. We launched the new version of Tate website as a result of a two-year project prior to which it had never been revised. The focus of the last two years has been getting heads down, tearing down the old website, moving everything across and adding all kinds of new features. Now that we are in a position when we know it is successful we can start to ask different kinds of questions. As a result we're working on a new digital strategy. Initially I thought it would be a new stage of activity, an extension of the re-launch, but actually it is turning into something more broad and exciting.

PETER: In many organisations a digital strategy can be a list of the current limitations of their website in relation to key opportunities that they need to address. How is yours different?

JOHN STACK: Our new strategy has become much larger. It's asking how are we going to address our digital presence throughout the organisation, and to retool and regroup to look at it. Significantly the new strategy is called the Digital Strategy not the Online Strategy.

PETER: Is this a direct result of having re-launched the website and having developed a critical framework to examine what you are doing?

JOHN STACK: What has happened is that in the last two years digital activity has gone from being something that was to one side of the organisation's activity. But now, concerns with digital, online and social media have begun to appear in the strategies of most departments within the institution. This has led to staff responsibilities and the creation of new digital roles which five years ago would have reported to me but now sit within other departments. As a result we are starting to move to a hub and spoke model for digital activities rather than a centralised department. For example, a digital marketing manager sits within the marketing department rather than the online department as they would have previously. And in the medium term I think instead of there being a digital marketing manager all the marketing managers will have 'digital' within their jobs descriptions. So the transition is institutional, not just concerned with the Online Department.

THE ROLE AND FUNCTION OF AN ONLINE DEPARTMENT

PETER: What is the role and make-up of the team for which you are responsible?

JOHN STACK: In the Online Department we have computer programmers looking at systems development and integration, designers doing front-end interface, a production team of people overseeing projects, and a small editorial team. One of the issues we had with the old website was that it was not being maintained consistently so we centralised editorial control to address this. However, as a result of the new approach less and less content will be sub-edited, overseen or shaped by people on my team.

PETER: Can a devolved structure of this sort have disadvantages, in terms of management, as well as advantages?

JOHN STACK: Of course the risk is that it can become an incoherent mess. University websites are shown as an example of what can happen if departments head off in their own direction, which may not matter as they may have different

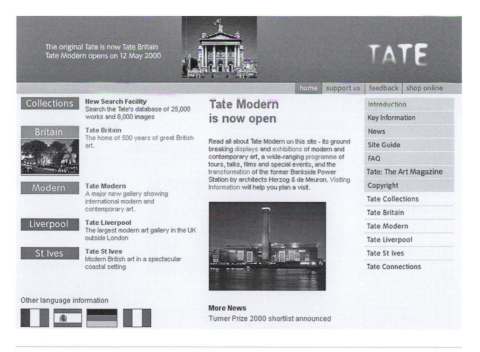

FIGURE 6.1
Screengrab of Tate website (2000)

FIGURE 6.2
Screengrab of Tate website (2004)

Sigmar Polke
History of Everything
2 October 2003 - 4 January 2004

This is a significant opportunity to see recent work by one of Germany's most renowned artists. Polke's distorted use of mass-media imagery explores controversial themes such as the hunt for the Taliban and America's obsession with guns. This major exhibition is both visually stimulating and thought-provoking.

▶ Find out more   ▶ Book tickets

FIGURE 6.3
Screengrab of Tate website (2006)

Kandinsky: The Path to Abstraction
Until 1 October

This exhibition follows Wassily Kandinsky's intriguing journey from landscape painter to modernist master, as he strove to develop a radically abstract language. We recommend booking in advance for this blockbuster exhibition.
Find out more >
Buy tickets

Holbein in England
28 September 2006 - 7 January 2007

Through an outstanding collection of paintings brought together from around the world, this exhibition documents the thrill of the court and life in Tudor England.
Find out more >
Buy tickets

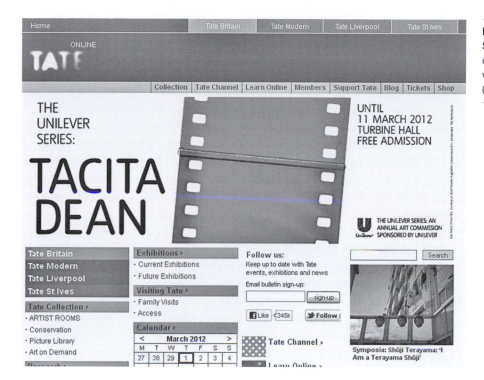

FIGURE 6.4
Screengrab
of Tate
website
(2012)

audiences. Whereas with Tate, there is more of a commonality of interest between different people who make up our audience from teachers to researchers to visitors. As a result the content is more broadly applicable to all of them, and there is more need for a more coherent whole. Therefore one of the roles ahead is that of an editor in chief, though this person will not be responsible for deciding what is or isn't created but for creating the coherence of the whole.

CREATING THE STRUCTURE OF A WEBSITE

PETER: What you are describing as an outcome of the re-launch of the website appears to be a profound conceptual change. How is this reflected in the structure of the site?

JOHN STACK: For a start the site is no longer called Tate Online, it's just the Tate website. In terms of its organisational structure it has gone from being vertical to horizontal because it needs to work in a networked form across the organisation rather than in a vertical form with one person in charge leading it.

PETER: Often institutions design their websites so that they reflect the organisation and have an organisational presence like a building, an entity that visitors can come to. Is that one of the roles of the Tate website or does it have a different notion of the way an audience will use it?

JOHN STACK: The old website was very much based around the structure and functions of the organisation, which is a typical way for museums and galleries to develop their sites, but wasn't really servicing business requirements or audience needs. Instead the new site has been restructured around what audiences want. As a result lots of sections of the site that were named after departments disappeared and their content re-positioned across the site, and interlinked.

PETER: Do you think that visitors have a singular sense of what the website is for?

JOHN STACK: I think what we have created has a unified presence and the whole site has a homogenous design now, but within that there are various sections that have their own character and purpose. The site is huge, there's hundreds of thousands of pages and so no one really can have a grasp of the entire thing. In that sense it has to be seen as a whole.

PETER: Reorganising the site so that content is distributed and retrieved dynamically and laterally, rather than to use a hierarchical file-folder structure for navigation, would appear to be a logical thing to do for a complex organisation. But are there additional issues of scale if you are working with a vast amount of material?

JOHN STACK: One of the challenges of this approach is that not only was it a tricky thing to do once, it was not a one-off activity. Anytime someone comes with a piece of content we have to ask where does that content go, where is it linked from. This is a conversation you have to have every single time.

PETER: We could say that a site like Tate's website has to serve multiple purposes because you have multiple audiences. But at the same time, are there institutional priorities that are reflected in the site?

JOHN STACK: You could look at the home page of the website and say that it prioritises marketing and communications especially relating to exhibitions. But at the same time we know that only a third of the website visitors are planning to make a visit to the organisation. So you could ask, why should we give the majority of attention to a third of the audience. But there are reasons why this should be so that are to do with institutional agendas and strategies. Consequently, navigating these challenges and setting priorities is very challenging because there is no shortage of ideas but there is a limited capacity. However, it has to be said that if you ask anyone in the organisation what the website is for they will respond from their own perspective.

ENABLING NAVIGATION THROUGHOUT THE SITE

PETER: Do most people access Tate's website from Google or another search engine or do they come via front-end navigation?

JOHN STACK: They come into the site deep via search engines. So most visits don't include a visit to the home page.

PETER: That adds to the complexity of the question of whether or not the site prioritises visitors who may visit Tate, if most website users bypass the home

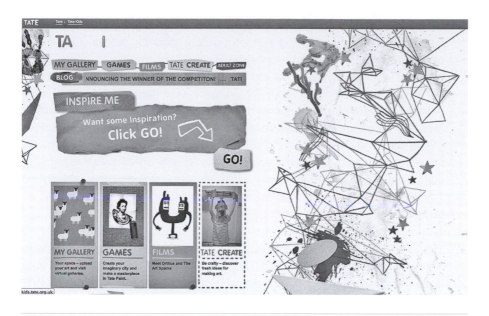

FIGURE 6.5
Screengrab of Tate Kids section of Tate website (2013)

page. When visitors are within the site how do you want them to experience it? Do you encourage people to move laterally or to use a navigation structure?

JOHN STACK: One of the things we were very keen on was to try and push people sideways from one place to another. We've done that very successfully in the online collection where users will select an artwork but then be given an option for 'other artworks you may be interested in'. But it deliberately tries to give you not what you'd expect, it tries to give you things that are a little bit off the beaten track. That way people can click around the whole collection without having to go through the search feature. The intention is to move away from having an online collection that is like a reference card taking users to where the actual content is. In contrast it offers something that's more browseable. These sorts of things of design approaches are what you see on Amazon and commercial online platforms all the time. These approaches give ways to increase the sideways journeys from content to content, rather than expecting people to use a formal navigation structure.

BRANDING A SITE AND CREATING ITS IMAGE

PETER: How much does a site need to have a consistent brand or image? Most organisations are very determined to maintain their visual brand in marketing and print materials though design and typeface. But on a website, if visitors come in at deep points, through external search engines or links, does it matter if they have a sense of being part of the Tate site? Or is it enough if they sample the content and move on again.

JOHN STACK: I expect most of us visit new sites most days, and we constantly find ourselves exposed to a new organisation or individual. We might ask if we are reading a reputable journal or at some random person's blog posting. And in a sense we don't care, because we will make our judgments based on the quality of the content and experience. It is important to recognise that capacity in audiences. So we need to deliver quality content. But in terms of our brand, it's also important that audiences will know that they are on the Tate site. For that reason every page carries a logo.

PETER: So we could say that branding has to be handled with subtlety but also with consistency?

JOHN STACK: Especially since our digital presence is increasingly all over the place, it's on Flickr, on Facebook, on YouTube and on iTunes. In that sense the Tate brand does become important because it becomes a signifier of high quality arts content no matter where it is. It needs to be something that audiences are aware of but not necessarily at the front of their attention, because they're usually not necessarily interested in Tate, they're interested in art.

WHAT IS THE CRITERIA FOR MEASURING THE SUCCESS OF A WEBSITE?

PETER: What is Tate's criteria for the success or value of the website? Google Analytics gives you detailed information about where your traffic is coming from and how people moving through it. But the larger questions that we've been talking about are how philosophically the online presence helps the organisation understand itself.

JOHN STACK: We have Key Performance Indicators, for example, revenue, number of visits and dwell time, but these just give part of the picture. But there's not a large enough understanding within the organisation of what success looks like in the digital space to currently engage colleagues in the dialogue that we want. As a result we have recently created a new role for a Web Analyst who can spend time on surveys, analytics, reports and projects we've initiated to ask 'what does success look like here?' Through this we want to get to the point where colleagues in the organisation are making decisions based on qualitative and quantitative research rather than gut instinct. Gut instinct can, of course, produce good things but it needs to be backed up by substantiated information.

PETER: Does this help you evaluate relatively ambiguous but necessary goals such as 'increased participation' and 'engagement'?

JOHN STACK: Words like engagement and participation and interaction are the ones that get bandied around, interestingly by all kinds of different departments meaning all kinds of slightly different things, and so it's not necessarily a straightforward thing. If you want the website to be more social, to be based more around the community, it's actually a hard thing to measure. You can do it quantitatively and measure the numbers of comments on an article or qualitatively by evaluating what kinds of comments you got or how many discussions took place. But neither gives you an entire picture, and sometimes you have to make a personal assessment that takes account of the context.

CREATING PLATFORMS FOR PARTICIPATION, MULTIPLE VOICES, DISCUSSION AND DEBATE

PETER: How does participation play a role in the Tate website? One of your goals is to 'develop engaging platforms for multiple voices, discussion and debate'. However, traditionally the online presence of most gallery or museum websites has been about providing the user with the authoritative presentation of information, such as presenting its collection, scholarly material and research as well as information on its current activities. How does an institutional website such as this open itself to individual voices, communities and interactions or enable an exchange of voices and opinions?

JOHN STACK: Fundamentally this is the direction in which we are moving. Many of the projects that we will be launching in the next year are starting to address how the audience can write back to the museum. On the website there is a greater freedom to do that than in the physical museum, but I think this will start to spread out into the museum more and more. We plan to have audience members being able to take works from the collection online, comment on them and start to upload their own material next to them. We are also looking at incorporating crowd sourcing knowledge or adding personal feedback. A lot of these sorts of things are design challenges, by which I mean design in the broader sense because putting a comment thread on everything is not actually going to offer a solution. But within the institution there is a strong belief that artworks are there to generate new meaning and therefore we are able to ask what are the platforms on which those meanings can be expressed. And obviously online gives us this possibility.

PETER: Do you anticipate supporting open content platforms and allowing the distribution of content to other sites?

JOHN STACK: We have the possibility to develop our own platforms but we can also facilitate the use of other people's platforms. This leads us to ask how can we enable people to take and do things with our content elsewhere. As a result we are looking at Creative Commons licensing, and reuse of content. On one hand this is to unlock the value of our content. But it leads to a deeper question – it is a way of asking why would you come to our site and write a blog about this when you could take our image and put it on your Facebook page and write something there.

PETER: From what you are saying a site like this can do is to explore the ethos around what participation and community is. So as an online user I may be accessing high quality information about art but I may also get the sense that the site is open to my existence and that two-way connections are being made, that it's not just a broadcast medium.

JOHN STACK: This has had an effect on the way we work with content. Previously projects might have featured a major Flash animation but instead they are more likely to have a blog, or a Tumblr account, or a page with a Twitter account. Instead the money that would have been spent on creating expensive content will go towards employing a community manager who will shape the project: locate existing or external content, commission films and control the social engagement. These kinds of roles are ones that we didn't have previously. Another interesting thing about participation is that different people in the organisation want to do it for different reasons. The Marketing Department may want to do it because they want to expose the product to a network effect

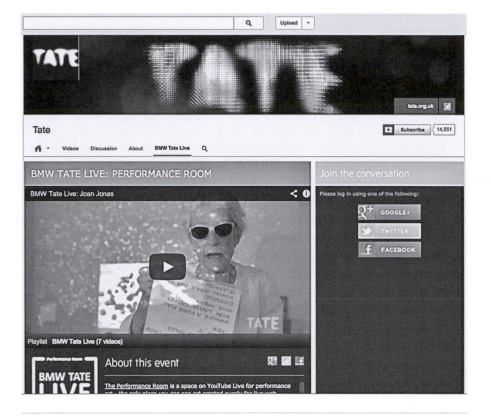

FIGURE 6.6
Screengrab of Tate channel on YouTube (2013). Tate connects to content on other platforms from its own website (www.YouTube.com/user/tate/tatelive)

that will happen when people re-tweet their tweets. However, other departments might feel this approach was a shallow level of engagement and want the deep engagement that comes from asking meaningful questions and getting people to contribute to a dialogue.

WHO PRODUCES CONTENT AND HOW DO THEY PRODUCE IT?

PETER: This marks a shift from websites being online content providers to being community facilitators. How do you envisage these different approaches taking place?

JOHN STACK: It points towards the question of whether with these different activities within the organisations are there different audiences or are they the same audience. And in what ways do we need to join those things up and at what level do we not need to join them up. Given that the institution is going to have more voices maybe it will be inevitable that separate communities of interest are going to grow.

PETER: There are many ways in which the structure and approach of a website can indicate a new approach to generating content. Do you find that as the new site develops it starts to appear to be more spontaneous in its style?

JOHN STACK: One thing we had on the old site was a lot of little micro sites, or project showcases, that were at the end of projects. But we wanted to move away from a research project simply having a number of outputs often published in the last six weeks of a project to ones where we are encouraging blogging as we are going along. However, this creates a tension between the highly polished, potentially peer-reviewed output and then a rougher material that emerges as you go along. There is a tension between those things, but I am comfortable with this and I think as an organisation we need to accept that is how it is, and that polished content such as short films and articles have become an important touchpoint to us.

PETER: Does this only apply to content from curators or does it apply to content from other departments?

JOHN STACK: It is an integrated approach. So it is much more common for an email or a tweet from Tate to link not to an exhibition page with marketing information to encourage you to buy tickets but to a video of the curator or a curators blog post and from there to try and engage you before taking you to a 'book now' link.

PETER: You used the term 'rougher material'. Does having content that is produced by members of the organisation in a more spontaneous way mean that it has to be categorised as having different value or style from more traditional forms of material?

JOHN STACK: There will still be certain material, that has a number of people working over it, with the communications department, the marketing department, even the curator writing it and then having it sub-edited, so it's pretty polished content. But on the other hand there could be a blog post by me or another person for a research project, and we will not run this by anybody, we will just post it. The first will be on a page with a huge amount of traffic, and the second will have a smaller audience because maybe only 50 people in the world will interested in the subject. And one is pored over and worried about by a team and the other is just managed by one person. This is because it is not institutional communication it's a personal voice from one person. But in terms of the website they have the same status they are just posts.

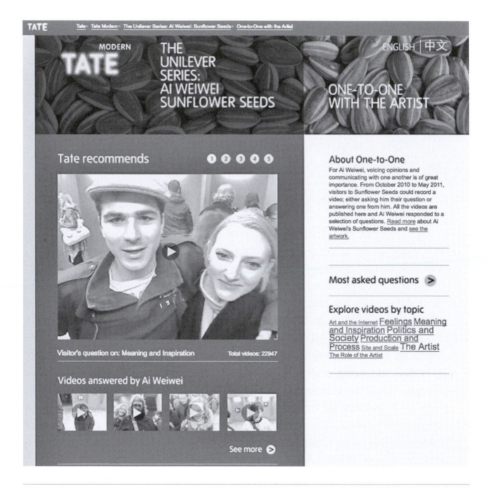

FIGURE 6.7
One-to-one with the artist, The Unilever Series: Ai Weiwei, *Sunflower Seeds* (2000). The site enabled audiences to upload questions as video clips to the artist, Ai Weiwei, about his installation *Sunflower Seeds*, which was shown at Tate Modern in London in 2010–11. The artist would then respond by posting his replies online

OPENING A SITE TO AUTHORED CONTENT
AND PUBLIC OPINION

PETER: This might make perfect sense to an online visitor but websites still reflect an institution's value. Traditionally most museums and galleries would have an institutional voice that conveyed its authority. The same would be said of many commercial organisations. What effect does allowing an individual voice to be heard, that is not the institution's voice, have on the organisation?

JOHN STACK: It's very interesting because on the old website very few things had a byline, except for parts of the site like our peer-reviewed journal where the authors had copyright of the articles and therefore had credit. Now lots more content has a byline so multiple voices and multiple personalities start to appear. I think the result will be that the website will end up being like a newspaper, which is full of voices.

PETER: Giving space to the individual's voice also relates to allowing the online public discussion and opinions. When an organisation is opening itself to discussion, what the extent to which you would want to have an editorial control? Are there times that you need to exert it?

JOHN STACK: The debate about dialogue and discussion is very complex. Should we become an open platform for discussion around arts in which case we could not control the nature of the contributions? There is a certain code of ethics around what a curator may or may not say. But public contributors might say things we don't like or would not chose to say. For example, they might have controversial opinions about artists and this could not only create public discord but affect our relationship with the artist. Or they might use the opportunity to promote or interact with the commercial art world, which is something we would never do on our site for reasons of professional impartiality. As a result we have to ask if we ought to challenge the idea that we can have control.

CULTURES OF CHANGE WITHIN TATE,
FAILURE AND RISK

PETER: Often the criticism of big organisations is that they are slow to change and slow in responding to other things that are happening in the outside world. But as you've just said the positive side has so much attached to it.

JOHN STACK: The digital is going so fast that you find something is going to be obsolete in three years. Digital doesn't care about the departmental boundaries, so sometimes it's forcing change faster than the organisation can handle it, and one of the challenges there is that it comes down to individuals to being very open-minded about rethinking how they can operate and what their departments should do. Digital thinking, digital skills and digital literacy are going to become important and I think the organisation is capable of dealing with this.

PETER: A lot of what you are trying to achieve is clearly experimental, maybe not necessarily in terms of applications of technology but in the way that the online presence is being developed. Does this mean that you have to calculate risk and anticipate that some things will be unsuccessful?

JOHN STACK: Within the museum and gallery digital sector there is a lot more talk about projects that have been unsuccessful and what can we learn from that. The freedom to fail is really quite important.

PETER: What kind of organisational culture will support that approach? Do you think that the scale of an institutional affects the way that it can accommodate an experimental approach? Maybe it is easier for large cultural organisations because they are used to handling different projects from exhibitions, publications or films and know that some will be successful with audiences and some of them won't. Whereas a small organisation that is putting all its eggs in one basket could get burned by failure.

JOHN STACK: I think it takes a kind of entrepreneurial approach which Tate is good at. To make an analogy, plants produce two types of seeds, the seeds fall near the plant because the ground around it is likely to be fertile, and therefore successful. And then there are plants with seeds designed to be blown a long way, and they may reach new areas but they will have many failures. And on one hand institutions like Tate are slow-moving and bureaucratic so propagate by dropping seeds close by, and on the other hand the digital space lends itself more to experimentation and analysis and an approach that is about doing lots of things that may lead to failure then trying again. So this is more like the second. And I think in our department we have quite good culture of understanding what takes root. Maybe that is part of our success.

WHAT MANAGEMENT SKILLS MAKE SITE SUCCESSFUL?

PETER: As a head of an online department, is being critical an essential management skill that is required to make a website operate successfully and to go forward? By this, I mean looking out at what's happening in the wider context and responding to it, and then looking in to work out what your unique needs are as an organisation.

JOHN STACK: It's both looking out and looking in. That's the core of my role as Head of Tate Online. Looking in means talking to people in the organisation to find out what they want and devising the best way of achieving that, but also putting some rigour around that process. Everyone wants to be involved in design because they think it's the fun way of solving a problem, but it's not a way of finding out what we want to achieve, nor of responding to it. So I keep the focus on our goals and push people that bit further. Then in terms of facing out I am always researching the sector. I read an enormous amount of research papers, I look at other platforms that are emerging and ask what are the trends. I need to know when we should innovate really fast, because there's a first mover advantage, when we experiment and when we choose keep up with trends. All these things are important.

Part II

Convergent media

CHAPTER 7

Convergent media

What is convergent media and how does it differ from other separate and distinct media? As this section goes on to detail, the convergence of previously separate cultural and media forms and practices has created a new working environment for the production of media, the common feature of which is networked computing. Computers and the screen interface constitute the space of convergence of previously separate forms of the production and consumption of media-based communication. Convergence is a consequence of the digital tools used for media production in which software combines the manipulation of the moving with the still, the graphic with the photographic, the typographic with the filmic, the visual with the sonic. Having said this not all media is produced in the convergent environment and, imagined as a continuous line, there is a high-end of applications, in major feature film production for example, where dedicated software and computers are used to manipulate and render large files and a low-end where digital processes interface with analogue systems. Each point on this continuum entails the use of specific software, requiring specific skills while at the same time there is a generic set of skills and familiarity with software use.

HYBRIDITY

The revaluation of old media through the prism of digital media, or the visioning of digital media possibilities through the lens of old media is a response to the phenomena of convergence in technologies and media ownership. Convergence is also a way of thinking about the current state of digital media languages. Practical developments in digital media language, as well as the cultural conversation about digital media can, at best, be regarded as a patchwork of knowledge and understanding. We can look at what some of the key knowledge and skill transfer consists of in terms of what is specific to digital media and what remains generic to cultural language. From such an exercise it is possible articulate what the 'new' or 'emerging' practices of digital media are. Convergence suggests three identifiable processes, which we might expect to find in both film and digital media:

- overlapping practices;
- dissolving of conceptual boundaries of potential meaning;
- emergence of new hybrid practices.

For the creative practitioner working in convergent media the degree of technical knowledge needed is always depended upon specific application along the continuum of file sizes and outputs. Acquiring software skills for use in media production is largely a matter of apprenticeship, involving repeated use and practice in order to be able to confidently deploy the features of a specific programme. Given the division of labour in digital media production it is the case that individuals become highly specialist in the use of specific applications within the chain of production, for example the use of Adobe Photoshop or After Effects CS6 in video and photography montage and editing for media production for the web. Having both generic and specific software skills means that it is relatively easy for practitioners to pick-up how new software works as well as updating existing skills as software changes. The skill set for digital media practice in the networked environment is then a reflection of the use of software programs, which are themselves a convergence of digital tools, which are deployed in a convergent media environment. In parallel with the acquisition of what might be thought of as hard skills, there is also a requirement for a knowledge and understanding of the uses and potential of the combination of programmes operating within the network. This broader cultural knowledge and understanding of hybrid media in network culture originates from two primary sources, the history of new media and theories of technology and its relationship to human needs and social organisation. Of course experience of living and working in a network culture provides valuable insight and accounts of what hybrid media entails, from both user and producer perspectives, yet without more systematic knowledge, such experiential learning can remain descriptive and without analysis.

So far we have been making observations of network culture in terms of its continued wide dispersal, increasing use and new ways of associating and communicating. We now need to consider the ways in which what we have come to call media enters into and is indeed centrally part of networked culture.

MEDIUM SPECIFICITY

A useful starting point for understanding media is to consider both the concepts contained in the terms media and medium. The derivation of the term 'medium' comes from the meaning of 'a middle state or condition', and 'an intervening substance or element'. These two definitions are helpful in thinking about a medium as being both a material property and mental intermediary, combining conceptual position and physical element in order to connect things. Three examples of different uses of the term medium illustrate the point. The air we breathe is the medium necessary for life and is a conduit for the oxygen cycle, just as water is the medium of the aquatic cycle. Clay is a naturally occurring substance, which is used as a medium for sculpture and pottery in which the clay, a malleable substance of even density, can be manipulated into spatial forms. Graphite, another naturally occurring element, is used as a medium for making organised marks in the medium of drawing. The air, water, clay and graphite are all substances, which carry, or relay something between one state and another. So a medium, defined as a carrier and an intermediary, is a good starting point for thinking about media as material organisation and historical development of the intermediaries of communication. In the case of mark making with graphite, the physical substance, used in conjunction with material flat surfaces, developed into the medium of drawing. Drawing as an example of a medium clearly demonstrates both the technical means and mental concept of registering meaning and is therefore a paradigm example for contemporary technical media in which the registration and transfer of meaning takes place across a number or related materials, concepts and processes. Mediums are evolved forms of transmission and reception and as such constitute collectively means of human communication. In computing as we discuss the medium of electricity is converted into a signalling medium.

COMMUNICATION

Communication is the central purpose of any medium and the central abstract purpose of communication is to share. In network media practice communing with others takes place through electronic relay. However, the remote relay of computer terminals still relies on human commonality of conditions, experiences, interests, needs and meanings. Given the centrality of communication in human affairs communication has become a major field of research and study within and across the disciplines of psychology, sociology, anthropology and linguistics. Language constitutes the root of all studies and theories of communication, derived from *structural linguistics* and the development of *semiotics*. For the study of communication in digital media the emphasis within language is now upon systems of communication, which have given rise to independent theories of information and to the regulatory function of systems in cybernetics. Communication is generally understood as the cycle of encoding, decoding, transmitting and receiving messages, either in a simple model of a *one-to-one* communication, through the *one-to-many* model of mass communication, to the contemporary situation of the *many-to-many* model of networked communication. In all of these models of communication the environment or context in which communication takes place needs to be taken into account as an essential ingredient in the formation of messages. The process of communication involves a cycle of who is communicating, with what intent, about what, with what means and to whom. Communication is far from, if ever, direct. Even when we think we are using a direct and simple means to convey a message: (a) the medium, the intermediary, imposes its own means and meanings as an inseparable element of the process and; (b) reception carries with it an interpretative context. An easy way to think about the indirectness of communication is to consider the obvious examples of being at 'cross purposes' in an exchange, in which, at first, it is not clear that two different things are being talked about as if they were the same thing and this 'miscommunication' only becomes clear in the course of exchange and often by an apparent 'accident'. Now if we say that all communication in some ways contains cross purposes, whether we recognise them or not, we are getting closer to seeing how complex the process of communicating exact meaning is.

THE SOCIAL ORGANISATION OF MEDIA

Media is now a somewhat confusing term because the socio-technical organisation of communication to which the term media referred in the second half of the twentieth century has changed significantly. At one level the term media no longer carries sufficient specificity to be really useful and yet there is no easy linguistic replacement to the complex organisations of communication to which it refers. The term media as it came to be defined was used as a singular collective term, as the plural of 'medium', such that it became possible to talk of 'the media'. In this now established sense media refers to 'communication media', a term closely allied from the mid-twentieth century with 'mass media', whose major definition came with the rise of television. In this predominant use of the term media refers to all of the arrangements that make up the production, distribution and consumption of media products, such as newspapers, magazines, radio, music and television. On such a definition media included the institutions, organisations, corporations, companies and forms of work, as well as the material technologies for producing media, for example, printing presses, television studios and cameras and their equally material forms of dissemination in broadcasting stations and newsstands and newspaper vendors. By the end of the twentieth century the grouping of cultural communications known as 'the media' was given a new emphasis in the term 'media industries' and was extended to include an even bigger list of activities including popular music production, print publishing and advertising, alongside of cinema and photography. This stress upon media as an industry was an important redress to a prevailing idea that only the production of necessary goods and products were central to the backbone of the economy and that media communication was a kind of non-essential add-on. The recognition that media communication was an important economic as well as cultural set of activities coincided with broader economic changes in Britain, Europe and North America from the 1980s, associated with a growth in service sector industries.

THE GLOBALISATION OF MEDIA

In what can only be a schematic simplification we can say that media of the later part of the twentieth century was being transformed by the greater movement across national borders of capital and labour. The historical background to these changes represents the older mode of colonialism and the industrial revolution. The mode of industrial production of European nations during the nineteenth century had benefited from the capital resources gathered during periods of colonialism and the movement of raw materials from colonies to be turned into products in the industrial centres of Europe. The processes of European industrialisation were given specific shape and force by the needs of military technology during the first and second world wars, including, importantly, communication technologies. The strong European economies, in which nation, capital and labour were vertically aligned, began to be restructured in the second half of the twentieth century by forms of international and multinational capital accumulation in which production was globally dispersed. What has been termed as globalisation is founded upon new forms of economic activity organised across the world, which has led to the rise of newly emerging industrial centres and economic migration. A necessary condition of the greater flow of capital and labour across national boundaries has been the need for more extended, reliable and faster communications. The

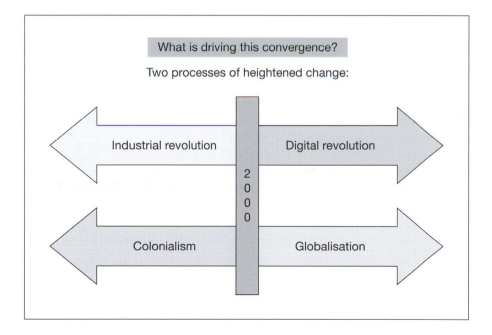

FIGURE 7.1
What is driving this convergence?

development of the Internet and the introduction of digital technologies provided the new, global means of information exchange. By the end of the twentieth century the production of certain kinds of information – news, for example – was operating instantaneously, on a world scale, 24 hours a day, seven days a week. The impact of new forms of global economic and technological change was experienced within the older European nations as a restructuring of industrial production and with it changes in work processes. From the 1980s onwards digital technologies were being increasingly introduced into the production processes of major media producers in ways, which began to change the previous analogue production processes. Older forms of production began to be replaced by new technologies and with that a whole range of specialist jobs entailed in older processes became redundant.

NEW TECHNOLOGY IN NEWSPAPER PRODUCTION: THE WAPPING DISPUTE

On 24 January 1986 some 6,000 employees went on strike after months of protracted negotiation with News International and Times Group Newspapers. The company management had ostensibly been seeking a legally binding agreement at their new plant in Wapping which incorporated flexible working, a no-strike clause, new technology and the end of the closed shop, but it had long since determined not to settle and instead sought to provoke a strike. Immediately after the strike was announced, dismissal notices were served on all those taking part in the industrial action. As part of a plan that had been secretly developed over many months, the company replaced the workforce with members of the EETPU and transferred its four major titles (the *Times*, the *Sunday Times*, the *Sun* and the *News of the World*) to the Wapping plant. And so began the Wapping Dispute.

> Within two years all national newspapers had adopted the technologies News International introduced and had adapted their working practices accordingly, precipitating an exodus of newspapers from Fleet Street, largely to Docklands. After hundreds of years of ascendancy, Fleet Street was no longer the centre of the UK newspaper industry, no longer able to resist the influence of new technology, changing employment practices and the demands of a more competitive business environment. The Trade Union movement, and the print workers unions in particular, found themselves in a spiral of decline, increasingly unable to muster a response to the changing industrial landscape.
>
> (Oatridge 2003)

A good example of sudden change in media technologies, one that produced a very fraught shift in newspaper production working practices, surrounded the events of the new production plant built by Rupert Murdoch in Wapping, London, in 1986. The newspaper publishing companies, based in Fleet Street for over a century, used Linotype machines, which were mechanical devices for typesetting the text, and manual pagination prior to the plate-making process; these production processes were detailed, and involved specialist divisions of technical skills to print newspapers. Murdoch wanted to introduce an offset litho printing process, connected to computers that could compose pages electronically, for the production of *The Times* and other News International titles. This new method would allow journalists to input copy directly and would make the older process redundant and with no further need for skilled print workers. Under a cloak of secrecy and with no consultation with the trade unions Murdoch built a new production plant away from Fleet Street in Wapping with the plan to transfer to the new technology and its working methods in one radical move.

CULTURAL CONVERGENCE

At the beginning of the new millennium the grouping of communication processes known as the 'media industries' in the 'post-industrial' centres of the world, had begun to overlap and at points merge with a growing service sector economy. In Britain the 'creative and cultural industries' emerged as a new grouping bringing many former aspects of media together with contemporary arts, heritage and popular entertainment under one umbrella term. While there are clear cultural distinctions between what are still understood as high, or elite, cultural forms and low, or popular, entertainment, the boundaries between them have softened and there is a greater degree of overlap and merging of forms. Cultural convergence has come about for a variety of social and economic reasons related to new forms of consumption where demand for goods is market sensitive. In the arts a number of trends are discernible that follow the pattern of consumption-led production, such that traditional art forms are now marketed using branding techniques, much as with any other product or service, including networked social media.

In addition, arts broadcasting has become a significantly larger part of the media landscape. Digital projection and download facilities in cinemas have made it possible to have live screenings of opera for example and the output of arts based factual programming on television has increased. In the visual arts the 'blockbuster exhibition' has extended audience figures and successful contemporary artists have become celebrities. The reverse trend is equally true as 'ordinary people' can appear in reality television programmes and gain the status of television personalities. Previous subordinate cultural practices (sub-cultures) of young people in music, fashion and dance, have been taken into 'mainstream', culture through the fashion and music industries. On top of this consumer driven phenomena of cultural convergence, the advent of Web 2.0 has created the tools for all cultural activity to be uploaded and shared, bypassing the previous 'cultural gatekeepers' of broadcasting and publishing.

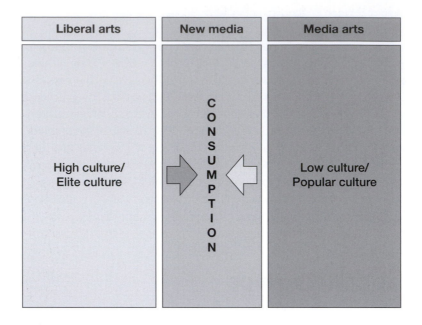

FIGURE 7.2
Cultural convergence

TECHNOLOGICAL CONVERGENCE

Technological convergence is discussed at many places throughout the book, but its basis in computing and digital code needs underlining at every turn. Digital code is the technological basis for media convergence, enshrined in Negroponte's phrase 'from atoms to bits', in which he recognised the transformative power of converting words, sounds and images into bits of electrically stored information. The characteristics of computer representation were importantly outlined in (Manovich 2001) when he pointed out that new media objects are based upon mathematics. From this he went on to deduce five principles of new media; numerical representation, modularity, automation, variability and transcoding and his schema remains important today and each of the characteristics he identities is a relevant conceptual dimension of digital code. However, with a further decade of development it is possible to see that while the five principles of digital code are important as an account of the formal principles of digital media, they do not by themselves amount to a language. With the expansion of the extent and reach of networked computing in all aspects of human affairs, the question of whether it is possible to define a language of new media has returned in a series of further questions about the human computer interface, questions that direct attention away from human control of a new language, to the control by computers of its own systems (Galloway 2012). In doing this attention is once more directed to questions of interface and interactivity.

MEDIA INDUSTRY CONVERGENCE

Over the past two decades the tendency within digital media technologies towards convergence has been an object of attention, in both critical and commercial contexts. One of the most powerful examples of media industry convergence has been between television and computer companies. The possibility of merging the domestic television and the personal computer became a battle between television producers and distributors, who were content rich using the existing means of terrestrial and satellite distribution and the manufacturers of computers and Internet service providers, who had the digital means of transmission and reception but not the content nor distribution channels. In the 1990s the TV/PC convergence was largely seen as being based upon the optical fibre cable TV network, which could also be used to receive fast connections to the Internet. This was in fact the dream ticket envisaged in the AOL-Time Warner merger, since at the time the latter controlled 20 per cent of the US cable TV market. In the 2000s the global expansion of the Internet, increased WiFi coverage, the battle has shifted to Internet-based providers who also control content, or who can merge with media companies with content. However, we need to remind ourselves that there is much more at stake in convergence of television and the Internet than technology. Television is both a medium of communication and a technical transmission and receiving system, which is to stress that television is a cultural medium, with developed institutions of programming and control and forms for the production of content. The domestic television receiver was developed specifically to receive that content. The Internet on the other hand, as with the telephone, developed as a transmission system without any institutionally produced fixed content. It is the World Wide Web, which has developed HTML pages with graphics, images and texts that can be said to be the content of the Internet. The Internet is an electronic network designed to transmit code to computers that contain software programs, which can convert the technical code in to humanly legible documents. The convergence of the TV and the Internet is now almost complete, or at least the convergence itself is settled since the flat screen of the PC and that of a digital TV screen are one and the same thing and both connected to forms of downloadable content. What is not yet completely settled are the new lines of corporate ownership of content and its distribution as well as the future shape of programme making, which on the one hand requires huge budgets and assured markets, and on the other is increasingly low budget with niche audiences.

In the 1990s the concept of the convergence of television and the Internet ran ahead of the technological ability to deliver a unified media system, if that was indeed what was being collectively aimed at. At the present moment the meaning and potential of digital media convergence is regaining interest because of further technological developments in digital video compression, higher definition image capture and broadcast formats and greater bandwidth. However, while the actual technologies for producing an integrated system for the delivery of high definition,

EXAMPLE: INDUSTRY CONVERGENCE

In 2000 the American film and publishing production conglomerate, Time-Warner combined forces with the Internet Service Provider, America On-Line (AOL) to create the world's largest media corporation. This merger represented an important new level in the convergence of the industrial and economic organisation of media production and distribution. At the time of the merger Time Warner controlled 20 per cent of the US cable market, which was a major factor in AOL's decision to merge, because it would allow fast connections for their subscribers. After the merger AOL-Time Warner's brands included, AOL, *Time*, CNN, CompuServe, Warner Bros., Netscape, *Sports Illustrated*, *People*, HBO, ICQ, AOL Instant Messenger, AOL MovieFone, TBS, TNT, Cartoon Network, Digital City, Warner Music Group, Spinner, Winamp, *Fortune*, AOL.COM, *Entertainment Weekly* and Looney Tunes. This was a media corporation that could have the vision to provide a total integrated system of technical communication services and media entertainment content for a domestic market across all media platforms.

multi-media and hypermedia digital media now exist, the short term economic imperatives of differentiated media ownership make it unlikely. Indeed the idea of 'one black box' through which households receive all news, entertainment and two way communications is an extremely unlikely outcome of convergence, since the proliferation of media products in a digital form, suggest a multiplicity of systems and devices. However, the common deployment of digital technologies across a wide range of applications continues to expand the processing and transmission of digital information. This suggests that further digital convergence is highly likely for a number of reasons. The technologies for digital, capture, encryption, storage, transmission and display are increasingly cheap and ubiquitous with prices falling as markets increase. Workstations, laptops, palmtops, cameras, mobile phones, music players, digital televisions, and digital converters are part of everyday life in the Western world and continue to replace analogue domestic technologies. The quality of digital objects and materials continues to match the cultural fascination with verisimilitude and hyper-sensate representations in all media. It would appear that we want media to be fully equivalent to, if not surpass, the reality to which our senses give us access. In addition digital technology now makes it possible to transmit higher definition video streamed material from anywhere to anywhere in real-time. For these reasons alone technological convergence in the transmission and reception of media is only likely to increase. It is important, however, not to confuse what are real differences between technologies and media and within the later, between media forms and media economics. What the AOL-Time Warner merger indicates is that convergence needs to be thought of in more than the technological dimension. Media ownership has been converging for most of the twentieth century in the print, television and film production industries as Time Warner, prior to its merger with AOL, is an example.

CULTURAL CONVERGENCE

Jenkins (2001) distinguishes five distinct kinds of convergence, which allows him to predict 'no single medium is going to win the battle for our ears and eyeballs'. Jenkins's distinctions are more refined categorisations between technological, economic and cultural convergence. Jenkins would agree with the technological and economic levels of convergence exampled here, but he goes on to distinguish three types of cultural convergence. First, social or organic convergence, which can be defined as social practices in which we are engaged in more than one level of media attention. Multitasking in the workplace would be an equivalent to the organic convergence of watching TV and texting a friend at the same time. Convergence here is one way of discussing new patterns and modes of attention to and engagement with mediated realities. Second, Jenkins defines cultural convergence as new forms of cultural creativity at the intersections of media technologies. Here he is pointing to the emerging forms of participatory culture in which users can 'work upon' media content and digital information, through annotation and on. Third, global convergence recognises that there is two ways 'cultural traffic' in a global communication network, which leads to cultural hybridity. However, such two-way traffic is not equal and the domination by major transnational corporations, who are 'content rich' and have the means of transmission, outweighs small and emerging local and national producers and providers. This structural inequality in globalised communication networks ensures the cultural dominance of the West or even more specifically the cultural norms and products of Hollywood. While such Western dominance of globalised media is evidently the case, digital media convergence has made this process of cultural Imperialism more globally visible and given local communities 'plugged into' the network a means of 'acting back' upon dominant values as well as using it for their own purposes.

The discussion of convergence is at one level inimical to all aspects and dimensions of new media in the sense that convergence is technologically written into digital media. But as others and we have indicated convergence does not mean an irreversible tendency towards all media becoming one medium nor all broadcasting and communication systems becoming one global corporation. Both of these scenarios are dystopian and technologically determinist and while convergence is a real fact of the media landscape, there is historical and current evidence as well as theoretical perspectives to support the view that we will continue to have differentiated and heterogeneous forms of communication. One of the most simple, yet powerful reminders of this is that a medium, of whatever kind, is more than a means of transmission. A medium is a deeply coded form of human communication, meaning and value, which emerge and change over time. Technical changes to the means of transmission of a particular medium clearly have affects and effects upon what is and can be communicated or expressed, in effect how a cultural message is technically coded. Digital technologies are the latest in a long line of technical developments that have been applied to specific media forms, radio, television, film, photography, music and the contemporary arts. One limited version of this understanding of technology suggests that digital media applications are simply new tools for longstanding and established human purposes of communication. This is at many levels hard to deny and is a kind of truism illustrated by the fact that typing this text on a laptop, rather than on a portable typewriter, is, for example, simply swapping one tool for another. On the other hand, the more complex point lies in the recognition that the tool is a 'mediator' between the intended message, to follow the example, the thought in my head, formulated through language, which I then type into the laptop, which is eventually read and interpreted by a reader. The ways in which computer generated type mediates the process of writing are hard to fathom, but in some obvious respects it is clear that the digital tool proliferates versions of text. The electronic 'cutting and pasting' of sentences and paragraphs on a screen is seamless and fluid. The copying and 'saving as' of text to different files, formats and other computers gives onscreen text a temporary, unfixed and ultimately more relative feel that changes the status of text itself. The impact of digital technology upon the cultural forms of writing are clearly evident in how email has changed the institutional memorandum and the personal letter, how blogs are changing forms of journalism and how text messaging is changing language. We should also note here the highly developed discussion and debate about the relationship between hypertext and forms of literature.

The argument about whether digital media are simply a collection of technical tools or a new cultural medium is an important one that runs throughout this book, but another way of looking at the problem is to say digital media are both a set of tools and a new medium. Technical convergence has reordered the toolbox, recasting the separate tools of analogue media, into a common digital matrix, allowing sound, image and text to be captured, encoded, edited and outputted in the same technical 'studio' using the same 'apparatus'. Of course this does not mean that what is being worked upon is necessarily experienced as converged media. Film is still film whether it has been digitally edited or not. Music is still music and novels are still novels and so on. The cultural forms of media persist, but in the converged world of the digital toolbox, we also know that changes are taking place within the cultural media forms themselves. Hybridity is one of the obvious outcomes of convergence and this is evident in the content, structure and language of particular forms. Digital 'special effects' are an example of how the digital toolbox is creating hybrid styles and types of animated film sequences in feature animations, live action films and computer games. Photoshop is also a part of the digital toolbox, which had produced a new typology of montage in photographic images across art and advertising. Interestingly enough the application of skills using the digital toolbox in the digital workshops of the world remain highly differentiated and specialist. The application of software skills follows the media forms in film editing or sound mixing for example and even in the new areas of online media services the preservation of specialism and demarcation of specialist skills is maintained. Yet while this is the case for high-end production companies, software development is driving at greater audio-visual convergence in immersive graphics for use in advertising in order to match the higher expectations of audiences for the immersive special effects of computer generated imagery (CGI) rendered sequences in Hollywood films and the computer games industry.

SOFTWARE CONVERGENCE

Motion graphics is an example of software development driving at convergence, although most graphic software used to produce 'infographics', or interactive data visualisations, are based upon the convergence of previous analogue graphic forms such as film, photography, typography, drawing and painting. The new element in motion graphics is the inclusion of video footage and audio, producing a hybrid form of animation. Motion graphics produce datasets that are closer in character to film in that while nonlinear in construction, they play linearly in a timeline within a frame on a computer screen. Motion graphics bring the representation of space and time to previous forms of static graphics. While this is not new in itself, since frame-by-frame animation also created the effect of space and time, computers can use less information space in automatic randomised calculations of apparent movement between static shots of objects. Through 'automacity' (one of Manovich's key principles), computer software algorithms can render key changes of images in a timeline in a process known as 'tweening'.

Motion graphics is located in film animation history dating back to early experiments with flipbooks and mechanical devices such as the zoetrope, in which a series of static images were 'made to move', or created the illusion of movement. The recent history of motion graphics can be found in developments in film and television titling sequences, where image, sound and typology are combined in a movement sequence. Producing motion graphic sequences in the film and television industries of the late twentieth century was, like all film animation very time consuming and hence costly. With the advent of computer graphic systems dedicated industry-based software was developed meeting broadcasting standards, for example by the British company Quantel, which developed a number of proprietary computer graphic systems for industry use such as Paintbox. The subsequent development of widely available graphic programmes, such as Photoshop combined with Adobe After Effects, have made the production of motion graphic sequences less time consuming and expensive, which has encouraged its wider use. The current popularity of motion graphics across a range of digital media productions continues and new features drawn from film practice, such as camera movement and greater rendering in 3-D.

Motion graphics software represents the most hybrid form of media convergence in increasingly general use in online digital media. It is adapting features of much more complex compositing and rendering bespoke software programs, such as Maya and 3-D Studio Max, used in film and games CGI productions for general use. Motion graphic sequences used in online media represent the latest in a continuous line of interest in making 'rich media', or 'embedded multimedia', for the interfaces of our computer screens and this increase the twin tendencies towards both more *immersive* and equally more *hypermediated* interface designs.

INTERNET CONVERGENCE

As we said at the outset of this section, convergent media also represents an environment and above all that is the Internet and it screen Interfaces. Google and Facebook represent major examples of Internet screen interfaces, which are driving greater convergence by creating customised sites through which personalised networked information takes place. Google and Facebook are the personalised department stores of the twenty-first century, which virtually assemble your friends and customise your products. Google and Facebook present themselves as the 'one-stop-shop' for all your communication needs, they are a convergence of previously different functions and sites of search, send, receive and upload. In becoming the giant sites by which the WWW is mediated, Google and Facebook in turn gather vast amounts of personalised data on users, which they use to further personalise and hence select web traffic. Convergence in customised web traffic presents both looked for and unlooked for outcomes and currently attention is focused upon the control and use of personalised data by private commercial interests, whose processes are not transparent to users.

CHAPTER 8

Case study

Audience attention

Dialogue with Matt Locke

What are the new patterns of engagement with digital media? Broadcast media has seen a new development in its understanding of the way that audiences operate on digital platforms. This study, with a media consultant and producer, considers how understanding patterns of audience attention, how it spikes and what makes it sticky, is now more significant than measuring audience figures in broadcasting and in business. It also demonstrates how other sectors, such as publishing, can use the concept of audience attention to change the way that they promote their product and find new ways to engage a readership over a longer period of time.

Matt Locke is the Director of Storythings, a company that was set up to experiment with the ways that we tell stories in the digital age, by facilitating consultancy events and creating experimental projects. Matt has worked in the digital media industry for over 15 years in both strategic and delivery roles at major media organisations and within cultural organisations. Before starting Storythings, he worked in the UK TV industry for the BBC as Head of Innovation for BBC New Media (2001–07) and for Channel 4 (2007–11) as Head of Multiplatform Commissioning, where he was responsible for commissioning many cross-platform and transmedia projects. Prior to working in TV, Matt began his career working with photography and new media arts organisations.

Matt argues that innovation is a critical driving force that directly affects what we do online but that there are many different ways to talk about innovation. An important aspect of this is how users respond to innovation. Through his work, Matt has become particularly interested in user-centred innovation because one of the things that distinguishes patterns of use is that it is not always based around the most expensive or technically sophisticated equipment. He perceives that we are now at a point where we have started to see very mature patterns of use and consumption of new media online, which are brought about by the way that users respond to innovation. These patterns of use can be seen in the way that audiences work with new forms of media content but they can also be seen in the way that traditional media are being accessed and consumed by people.

SHIFTS IN AUDIENCE PATTERNS OF USE

MATT LOCKE: The big shift in thinking over the last ten years is that there is no longer seen to be a tension between new and old, or a binary opposition between the way we do things now and the way we used to do things. Instead a much subtler, and harder to track, series of changes have taken place as the new technologies have gone mainstream.

Previously, we were focused on innovation and the question of what drives technology. I was concerned with whether innovation was going to be driven through the public or private sector or whether it was led by the users or the market. I think we are past those arguments now because, in a strange type of way, I think the audience has won. So many people are engaging and performing with digital culture that their patterns of use are now quite mature. As a result new businesses have been built very successfully on how people want to engage, such as YouTube and Facebook and this can also be seen in Apple's whole way of operating.

The challenge in the early 2000s was seen as being to define the new forms of content that could replace traditional material and to find new ways to produce material for cultural consumption. Now, in comparison, the big question is how do you release culture? In systems which are based around these new patterns of engagement how do you make sure that culture can find its audience and their patterns of use. We used to ask what are the different networks we can release our culture into. Now, instead, we ask how are we going to manage the different patterns of attention. Even with the simplest cultural project we are now faced with the challenge to manage the information about the project or event prior to launch, to get people to talk about it during the period when it is being shown or newly released, and to keep and maintain the conversation afterwards so that there is a continued set of relationships around the activity.

Many people like Matt who worked in broadcast and the traditional media industries have seen big shifts in attitudes within them. Although there had been some predictions with the onset of new media technologies that traditional broadcast media would be rapidly superseded, what became obvious instead over time was that the major stakeholders in the industry were not going to be replaced immediately and traditional ways of working with media were not going out the window in the near future as they found ways to adapt to the new technological environment. As a result these industries started to consider how patterns of use were changing and how this impacted upon the financial models that they were operating with and upon their understanding of what their audiences wanted.

Working at the BBC and at Channel 4 in the 2000s Matt saw the sorts of changes in user behaviour which had never been accounted for before, such as people using mobile phones while they were watching TV to exchange and look for information, or go online to follow up on things they had just seen for added cultural experiences. Behaviours of this sort went from being seen as marginal or radical to being predicable and mundane. Many professionals within in the industry and media strategists thought that the new role of the big media organisations like the BBC was to shift the position and focus of public service culture away from being mainly a provider to becoming a facilitator.

MATT LOCKE: Many of us were talking about big organisations changing from being publishers and distributors to being facilitators of other people's content. But although there were many attempts to operate in this way there was never any public sector project that made that work at scale which would mean operating more as platforms. The companies that did get that right and created platforms in which people could provide their own content, or worked with pre-existing content, were those like Facebook, Twitter and Google. These companies managed to create business models around millions of people interacting rather than the distribution of content from one too many.

NEW BUSINESS MODELS AND CONTENT PROVISION

Matt identifies that if we examine the way that facilitators of this sort operate it reveals a complex series of interrelationships. These are very different from the service or commercial models in the past and they can be best thought of as ecosystems.

MATT LOCKE: One of the big things I'm doing is helping understand that it's no longer a world of networks but world of ecosystems. There are four companies in particular that work with an ecosystem model and a value chain of content: Amazon, Apple, Google and Facebook. They all have a range of services that start from cloud storage and cloud services to give the ability for the user to store their content and go through to the interfaces and operating systems. These platforms allow users to use that data through to the marketplaces that enable users to buy and share that content. They then extend to the social networks that allow users to talk about it to the actual devices themselves, such as the mobile phones or the tablets on which they use it. Finally it continues through to the advertising companies in which the companies use and sell the data generated by users through being part of that system. This provides a whole value system through from storage to use, to device to socialisation. Each of these four companies has one or more products in each of those parts of the system. And what all are trying to do is create a single seamless value chain around content in all of those sectors.

MEASURING PATTERNS OF ATTENTION

The issues that are presented by companies that work with chains of content are very different from the issues faced by media organisations in the twentieth century. The predominant issue was previously one of scale and how to distribute the same content to millions of different people at the same time. The industries that had control were those that had the license to broadcast or to distribute their content. The way that these industries referred to their audiences reflected the way in which their technology operated and value was placed on measuring audiences as absolute figures or percentage shares.

MATT LOCKE: In the last century, at that point of time in what was called the 'Golden Age' of broadcasting, the competition for attention was quite slim. Conversely, the challenge in the twenty-first century is longevity. In previous decades the networks controlled the limited amount of content that was available. Therefore when producers were able to launch content they were able to keep it there for a long time. So the significance of attention is in the patterns that attention creates, rather than absolute measurements or charts.

The big shift in the last ten years has been in the way in which audience attention has been measured, from measuring it in terms of ratings or metrics into measuring it in terms of patterns. As audiences have been able to access content across different platforms, search for it and respond to it digitally, their experience has changed often long before the content itself becomes digital. Many parts of the industry have waited until their content has become digitised before they change the way they operate. For example, many publishers became serious about the way that digital content was important in the industry when e-book sales became significant however the way that people found and bought books had already been disrupted by Amazon. The same thing has happened with TV which has yet to see a total change in peoples viewing to being an online experience. In the meantime most of the searching, discussion and the viewers' exchanges around the experience of TV content is happening online. Yet TV programmes remain in the format they have traditionally been, for example hour-long slots with advertising breaks throughout.

THE IMPORTANCE OF SPIKES OF ATTENTION

The changes in the way that audience attention is understood can be seen as a shift from representing attention through charts to seeing it occurring in patterns. Previously the criteria of success was largely based on sampled metrics from networks, such as sales of music in shops or ratings figures of people watching television at any one time. This is now shifting to a much deeper understanding of dynamic audience patterns. This results in a change in thinking about audience attention in terms of a 'longevity of attention' to a new understanding of 'spikey attention'.

MATT LOCKE: The consumption of culture now has a lot of different effects. We live in an era of spikey attention. Not only can people find and access culture in their own time but they feed that information back to their networks. Spikey attention deals with things that rapidly rise and fall again. This is best demonstrated by the way that Twitter identifies 'trending' topics among what is being tweeted. Twitter shifted very quickly in the way it measured trending from measuring the overall volume or intensity of topics into measuring the velocity or the rate of increase of a certain topic.

The challenge in the twenty-first century is to know how to build relationships so that people come back to content beyond its initial spike. The big networks through their marketing and distribution, still have the power to drive spikes of attention but it is getting harder and harder to maintain this because the challenge for the audience's attention is now huge and there is always the potential for other spikes to arise that reflect the traffic on different networks. So the big networks try to drive attention on a number of different platforms simultaneously. Sometimes this is about organising content so that it can be placed in different niches at the same time. The choreography of niches is what marketing in the twenty-first century is often about.

In the 1980s and 1990s there was a limited number of networks which were controlled by a small number of media operators. There was a limited number of cultural products that could operate in the mainstream so, for example when punk came along it needed to develop a solid niche following before it was recognised and space was created for it within mainstream culture where it could be recognised as having significance. For many of us that grew up in the twentieth century this is our understanding of how culture happens, where cultural forms move from the avant-garde into the mainstream. But the changes that we are going through now indicate to us that the mainstream is only a temporary consensus, and overlap of all our taste profiles.

In many ways what I have realised in the past few years is that we have seen the maturing of a different type of attention – one that we are only just beginning to understand. Companies like Google and Amazon, Facebook and Apple have built new value chains based upon their understanding of patterns of attention. And they have encoded them into the advertising networks that they control.

GATHERING INFORMATION ON TRENDS AND USING QUANTITATIVE DATA

As a result of changes in the way that cultural content is created and disseminated, the patterns of attention can now be measured in many ways. Trends, occurring over a short or long period, are an example of this. But it is also possible to monitor how people are spending time consuming culture though products, such as broadcast entertainment, and what they are spending time doing, because the feedback mechanisms can be built into the way that cultural products are constructed. As a result we have more quantitative data profiling the way that people consume culture.

MATT LOCKE: Our methods of quantitative measurement are more sophisticated now. Previously it was hard to broadcast culture in a way that the audience might have actually wanted, and in fact audiences found their own way of engaging with culture in their own attention patterns but this was rarely recognised. For example as early as the 1960s, people were using early recording devices to tape and share television and radio programmes and to watch them whenever they wanted to. But broadcasters were never able to know what was being done. But now broadcasters can be aware of the way that audiences are choosing to engage with their product with an incredible amount of fidelity. They can see if it's being watched at different times and also when, and how, people are commenting or exchanging information about it.

AUDIENCE ATTENTION AND LIVE BROADCAST

Producers now r- ed to be aware of the way that audiences respond to cultural content in different ways, according to their interests and how it will fit into their patterns of attention. This is now becoming an important part of designing cultural products. It also means that producers or broadcasters may try to reconstruct their products so that they can make use of new patterns of attention. Social media requires special attention here because of the way that it can amplify the effect of a product, for example with a live event such as a concert or theatrical performance.

MATT LOCKE: We see this particularly in the way that broadcasters of live TV now encourage audience participation as a way of managing how attention spikes. This emphasises immediacy and creates the sense that people need to be engaged with the programme then and there or they will miss an aspect of the show, for example one of the ways that reality TV shows do this by is by enabling the public to vote contestants on or off. This has resulted in genres of live TV that have never been seen before, even game shows, which are as expensive to produce as live programmes but gain an extra dimension that they cannot have if they are pre-recorded. Many broadcasters are dependent upon selling the attention of their audiences to advertising companies in thirty second commercials slots built around TV programmes, and so they obviously want the audience to conform to the pattern that suits them. Therefore they encourage the spikes of attention at the periods that work with their commercial model and to discourage people from recording, fast-forwarding and watching in their own time. Whereas for other cultural producers such as games manufacturers or app designers it doesn't matter when users play the games or download the apps and so as a result they can have long spikes over a continued period of time.

WORKING WITH STORIES IN MEDIA AND CULTURAL INDUSTRIES: STORYTHINGS

Matt set up his company because he felt that there was a need to explore how new patterns of attention were impacting on the media and cultural industries and how it affected the way that stories were being told. 'Storythings' was chosen as the name for the company because Matt wanted a title that crossed boundaries and was not sector specific to TV, film or the web. Fundamentally he wanted the company to be able to address the key question that was arising across these industries: 'How do you make cultural products in an era of spikey attention?'

MATT LOCKE: I had been going to a lot of conferences about TV, web, games, film and digital media conferences over the past ten years. Mostly they were about the political issues of that subsector or its economics or about the underlying theories of the work. However, I was particularly interested in the practice of the sector – the approaches that professionals were taking and why that was interesting. I wanted to talk about what it meant to work with stories now.

One of the reasons why I wanted to work in this way was because it felt as though suddenly all these industries, in different ways, were asking questions. They were all asking how they could shift their methods from a world where their business models are based around linear distribution models and control into a world of patterns and spikey attention. But also they needed to know how to understand what the flows of attention are and what directs those flows both from users' needs and technological capacity. Only by knowing this could they create ways of entering into those streams of attention and having impact.

CASE STUDY: BOOK PUBLISHING AND SPIKES OF ATTENTION

Matt works with a diverse list of clients: with film and television companies, with magazine publishers, book publishers, government and funding agencies, arts organisations and festivals, news networks, individual artists and photographers. As well as investigating current practices and creating strategies Matt wanted his company to produce cultural products. A particular goal was to work with clients who produce media content and to see if they could create returning spikes of attention by making new content. An example of the way that Storythings works can be seen in a project with the publishers Faber & Faber around the release of a novel *Capital* by John Lanchester.

MATT LOCKE: Faber & Faber knew they had an attention problem. Their traditional marketing efforts were designed around a book launch and were directed at the print and broadcast media. They knew from experience that a book could sell in large numbers for approximately a year due to their marketing. Sales patterns also showed them that, partly driven by the algorithms of Amazon, they would see unexpected spikes of attention due to the fact that the book would appear within peoples search streams and recommendations. In spite of this they had no specific knowledge of how to engage with this and to drive further spikes after their initial marketing had ceased.

Even if a cultural product is analogue, the way that an audience discover it, organise their time around it, share it with others and how they talk about it afterwards has all become digital. So although the cultural object may be the last thing to become digital the interesting thing about it is the shift that has taken place in attention patterns around the object – sometimes years before the object itself is in a digital form.

The usual answer for publishers is for an author to develop a strong presence on twitter and to develop a Facebook profile and that way to gain thousands of followers. In some cases this is highly successful and some authors, like J. K. Rowling, can control a very powerful network that determines aspects of the way that their books will be promoted and sold. However, this is not always the case, it need not be the solution that the author should become the network. In our project the author wasn't interested in doing that and I agreed with him that the book should be the object of attention, not himself.

CREATING A DIALOGUE WITH READERS

For the project with Faber & Faber, Storythings created an online programme called *Pepys Road*, also a work of original fiction by John Lanchester, but one that worked in a very different way as an episodic story. *Pepys Road* was designed as experience that audiences could join and that would engage them in a dialogue, over ten days, by asking them questions about their feelings about living in London and their expectations for the future. The structure of the programme therefore was predictable and had repetition.

MATT LOCKE: The book *Capital* deals with complex issues about living in London, its social and economic make up, and how our lives are determined by social and economic structures. We felt that this would resonate with a lot of people who were thinking about their future in London and an uncertainty about where the world is going to be going over the next ten years. We used a Google adwords campaign which would pop-up when people did searches on relevant things to do with future concerns, and with capital, and this would take them to a site where they would be asked a series of questions over ten days, and at the end of the ten days they would be told if they would do well in ten years time.

The online campaign started by asking users questions about ideas that are central to the book. Gradually, through the questions and through new extracts written by John Lanchester the audience was taken into the subject of the book itself. So the object was to get people to pay attention to the book and to lead them to buy it by getting them involved in part of the story and offering them something that could fit within their own patterns and attention span. In the first months of running the project, the conversion rate from people taking part in the online project and buying through to the Amazon site was at 34 per cent, which is extremely high for a campaign of this nature.

FIGURE 8.1
Pepys Road, detail from registration page

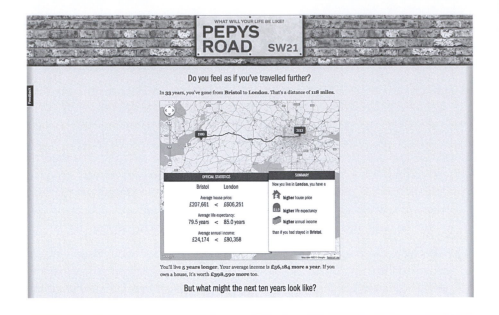

FIGURE 8.2
Pepys Road, detail from second page, which engages with information submitted by
the reader

CONTINUING THE CONVERSATION

The additional challenge faced by Storythings in developing *Pepys Road* was to
keep the conversation with the audience going over a year. This extended the
traditional pattern of marketing for publishers, which is normally based around
promoting the immediate release of a book, getting press and TV coverage and
getting it into shop display to propel it onto the best seller lists.

MATT LOCKE: We knew that there was a large number of readers who knew the
author's work. They would come across the book through reviews, television
features, interviews with the author or any of the other ways that it was being
promoted in the broadcast and print media. This was an audience we could
easily attract but who we needed to keep. We realised that if we wanted to
create regular and returning interest from our audiences we had to find a way
to slip it into their daily patterns of activity rather than try to make then come
to us. This is why it was important that the campaign had elements that were
predictable and had repetition. And one of the ways that things register in the
spikes of attention is that people get used to noticing them.

Normally for a product launch you are lucky if you get an immediate recognition
that may lead to a spike in attention. As a result it may get written about in
blogs, people link to it and comment on it but then it dies down. We realised
you need to constantly re-engage people. People need to be reminded of

things that they might not have noticed the first time around or might not have acted upon the first time around. To do this the project had a second stage where information that had been gathered from people was fed back to them, followed by a third stage some months after that were Storythings created another wave of debate around the product to encourage people to be more aware of it. And all of these were designed to lead to sales of the book.

What this teaches us that if cultural products are to operate in an era of spikey attention they need to be built to accommodate new stories within its lifespan. So we are not designed things that have only than 'one bite' but that they are designed as things have many bites over an extended period of time.

DATA TRAILS THROUGH CONSTANT FLOWS OF INFORMATION

Gaining information from people who engaged in *Pepys Road* allowed Storythings to develop a mini data-history that could be presented back to them, which offered little moments of reflection. It allowed the campaign to tell mini-stories that could

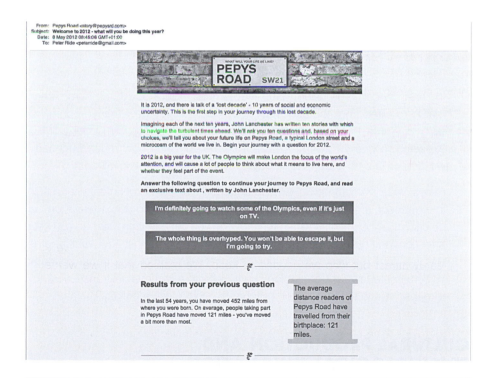

FIGURE 8.3

Pepys Road, email from the project to the readers, keeping them connected to the project site and engaging them in further questions

be presented back to the users, recording their own decisions but also the decisions of the crowd reading and taking part in the same project. This illustrates Storythings' approach to handling data trails, which are being constantly built up online, by finding story elements within them that people can then relate to.

GETTING PEOPLE TO READ

A further aspect of the *Pepys Road* campaign was to get people to read. Matt argues that a weakness of marketing can be that it can try to get the audiences' attention with one activity but the end goal being promoted is quite different. This can create a stumbling block in getting people to move from one behaviour to another. Therefore the behaviour that Storythings wanted to base the project around was reading.

MATT LOCKE: It's not just enough to launch culture into a network but it is also important to help the audience find the time to consume it. The attention profile of the media world of the twentieth century was the schedule that determined how TV programmes were organised, music released, more books published. The attention profile of the current media world is the stream where a vast amount of material is available at any given time. We live in a stream of a constant publishing of content. As a consequence we are constantly filtering the stream through things like search engines which gives us automatically generated lists of things – and these are all things that we could possibly spend your attention on.

Increasingly culture is being made that is quite explicit about the commitment that is required from the audience. A box set will say how many hours it will take to watch that programme, or a game will say how long someone is expected to play it. Making it explicit to the audience how much attention it will cost is just as important as saying how much money it will cost.

Pepys Road is a commercial experiment but it is also an experiment in attention. In retrospect, I realise in that way that most of my work in public television can be seen as experiments in attention: how do you get attention, how do you keep attention, and how do you turn attention into the output that you want whether that is a public service outputs such as to get people informed, better educated or better entertainment or how do you turn it into a commercial transaction how to get someone to buy a ticket, purchase a book, take a holiday.

CULTURAL PRODUCTION AND TECHNOLOGICAL INNOVATION

Matt argues that in the past companies like Storythings working in the culture and media sectors had an important role as trend identifiers and predictors of the future, but this is less important than before. Discussions in previous years had often been based on issues around how cultural production would respond to technological innovation, but this is now less of a concern.

MATT LOCKE: I think the reason why we talk much less about the future now is that it's here now. In the past I talked a lot about user-centred innovation because it was quite hard to pick up on the relatively weak signals of the audience's patterns of attention. It was much easier to plot innovation in terms of technological changes, in particular what the big media companies were doing, and to see things as being driven by innovation. Now we have come to understand that the audiences are the most important thing to hear. Those participatory networks have now become the landscape in which the culture is formed. That shift has happened in the last ten years and it has happened pretty much universally.

If we take a broad view I think what has happened is that now in the developed world the vast majority of the audience have the ability to find and engage with culture using some sort of digital network. Ten years ago we would not have said that this was the case. In the early to mid 2000s Web 2.0 was just becoming established. Blogging was only just starting to reach a critical mass. Participatory culture had not developed. Our mental models of what media culture was were only just starting to develop and much of the conceptual language was based around the idea of sites and locations. The language that was being used to describe the web was quite architectural. What has happened now is that a different language has come into being in which the references are those about velocity, pattern, streams more than about position. And I think this is because we've had a number of years where we can see what audience patterns look like when things move in big ways and we have seen the culture of memes.

As a result, irrespective of whether the big companies and institutions in the current ecosystems survive or not the new patterns are likely to stay. People will want to talk about and share culture and in ways we are developing now. We will want to search and discover using social networks, and engage with it using time-shifting, clouds and access it on devices that are increasingly more flexible to our needs. These patterns are getting stronger and stronger so in many cases what the future is about is building culture and finding out what works and what doesn't and what fits these ecosystems.

WEBSITES

Storythings, at www.storythings.com
Pepys Road, at www.pepysrd.com

CHAPTER 9

Case study

Creative convergence

Dialogue with Frank Boyd

How has the digital convergence of media impacted upon creative industries? Creative industries have often been thought of as important hub of digital activity since they include computer games, web and interactive design and software creation, among other things. However, as this case study demonstrates converg- ence does not only relate to media forms but to sectors as well. With increased pressure to innovate in the creative industries it is beginning to ask itself what makes it unique. This case study also considers the implications of the 'Internet of Things', in which physical devices and connected to the virtual world.

For the past decade convergence has been the defining characteristic of the emerging digital media ecology and economy, argues Frank Boyd, the Director of the Creative Industries Knowledge Transfer Network (KTN). The Internet, particularly the web, brought standards that meant that any screen, on any connection, was capable of delivering pretty much the same media and the same services. But while platforms may have similar capabilities, it is increasingly clear that, in different contexts, people use different devices for different purposes. Technological converg- ence has brought with it increasingly divergent patterns of user behaviour.

The role of the Creative Industries KTN is to stimulate and encourage innovation in the creative industries in the UK, helping people to realise the potential of the creative industries and to motivate lasting change. In his capacity as Director, Frank Boyd is keenly aware of the way that innovation through digital technologies has impacted on the way that creative industries operate and even how they can be defined.

Creative industries are becoming increasingly important components of modern post-industrial knowledge-based economies around the world, according to

UNESCO (2006). Not only are they thought to account for higher than average growth and job creation, they are also vehicles of cultural identity that play an important role in fostering cultural diversity.

During the last decade a number of governments around the world have recognised this fact and started to develop specific policies to promote them. This mainstreaming of what was once considered a sector of marginal interest, which received limited attention from researchers, has led to a growing body of analysis, statistics and mapping exercises on the relationship between culture, creative industries and economic development (UNESCO 2006).

Creative industries are usually taken to include advertising, architecture, art, crafts, design, fashion, film, music, performing arts, publishing, R&D, software, toys and games, TV and radio, and video games. The creative industries are those in which the product or service contains a substantial element of artistic or creative endeavour.

The UK government places great emphasis on the creative industries and their contribution to the economy and culture, and sees them as increasingly positioned at the heart of global economic and social life. They argue that UK creativity inspires the world, producing a stream of brilliant individuals and creative teams who are hugely influential in global media, entertainment and the arts (DTI 2012).

The UK government describes the creative industries in the following way:

> Our creative industries generate £70,000 every minute for the UK economy; and they employ 1.5 million people in the UK. According to industry figures, the creative industries account for around £1 in every £10 of the UK's exports. With the right support, they have the potential to bring even more benefits to our culture and economy. Digital technology and innovation is seen to lie at the heart of contemporary creative industries and a hugely significant component of the digital economy. The sector is supported with legislation, regulatory frameworks, digital intellectual property and communications structures.
>
> (DCMS 2013)

However, the developments of digital media and the effects of convergence are making the definition of a creative industry increasing more ambiguous.

FRANK BOYD: Currently we are reviewing the Creative Industry Strategy of the Technology Strategy Board of the UK. And the more we look at it and the closer we look at it the more complex it becomes in terms of what is part of the 'creative industries' and what isn't. On one hand you can say that everything is becoming part of digital culture and the digitisation is affecting every part of culture and the economy. It's almost possible to describe what we are talking about when we use the term 'creative industries' because they affect and play a part in so many parts of culture and the economy.

CONVERGENCE

Nevertheless, as Frank also explains, while it is important to recognise the fluidity within the sector of what creative industries can be it is also important to recognise that there are specific cultural frameworks that professionals work in. This leads to interesting challenges when addressing how innovation can lead to convergence and what the implications of this might be. Convergence is one of the important focuses of the network and one of Frank Boyd's interests is in investigating what makes it possible – or difficult – for professionals and companies in the creative industries to collaborate successfully with people and other professions.

FRANK BOYD: I'm finding this very interesting space to be in. I have spent many years working with media industries asking how we can find new ways of telling stories and finding experiences for audiences across various platforms. But now the space we are in can be thought of as virtual value chain of the creative industries. As a result we are doing more and more work that looks at cross sector innovation. For example, one of the things we are addressing at the moment is the impact of digitisation on health. The health service in many countries is a huge part of the economy but unlikely some other countries, the UK has broadly ignored the Internet as a way of delivering services. Think about the relationship you had with a bank ten years ago. This has totally changed because of the affordances of the Internet. But the relationship you have with your doctor is almost exactly the same. So there is a huge scope for change there. Creative industries can be part of that.

Frank argues that many independent producers are now capable of designing services that engage users in multiple ways, on multiple devices and in multiple contexts. In this context innovative media producers who have come out of working in entertainment or with media might easily use their expertise to produce products for the health industries. These results represent a convergence in terms of sectors working together but also in terms of approach and design.

FRANK BOYD: Internationally there are many companies developing projects aimed at the health services and about well-being more generally. I think we will get to see more and more activity in that space, for example we can see that in the trends towards the consumer items produced by corporations like Nike or Apple with wearable computer devices incorporated your sport shoes or in your iPhone that measure your pulse or monitor your bodily processes. We can think of this as part of movement around the quantified self. So one of the big challenges is how to integrate this range of products and platforms into the health services.

Frank argues that one of the outcomes of convergence is that it raises issues about data ownership and that established patterns and ways of operating with data may become contested. For example the question can arise of who owns the data about individual's health because at the moment individuals don't own it. Although they may be able to get access to it they may not have the rights to can share it. Therefore producers who build apps for health and well-being may have to negotiate to use the data owned by the health service – or may in turn, contribute data to it.

One of the things that make innovation possible is when one sector influences another or offers solutions to its problems. When this happens, the expertise that makes a company viable as a product and content developer in an area such the heath sector may be seen to have come out of other industries such as the cultural sector. Convergence, or 'converged products' can therefore demonstrate a subtle hybridity of approaches and skills and as a result sometimes the distinctions based on the traditional areas or marketplaces of a sector may become redundant.

FRANK BOYD: One of the developers that we are involved with had established a digital entertainment company, in the private sector, for digital broadcast but there was not enough demand and so it had gradually evolved to working in the public sector. As a result, the developer has set up a company which is entirely structured around delivering digital services for health and life sciences. But when I think about what the developer does now within heath and life sciences is that part of the creative industries? He is doing essentially what he did when he was running a company that made digital entertainment, but he is now applying that knowledge in a different market. So is that a creative business or is it something else? These are distinctions that don't make very much sense.

AUDIENCE AND USERS

Many independent producers are now capable of designing services that engage users in multiple ways, on multiple devices and in multiple contexts according to the Creative Industries KTN. The migration of content across different media networks and platforms – TV, mobile and the web – has been underway for some time. It offers opportunities to extend services, grow audience interaction, target different demographics, and develop completely new service and experience formats. The range of devices and environments in which we consume content is widespread and increasingly portable and ubiquitous. Whether consumers watch high definition, full screen movies at home or play games on phones while travelling, the potential for enriching, deepening and extending those experiences across and between platforms has a new currency across a very wide range of the arts and media. But at the same time the fragmentation of audiences has undermined the established metrics for assessing the value of attention. Frank argues that one thing that is of fundamental importance if producers are trying to work in the digital networked environment with a cross platform approach is that they have to understand that, and how, the intended audiences relate to the devices they have in their lives.

FRANK BOYD: One of the issues facing industries is how to understand new forms of audience engagement. Often there are still clear distinctions about the way that people perceive their roles in relation to content production and audiences and users. Bizarrely you see it within sectors where you would think that this would not be the case, such as entertainment. However, in industries there are silos and differences, between people who operate in different fields, for example, sometimes people who know how to make linear television programmes have very little concept generally of how to exploit networks and work with digital media. They are very good at telling a linear story. But directors of productions report it is hard to get various people in one room devising together because they have fundamentally different cultures and different ways of understanding what they are doing.

USER-CENTRED DESIGN

FRANK BOYD: One of the core things that I have worked on in a creative context over the last decade is the notion of user centred design, experience led innovation, and human centred design. Often I have used a diagram that I developed to explain this in which there are three overlapping circles representing 'conception', 'production' and 'distribution'. But at the overlapping centre the circles was the user. The purpose was that what you have to do throughout the processes of conception production and distribution is to hold your understanding of the point of view the user at the centre in order to ensure that what you develop will communicate to the intended audience.

This idea of user centred design which makes sense to many people in the industry who work with digital platforms but it can also be hugely contentious with creatives who will protest that is was not the way they work at all. They often argue that these are processes that are derived from product design and that they make programmes, they do not make products. But, to me, this seems to be meaningless because the programme is a product of a particular kind. However, I understand that the way they are coming from is that they are driven by a need to communicate.

BARRIERS TO COLLABORATION

FRANK BOYD: What is implicit in this situation is that the spark doesn't come from thinking about the audience it sparks from thinking about the concept. And I think that it is fine to start with the idea, but if you're going to create an experience that operates across platforms you have to take the audience into account. You have to think what is the context in which they going to experience this. You need to ask how can you frame this to take account of these conditions and if you are going to make something that doesn't have a physical location that can now be received on one of the many types of mediated devices from tablets, laptops, phones to televisions you have to think about the environment in which people are likely to consume things and design for that environment this becomes fundamental.

So as a result I think we have to say that while everything is becoming part of digital culture, but still within it there are specific cultural frameworks in which professionals are working. And that they are operating in 'languages' and with concepts that are highly specific to those professions which makes it difficult for them to collaborate and to communicate successfully with people and other professions.

EXPERIENCE ECONOMY

Frank considers that in an environment affected simultaneously by convergence and divergence, creative businesses face significant problems, which can sometimes be described as having to do with communication. For example, not only do producers need to collaborate across sectors on 'converged' projects but they need to work in different ways within their own sectors, but to do this are hampered by traditional ways of working within their professional cultures that may not easily open them up to change.

FRANK BOYD: One of the questions we have been asking is: where is the need for investment in R&D into innovation to help businesses in the creative sector grow within the next decade? One example is that the film industry understands how to use the technology to make content, but what they don't understand is what's happening to audiences. They now have a problem with marketing and find that the old patterns of marketing don't work because audiences congregate in different places, they display different behaviours and use different devices. Yet understanding what people are doing, how you reach them and how you engage with them is something that filmmakers don't get. This is partly because of the legacy of specific ways of doing business which they find hard to move beyond. So they are, in effect, tied up in the old way of doing things. This is like the music industry, which has spent years trying to protect twentieth-century business models at the expense of trying to figure out how to how to make money in a new environment.

This emphasises that people in the creative sector need to address the growing importance of the experience economy. Something that is being regularly argued now is that successful businesses have to focus on experience. Instead of thinking of the product or the service they need to address the complete experience the audience or user has of interacting with whatever the brand is, or the product is, and that is where the value of the transaction lies.

The difference between analogue and digital has been the subject of a huge amount of conversation in the last two decades. Frank considers now that something else that has emerged as a concern is the relationship between the physical and virtual. Although the concepts are not in any way new, in the current context of innovation this creates a new set of challenges that emerge from the relationship.

IP AND THE 'INTERNET OF THINGS'

FRANK BOYD: This is indicated for me by the phrase 'the Internet of things' which for me is this decade's version of 'information superhighway'. In other words this is a phrase which means there's something happening over there but we're not sure what the implications of it are – though we recognise that it is going to be massive. And as we begin to understand what it means in more granular detail, we realise that we are talking about specific instances of what IP can offer us as part of a world where objects are connected through an Internet of things. This presents huge challenges for an organisation or business that is used to working in a physical environment and now trying to operate in an environment where it's very difficult to tell where the physical stops and a virtual world starts. It asks questions about what an object is when it is in that environment, and who owns and what it produces or generates.

As a result it may be that the different relationship of the virtual and physical will increasingly be the territory that we are going to be exploring through augmented reality and 3-D printing. This can lead to the possibility that a lot of the issues for example that have plagued the music industry and television industry in terms of piracy may start to become possible in terms of physical objects. The rapid advances in 3-D printing mean that users can download data sets to and replicate small sized objects but new printing developments are pointing to the production of large objects.

FRANK BOYD: I think this is a space where there will be a lot of activity and innovation in the future. I think this will have significant reverberations because there will have to be new models in the retail sector around the advent of active printing, or 3-D printing. This could challenge existing patterns, and create new ones, of relationships between producers and customers or users. It indicates how the 'weightless economy' is now becoming very important in the physical world, as had been theorised some time ago. Again, the Creative Industries sector will prove to be very significant here, not just as a sector that includes design, but because a lot of the experience that has been gained in the Creative Industries over the last decades, and so it will contribute to the way we understand how to work with new developments in virtual and real objects.

CHAPTER 10

Case study

Design and digital experience

Dialogue with Richard Sedley

How does a business go about developing a product or service that is designed for the optimum customer experience? This study looks at the way that digital media has impacted upon businesses and brands – not just in the way they make goods and promote them but in the way that they relate to their customers and how their customers relate to them. It looks at the way we have moved from selling objects to selling experiences in response to the way that people now operate within a multichannel world, using many platforms simultaneously. And as a result product designers need to understand how the public will engage with what they have on offer.

Richard Sedley is Director of Design for Seren, a customer experience consultancy, one of the leading international companies that works through research, design and measurement to understand how customers feel and interact with brands, and businesses.

Richard's work illustrates how the social use of digital technologies has impacted upon a fundamental basis of much commercial marketing and its mission to attract and grow a vital customer base. It also shows how concepts of business to customer relationships have changed because of digital media platforms.

THE BEGINNINGS OF RESEARCH INTO ONLINE ENGAGEMENT

Richard Sedley began his career as a web designer, and the trajectory of his career indicates how the concept of experience has become synonymous with our understanding of the online environment. Richard initially trained as a fine artist, worked as a picture editor before starting up his own digital design company. After working with a series of high profile and eclectic clients in the 1990s and early 2000s Richard began to move away from pure design and to start working more closely with clients. This began a shift towards planning and strategy that has marked his recent career.

RICHARD SEDLEY: The less you work on the look and feel of sites and the more you work on the structure and planning behind them you have to take on a different mindset. You have to involve yourself more in understanding the business that you're designing things for and the strategies they are working along.

In the early 2000s, Internet marketing and design companies began looking at online engagement. This was in recognition of the growing awareness within digital industries that good design went beyond quality and functionality and that it was important to understand how people were looking at and using websites. As a result companies began to use this research to build a relationship with their customers.

COMBINING BEHAVIOURAL AND STATISTICAL RESEARCH

Over the last decade, the development of this approach has developed to a highly sophisticated level. Seren, the company where Richard is based as Director of Design, undertakes sophisticated analytical research into the way that people are accessing websites, how they are accessing them and how they are spending time on them.

RICHARD SEDLEY: One thing about the digital space is it provides you with an extraordinary opportunity for gathering data. Many of the people I work with are human interaction designers or psychologists. We go out globally, find customers, interview them and work with them to develop insights about the way in which they engage with a product and then bring that back and design solutions. We then build that back into the way the company develops what it does.

The analytical research carried out at Seren uses as combination of two methods of research, statistical analysis that tracks users online and behavioural research. These research methods extend from interviews and observation of users to eye tracking and brainwave measurement so they are able to measure an individual's stimulation or boredom. This enables researchers to have greater insight and a more sophisticated interpretation of the qualitative and quantitative analysis that it is normally possible to get through usability testing, focus group research or surveys. This mixed range of approaches gives the researchers a complex level of understanding of the way that people engage with websites, products or applications.

WHAT DOES DIGITAL EXPERIENCE MEAN?

Richard's work raises fundamental but hypothetical questions. What does it mean for a company to specialise in digital experience? How can we articulate the way that experience is built into design in the digital technologies sector?

RICHARD SEDLEY: What we do can be described in a straightforward way: we help companies make decisions better. The goal for companies is to become more effective with their marketing and to develop stronger relationships with their customers or users. So we go some way to helping design the experiences that their customers will have.

However, this poses the question whether or not there is something that is particular about 'experience' in the context of digital technologies. It could be argued that any company that works within marketing and design solutions is inherently working with information and how people respond to it. However, people's understanding of how information is processed and delivered is inherently bound up with the way that digital technologies structure, process and represent information. The industry as well as the users are operating in a context where new technology has had an ever growing influence on the way that people experience interactions, as human to human, or as human to machine, or human to network. So even though the products that a company is developing and promoting may be physical objects or analogue media and not digital entities in themselves, such as newspapers or film, clothing or holidays, they are experienced within a social and commercial environment inherently bound up with digital experience.

THE DIGITAL EXPERIENCE IS MULTI-CHANNEL

Richard's work demonstrates that the digital space is one of the main drivers that is affecting how companies now understand their relationship with their clients and users, and how that experience shapes their response. He argues that the way we now communicate and undertake tasks now is essentially what is described as being multi-channel or multi-nodal.

RICHARD SEDLEY: It's quite rare to experience or do anything now without interacting with any number of particular items. If we take personal relationships as an example, in the eighteenth century they would be face to face or by letter. Most of the twentieth century it would have been face-to-face, letter and telephone. In the twenty-first we have face-to-face, mobile, email, instant messaging, social network, avatar, the list goes on and on. Even the experience of football is different now. No longer do you only go on a Saturday to the ground and watch a game. Nowadays you go to the match, you text at half time to see if you can win a signed football shirt, go back home and plug into your Sky box to check whether a referee really did whistle at the right point or not, and then communicate online about that with your mates. The whole experience of what football is no longer just sitting in a stand. It is entirely mediated through a multi touch-point, multi-nodal, distributed experience. And this is something those interested in fostering customer engagement need to understand and relate to.

Over the last decade the explosion of multiple channels has dramatically changed the way that business understands their customers' behaviour. The concept of the multi-channel experience reflects the direct application of this concept in the marketing sector. The growth of the multi-nodal experience has led to people accessing information across different platforms and channels. And the direct result of this in commercial terms has meant that the way people do business now takes place through a range of channels that in particular give digital access, often by interacting through multiple channels per transaction, gaining information from one channel and then switching to another. They may get their initial information on a product or activity using a smart phone, to use social networking to see how other people respond to the same item and to make a purchase or take part in something while at their PC. This has led to the development internationally of customer experience management companies providing research, tools and software. 'Customers today want to interact with you through their channels of choice, whether it's online, over the phone, in store, via email or text' states the website of a typical company. 'In most cases, they interact with you through multiple channels per transaction. To succeed in this multi-channel environment, organisations need to connect the dots across channels to ensure smooth customer experiences across all touch points' (Tealeaf, www.tealeaf.com).

'DISINTERMEDIATION' AND THE DISRUPTION OF THE BUSINESS-TO-CLIENT RELATIONSHIP

Richard Sedley explains that to understand the impact of multi-channel relationships between businesses we need to recognise how digital platforms have offered different patterns of connection in the business world.

RICHARD SEDLEY: At the start of the century the Internet had the effect of what we now term 'disintermediation', which means allowing customers to relate directly to many brands for the first time. Prior to disintermediation most big companies or brands would be unlikely to have a direct relationship with their customers. Well-known brands would not expect be in contact with their customers because shops would sell the product. The brand would only deal with the retailer because of the model of distribution that it was using. However, the web put the consumer in a direct relationship with the brand and the consumer was able to talk to the people who made or designed the goods that they were purchasing. This suddenly put pressure on companies to have the right stories, the right information, the right attitude and the right way of conveying what they do to the people buying the product. This was an incredibly disruptive period for many businesses because it confused the way in which distribution and supply chains had traditionally operated. It's only recently that companies and brands have got used to the idea that you can talk to anyone and anyone can have a conversation with you. Even celebrities have recognised that they need to see themselves in this way, which is one of the reasons why social networking has been very important for the brand of the celebrity.

CHANGING BUSINESS MODELS FROM OBJECT TO EXPERIENCE

The changed relationship between customer or user and the business or producer can be seen in terms of the relationship and the way that feedback and conversations take place. But it is also implicit in the way that the supply chain between businesses and customers has taken place and how it has disrupted traditional business models and created great anxiety and uncertainty in different parts of the cultural sector. Much talked about examples of this are the publishing and music industries. Publishing is very concerned with the way in which the book can operate as a commodity and whether publishing can continue with the traditional model in which authors produce work that is represented by agents who promote it to publishers who print and distribute to bookshops, which then sell the item. This has been disrupted by the model of selling through Amazon and then increasingly it has been fragmented by the development of e-books and Kindle. The music industry has also dramatically experienced this and gone through a period where downloads and file sharing have had a huge impact on the way that the industry understands how it can operate and make profits, with the closure of formerly powerful giants in the music sector. As a result, the music industry has had to reconfigure the point at which money is made from being at the sale and distribution of the recorded music and to being at the live event or concert performance. Under this way of doing business the model of financial transaction shifts from being one of the sale of the consumable item to an experience.

Richard argues that the changes in financial models should not just be seen in the terms of digital technologies, but also as part of a wider evolution of business models in which we ask where the important experience lies.

RICHARD SEDLEY: We don't have memories long enough to be able to embrace the continuity of these things but we could look back to what was being said when radio began to broadcast music. When radio began broadcasting, publishers of sheet music claimed that music was being away for free. But what happened is that the world changed and a new business model was created where radio provided the advertising space, and the demand for the music, which was then sold as records and discs. The music industry has had a tremendous upheaval recently because recorded music has ceased to be the thing that people want to pay for but prefer to download or copy. As a result recordings have become part of the access and distribution chain rather than the endpoint. This doesn't mean that businesses and musicians can't make money out of music but it means that they have to employ a new financial model. What we are seeing now is that the important product is now no longer seen in terms of singles and albums. The key experience is not in owning the music but in going to see the performance.

AMPLIFICATION IN THE DIGITAL SPACE AND THE 'AUTHENTIC' EXPERIENCE

An important aspect of the online space is that it has provided an environment which has lowered the barriers for entry. This enables people to engage with business and each other, and take part in conversations on multiple channels. At the same time, the openness of online space provides an opportunity for new companies to come in and compete in the same space with existing companies, which offers new options to customers. But it also provides opportunities for people to represent themselves and their interests at an equal level with companies, with as much authority. Or if they wish, to set up a dialogue about companies or products that entirely bypass what is considered by brands to be 'legitimate' information. As a result the experience that people have with products, events or services is changing in the way, that is demonstrated with music and publishing, but in addition the ways that they can communicate this experience to each other and to the businesses have become much more diverse.

Richard defines this as being part of the amplifying effect of the digital space. The adoption of social media has had an effect on customer-to-customer interactions. Much of this customer-to-customer exchange happens digitally but the subject of those exchanges cover every, and all, customer touch-points, on- and offline, managed and unmanaged. Online is now the place to share and to engage. The net effect is an amplification of the impact of both positive and negative customer experiences. Richard argues that an important aspect of the way that people communicate their experiences is that they articulate what makes an experience worthwhile to them, what they want to engage with and how they do it. This has created the concept of the 'authentic experience'.

RICHARD SEDLEY: There is an understanding that differentiation can come from experiences. It's not just about having bad experiences and being able to go onto a social network and tweet or post onto Facebook if you are dissatisfied. It's that the more you have an authentic experience with brands the better you are able to know when you've had an experience that is not authentic. And being in touch with other consumers who are talking about their experiences makes this very possible. This has resulted in a shift in the significant idea as being a 'good' experience to an 'authentic' experience. An example would be that if you went on a cut-price airline and they gave you a big seat with a huge amount of legroom and served you proper food during the flight you would start to disbelieve in the budget airline experience because this was not what you paid for. Instead, the airlines brand experience is delivering on time with a no-frills experience.

At our company, Seren, we believe that what brands say about themselves is less important than whay they actually do. We talk about the experience they can create around what they do. Sometimes this is about helping them express the way that they understand themselves – to complete their brand promise. At other times it might be specifically about the products that they have on offer in the online space and how to get more visibility.

This leads to a re-conceptualisation of design that now encapsulates understanding what experience means to customers and users. It includes learning how to provide an experience that customers will think of as 'authentic' and anticipates how they will interact with it in a multi-channel way. It also indicates how the design of customer experience can affect sectors in a substantial way, not just in terms of specific product lines but also in the way that people think about the type of service they expect to get, and therefore how they could switch their loyalties from old models to new ones.

At the same time, the openness of online space provides an opportunity for new companies to come in and compete in the same space with existing companies, which offers new options to customers.

RICHARD SEDLEY: It is now well established that lowering the barriers for entry in the online space has not only created opportunities for individuals and customers. We can now also see what happens when companies use the opportunity to create new business models, which they can then introduce into the same space with existing companies that previously might have been very hard to compete against. For example, in the financial sector there are a number of new online banks which are offering a very different customer service which is highly attuned to what customers actually want in terms of their financial provider. They may not have the legacies of the large traditional banks but this may make them more flexible. Potentially these banks could end up owning a substantial amount of the customer layer because they could offer a better service which is appealing to people who want to feel that they are getting a return on the money that they are paying to have a bank account. If the online space provides the opportunity for new players to come into the market at a relatively low cost then this could very feasibly present a challenge to the traditional banks that have always monopolised the market.

DESIGN IS THE BLUEPRINTING OF EXPERIENCES

Richard Sedley argues that we need to think of design as operating right across the spectrum of product or service development. 'We think of design as the blue printing of experiences.' This reaches from proposition development and innovation to the day-to-day design and optimisation of apps and website pages. His experience demonstrates how companies have changed their approach because of digital media. Not only has technological innovation led to new approaches in design, but in addition it has also enabled them to have new ways to operate with clients and their customers.

RICHARD SEDLEY: At my company we spend a great deal of time with customers. We talk to them, we watch them, we test them, we survey them and we listen to them. Time and again we see their frustrations when they experience disruptions in their engagement with brands, but equally their awe and wonder when their journeys are frictionless and even enjoyable. This is important because ultimately customers will gravitate towards companies that will offer clean, lean and enjoyable experiences.

ILLUSTRATED CASE STUDY 2: AUGMENTED REALITY

Pure Land: using augmented reality for museums and heritage

Augmented reality installations are becoming important in museums and galleries and to the heritage industries because they can allow visitors to gain tangible experience they cannot otherwise have. A new generation of handheld and mobile technologies can provide the means for visitors to encounter fragile and rare artefacts with depth and subtlety, from places they might not be able to travel to, or from collections that only experts can access.

Pure Land: Inside the Mogao Grottoes at Dunhuang is an augmented reality project that immerses visitors in the quintessential heritage of hundreds of Buddhist grotto temples, an art treasury abounding with murals, statues and architectural monuments. This UNESCO World Heritage site, also known as the Caves of the Thousand Buddhas is located at Dunhuang, a small town in north-western China that is an oasis in the Gobi desert. It was a gateway to and from China on the ancient

FIGURE 1
Visitors experiencing *Pure Land Augmented Reality Edition*

Silk Road, which carried trade between China, western Asia and India for over 1,000 years from the 2nd century BC. There are over 700 caves at the site of Dunhuang, of which 492 still contain rich murals and sculptures. In order to ensure their long-term preservation, the Dunhuang Academy only opens a few caves at a time to visitors. At Dunhuang there is an obvious tension between the desire to show this rich and important treasury to the world and the ongoing protection of the caves.

Pure Land is an exemplary new heritage application devised by the Applied Laboratory of Interactive Visualization and Embodiment (ALiVE) at the City University of Hong Kong, under the Project Conception and Direction of Dr Sarah Kenderdine and Professor Jeffrey Shaw. It brings to brings new life to the aesthetic, narrative and spiritual drama of the extraordinary cave paintings and sculptures. The *Pure Land Augmented Reality Edition* provides ground breaking conceptual, technological and operational paradigms for the future of digital preservation and cultural heritage interpretation.

Visitors entering the installation room of the *Pure Land Augmented Reality Edition* find themselves a space that reproduces the dimensions of one of the caves, and which has white walls and graphic representations in black-and-white of the paintings on the cave walls. Holding up an iPad or

FIGURE 2
Visitors experiencing *Pure Land Augmented Reality Edition*

C@SE STUDY

FIGURE 3
Visitors experiencing *Pure Land Augmented Reality Edition*

C@SE STUDY

tablet to the walls they see a one-to-one scale of the ancient images. As they move the iPad around it reveals to them the paintings positioned in relation to them as if they were in the cave itself.

The tablets operate as mobile viewing windows that present the features of the actual cave within the space of the installation room. This is made technically possible by a number of infrared cameras that accurately track the position and orientation of the tablet-PC's as they are being handled by viewers. Computers then render the appropriate views of the actual Dunhuang cave, which are sent to the tablet screens via Wi-Fi. Original 'point cloud' laser scans have been converted into a 3-D polygonal mesh, which form the virtual surface structure onto which the Dunhuang Academy's high resolution photographs of Cave 220's paintings and sculptures are rendered. This composite 3-D representation is then seen by visitors on the tablet screens.

Augmented reality of this form makes use of devices that are easy for the participants to use, and although they are driven by highly complex data sets they have the advantage of seeming simple and straightforward. It requires no prior knowledge to use the interface and the information that is received appears instantaneous to the user.

C@SE STUDY

FIGURE 4
Visitors experiencing *Pure Land Augmented Reality Edition*

Pure Land augmented reality edition (2012) was directed by at Applied Laboratory of Interactive Visualization and Embodiment (ALiVE), City University, Hong Kong.

Part III

Creative industries

CHAPTER 11

Creative industries

The term industry has been progressively applied to the arts and media over the past 25 years as both an argument and an established fact. Historically the argument has been about the relatively poor levels of public and private economic investment in the arts, set against other government spending, for example in health, education, energy and defence. Those working in the arts have been put in the defensive position of having to justify the contribution the arts make to public life and the economic argument has come to the fore. The arts represent a large employment sector that regularly turns out profitable products, theatre or the film industry for example. The arts are also central to the tourist industry, with record numbers of people visiting museums and galleries. Where the arts were not seen as an organised industry contributing to the national economy in the past they are now recognised as making a strong contribution to economic life and as such there has been a steady process of professionalisation within all aspects of the arts, which now contributes to the idea of the cultural industries. In contrast, media has been seen for a much longer time, if not from their inception as mediums, as part of many industries, the print industry for example, as well as forming a definable sector of economic and industrial production in newspapers, television and film. The Internet and computing has enlarged the field and scope of the media industries to include computer gaming, Internet advertising, software and sale services. The further convergence of digital media within networked operating environments is creating new positions, occupations and practices and this section looks at the current and future contexts of digital media practice. The convergence of arts and media industries is expressed in the terms, cultural industries or even more so in the creative industries.

RECOGNISING CONTEXTS

The practices of digital media are necessarily embedded and contextualised, which is to say that digital media practice always comes out of and relates to a given set of institutional and cultural arrangements. In most senses of digital media practice, the term 'practice' denotes work. That may be in the form of permanent or casual wage labour, or the elected work of being a student of digital media, or working as a freelance independent on speculative/commissioned briefs. Digital media is entailed across the creative media and cultural industries from employment in large corporations or in small to medium enterprises (SMEs). Digital media is also present in many aspects of the public sector in marketing and publicity, information and communication technologies (ICT), or in education and training. Alternatively employment in digital media can be in singular, independent freelance practice. Across the employment spectrum of digital media there is an organised division of labour, in terms of roles, skills and specialisms. This division arises from the needs of production and the technologies employed. As a consequence of these divisions and organisations people become involved in digital media practice within a set of functional roles. It is important to understand that such organisational contexts provide the framework of meaning for the activities of both production and consumption and that the good practitioner needs to be able to reflect upon their own context. To see work and employment as having a context is to get nearer to being able to scrutinise and reflection upon the conditions of production. The context, therefore, has a shaping role in how digital media practices are understood and valued, because the context stands in a determining relationship to the practices themselves. The context of digital media can be reduced to a baseline in terms of wage labour and the common example here is that it is highly unlikely that you will ever be paid, however it is calculated, enough for the hours you expend. However, context is also about the values of the organisation you work for, the social or economic value of its products and what role you occupy within the organisation. Working as an assistant on *The Guardian* picture desk is a very different experience from working for a small digital media company on a day rate creating title sequences using Flash. Working in a regional city will be different from a capital city and so on. Reflecting on the context of practice, helps to explain the purposes of production, why practice is organised as it is and the role of individual practitioners.

At the general level we can distinguish between *private sector* and *public sector* contexts of the production and consumption of digital media. The private sector context of production embraces all commercial activities that are organised on a 'for-profit' basis. The private context of consumption is synonymous with the consumer market for products and services and the activities that are predicated upon them. The public sector of production and consumption encompasses all publicly funded institutional uses of digital media. The public versus private distinction, at the level of production, is broadly a distinction of for-profit or non-profit organisation, while the public versus private distinction, at the level of consumption, is broadly between institutional and domestic use. This is not a neat and exclusive categorisation because public funding in digital media does support production that is privately organised, we are thinking here of the outsourcing, freelancing and franchising operations of government offices, public broadcasting or education for instance. Commercially organised digital media activity is subsided by and contributes to public institutions that procure digital media products, which are in turn used to deliver services that involve digital media. However, the alignment of the distinctions – public versus private; non-profit and for-profit; and institutional and commercial – indicates some general characteristics of contexts. A private, commercial, for-profit company will have a culture and organisation that subjects all processes towards the end of increasing profit, through tight cost control and expanded productivity and business. It will typically follow all the norms of business practice, such as, the clear identification of itself in a segment of a market and its position in relationship to its competitors. Of course there is not one monolithic commercial culture and organisation. The private sector of digital media production involves different economies of scale, from the individual freelancer, to the large corporation and everything in-between. Even though the technical role and performance of your skill might be similar, you would expect to experience differences between the working practices of a three-person 'start-up' company and an established, large corporation.

INDUSTRY AND CULTURE

Digital media has been inscribed into ideas about both culture and industry in intensively practical as well as highly abstract ways. Practically digital media is already an established area of employment ranging from large international corporations to the cottage industries of small and medium enterprises, united around a number of sectionalised professional journals and sections in the national press. Digital media can also be identified in the public sector in institutions of government, education and research. Digital media has become an umbrella term to cover this variety and diversity of sites and activities. Digital media is a kind of loose collection or sub-category for a range of practices in the more overarching category of the creative and cultural industries. Digital media applies as a term whether we are discussing social media, web design, or digital art. As much as digital media is a loose and inclusive term for industrial, commercial and professional practices, still possibly being worked out and claimed by various interest groups, it is also being discussed, as we will see, in much more abstract and theoretical ways as a radically new and distinct medium, as a new cultural and symbolic form.

THE ORGANISATION OF DIGITAL MEDIA PRACTICE

Remaining with a wide definition of the digital media practitioner, as someone using computers for expressive and communicative purposes, encompasses the use of the computer at work and in the home. Digital media practice can involve using the computer to communicate, to access and organise information, to play interactive games, or simply to surf the net. Computer communication importantly crosses the world of work and leisure, or, as it is currently put, the work/life balance. At its largest definition, anyone who uses computers can be defined as a practitioner of some sorts. The importance of this inclusive definition of digital media practitioners as users, relates to the organisation of the self-selecting structure of the various communities of users.

Clearly there is a distinction between professional and amateur practitioners of digital media, but that distinction is not necessarily made along the conventional lines – the distinction between professional training and earned income, on the one hand, and self-taught amateurs who engage in practice as a leisure pursuit. Many lucrative e-businesses were originally the good ideas of amateurs and many successful websites have been produced by self-taught practitioners. The commercial opportunities presented by the Internet a decade ago, in what is aptly referred to as the 'Internet gold rush', were eagerly seized by many individuals with little or no formal training. However, a greater percentage of new e-commerce is developed along much more conventional business lines, requiring business plans, investment backers and specialist divisions of labour. Another way of putting this is to say that, in the same space of time as the growth of networked, online commerce, a new service industry has emerged to cater for its growing needs. It is an industry that is young enough to still be evolving new roles and forms of labour. It is, more accurately, not one unified industrial sector, just as all photography is not one kind of photography, but a series of separate, related sectors.

As we discuss elsewhere the convergence of media, through technologies, distribution and ownership creates an exceptionally complex picture. The older organisation of media, with vertically organised companies, distinct analogue technologies and clearly defined work operations and skills, has given way to cross media platforms and deregulation of media production. Since the deregulation of television in the 1980s there has been a widening of the base of media production, if not media ownership. Across the spectrum of ownership, media production makes great use of the freelance practitioner. One of the contributory factors that led to the break-up of the older forms of highly concentrated corporate media production, in the print and newspaper industry, was the introduction of new technologies. Digital media operates along the 'fault lines' between the old and new modes of production, in the sense that digital media is highly present in large corporations, the BBC for example, as well as being a new, relatively low cost, independent and accessible medium. It is the case that 'professional' level editing and design software for image, sound and text is as available to the amateur as it is for the professional in the PC. While there is a burgeoning market for 'low end' amateur digital cameras, 'professional' level video and still cameras and digital audio recording are within the reach of the graduate student. Bedrooms and bed-sitting rooms are the new recording and editing studios of digital media producers. It is possible for a budding film maker to shoot and edit on low-end digital equipment and send it electronically to a Hollywood producer, just as it is possible for any practitioner to showcase work on their own website.

This is not to say that high-end technology sectors in digital media don't exist. In the entertainment industries, special effects and animation, for example, remain expensive, involving technically complex computing digital hard and software. Large corporations and companies run big databases, with the need for system managers and engineers. The point that is being made here is that the digital media sector is differentiated along the lines of scale of operation, more than it is along the lines of types of technology. The operational and organisational skills of digital media practice are, in this sense, therefore more generic than those of previous analogue media.

Much of the thinking that limits the idea of the digital media practitioner to a narrow industry specialist is based upon the organisation of large scale and mainstream media production. In the established media forms, of newspaper or television production, for instance, there is a rigid division between production and consumption. Millions of people read newspapers buy magazines, watch television, and a relatively few people, divided into specialist roles – editors, journalists, copywriters, compositors actually make the products. This model of media production is understood as that of the few talking to the many, or the one to many and was the model of broadcast media defined more generally as 'mass media', a term, which in research and study, is now used with caution (Spurgeon 2008:5).

WHO ARE THE DIGITAL MEDIA PRACTITIONERS?

It is important to resist hard and fast distinctions between producers and consumers of digital media. The interactive and social nature of networked computing requires a consideration that all users are, initially at least, practitioners of one kind or another. An instructive parallel can be made here with the historical development and use of photography. In photography there is a very large market supporting domestic, amateur and professional photographic practices. News, fashion, sports and reportage photographers, high street portrait photographers, wedding photographers, fine artists, camera club amateurs and snap-shooters all use photography and they all produce photographs. The products of all these different photographic practices are valued in different contexts and frames of reference. The same can be said for many other media practices, writing would be another good example, where many more people sustain the practice of writing than those whose writing is subsequently published and far fewer still whose work is given marketing and media prominence. In social media there is a constant exchange between different types of labour put in and labour taken out in the production of data.

DIFFERENTIATING TYPES OF USERS/ PRODUCERS

This inclusive definition of the digital media user/practitioner, which embraces the user of the Internet, the routine information worker and developers, could be taken to be confusing the line between professionals, who produce media services or content and the users/audience, who consume products and services. Surely, any meaningful definition of the digital media practitioner should be limited to, the scientists and engineers who conceive, design and build hardware and the creative directors, editors and designers who produce products. So far we have resisted this standard definition because it simply reproduces the already well-established organisation of media production and consumption, which digital media does and doesn't follow. We have already proposed that digital media practice operates on a kind of fault line between established forms of production and new and different

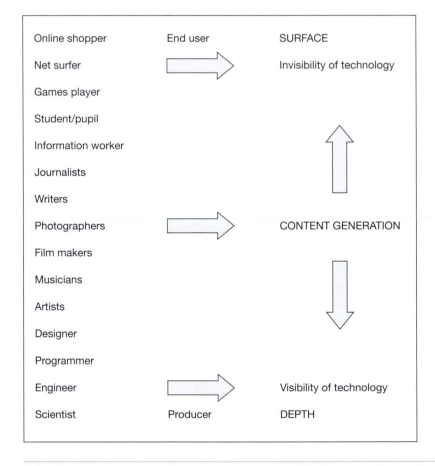

FIGURE 11.1
User–producer continuum

forms of production. We also go on to say that one of the defining features of the medium itself is that the division between author and audience is challenged by digital media's interactive quality.

We can move the discussion forward by expressing the relationship of user/producers as a continuum, from the computer scientist, engineer, programmer, to the designer, writer, office worker, college student or school pupil, games player, net surfer and online shopper. At one end the continuum, the computer scientist is involved in defining what lies 'behind the screen and code', while at the other end, the online shopper is decidedly in front of the screen using a highly prescriptive, coded piece of software. The shopper engages with the surface of the screen, through the Graphical user interface (GUI), while the programmer engages with the 50 million odd lines of code, each with approximately 60 characters, of the Windows Operating System. Between the shopper and the programmer, the designers, writers, photographers, musicians and artists engage somewhere above code in using the tools of dedicated software to generate, manipulate and organise specific content.

NETWORK PRACTICES

On one view the Internet is a self-publishing industry with millions of people involved daily in publishing themselves through social media activities on smart phones, tablets and PCs. The massive expansion of social networking since 2004 has meant that most users will make media files of some order or another and share them of a specific site. Internet users are disclosing, composing, exhibiting, writing histories, biographies and narratives on a continuous and currently still expanding basis. Such activities fall well within a broad definition of a digital media practitioner. How well, or badly, people perform on Twitter or Facebook social media or the quality of the content of personal blogs and websites is irrelevant to their existence within an unregulated global network of communication. Unlike print the Internet has no publishing house gatekeepers, controlling what is considered worthy of publication. The absence of editorial control on the Internet is, of course, a much debated dimension of the new medium, which above all raises the issue of the quality and provenance of information.

GLOBAL USE OF THE INTERNET

Some idea of the scale of the new medium and its use can be glimpsed from its growth. In 1989 the number of worldwide Internet users was estimated as 1.1 million world and about 86 per cent were in the US, but by 1995 that figure had dramatically risen to 45 million. Currently the number of Internet users is over 254 million and is predicted to rise to over 2.8 billion users over the next two years, with most of that growth coming from Asia. The world population is predicted to rise to over 9 billion by 2050, but the Internet user population is rising at a much faster rate. Currently China has the greatest number of Internet users, with approximately 310 million and the USA is falling behind other countries in Internet users per capita.[1] The phenomenal growth of a new medium has happened in just over a decade; however, the distribution of Internet use is uneven between socio-economic groups within countries as well as between countries. The development of a 'digital divide' between those with knowledge and access to the new medium and those without has been recognised at an international level by researchers and government agencies. Not forgetting the uneven growth, the general world trend in the spread and use of computing and the Internet is uniformly upward. The highest penetration of Internet users per head of population is in North America, Australia and Europe, while the largest number of users is in Asia (China and India), and Asia and Africa have the lowest penetration rates. Increasing usage of wireless devices will count for much of the Internet user growth in developing countries.

STRATEGIES FOR DISSOLVING THE DIGITAL DIVIDE

Strategies for crossing the various levels of the digital divide are central to the creative development of digital media practice. Without such strategies and the work and struggle that goes with them, we may well face the vision of the digital divide of the future presented by Castells[2] in his account of the networked society. This is a world that is doubly divided, first, into the information rich and the information poor and, and second, into users who will only have access to the limited commands of a highly structured market of consumption, and those that have the knowledge to both access and author the full resources and assets of the networked society. Such a divide, with its hierarchical structures of power and control, is not unfamiliar to us when we consider the current organisation of global television, in which a small number of large corporations control the production and distribution of programming for a large (and traditionally passive) audience. There are several arguments wrapped up in the idea of the digital divide, which we discuss in section two. But it is important to note here, when we are discussing the digital media practitioner, to grasp that digital media has the potential to radically alter the traditional one way model of transmission and reception. One of the un-looked for outcomes of the advent of digital code and convergent communication technologies is that they have changed the relationship between producers and consumers by substituting the idea of the enlightened user/author for both of those previously separate positions. Having said this, large parts of the world of commercial digital media practice(s) are a world of conventional divisions of labour, most of which have been and are being translated from divisions of tasks performed in existing media industries.

There are areas of digital media practice, many of which form the basis of our own examples, where the pressures that drive the digital divide are not so immediate and in which there are various imperatives to cross or expose 'levels'. In such practices as digital media art or in research projects the emphasis in to explore both the technology and its use, to be more lateral in thinking and less concerned with immediate outcome. Many digital media artists adopt strategies of transgression when working with proprietary software in order to question the ways in which the users has already been programmed to respond, or to confront the ways in which hierarchies of information are thought to be organised (Manovich 2001) touches upon the same problematic of the digital divide in related terms when he advocates the use of the term 'digital media object', rather than product, artwork or interactive media, to denote what is made by the digital media practitioner. For Manovich the overall importance of referring to a website, or game or digital still as an object is that it relates to experimental models in science and art. In computer science and the computer industry, 'object' is already a standard term, as in the modular nature of object-orientated programming language. 'Object' also has connotations with the Russian Constructivists, who wanted to emphasise the role of design in industrialised mass production, and it invokes the idea of the laboratory experiments practiced by the European avant-garde in the 1920s. Manovich wants to hold the digital media practitioner to the task of experimentation at a point where he sees the media has yet to develop. In fact he observes that, few artists using digital media are willing to undertake systematic, laboratory-like research into its elements and its basic compositional, expressive, and generative strategies'. He goes on to say:

> Today, those few who are able to resist the immediate temptation to create and interactive CD-ROM, or make a feature-length 'digital film' and instead focus on determining the digital media equivalent of a shot, sentence, word or even letter, are rewarded with amazing findings.
>
> (Manovich 2001:14)

This is a call for critical reflection upon the technology and its software by means of slowing the process down in order to look at each constitutive element of how meaning is formed.

Another strategy aimed at the same problem of over prescribed-programmed choices is identified by Lisa Blackman in the work of a number of artists using interactive software. Blackman points out first of all that the notion that the interactivity of proprietary software while promising 'free choice' or new freedoms to the user is in fact highly prescribed. One of the principle strategies employed by many of the artists in the exhibition was to disturb the choice offered to the user. The user's expectations were deliberately played around with by introducing into the electronic artwork 'bugs; and 'malfunctions'. In this way these works not only critically comment upon mainstream views of interactivity, but also attempt to force the user to reflect upon their own preconceived expectations and desires within virtual space (Blackman 1998:136).

PRIVATE HARDWARE AND GLOBAL MANUFACTURING

The digital divide is one way of expressing a set of experiences and observations, which arise from the global organisation of the computer industry and the commercial and institutional contexts in which computer mediated communication is deployed. There are conflicting and opposing interests at work between the economic and cultural, which the concept of digital media can, if we are not vigilant, ignore. At its simplest the argument follows a familiar, yet still relevant, line of analysis, which has been advanced about other powerful communication forms, television for instance (Williams 1974). The argument is looked at in more detail in the next section, but suffice it to say here that the core conflict within the production of media lies within the organisation of media for maximum economic profitability against the organisation of media for creative communication. The computer industry, like that of Kodak in the case of photography, is organised primarily to drive up its profits by a continual expansion and renewal of its products, selling faster, smaller and more powerful computers to more and more people is a goal in itself. The potential uses of the computer are not as important to the marketing of the technology as the total sale of computers. But as the average lifecycle of a computer decreases, so does the number of computers being discarded grow each year. By 2005, the average lifespan of a computer will be just two years. An unplanned by-product of this built-in obsolescence is that electronic waste is being recycled in third-world countries where poor regulations threaten the environment and people's health because toxins, lead and mercury, will contaminate local water and soil. The United States is shipping the majority of its electronic waste to India, Pakistan and China (Markoff 2002). The same phenomena of mountains of obsolete hardware can be observed with the mobile phone, where handset upgrades are currently running at less than 18 months. There is a veritable mountain of redundant handsets lying around in millions of desks and drawers across the world. There is nothing intrinsically wrong with a system of technology that creates privately consumed hardware, everyone should and could have mobile phones and laptops with access to WAP. Phones and laptops are objects of practical utility, not items of luxury and status, and their production could be organised along the lines of environmentally safe, sustainable and renewable resources and processes. This is something to aim at, as with all consumer products, but it is far from current practice. The organisation of technological production along the lines of maximising profit reproduces deep divides between people and cultures and it does this within the production of technologies that offer the promise of universal access to the wealth of human knowledge and global communication. This is a stark contradiction that stalks the digital media world and tempers the most ardent accounts of the emancipatory potential of the phenomenal growth in the use of computer mediated communication (CMC) globally, and especially in the richest countries is in large part due to making computer hardware affordable to a wider economic group. To produce computers cheaply has meant siting the manufacturing operation in countries where labour is cheap and stable.

As with cameras and television sets before, digital media technologies represent powerful communication tools and systems, which are being organised along the lines of the consumption of products for known and established purposes. Most of the consumption of hardware is organised and marketed around increasing the technical quality of delivery and access to existing entertainment content.

PERVASIVE MEDIA

The question of context, which it is argued, is an important factor in understanding the specificity of digital media, becomes much harder to define when we consider the Internet itself. Is there, or can there be, a single context or indeed any context in which to locate the Internet? In one sense the Internet is now everywhere and anywhere. It can be regarded as a parallel and complete world, and yet we can't live in it. It can be understood as our life on, or in front of screens, but screens that have many differing social and physical contexts. The Internet can be the world of work or the world of leisure, the place of identity or a space of anonymity. The communicative context of the Internet is both profoundly social and communal as well as deeply individual and isolating. The material context of the Internet is the network of networked computers, in our homes, about our body, in institutions and connected to a growing battery of server centres dotted around the world, shrouded in secrecy and sucking up enormous electrical energy supplies. In its most direct and concrete sense the context of the Internet is the screen and its interface, although even this context is illusive when we consider what we think we are doing through the interface and what the computer is doing with us. Because of the multiplicity of contexts the Internet is not easily assimilated by media contexts, rather the Internet is in the process of assimilating all previous media. The Internet is characterised by being an interactive media, whose operations are still evolving. Online interactive media is not a case of a digital technology being applied to an existing medium, but rather a new medium, which imports an assortment of languages from existing media. This accounts for the hybrid nature of its practices, part graphics, part programming, part scriptwriting, etc. Online screen-based interactive media still displays the ways in which the digital simulates the photographic and graphic, and borrows the journalist conventions of magazines and television in the screen interface. In the early days of digital media production small companies working on web development often had a less differentiated division of labour, a culture which encouraged an everyone does everything philosophy, with a 'flat hierarchy' or more collectivist principle of management. The rapid expansion and increasing profitability of the digital media online sector has led to the adoption of more conventional divisions of labour and traditional lines of management. With this 'professionalisation' of online media production, the divisions of labour as well as its organisational form reproduces some of its origins in television and print organisation, with editors, features writers, typographers photographer and graphic designers.

'BEHIND' THE SCREEN

It is the architecture of the network, through which the interface and hyperlinked navigation operates, whose practices have little obvious historical precedence and whose effects are largely invisible, which remains elusive to the creative practitioner, and yet whose operations are essential to the operations of the screen and interface. The architecture of the network and web is central to an understanding of how users interact with data, how data is made available, selected, differentiated and 'pushed', as well as how data uploaded by users is operationalised and monetised by the owners of proprietary software, such a Google and Facebook. The architecture of the Internet and web represents the most radical and novel element of a new medium, containing the greatest scope for its development as well as the greatest threat to its uses. Understanding what is currently at stake between how Internet data is being capitalised through data mining and how the network is used for creating and circulating social and cultural value is perhaps the central contemporary context of the Internet. The account of the technical, social, commercial and ultimately political context of the Internet is discussed across this book and cross referencing here is useful.

CREATIVITY AND THE IMAGINATION

The discussion of what we mean by creativity and the imagination becomes a means of approaching what we understand as the new in digital media. By placing the question of what a digital media object is and how it was achieved into the context of why it was undertaken we are posing the question, how was it conceived. Thinking digital media draws attention to the fact that what we do with a medium depends almost exclusively on the values, or sets of values (paradigms), which are inextricably bound up with its organisation and practice. There is then a discussion to be had about how digital media is being thought as well as organised and practiced, and there is of course a crucial connection between all these three elements, between conceptions about what digital media is, the conditions under which it is produced and received and what actually stands as the artefact or object.

The production of digital media artefacts is strongly linked with the creative arts creative in which creativity and imagination are considered essential ingredients. Arts prizes are awarded, reputations are made, marks are given and jobs are secured precisely on the judgements people make about how creative or imaginative digital media objects are. This is true across the spectrum of digital media production, whether it is a single digital montage, an edited film sequence, an animation, the design of a splash page, the interface and navigation of a website, or an elaborate interactive installation. In these examples the issue of creativity and imagination will be translated into specific team discussions about how good the concept is and how it interprets the original brief or aim. In turn there will be constructive feedback about how well a concept has been realised. The realisation and reception of work will involve very detailed discussion of the ways in which something was put together using particular technologies and software. From broad to detailed, abstract to technical, discussion will take place in relationship to a body of shared knowledge and experience, leading to judgements about whether the artist(s) or producer(s) have come-up with a creative solution, or that the work is an imaginative answer to the project brief. Alongside this regular, embedded discussion and evaluation of digital media artefacts and products, usually a discussion among a community of users who have the 'know-how' to consider what alternative possibilities and solutions might have been considered, is a wider discussion of why such objects are made in the first place. The question of 'how' something is achieved will always contain, implicitly, the question of 'why' it was produced. In established and long standing cultural activities, we rarely ask why and what for. Think of football, or feature films, we know what they do, they are self-evidently valuable, they are supported by large organisations and have extensive audiences and followers who appreciate them. Rarely do supporters or audiences have to ask, why football, why cinema, what are they for, even though both football and cinema have undergone major change. Digital media presents us with a different case, precisely because of its newness and its difference, which leads us to ask, not only how well something was done, but why it was done at all and for whom. As we go onto to consider, not everything that is new in art and media is easily recognised or accepted by the social and cultural institutions in which it is, or seeks to be, produced. If we accept that there are digital media practices that are literally exploring new areas of experience then it follows that the reception of that work may be uncomprehending and sceptical. Equally everything that is new is not necessarily eventually going to be valued.

KNOW-HOW

How digital media is thought about by its practitioners impacts upon what kind of digital media is produced. The projects of digital media across many different contexts are informed by the ways in which the digital is conceived. If we think of digital technologies being a central feature of the mode of reproduction in our own period, in a similar way as mechanical reproduction formed the basis of the Industrial Age, then we would expect the digital to be a defining logic of post-industrial culture and society.

We say that the rules of practice are implicit because they are most often not written down or communicated separately from the making of work. There are plenty of software manuals that are organised procedurally around the functionality of the tools, but have nothing creative or critical to say about what you do with them. It is worth saying here that software manuals do carry an implicit set of assumptions about what the user will be doing with the program – that is, manuals address a proto-typical user rather than a wayward one. Here we would say that manuals are just another version of the implicit codes of practice. Practice rules are, by definition learned on-the-job, from show and tell sessions in studios and classrooms, from the culture of the computer and media labs where ways of doing things, short cuts and achieving effects are demonstrated and tried. In most respects learning-by-doing is how it should be and is the modern equivalent of the medieval guild system of apprenticeship. However, the cautionary note is, as ever, that know-how, that ways of doing something acquired on-the-job, is not the same as know-why, which is acquired by critical distance and reflexivity, normally associated with the work of theory.

Solutions to practical problems of how to achieve a desired outcome in a digital media production can involve a complexity of different orders of applied knowledge and understanding all of which are often subsumed in the idea of creative problem solving. We tend to think of problem solving according to a set of binary analogies, lateral rather than vertical, thinking out-of-the box rather than confined, non-linear rather than linear, breaking a rule rather than following one and so-forth. The strategies of long established creative practices are extended to digital media, for example, the inspired leap, playfulness, non-directed thought, the intelligence of feeling and subjective introspection. These are some of the ways in which the process of creative production has been described by and about painters, musicians, writers and architects. The general point to make here is that digital media practice(s) are not only building upon the languages and forms of older established media, but also, in doing so are taking on aspects of their modes of production, which in turn carry with them the know-how we have been discussing. In this respect the small digital media production companies that have survived since the Internet 'gold rush' of the mid-1990s have increasingly organised themselves along the lines of more specialist producers displaying skills in the use of software for the production of still and moving graphical sequences. The major example of digital media organising the division of labour along the lines of older media is more clearly seen in the in-house digital media production of larger media corporations of television and newspapers, where there is a conventional set of editorial and technical functions. Upon reflection it is hard to imagine any other outcome for mainstream digital media than a conventional mode of production and the rapid establishment of a division of labour, since both product and production is being structured and determined by the demands of profitable exchange in the market place. The point here is the recognition that digital media business has now incorporated the languages and hence the values of established media production.

WHAT 'WORKS' AND WHAT DOESN'T

For most of the time the language of judgement about what is creative and what isn't, what 'works' and what doesn't, what has a 'wow' factor and what is mundane is assumed and shared among a group working in a common area. Designers know what colours, shapes and proportions 'work together'. Interactive designers can judge whether an interface integrates functionality and feel. Programmers to can spot the 'cleverness' in the use of a code, photographers can 'appreciate' the consummate use of Photoshop in a digital image, animators get impressed by the qualities of movement or rendering and so on. Such judgements constitute a routine and everyday practical know-how. Knowing what is good and bad in your field is always based upon an implicit and shared set of rules of the community of practitioners. It should also be considered along the way what the various kinds of know-how brought together in new production are. This question has obvious implications for the organisation of the education and training of digital media practitioners. The syllabi of the expanding range of further and higher education courses in digital media, multimedia, interactive media and convergent media, are themselves expressions of what knowledge and know-how is thought necessary.

WORK PLACE CULTURES: WORK/LIFE BALANCE

All workplaces have a culture of work, which reflects the owners', directors' and managers' values and the context of production we've discussed such as differences in public and private sector organisations, the timescales, schedules, deadlines and standards they work to. Within these two factors workplace cultures also depend upon the ways in which people associate and get on with each other. Working in digital media can be social and in can be isolated, it can have common and differential conditions such as contracts, hourly rates, working hours, holiday entitlements and other benefits. The digital media developed within the creative and media industries during a period in which trade unions ability to negotiate over conditions had been deregulated by central government and in which membership of trade unions declined. In the world of small companies and freelance working trades unions were never strongly represented and individuals replied upon individual negotiation, or simply non negotiation over conditions, depending upon employers to set and change the terms of work.

Still considering the question of the contexts of digital media practice, getting the right balance between work and the rest of our lives is important. Working in digital media can be exciting, it is certainly demanding and often led by tight deadlines, which require long hours leading up to the completion of a project. Working in digital media can also be very isolating during the long hours spent in front of a computer. Equally the increased use of online computing both in work and in leisure is increasing the amount of time we spend communicating through the computer interface. The results of these changes to our general patterns of living have yet to be studied in any great breadth or depth. Interestingly enough the cultural discussion of life in cyberspace is highly aware of the 'redundancy' of the body as we engage with our mind in the various forms of hypermediated and immersive screens. The effects of working with technologies upon the mind, consciousness and our concept of self have also been given attention at the theoretical level as we go on to discuss in Part IV, Reflections upon 'life in cyberspace' seem to be of three orders. At one extreme there is an argument for a full positive 'cyber-embrace', often based upon the inevitability of scientific and technological progress, which suggests that our very notion of what it is to be human is changing as our relationship to computer mediated communication increases. This view also argues that we have already accepted a great deal of medical technology that 'improves' or maintains the body and that we are therefore at the early stages of the actual merging of the body and machine, The counter to this position is that the application of machines to the body increases our alienation and estrangement from ourselves and each other. Such a view was in evidence, in the British trade union the Allied and General Workers Union's (AGWU) critical response to the introduction of armband computers for warehouse workers in order to direct them physically through computerised storage systems in order to speed-up delivery times. The second position is another kind of positive endorsement of the cyber-embrace, which recognises the separation from machines of what it is to be human but recognises the positive benefits of augmenting and extending our social. psychological and phenomenological reality thorough an engagement with online communication. Such a position would say that it is great to be part of an online community and to explore our ideas and identities in virtual communities, but then to acknowledge that we need to turn the computer off and engage in face-to-face community activity, The third position is less interesting to us as it is one that does not recognise the creativity of the computer and wishes to limit the use of computers to a range of utility or automated procedures for tedious human activity. There are, no doubt, other more subtle positions than those characterised here, but in all of our understandings about the effects of working with technologies there is a necessary and practical conversation to be had about how we integrate increase computer mediated communication into our everyday lives. The question for us is one of checks and balances in which the fascinations and benefits of working with technologies also lead us to value and sustain a rich an varied set of social and cultural activities in which we look after our mental and physical health through striving to maintain connvivial work cultures.

NOTES

1   Source: www.etforecasts.com/pr/pr1202.htm.
2   Castells discuss the difference between information rich and information poor.

CHAPTER 12

Case study
Designing a mobile app

Dialogue with Jane Prophet

What makes a mobile app a viable proposition? Games or programs can be output to different platforms so what are the distinguishing qualities that make something appropriate to work for mobile and handheld technologies? This study looks at the development of an app, TechnoSphere, with lead creative artist, Jane Prophet. The app is based on a program first developed in the 1990s as an Internet artificial life project. It is now being redeveloped as a mobile app. The case study shows how the same core concepts can be kept but a new version can be developed that explores the potential of different platforms and delivery systems. The case study also discusses the design stages used in making the app and how various subtleties of design are being considered, for example what makes something appropriate for a Chinese market.

The *TechnoSphere* app is a mobile app in development. It is unusual as an app because it is in itself a living history. It is the latest version of a project that has existed on digital platforms for nearly 20 years.

ARTIFICIAL LIFE SIMULATION

Created by Jane Prophet, Gordon Selley and Mark Hurry, *TechnoSphere* is a project in which users can make creatures as part of an artificial life simulation that is inspired by complexity theory, landscape and ecology. Originally *TechnoSphere* was developed for the web in 1995 and was online from 1995 to 2002.

Audiences or users who joined the *TechnoSphere* website were invited to build a creature to 'inhabit' the *TechnoSphere* 'planet' by designating them as being either herbivore or carnivores. They selected body parts, from a range of pre-fabricated elements, which determined speed, visual perception, or rate of digestion, and other attributes. The creatures were then placed in a landscape environment, where they fed and roamed. When creatures met they could graze together, fight or mate, which might lead to the creation of a new 'baby' creature. *TechnoSphere* automatically emailed the user of events involving their creatures, which kept users informed of such events and built up a loyal following of over 100,000 visitors,

Jane Prophet explains why *TechnoSphere* has is now being developed as an app. She accounts for why the project has had a lasting appeal to users that has led to it being revived and why the ideas behind the project are particularly suitable for an app.

JANE PROPHET: When we made *TechnoSphere* as an Internet project in the 1990s it dealt with two things. On one hand it was designed to present ideas about artificial life, complex systems and agents. But on the other hand, what the users of the website made it into was a very different project. They saw things, did things, and requested features that we hadn't seen and predicted. The users of the net version of *TechnoSphere* in the 1990s made creatures fairly rapidly, maybe without spending a great deal of time making choices over

FIGURE 12.1
Rendering of a creature in the online version of *TechnoSphere*, *c.*1997, showing how users could select different body components which gave the creature different attributes and abilities

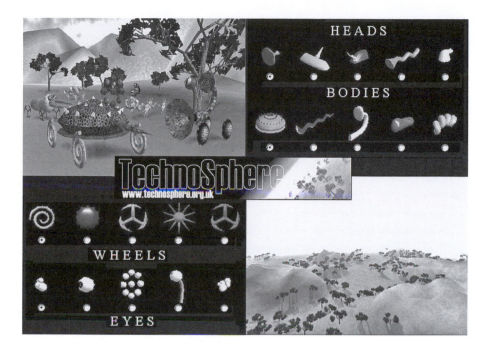

FIGURE 12.2
Promotional image for the online version of *TechnoSphere*, *c.*1997, showing the body components and the a-life environment of *TechnoSphere*

head, body, wheels or eyes, which were the things that gave particular behavioural characteristics to the creatures. What was obviously very important to them, however, was to name creatures and to have a relationship with them.

In the mid 1990s the Internet was much less guarded and protected than it is now, because this preceded concerns about privacy and data protection. Sites were allowed to publicise what we would now consider to be private data such as users e-mail addresses.

Users of *TechnoSphere* would get an e-mail message telling them that their creature had mated with another creature and now had an offspring. The email would also give them the name of second creature (the co-parent) and the e-mail address of the person who had created it. Quite quickly the users started to e-mail one another as well as the *TechnoSphere* website. At that time no-one used the expression 'social networking', but what resulted was a simple form of social networking. The creatures became connectors or interlocutors between the users. Many users would travel and meet up with one another, both locally and in different countries, and all sorts of online social activities would happen that were completely outside of any idea that we had at the time we designed the project.

REAL-TIME OFF-LINE VERSION OF
TECHNOSPHERE

TechnoSphere demonstrates how a project can bring people together in a virtual platform and a real-world environment, and also how a feedback loop between the project and the users leads to loyalty and renewed enthusiasm for taking part. Jane also explains how the project was later developed as an off-line, real-time 3-D version that gave a much richer visual experience for the users and also explored different ways that people could interact with their creatures.

JANE PROPHET: The initial plan with *TechnoSphere* was to move quickly towards situation where people could order images of their creature and see where it was at any time in the virtual world. However, we couldn't implement that because of bandwidth issues and restrictions. Because the project became popular it couldn't render the images on demand the way that people wanted as we didn't have the system power or the bandwidth for that.

A few years later we were commissioned to make a 3-D off-line version of *TechnoSphere* for the National Media Museum. We knew that we could do some of the things that we could not achieve with the online version, for example, we could enable users to render images of their creatures and follow them in the virtual world on display screens in the museum. However, we also realised that the users were not going to have the day-by-day or week-by-week relationship with the creatures that the online users had, but instead they were going to be in the museum space for possibly only 15 or 20 minutes. Therefore they had to be able design a creature and see something happen immediately.

In the online version when a newly-designed creature was instantiated into the artificial life environment it was created as a baby and took days to grow to adulthood. Instead, we designed the Museum version so that the creature was dropped in as an adolescent and could immediately seek mates, eat, fight or be eaten. This was a substantial difference in terms of the artificial life engine because on the Internet version those rules didn't apply to the baby creatures. Therefore, an important aspect of the museum version of *TechnoSphere* became about watching the creatures, and many of the things that we couldn't implement with the online version we could implement in the museum.

What the museum didn't have was the follow-up factor, so when visitors left the museum they heard nothing more from *TechnoSphere*. However, there was also a different level of interaction between the users, because people tended to gather around the control terminals to design creatures as a social activity and share the terminals where they could use virtual cameras to tag the creatures or fly through the space. There was still a design element to the Museum version but the user-to-user interaction through the interface of the creature was gone.

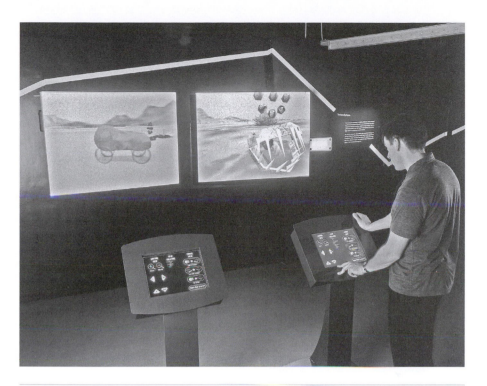

FIGURE 12.3
A museum visitor uses the real-time version *TechnoSphere* at the National Media Museum, Bradford

DESIGN OF AN ANDROID APP, ITS INTERFACE AND VISUAL QUALITY

Each version of *TechnoSphere* presents different aspects of technology. But they also show how, across time, different digital platforms shape the way that users can interact with them and how their expectations change. Jane considers why an app can take *TechnoSphere* in a new direction while still retaining many of the characteristics that made is so memorable for its previous audience.

JANE PROPHET: We are now designing an Android version of *TechnoSphere*. Interestingly, every month we still get e-mails from users of the old Internet version asking if we will put it back online. But the question of why to do something with it now is an interesting one. With Android and mobile technology now the technology has developed to the extent that we can explore the specificities of handheld devices in a new version, which is really what we did with the real-time 3-D museum version which was in many respects a very different experience from the Internet version. Each version of Technosphere has been an exploration of the potentialities of different technologies while still having the same core concept.

At the same time, designing an app presents interesting challenges for the graphic user interface design. With an app, users may wish to spend a lot more time on the process of designing a creature since they can choose a texture, see it render in real-time 3-D on a handset, change and modify it which has interface implications. We are having to decide where the creature resides once the user makes and then installs on their handset. Should it be limited to the handset or should the user be able to upload the data into what we call a stand-alone 3-D environment? These questions are presenting interesting challenges for the graphic user interface design.

The visual quality of the app is also an important consideration. We want to keep the connection to the 1990s version which has now become retro but this also has design implications because it means re-creating the style. We are only partially modifying it by upgrading some of the graphics but we don't want to take it far away from the characteristic look and feel that *TechnoSphere*

FIGURE 12.4
The design for the interface of the *TechnoSphere* mobile app

had in the 1990s. For example the *TechnoSphere* creatures were designed to appear quite mechanical and clunky with simple surfaces, so we don't want to make them more sophisticated by having particle system skins or fur because that would lose the sense of the legacy. But we will update the visual quality of the virtual environment and so the landscape can be more highly rendered and complex.

DATA MANAGEMENT AND ITS DESIGN IMPLICATIONS

Having stand-alone virtual environments so that each user is in charge for their own online world, rather than a multi-user artificial life environment is an elegant solution to the problem of adapting a community project as a small scale app. It prevents having to deal with complex data management issues that would arise from holding the meta-data generated through a multi-user platform. But as a result there is no 'single' *TechnoSphere*.

JANE PROPHET: We have been thinking about the multi-user environment options but we are also reluctant to do an online version that works the same way as the original Internet version because of the high cost of maintenance. But what we are interested in is a user version where for certain exhibitions we have a version like a real time 3-D version and users would be able to take their creature on their Android and be able to upload it into the system. However, if we can solve the maintenance and support issues for a multi-user system we may deliver one.

INCORPORATING DATA FROM MOBILE DEVICES

Jane explains how functionality of *TechnoSphere* can be enhanced with the new app using the characteristics and affordances that come from mobile technologies. In the previous versions of *TechnoSphere* it was the interaction of the creatures, created by multiple users, is what enables the virtual environment to progress along the rules of the a-life algorithm. Instead, on the app, any available datasets can be used to interact with the creatures and therefore produce outcomes. As a result, the potential of designing *TechnoSphere* as a mobile app is that it could draw on all sorts of other data that is available on the phone, including data drawn from phone usage and the users' patterns of movements.

JANE PROPHET: The first step of the design has been to create the 'user stories'. This means planning out the stages that allow the user to make a creature. This is a series of sequences where they designate it to be either a carnivore or herbivore, then go through the process of choosing components, such as bodies, wheels and eyes, and choosing the textures that are mapped onto the components. The next sequence is naming and saving their creature. These are the standard procedures that happened before in the earlier versions. This basic functionality is then supplemented by an additional level of functionality. To do this we have been examining the characteristics of the handheld and Android technologies that can be brought into the world of *TechnoSphere* – devices such as accelerometers. In *TechnoSphere* the creatures moved around a virtual world and they grazed hunted for food, looked for mates and were pursued by predators. We are asking if some of those behaviours could be determined not by the virtual environment but by the real-world environment that the user is in according to the GPS on their cellphone. For example, if they go to a restaurant or supermarket this could create a food location for the creature. We've also talked about doing an augmented reality version. What we learned from making the Internet version and then adapting and changing it into the 3-D version was to respond to the particular characteristics of those very different platforms and delivery systems, so augmented reality makes sense in certain situations because it is about gearing the project to the handheld device.

MODULAR DESIGN AND PRODUCTION

The development of *TechnoSphere* also demonstrates principle behind this form of design is to approach it in a modular way. This enables producers and designers to be realistic about what they can deliver and test outcomes as they are being developed. Jane explains how this process is implemented through Agile processes, or incremental software development methods.

JANE PROPHET: By designing the app in a modular way we can start off by having one or two creatures living on a phone and examine how the environment of the creature can be affected by the environment of the actual phone. We are using a process called agile which is commonly used in the business world. The project is structured into 'sprints' each having a two week period. This is a very different approach to software development from the way in which we worked in the 1990s which was to operate with a large-scale plan and pro-gressively work through it. However, the danger of this method was that if something fundamental didn't work out it might not be evident till later and the project would be stalled by a major failure. But the agile way of working, which is now industry standard in app development and other sorts of other software production, the producers or designers scope out the design brief, break it down into tasks and estimate and assign an amount of time per task. This method enables a lot more self-reflection and commenting on the part of the programmers. This also makes it easier to plan and predict for future development because it contains all the necessary date so if designers want to repeat a process they can see how long it took last time.

In addition we use a process called Fragments, which is standard for development on Android phones. This enables us to create screen designs so they automatically display according to the orientation and size of the screen, which is crucial for *TechnoSphere*. If the user if is designing a creature on a tablet or an iPad possibly six components would show on the screen but if they are looking at the product with a much smaller screen there will be only one or two components displayed at a time. This process allows us to plan that out.

TECHNICAL PRODUCTION SKILLS

The team working on *TechnoSphere* is small, and working across two geographical areas, which means that the production management needs to be handled with the greatest efficiency. Working this way also requires a combination of generic and specialist skills.

JANE PROPHET: The Chief Technical Officer and software engineer is Mark Hurry, who is based in Australia, and we have a team with me, based in Hong Kong, who are programming and 3-D modelling specialists. Because of the size of the team we have to be quite careful about the way we plan the technical management, ideas management and project management. The combination of generic and highly specialised skills is necessary because programmers are using certain kinds of protocols and operating systems and so there are design issues that they need to be aware of. In addition, we realise that the project benefits from having younger input, and a different point of view, and so our two programmers are recent graduates. App creation is now standard knowledge through computer science training so I would expect most graduates to be trained to design and build apps as a base level of expertise and to have specialist graduate programmers using Java-like or C++ programming.

3-D PRINTING AND DATA EXPORT

TechnoSphere also demonstrates how online gaming and other apps need to be seen as part of a wider pattern of user engagement. The *TechnoSphere* app is being designed so that different aspects can be built into it such as the export of data so that creatures can be printed.

JANE PROPHET: Other ideas that we are interested in come about because some of the technologies we have always been interested in have moved forward since we developed the last version. For example, we are investigating the potential for using 3-D printing technology to print the *TechnoSphere* creatures. We are exploring if we could have open source 3-D printing, bespoke high end 3-D printed models, or self-assembly 3-D models that are made not with a 3-D printer but from flat graphics. One of the things we did with *TechnoSphere* in the 1990s was in effect open source design since we had a very large group of committed users that had a lot of ideas about how they thought the project should develop. When we had a major upgrade of the Internet version we asked for, and then implemented, the users' most popular requests. So in developing the Android version we have been asking where open source communities are active and one of these is the 3-D printing community. People develop strong affective connections to the creatures that they have made so it's not a particularly big jump to imagine that they may want a real physical version of the creature. This also builds into the hobbyist culture of creating models from game characters. However, this also raises design complexities because what is generally ideal for a mobile app is low res graphics but a 3-D printer needs is high res graphics. So we have to deal with that complexity.

CHOOSING ANDROID AND QUESTIONS OF CULTURE

TechnoSphere is being designed as an Android app for a number of reasons, which demonstrates different considerations about the way that digital platforms are used and how technology can also be culturally sensitive.

JANE PROPHET: We have found that it is much faster and easier to develop for Android than iPhone and it's much easier to be able to sell the apps. Also we've looked at the market that we think is our target and the market share is massively more weighted towards Android than it is to iPhone. *TechnoSphere* has always been used by people on lots of different platforms. But also both Mark and I are aware that we are working in an Asian and Australasian context and Asia is predominantly an Android market. When we consider our initial user testing we will be user testing in Asia and we are very aware that that probably the biggest market going forward is China. It is very challenging though because of course the Android phone has such a huge variety of screen sizes so we have to be quite careful about the way we create our design and its functionality.

Cultural subtleties can be important too. As I am based in Hong Kong, one of our programming assistants is a first language Cantonese speaker and the other is the first language Mandarin speaker. However, even if I was based in the UK or the US I would want a Mandarin speaker involved in the team because issues about how we develop the graphic user interface is to do with the subtleties of the way that visual information is constructed and conveyed. This is at a much deeper level than the way written instructions operate for a program because of course the phones themselves can handle that kind of translation.

REVENUE MODELS

An issue for any media producer is how their product will sit in relation to the other products available to the potential user and what strategy is best to adopt if they want to earn revenue through distribution and downloads. *TechnoSphere* demonstrates how producers can present an app as freely available cultural property in order to ascertain if there is a financial viability and then introduce costed components. It also shows that at the level of independent small-scale production, it is not a matter of extensive market research but instead local and personal knowledge can give an important understanding about who is using products and how they use them.

JANE PROPHET: We are very circumspect and conservative about whether we think this could be a success or not but we just think it's the right time. I think we have to make sure we don't put the cart before the horse because there is no point in going down the revenue route until we know whether there is actually interest in the product. We expect to release a simple, free, version and see what the take-up is and then add layers of complexity. Therefore we have a mixed model of revenue streaming by identifying what elements have potential for revenue generation and only charging for parts of the project. For example, we may say that users can have one creature for free but if they want more than one creature they have to pay something, so this is a sliding scale model.

Working on a project with the history of *TechnoSphere* gives us a long viewpoint. In the 1990s we were planning a venture capital deal for *TechnoSphere* when the financial crash happened so we had a very substantial revenue streaming idea for a commercialisation that never came into being. But the lessons learned from that is to do things smaller and to be in a responsive mode, which is one reason why we have decided to release quite a 'cut down' app.

We have done broad market research top underpin the development of the project and secured initial financial backing for production but on top of that our own experience and anecdotal experience tells us the time us right. In Hong Kong, where I live, the mass transit system has full wireless provision and I mainly see people looking at videos, playing puzzle games or strategy games. This is one specific place but what is experienced in Asian countries with the use of handheld and mobile technologies is consistently a few steps in advance of much of Europe and North America. And it is evidence of the capacity for apps like this to be part of people's lives.

CHAPTER 13

Case study
Video games development

Interview with Maria Stukoff

What determines how games are developed? Are they led by technological innovation, social interests or market opportunities? This discussion covers how the games sector currently operates, the roles professionals play in games development and the skills it requires. It also addresses the future of gaming and how 'constant play' may be a feature of life in the future and how games may converge with other platforms to mix information, data gathering and gaming together.

Maria Stukoff says of herself:

> I am head of Academic Game Development for Sony Computer Entertainment Europe. My role focuses on providing universities with access to the PlayStation hardware and software and ensuring that best practices in game development are taught using the PlayStation platform. My activities span project management, setting up PlayStation incubation hubs and maintaining industry, government and academic partnerships.

THE SHAPE OF GAMING – TERMINOLOGIES AND DEFINITIONS

PETER: How would you describe the way that the games industry is changing and how it has developed? Starting from an overall point of view, when we talk about the 'games sector and games industry' are we talking about games that are delivered on a range of platforms from iPhones through to PCs or just high end games?

MARIA STUKOFF: Over the last decade, the definition of gaming has shifted from being an exclusive description of high-end and console games to be one that is inclusive of all digital formats. Microsoft, PlayStation and Nintendo have all expanded to join the market for mobile and hand held games. On top of this, there are other non-traditional content creators such as Channel4, in the UK, who have started to make an impact in the games industry.

PETER: Does this mean that the distinctions and terminologies used to describe the games sector consists of are themselves evolving?

MARIA STUKOFF: Terminologies are often used in different ways and the games industry is now also referred to as the digital entertainment sector and it can cover everything from hardcore to family entertainment to casual gaming. Ten years ago you would have probably heard more about the videogames industry. The videogame industry became determined by hardware that was linked to consoles and screens and where the game was hard pressed, and AAA studios run by the global companies like PlayStation, Microsoft and Nintendo, which are first party, internally owned development studios, drove the 'videogame industry'. But now when we are saying 'games industry' it is inclusive of mobile devices, so games industry becomes an umbrella term covering different forms of digital entertainment. But what is often categorised as hard-core gaming we would still categorise as the video games sector. So there are particular distinctions within the industry which depend upon the scale or the financial investment of the producer. I define my work with PlayStation as being in the video games industry or part of the digital entertainment sector

Depending who you talk to digital entertainment also brings in digital effects and animation which might not necessarily be gaming. The advantage of a term like 'digital entertainment' is that it can include all experiences of game related play. And playfulness is a great term to look beyond just the experience of video games. Playfulness could be digital entertainment for learning, or digital entertainment for medicine. So I find it a broader term for what we are allowing digital technology to do now.

PETER: Would you say, therefore, that gaming is increasingly taking different forms?

MARIA STUKOFF: Definitely. While gaming is partly leisure-based entertainment it can be many other things as well. PlayStation has expanded their PSP (PlayStation portable devices) handheld market to include the growing Sony tablet and mobile phone market as a gaming platform, which is the same for other leading producers who are using new forms of hardware.

HOW GAMING REFLECTS CHANGE: THE SHAPE OF THING TO COME

PETER: There have been important changes in games technology that have occurred over the last decade, which includes a significant shift toward mobile, byte size gaming and family orientated content on the consoles. To what extent do you see these technologies having an impact in the games sector and to games development?

MARIA STUKOFF: Distinct technologies are, overall, what drives the way that entertainment experience can be developed for each of those sectors and which leads to financial considerations. On one hand there is a console market with games that have a richness and offer an experience that will stay with the player over some duration, and are designed to last up to 45 hours of gameplay. These can be extremely costly to produce. But a player may also have a rewarding experience for a handheld device that is intended to give ten to 20 hours play depending on the scope of the game and these might cost between tens and hundreds of thousands to produce depending on quality and scope. When you reduce this down further to the tablet or the mobile device you lessen the investment.

In terms of the console games, technological change still dictates the way in which 'launch' titles are developed. For each new console launch there have to be key games that show-off the superiority of the technology to warrant its existence. Naturally the video games that are released for a major launch have to do this.

The videogames industry is right at the cusp of change. Because more than ever, technology is allowing people to do things that have not previously been possible for example the scope of networking and simultaneous play which is now possible without huge delays. We are now at a point where boundaries can be broken again.

PETER: How have the changes in games technology impacted on the way people play?

MARIA STUKOFF: On the console side, development of connected play has come to the forefront. This means players are connected into a game while on-the-go with mobile and hand held devices, which then plug or download into the game space once they are back at their home console. We also need to consider how free play and monetised models are also emerging because these are allowing the payers more choice in the way they digest games. At the same time we are seeing a development of family orientated content for consoles, featuring sports and family games where all the family can take part.

TECHNOLOGICAL INNOVATION, DATA GATHERING AND ITS IMPACT ON THE GAMES SECTOR

PETER: Do you think it is useful to think about technology as the thing that defines the gaming experience or do you think there are other thing we need to consider?

MARIA STUKOFF: I think the important issue is how we consume the technology rather than how has games technology changed. We have always used existing technologies for games, for example we have always had a gaming experience on mobiles even if it was textbased and the fact that we use it differently now because the processors have grown in capacity is irrelevant. What is relevant is what we can do with it. I think we can say that the content is not as important as the ways we experience our world through it and the software and the connectivity between these devices.

PETER: Is this because some of the technological innovations that affect how we experience technology in our daily lives, might not be about radical changes but about incremental modifications? Instead of major changes in the devices we use or the ways we connect, might they become faster and more minute, combined or have multiple purposes, which could be just as challenging?

MARIA STUKOFF: Certainly one of the big things driving technology is about making technologies smaller, more flexible and easier to contain on our bodies. This is concurrent with changes in our attitudes to technology and the way that we would expect those things to be on our bodies or in our lives. An example of this is the way that we have become very aware of the way we give over data and how we are part of constant digital surveillance. Yet at the same time there is an increasing appetite for people to give constant information about where they are what they are doing and how they are feeling. This helps to produce vast amounts of data about their activities both online and off-line. We may have concerns about data gathering and how it is used, and we may find it hard to conceptualise what may be happening. But we have no problem in understanding that the advertising we encounter online is increasingly tailored to our existing preferences, choices and interests.

PETER: Is it possible to anticipate how the gaming might develop in the future because of technological innovations?

MARIA STUKOFF: We have to consider the impact of technological innovation that comes from outside the games sector. For example, one of the technological developments at the moment that will have great impact on the way in which people work with devices is the development of flexible carbon mesh that will be used for new screens. The way that the IP for this invention has been handled has itself been innovative and strategic, and this means that it will enable flexible carbon mesh to become the material of the future. This might result in us having phones which are like a flexible card. These are the moments where an innovation enters the public consciousness because the vast number of products that might result will inevitably change the way that people incorporate technology within their lives.

HOW SOCIAL AND TECHNOLOGICAL CHANGES CAN IMPACT UPON THE GAMES SECTOR

PETER: Is it possible to have a long view and anticipate ten years in the future or are the developments in gaming too fast and furious to anticipate that far ahead?

MARIA STUKOFF: Maybe the most important issue is not one of gaming technologies in themselves but of connectivity or 'cross play' between gaming and other platforms we use. For example we can envisage a scenario when your phone will collect the data from you while you are on the go and when you get home it will upload it to your console and this may unlock something will give you further points in a game. So what you're doing outside in your daily life connected to your online activity, all transactions for GPS activity may get transmitted to your online persona and may allow you to get a key into another room in the game. This is not very different from the way that the script in a current game would fabricate this by requiring you to open a door or to follow a direction in a virtual environment. But this takes the same principle but uses real world experience instead of virtual.

PETER: One of the ideas that has been discussed a lot at the moment is the concept of 'constant play'. What you are describing seems to be a part of that.

MARIA STUKOFF: It is, and of course this can be accelerated by the convergence of different forms of hardware so that the television screen might be the console of the future and may be the interface that carries and transmits all this data. Much of this of course is already here and we are used to the pushing of data at some point this will just become synonymous with our everyday activity it is just a matter of connecting one dataset with another.

PETER: So the changes may also include the reasons why we are consuming it, and how it is experienced. Do you think this creates new opportunities for our understanding of gaming and what a 'game' is?

MARIA STUKOFF: To me this is very exciting because we have the potential now to think about moving aside out of the video games industry and beyond the digital entertainment sector. For example, how will we experience healthcare in the sector? It may be through one of our gaming consoles. You may be utilising the hardware you have for entertainment that may scan your body and access your hospital records and contact your doctor. How you feel may determine the television that is on offer to you and TV on demand rather than a pre-defined schedule. And your gaming console or mobile might be what is used to select what you might be interested in watching.

WHO ARE GAMES DEVELOPERS?

PETER: There is always a debate over whether games development is shaped by responses to technological innovation or if it is led by creative thinking. How relevant do you think this discussion is and does this lead to the products that we see?

MARIA STUKOFF: I don't think you can make those kinds of distinctions any longer. It's always been the practice for scientists to trial new technologies to advance their knowledge and know-how. At the same time we can see this as a necessary part of cultural creativity. No one would say that da Vinci was primarily influenced by technology, but technology and creativity go hand-in-hand. Within video gaming developers can be driven by a particular technology that they want to explore with no idea how it may transfer through a console or handheld device. Therefore, companies may have advanced technology groups or technology experts to look at how that might come to be. And on the other side you have designers and concept teams whose job is to make that experience come alive and I don't think one is superior to the other.

STUDIOS AND PRODUCTION IN THE GAMES SECTOR

PETER: What are the issues that affect the scale of the industry for example the role of the large studios and the development of smaller studios?

MARIA STUKOFF: At the end of 2012 we witnessed several closures of large studios, yet we are also witnessing the regrouping of expert developers with the rise of smaller studios. In this situation the 'indie' scene becomes very buoyant, with studios from the size of five to twenty people, because they can function like an outsource studio to bigger studios. Because they are smaller they might be more nimble and be able up to pick up some of the smaller applications that a larger studio might want to get done quite quickly so there is a market for them to operate in. This also has a run-on effect because bigger studios can operate locally rather than going to another country.

PETER: Are smaller studios easily able to produce their own content? What might be the factors that determine what they do?

MARIA STUKOFF: There are a variety of publication channels for games these days ranging from mobile content for example via iOS, Android and online browser games to platform specific games. However, the mobile market place is extremely saturated and smaller studios may face challenges to have their IP seen and be downloaded to generate enough revenue to survive. There are, however, success stories such as Rovio's *Angry Birds*, which topped the charts for several months running and led to a huge Angry Bird franchise and IP spin-offs. This success did not come over night though as Rovio created 51 other titles without the big financial reward! Sometimes it is pure passion and determination that see a smaller studio success, whereas others can benefit from links to larger development studios and operate on a work-for-hire basis.

PETER: As a result of this change are we seeing alternative ways of working across the sector?

MARIA STUKOFF: These days smaller developers have wider publication opportunities through online stores. But at the same time developers have to be aware of the requirements of different outlets, for example working with the Apple OS or with android and Windows market which will require them to change their code thus needing staff with the right skillsets. There is no quick fix or magic solution to do this. Choosing a publishing route can make or break a developer.

WOMEN AS CONSUMERS OF APPS AND VIDEO GAMES

PETER: There has been a lot of interest in the games sector over the last decade in encouraging women to become professionally involved, as well as getting women to take part as consumers or players. Do you think this is an important thing for the sector to consider and what impact does gender have on the products that come on the marketplace?

MARIA STUKOFF: A clarification has to be made between being a gamer and playing games. Many people define themselves as gamers and gaming is a continuous part of their lives and possibly connect to many of the other activities. This is the market sector we would often referred to as hard-core gamers and in this category men outweigh women by very significant percentage.

In contrast the casual gamer would dip in and out of various experiences, and move between different platforms. If you look at the casual games market you will find that there is a higher proportion of women who use it than men. There have been a number of studies have shown that in this market women will buy technology more readily than men, so this includes apps downloads the phones and smaller games in the videogames market. However, there is a reason why that market has not been captured for video console gaming. Because the industry is shrinking in the number of big blockbuster type titles which are produced. These are often tied in with movies and so the amount of IP or story and content is also limited. The big title games drive a certain market group which we would call hard-core gamers. Women of course might be hard-core gamers but if you look at the stats it's a very small representation.

PETER: So from this we can extrapolate that there is a direct relationship between content and gender?

MARIA STUKOFF: Unfortunately I find with the larger titles that the female market is not supported in that it does not cater for the experiences that they might seek. In other creative sectors we would find products with a wider palette and female user base, such as in film and in literature. On the flip side the indie developers have the freedom to create smaller games, designed to be experienced in small packages of leisure time as opposed to being consumed over several hours which requires a major commitment to video gaming. In this space the female ratio to men is much greater.

If you look at the titles that are released around Christmas, which is an important period in the publishing calendar, many of the titles will be action-based themes such as car chases, fights and war scenarios. The family-based titles such as the J. K. Rowling inspired 'Book of Spells' are rare. I don't think there is room for smaller more niche titles which would attract a different market because the revenue streams won't be able to compete with the big titles.

WOMEN IN THE PROFESSIONAL GAMES SECTOR

PETER: Does the involvement of women in the games sector as consumers also correlate to the number of women working professionally. What factors do you think play a part in this?

MARIA STUKOFF: Percentages of women involved in the games industry vary because it depends exactly where and how you are gathering your data, but this is probably not much more than 10 per cent. On the development side it is quite low.

Existing research shows that students' expectations on what kinds of employment they might go into are often set below the age of 16 so initiatives to encourage girls to become involved in the games industry need to be operational at an earlier age than higher education. Partly this is because the sense of self-worth, and what gives satisfaction, is affected before puberty. So if the sector is to support women as developers it needs to be done when they are quite young. This is often because the primary school environment can offer girls the space to explore the potential and the roles they might like to play in a way they may not get at home. This is important if girls are to become coders but it is equally important if they are to become managers, entrepreneurial, business savvy and trust in their own judgment. There are a number of stakeholder groups that are focused on this question, and they have been many groups over the past decade addressing this but maybe because of a range of social changes things might be different now.

REDEFINING THE ROLES WITHIN GAMES DEVELOPMENT

PETER: Can you break down for me the responsibilities and job roles that take place? Is everyone who works in the games industry called a 'games developer' or does it relate to a specific part of the sector?

MARIA STUKOFF: There are various departments or environments that will feed into what constitutes videogame development. One side of what we usually call the game development studio is the software development team that will work on concepts. This will require a pipeline of production from people developing concept ideas, programmers, plus programming specialists who understand how to drive the maths and physics within the game. It also includes specialists such as the artists to make backgrounds, character designs and games audio programmers. Some of these skills are interchangeable with skills used in film or other entertainment industries, and the same applies to many sub skills such as animators working with shading or highly specific areas, or skinning for characters, surfaces for costumes all of which requires very particular expertise.

PETER: What is the role of management within development?

MARIA STUKOFF: Coordinating the software development teams are project managers to make sure everyone is simultaneously growing their content together and ensuring that each of the delivery milestones are in place. And delivering milestones is crucial because these are the points at which money will be released so the managers will be looking at the flow of the studio. Then there will be games directors that make sure that the overall ownership of the IP and the aim is still on course as the project is developed through this pipeline. Studio directors make sure that while this IP is being developed and absorbs all the finances that the next IP is being anticipated so that there is a new project in development as you publish. So that is within the studio group. But if you have a small studio you would have a limited range of skills but you would also have a business person who are selling their skills to a larger company. And in a bigger studio you would also have a department specifically looks at marketing and legal rights departments.

SKILLS NEEDED TO WORK IN GAMES DEVELOPMENT

PETER: What skills do games developers need to have? Do games developers need generic broad-based skills or do they need to acquire deep and narrow skills? And alongside technical skills of software and programming what aptitude skills do they need such as team working, good communication or problem-solving?

MARIA STUKOFF: The requirement for skills and aptitude presents an ongoing tension because skills providers such as universities will want graduates have the best possible opportunities therefore they pursue a broad base whereas employers may want highly specific skills. So the tension is between those that deliver the training and those that determine who gets employed. A lot of people who study on relevant digital technology courses want to work in the videogames industry but they don't have enough knowledge that is specific to the sector. While other industries might offer training that is structured through apprenticeships or through in-house provision the games industry does not work that way. The videogames industry often wants people who have three to four years of intense programming experience because workers need a certain amount of know-how and skills to be able to come in at the required level. In a studio workers are expected to operate in a team, so although people may have been isolated into a particular skill set they need to be able to communicate within their team so that they can translate their expertise into a stunning experience.

PETER: Are developers required to have expertise with specific platforms when they come onto the job market? How should they demonstrate their capabilities to a prospective employer?

MARIA STUKOFF: Through my work I aim to champion the best practice in game development on the PlayStation platform and to work with PlayStation technologies and to get the best talent to our studios . . . That is not so different for graphic designs students learning digital imaging software or for film graduates to understand digital film camera! I want students to have access to our professional hardware and software technologies such as Playstation3 or PlayStation Vita development kits.

Furthermore the skills for C++ programming are transferable if graduates move to other game development job opportunities.

When students are looking to work in content development and storytelling I always encourage the, where ever they are, to show that they have made products because professionals will always be assessed on their ability to finish tasks and to visualise their ideas, alone or as part of a team. Students need to be able to show how they have understood how to develop a concept from sketch to a final version irrespective of the platform they are using. This is fundamental to being up to show the capacity to be part of the industry, whether it is related to concept and management or one of the specific technical skills. This of course demonstrates that the students can create a product but it also shows that they understand how the various elements come together.

PETER: What about the generic skills and aptitude required to work in a professional environment?

MARIA STUKOFF: There is necessity for anyone wanting to work in games development to understand professional skills that are not always taught. This is the sense of team-working, entrepreneurial-ness, conflict resolution and problem-solving. These are skills that give any person, the matter what technical specialism they are interested in, more rounded member of the workplace.

PETER: Does this include communication skills?

MARIA STUKOFF: We used to ask for people to have communication skills but I don't think that term is refined enough and so I call them 'translation' skills. Often I recommend to people coming into the industry as programmers that they don't just put programming on their CV, they should include something about themselves that is different from others but that is specific to themselves as a person. This way as an employer I can consider those generic skills that I might actually employ them for. Similarly for an animator I might tell them not only to show their portfolio but to demonstrate that they have submitted things to film festivals and to show something a bit wider to prove that they are a visionary.

WORKING WITH THE EDUCATION SECTOR TO PROVIDE THE NEW DEVELOPERS OF THE FUTURE

PETER: As Head of Academic Game Development what is the extent to which you are involved in the delivery of education or training in the higher education sector?

MARIA STUKOFF: My role is to assess courses in Higher Education and their curricula to see if they can incorporate teaching on the PlayStation platform and therefore provide opportunities for the students to use PlayStation as a development platform. The project that I run is called PlayStation®First and is a program to ensure that PlayStation is the platform of choice for the next generation of developers. I run this project globally, in particular across Europe, Australia, Singapore, South America and the Middle East.

The universities I work closely with in the UK have some form of industry accreditation such as Creative Skillset. This accreditation means the curriculum has been assessed by video game professionals to certify the course is industry fit and relevant. This covers different areas for example the hardware program is looking for future engineers for the PlayStation platform with computer science degrees, physics degrees. But there are also many new courses that are titled video gaming, software development, game programming all of which have strands of web programming or mobile game making part of their curriculum and they would want therefore hardware and industry expertise for their students in those areas.

PETER: Do students who want to work in games development need to be committed to game play themselves or do people with other interests provide new ways of thinking and useful approaches to gaming?

MARIA STUKOFF: If you don't taste your soup you don't know if it's salty enough! To work effectively in any industry people need to have a sensibility and passion of the industry they go into. Games developers would need to understand what kind of gaming there is and what kind of experiences people have across different platforms and as different sorts of gamers, causal gamers and hard-core gamers. To apply critical or theoretical judgments, developers need to have a critical framework based on their knowledge of the area. Even in my position I have to constantly refer to game mechanics which is the way in which you experience a certain narrative or the way in which you have to explore a space because those are the strong skill sets that determined the game narrative it's not just the story. But you can only make judgments about that by understanding how that affects you. And if you don't play games I think you would find it incredibly boring to have everyone around you talking constantly about gaming.

PETER: Are you looking for a diversity in points of view with future developers?

MARIA STUKOFF: Certainly, we should ask where do the new ideas, new designs, new experiences come from if not through a blending of thinking. The games industry needs a range of disciples and people. People who can demonstrate that they think in different ways can offer new ideas – that is actually really difficult to find. Often game concepts are developed within a studio where people share the same culture, for example, broadly watch the same movies, read the same books or are inspired by similar things such as gadgets or fads.

PETER: Are you looking for people to demonstrate a passion for the sector?

MARIA STUKOFF: The word passion is often used without ever quite explaining what it means, but I think what this passion is what is intrinsic to the individual and how this will let them contribute to the industry in a meaningful way

PETER: And can passion be linked to curiosity?

MARIA STUKOFF: It is surprisingly how often people will apply for a job in the games industry but not know what titles the company they are applying to has published so I always advise students to research as much as possible what the products are is and look for a studio that is part of an environment that they are interested in.

SKILLS AND KNOWLEDGE TO WORK IN MANAGEMENT WITHIN THE SECTOR

PETER: To continue to think about what it takes to work in the sector lets turn the spotlight on you! What skills and knowledge did you require to be able to work in the job you have now?

MARIA STUKOFF: In my job I need a broad skill base of interactive technology and digital concept design which I acquired during my media art practice and lecturing in this field since the early 1990s. I also need the ability to manage a diverse group of people with difference interests is extremely relevant to my work, and these are soft skills that I learned through project managing large festivals, teaching and setting up creative industry events.

PETER: Can you break down the work that you do and how you approach it?

MARIA STUKOFF: I need to be able to 'translate' between two different sectors – some people might call this being a connector or networker but I think it's the role of a social translator. I need to be able to explain to a university that is talking about knowledge and experience about business needs and I need to be able to explain how a curriculum is forged to a corporation so that they can understand each other. In other words translate from one sector to another. I need to process and translate certain ideas and ideals according to the client group that I'm talking to, because one group will be interested in what the other group is doing but not knowing how to connect to them.

PETER: So at a senior level people like yourself need a combination of technical, management and conceptual skills and expertise.

MARIA STUKOFF: I am better in my job for knowing how to do basic programming, working with animation tools, and knowing how to make product because the pipeline of product making is essential in this industry on a day-to-day basis, knowing how the studio is run, how the timing and the scheduling is managed. And I also need to know how these things balance against the university semester schedule, how these skills work in a curriculum and effectively teaches young talented people . . . Knowing what those skills entails enables me to translate between what the games industry wants and what is being taught. But it also enables me to evaluate quality and judge product, and as an art practitioner myself I can be a visionary and content innovator.

CHAPTER 14

Case study
Pervasive gaming

Interview with Matt Adams, Blast Theory

How can you play a game across a whole city? While many games are played with handsets and consoles other sorts of gaming takes place with players moving about real space like a city or a landscape. Blast Theory designs games of this sort and in this conversation they explain how, as artists in collaboration with leading technologists and media companies, they can create large scale hybrid events. They also demonstrate how collaboration across sectors can lead to experimental examples of pervasive gaming and incorporate ideas like 'outside broadcasting'. And they raise an important aspect of interactivity – how to enable people to contribute their own content to the narrative in which they are participating.

Blast Theory is renowned internationally as an adventurous group of media artists who use game formats, interactive media and create ground-breaking new forms of performance and interactive art that mixes audiences across the Internet, live performance and digital broadcasting. Led by Matt Adams, Ju Row Farr and Nick Tandavanitj, Blast Theory's work tackles interactivity and the social and political aspects of technology.

In recent years the group has been widely acknowledged as innovators in games, winning the Maverick Award at the Games Developers Conference, USA, in 2005 and being represented by Creative Artists Agency in Los Angeles for games design. The group's recent game projects have probed the fundamental laws of games and of play, posing questions about the boundaries between games and the real world that also have important ramifications for art, performance and virtual worlds. The artists have contributed extensively to debates about the development of games as an art form and how games may be conceptually, intellectually and emotionally demanding while also engaging a wide audience.

Blast Theory is also highly renowned in the creative arts and have won the Golden Nica for Interactive Art at Prix Ars Electronica among many international awards and commendations. Internationally, Blast Theory's work has been shown at ICC in Tokyo, the Chicago Museum of Contemporary Art, Sydney Biennale and the National Museum in Taiwan.

WORKING WITH A FOCUS ON TECHNOLOGY

PETER: Your website states that Blast Theory confronts a media saturated world in which popular culture rules, using performance, installation, video, mobile and online technologies to ask questions about the ideologies present in the information that envelops us. Would you say, then, that the most significant thing that connects your different areas of work is the focus on technology?

MATT ADAMS: There is an appeal of working with technology and part of this comes from responding to the dominant social and political transformations of our age and clearly technology is the driver of that. But part of that is also to do with the fact that technology is such a fast moving and fluid environment and it provides different ways to work. That applies to the people who are engaging with our work as much as to ourselves. So, for example, when we started working in 2000 with GPS most people were unfamiliar with what GPS did let alone the idea that it might offer possibilities for artistic or cultural uses.

CONVERGING GAMING AND OUTSIDE TV BROADCAST

PETER: Your latest game project, *I'd Hide You*, is described as operating at the intersection between games and television. It is also called an experiment in virtuality and physicality in real-time, and as a 'game of stealth and cunning like no other', so it raises a series of different expectations. What were you interested in exploring with this game.

MATT LOCKE: *I'd Hide You* is a typical project because it operates at different levels. At one level it is an online game, at another level it is an outside broadcast from the streets of Manchester with three guides showing you around. *I'd Hide You* is named after a classic club anthem.

PETER: What happens during the game?

MATT ADAMS: In the game there are three runners on the streets of Manchester, streaming real-time video and audio. The game they are playing is to try and film each other without being filmed. So essentially they are self-contained and off they go. But there is a second level to the game where anyone can go to the online site and enter a virtual model of Manchester with avatars of the runners moving around. Online players can click on any of their avatars to jump on board with them and see their video in full screen. If they do that they have the goal of trying to catch a snap, a screen grab, that shows another runner in the shot. They gain a point each time they get a successful snap of a runner on screen and lose a life if the runner they're on board with is snapped while they're on with them. It's a very simple game structure but with an interlocking element.

PETER: But it's also about the relationship between the real environment and the virtual world.

MATT ADAMS: Indeed, it's very much about the sense of presence. It gives a window onto the streets of Manchester in a busy part of the city in the evening when people are out and about, drinking. The runners chat to the people they meet, they show the online players around. Each one of them has a little refuge or secret hiding place that they may take the online player into to tuck themselves out of sight.

PLAYERS AS PERFORMERS

PETER: Are the runners volunteers or are they performers who need particular training or expertise?

FIGURE 14.1
A performer in *I'd Hide You* by Blast Theory 2012

MATT ADAMS: We have recruited a group of people through workshops with young people in Manchester. We work with them in advance to get them to think about what they're doing as cinematography and to think about what they are saying as being voiceover. They have a lot to do because they are playing a game at the same time. They are communicating with the online players as well who can chat with them through messages that come up on their phones so they are also operating in the virtual and the real.

PETER: Are you interested in creating a collaborative relationship between the two levels of players, so the online community can instruct runners where to go?

MATT ADAMS: They can tell them where to go, but whether or not the runners will pay any attention or not is up to them. I suspect it will be negotiated, because online players can help or hinder or distract. The game side of it could almost fall away and it might become something quite different. Part of the fear of these sorts of projects is how to create a structure that will be as broad and open as the players dare to make it.

GAMES AS TECHNOLOGY RESEARCH

I'd Hide You is more than a game. It is an example of the way that technological research can incorporate a creative project. It was developed as part of a much larger research initiative that brings together computer science and the arts and stems from a long term partnership that Blast Theory has with the University of Nottingham to examine ubiquitous computing and computer and human interaction.

PETER: How did *I'd Hide You* come about as part of technology research?

MATT ADAMS: The work for this project came out of an interest into the future of outside broadcasting. It is one of a number of projects funded by the Technology Strategy Board of the UK, and was developed with our key partners, the Mixed Reality Lab at the Computer Science Department at University of Nottingham and a London TV production company, Somethin' Else. We were asking if there could be a better way to do outside broadcasting then we currently have. Currently broadcasts are likely to depend on very inflexible high-end equipment. We were proposing that broadcast could also use HD cameras on mobile phones and other sorts of devices combined with increasing network facilities and bandwidth and multiple consumer products for encoding, streaming and delivery. If you put all those things together it looks like a completely new way of doing outside broadcasting. When there's a festival like Glastonbury with 50,000 people in front of the main stage, 49,500 of them are likely to have a camera on them, and our idea was that all those cameras could be part of the live transmission. If Bono jumps into the audience and puts his arm around a woman you want the camera right next to him not the HD camera 20 metres away on the stage.

APPROACHES TO WORKING WITH AVAILABLE TECHNOLOGY

PETER: As a result are you suggesting that rather than advancing the level of technology we have, the way that we operate with available technology could be developed and therefore new approaches could be taken? In this case what approach do you take? Do you look for someone to come up with – or invent – a technological solution to a problem? Or do you look at what is available on the shelf that you can re-purpose for your own needs?

MATT ADAMS: It's a little bit of both of those. In this case we tried to build our own software first of all and we did multiple tests with multiple mobile devices using netbooks, video cameras, iPhones and Android phones. But through this we found out how incredibly hard it is to achieve what we wanted. This proved to us some of the reasons why what we wanted to do had not been done more widely! We then focused our research on existing products to see if we could invest our resources and energy in a professional product instead of finding ways to stitching together things that work in different ways. As a result we located software which was not made for exactly this purpose, but essentially it provides a turn-key solution to a particular technological need. In terms of working method this is typical. We are always snaking backwards and forwards across a divide: creating our own resources allows us to keep ownership and enables us to really to explore the material but buying in products helps us get result is we know it will do exactly what it says on the tin.

You Get Me (2008)

You Get Me (2008) was a documentary game played between Mile End Park in East London and Covent Garden in central London. It used the Internet to connect two sites that although they are only five miles apart geographically are separated by a much larger cultural gulf. Following in the structure of previous pervasive game projects by Blast Theory, *You Get Me* used a game structure and then stretched it and extended it. It created an exploration of whether a game can be a conversation and whether technology bridges or reinforces social divides. Visitors could choose from one of the teenagers (known as runners) based on a picture of them and their question, for example 'What is your line between flirting and cheating?' or 'Would you employ me?' By navigating their avatars through a virtual Mile End Park, participants could find their chosen runner while avoiding the others. If one of the others got too close they were knocked out of the game.

You Get Me was a commission for Deloitte Ignite and was developed with the support of the Mixed Reality Lab of the University of Nottingham.

FIGURE 14.2
Detail from *You Get Me* (2008)

FIGURE 14.3
Detail from *You Get Me* (2008)

FIGURE 14.4
Gamers playing *You Get Me* (2008)

QUALITATIVE ANALYSIS INTO AUDIENCE ENGAGEMENT

Blast Theory is also involved in collaborations with groups doing other forms of research to look at the way that people engage with the projects they create. This provides them with deep qualitative analysis of the way that people chose to take part or play games, as players, participants or audiences.

PETER: How does the knowledge that you gain through this research help shape the way that you work? Do you think it gives added value?

MATT ADAMS: This really does shape the way that we work and that exists at a number of different levels and is always arresting and enlightening. The partnership that we have with the researchers at the University of Exeter, as well as the University of Nottingham, who are doing this work, brings a tremendously sophisticated philosophical and theoretical perspective to the work that we make.

PETER: Can you describe an aspect of the work that this research might contribute to?

MATT ADAMS: One piece of research looked at the nature of instructions in one of our projects. Its goal was to focus on exactly what goes on in someone's head when they are given instructions that are not completely clear, because sometimes instructions need to be ambiguous, and how the participant then assembles a mental picture of what these instructions might mean. People develop a mental notion and are then testing it in real time against what then subsequently occurs. But sometimes what takes place means that they need to go back and revise what they thought they were doing over the previous ten seconds and an idea just drops into place. This gives us a very detailed sense of how someone follows instructions in an artistic work or game environments.

PETER: Is it easy to do this sort of research into the way that people participate in game environments?

MATT ADAMS: It is very complicated and it's one that we try to decouple from the reception of the work so that participants are not required to be thinking about any of the evaluation at the moment that they are experiencing or taking part in a projects. We are very vigilant about even how much observation of people goes on when a work is active because to be observed is to change your experience – if you have someone with a clipboard asking you at this moment 'Are you lost?' It might be interesting for a researcher but it's just killed the experience of the person who got asked.

RIDER SPOKE – A GAME OF CYCLING PARTICIPANTS

Another of Blast Theories projects, *Rider Spoke*, took playing in a different direction. Like *I'd Hide You*, the 'game' also took place in city streets, this time with participants or 'players' cycling through the city. Following a short introduction the players would head out into the streets with a handheld computer mounted on the handlebars. Players were given a question and invited to look for an appropriate place where they could record their answer using the computer, which would then be stored, or 'hidden' at that location. The computer screen showed the questions and whether there were any hiding places nearby.

The other aspect of the game was that players could find the 'hiding places' where other participants had recorded their answers. When they cycled close to a place with a contribution, the computer would alert them to stop and show the question that that previous person answered and played their answer. The recordings that people made were only available in this context: played to a player, alone, in the place where they were recorded. Each hiding place combines two properties: the physical location and the electronic location as reported by the device.

Rider Spoke was a collaboration with the University of Nottingham and Sony Net Services, which was based in Berlin. Rather than using GPS, Rider Spoke used Wi-Fi hotspots for location. To enable this the University of Nottingham designed a system that used WiFi access points to determine the position of each rider.

FIGURE 14.5
A participant in *Rider Spoke* by Blast Theory (2007)

USER GENERATED CONTENT

PETER: Can you tell me how *Rider Spoke* came about and the ideas behind it?

MATT ADAMS: *Rider Spoke* is work that really came out of the phrase 'user generated content' and reveals our thinking about each of the three words in that phrase. We were interested in looking at the possibilities to create different kinds of contexts where the public could contribute creatively. In many ways for work like this the phrase 'publicly created contributions' is better than 'user generated content'. And in *Rider Spoke* we wanted the public to be co-authors of the work. Essentially what they do is listen to recordings made by other members of the public and make their own. We created a dramatic structure that sets a very particular arc in place but nevertheless invites people to engage with it on their own terms. One of the things I like about this project is that any member of the public can be performer and author as well as being the audience and listener.

PETER: And as a result people will see the work differently depending on what they bring to it. Do you think that it's important that your users or players, the public, understand that you have designed this as a kind of framework or scaffold into which they are able to make or put the content. Because most people would be used to using platforms that do this in an online media context, for example using Facebook, which has a specific structure but it's up to the users to decide how they are going to populate it and respond to the content that they or other people put in. Most of your public would understand the rules or the setup for this sort of thing. Do you think people respond to your work as operating in the same kind of way?

MATT ADAMS: Certainly there are ways in which projects like *Rider Spoke* offer containers that people can populate. Obviously a platform like Facebook is ideologically constructed in specific ways and they have already set a very strong trajectory in motion as to how people will use it and what they will do there, and every decision users make prescribes that ever more narrowly and tightly. All interactive artworks are also ideologically constructed but probably in different ways. But I do think that one of the interesting things about the last 20 years of cultural and technological change has been a loosening of roles in general and specifically in culture and particularly between who produces it and who consumes it. I think that's one of the fantastic and significant shifts so we've tried to make work that responds to this.

PETER: Does it follow then that projects like *Rider Spoke* can be a completely different experience to different users, because you leave it open for them to shift between being producer and consumer. Also, the different context in which you present the work in different cities will affect how people experience it and who takes part in it.

MATT ADAMS: When *Rider Spoke* was in Athens it was supported by the local cycling club. The people who were working on it were all advocates for cycling in the city and saw the whole thing as a kind of activism to make people realise that cycling is important and to encourage people to do it. In Australia, in Sydney it was at the Museum of Contemporary Art, and presented as an art project, but the following week we were in Adelaide at a film festival. So there were multiple permutations in the way that people see it. I really like that because is partly to do with asserting that the interest of the work is not dependent on its artistic heritage. So for me the question of 'is it art?' is a complete non-question. Instead is it interesting or is it rich or is it complex? Much of my cultural inspiration comes from people like Alan Moore, the graphic novelist, or from William Burroughs who paid little attention to the status of art. Certainly the work is interesting and relevant regardless of whether it has an art status.

NARRATIVE STRUCTURES WITHIN GAMES AND PROJECTS

PETER: I am interested in the way that even within open structures there are some things that you determine about the subject of the work. Within *Rider Spoke* there is a particular narrative and creative thesis that dealt with things like the way we experience a city, as a tourist or as a resident, and how we develop our sense of place through our memories and impressions and connection to other people's impressions. I think cycling is also an interesting device to use because sometimes the purpose of cycling is about getting from a place to a destination and sometimes it's about the physical pleasure of moving through a space. *Rider Spoke* lets the player experience the way they develop understanding of the city and create a sense of meaning. So as creators you don't determine the narrative that they come away with but you give me the space and the structure to construct it on their own.

MATT ADAMS: Part of the way that we make work is the rejection of the dualism of mind and body and there is a choreographic performative thread through the work that we make. In *Rider Spoke* the bodily experience of moving and freewheeling off into the night without a set destination, following your nose harks back to the flaneurs and the Situationists. This freedom from goals can then tie into reflections on the player's life that might be quite personal or private, but those things are essential to the experience of the work. They get asked the question then they choose where they want to go. They may know where to go or they may be looking for somewhere that will suit the conditions for what they want to record. But in the period between hearing the question and arriving at the place where they will stop and answer it, they are busy cycling. They may not be consciously thinking about their answer but in fact they are subconsciously processing it in and when they come to record their response they have had a period of reflection. That's the thing I love particularly about *Rider Spoke* – the physical activity primes the emotional and intellectual tenor of the way the work unfolds for people. It means people can inscribe those locations with real meaning.

CREATING NEW HYBRID SPACES FOR GAMES

Rider Spoke shows Blast Theory's fascination with how games and new communication technologies are creating new hybrid social spaces in which the private and the public are intertwined. It poses further questions about where games may be sited and what form they may take. It invites the public to be co-authors of the piece and a visible manifestation of it as they cycle through the city. It is precisely dependent on its local context and invites the audience to explore that context for its emotional and intellectual resonances. One of the main considerations behind the research for *Rider Spoke*, was how technological innovations could enable people to make location-based projects without GPS, which *Rider Spoke*, achieved by using Wi-Fi 'fingerprinting' and hotspots instead of GPS.

WORKING WITH TECHNOLOGY AGENDAS

PETER: Can we say that a project like *Rider Spoke* operates on many levels? For the users it might be a game or an art project but for some of the people involved in the development it provides a case study which can explore a technological conundrum or a particular applied research agenda through creative practice.

MATT ADAMS: This has real impact on the way in which we are able to work. In terms of the financial side of our work, those research relationships are absolutely essential because those are the things that give us our hinterland. By developing projects through our research relationships we are able to work together with partners over several years, which we did in the case of the project with University of Nottingham on pervasive gaming. We undertook to research the field of pervasive gaming as it exists economically, technologically, socially and culturally. The benefits are more than financial because through collaboration we get to learn a great deal from our partners who are working in totally different ways, for example in the research labs of Nokia and Sony. Those partnerships are incredibly meaningful part of our practice.

PETER: Presumably also the collaborations are crucial in terms of developing your creative concept but also because your partners focus is on the techno-logical possibilities of the projects because they are led by the exploration of innovation.

MATT ADAMS: And innovation vogues. For example 'location' has risen up and up the research agenda over recent years as GPS has become more widespread and smart phones have changed peoples ways of operating. At one level the impetus comes from government thinking that wants to lead change and social development, or research councils that want to pursue knowledge develop-ment and exchange into location-based work. All of whom have an interest in producing IP, new business models or new demonstrations of services and so on. Therefore the success of our projects and the involvement of our partners is due to their ability to bring people to support and work on them, which is entirely to do with how congruent they are with major technological and social research objectives. Our job as artists is to harness those agendas to our concerns, to use those as springboards and to pose critical questions about those agendas.

DEFINITIONS

PETER: Lastly, how do you describe Blast Theory? You are described variously as media producers, artists and game creators. So what defines Blast Theory?

MATT ADAMS: Part of the attraction of working in this sector is the instability of categorisation. We've always been keen to operate in a framework where things are not overly defined. In our early work we would often work in a club-like environment but the work we created wasn't something you'd typically find in a club. With later projects it wasn't obvious if they were a stunt, a prank, an artwork, a new media work or a moneymaking activity, and they deliberately left all those questions unanswered.

Part IV

Digital media

CHAPTER 15

Software as culture

What is software and why are we emphasising that it is cultural? Software is in essence any machine-readable set of instructions, which in computing is written as a program that directs specific operations of a computer's processor. The term software distinguishes a set of computer operations that are distinct from its hardware, which refer to the physical devices. Software and hardware comprise related dimensions of computer processes and the intermediary term, firmware, denotes software stored in hardware, which perform certain levels of computer operations. Software then is a general term which can refer to both the numerical binary code of machine instructions, as well as the source code, which is the instructions written in a code that humans can communicate in order that instructions can be executed by the machine. The writing of machine readable source code, the development of software and the uses to which it is put, represent distinct and different spheres of operation, which are not normally considered together. However, cultural scholars (Fuller and Goffey 2012) have recognised for some time that a full account and understanding of computer mediated communication needs to take all three moments of numerical coding, writing code and the execution of code into account. Synthesising the computer and cultural layer as the language of digital media is exceptionally difficult and software studies is an emerging area of research which crosses the disciplines of science and technology studies, computing and cultural studies. Another way of putting this is to say that there is a cultural relationship between the functional levels of platform and application software. In the historic development of computer software there has been a distinction between open-source software (OSS) in which the copyright holder provides the licence rights for users to study, change and distribute software without charge and proprietary software, which is commercially developed and where the copyright holder gives exclusive legal rights for use under restrictive conditions. Open source software is closely associated with the proponents of free software or public domain software that is not subject to copyright and which has been developed by a collaborative technical community.

The 'language' of computer mediated forms of communication, which we've characterised as complex and layered, can also be schematised as software. At the user level we can conceive of a language of the human–computer interface (HCI), which consists of software programs together with the data assets, the electronic encoding of written texts, images, graphics, sounds they make available. At the computer processing and programming level we can consider a language of code, the mathematical algorithms, which structure the computer processing and operating system. Our two levels are similar to what (Manovich 2001:46), distinguishes as the 'cultural layer' and the 'computer layer', which, he says, influence each other, or are composited in practice. Where, exactly, these two levels meet, between the design of computers and software and the ways in which a user engages with them is a complex, but important point of understanding. The design and production of any machine or technology needs to be understood as already containing cultural values or meanings, which are part of the structure of the language of any digital media product, but are not immediately obvious to the user. One way of revealing the cultural/linguistic meanings built into the design of computers, is through analysis of interfaces and software use. Thinking about software as culture leads us to see that software code is based upon usability concepts, based upon a set of assumptions and precepts about the purposes the machine or program has been designed to solve, or facilitate. The personal computer (PC) arrives culturally conceptualised, as a machine with user intentions and purposes already prefigured in its design. The problem with the distinction between the machine and its organisational function, one the one hand, and the human uses to which we put the machine on the other, is that it can lead us to assume the neutrality of the machine as a tool.

The distinction between our two levels of language (machine and its uses, or the computer level and the cultural level) is not recognised in practice, because the user experiences a seamless flow, from the interface metaphor (the desktop), through the controls its offers, through to the data it makes available. The user interacts with the computer, through programmed instructions embedded in software, which conceals the programming layer, while simulating the cultural layer of image, sound text. The end user doesn't 'see' the layer of code, or even necessarily need to use the programming language, and hence doesn't need to think about it either. The computer layer constitutes the invisible part of the grammar of digital media until, that is, something goes wrong with the operational commands, which forces the user to become, negatively, aware of it.

The recognition of 'visible' and 'invisible' levels of interface command, the former based upon mathematics, and the later on the simulated representation of existing forms of cultural communication, make the notion of a unified or consistent language

Table 15.1 Schema distinguishing between the human and computer level of interface communication

Level 1. Command	Interface
Metaphorical interface	windows, icons, desktop, toolbars
Physical interface	screen, keyboard, mouse, input devices
Level 2. Processing and Memory	**Function**
Operating system	software code
Central processing system	algorithmic code
	electrical impulses and switches

of digital media untenable. The reasons for this are threefold, first, digital media is, by definition, continually evolving and developing and could therefore be said to be at a current stage where it has no developed language of its own. This is a view adopted by a number of commentators (Rush 1999; Manovich 2001). Second, digital media is characterised more than anything else by its hybridity. The graphical user interface of the PC, the desktop and its current applications is the nearest we come to defining a coherent usable set of common communication tools. But the graphical user interface (GUI), is itself based upon the previous and distinct analogue media disciplines, i.e., typewriting and printing, 2-D graphics, animation, film and photography, as well as being founded upon computing (Bolter and Gruisin 1999). Third, there is a widespread social, cultural and institutional application of digital media, in the office, home, laboratory, school, college or workshop, which differentiates user requirements and access, what has been characterised as 'grey media' (Fuller and Goffey 2012). Within such contexts of computer-mediated communication, localised purposes, rules, conventions and understandings will be defined, which will contribute to the ways in which communication takes place. While there are distinct technical stages in digital media production and different cultural contexts and uses, it is their convergence in software, which form the basis upon which we say that there is something like a language of digital media. The current position of computer mediated language can therefore be summarised in the following way:

1   the language of digital media is at an early stage of development;

2   the language of digital media is highly dependent upon historical media forms and their discourses, which digital code simulates and represents;

3   the language of digital media is characterised by a high degree of hybridity, based upon convergence.

The question of the languages of digital media is further discussed in Chapter 2.

USING SOFTWARE

Increasingly there are very few 'old media' practices left in operation other than in very specialist types of production. In one sense the category of new media industries defines precisely new types of businesses, which have emerged with the development of the Internet and IT as well as the growing use of social media by most large institutions and companies. At the same time new media industries signals a set of new activities and practices, which have arisen through the application of software, within existing business organisations. So at times it is use of software, which is seen to be the common link in a chain of otherwise different activities and businesses, banking and newspapers for example require different kinds of software. At other times it is the form of digital media practice, which connects different contexts, both banks and newspapers have websites, for instance, which need to be set-up, designed, updated and managed. In addition there is a wide range of long established media related practices of communication, which have been deeply affected by the introduction of software to process media files. Film, photography, architectural and graphic design and music now all use software for the generation, compositing and editing of image and text, sound and movement. Because they use digital software traditional media industries, of broadcasting, the press and advertising are also included within the term new media industries, although their institutions and many of their practices are far from new. Currently the fastest growing sector of employment in digital media is in the management, optimisation and personalisation of web traffic, including the management of corporate presence within social media and all those new content managers are using bespoke software.

DIGITAL DISTRIBUTION

This current complexity in mapping the territory of the digital media industries, particularly in relationship to established, or old media industries, is a reflection of the different ways in which software has been applied to existing practices. The traditional media sector has almost universally developed an online presence for their business. The most popularly visited website in the UK is the BBC Online for instance. All of the major Hollywood studios have websites. While at one level a website could be simply a media organisation's calling card, or directory entry, it is also recognised by media organisations that websites are an important direct marketing tool. Additionally traditional media organisations perceive the Internet as a major means of advertising their products, as well as, increasingly, a means of product distribution, with proprietary and customised download and player services. Online publishing has massively expanded as publishers have found ways of selling electronic versions of books in line with the take-up of reading on portable screen tablets. Perhaps the biggest example of electronic distribution is music downloading, which has radically changed the economic and legal arrangements of existing forms of music reproduction and distribution.

DIGITAL COMPOSITING

The established media sector has also adopted digital software to carry out the functions previously reproduced by analogue technologies and autographic reproduction, such as non-linear digital editing, music recording, page layout and compositing, graphic design, architectural drafting and most recently the application of motion graphics. This has meant that photographers, editors, musicians, sound engineers, layout artists, graphic designers, cinematographers and architects have acquired the skills of operating computer software programs. There is a generation of 'creatives' working in the traditional media sector who acquired new skills and changed their practices 'on the job', as new compositing, editing and drafting technologies were introduced. As software programs and their updates were rolled out across the late 1980s and 1990s, a new technology training sector grew-up, alongside the industries to provide in-house and short course programmes for workers who needed to use computer mediated communication software. This was fairly quickly followed by the introduction of formal certified higher level courses in education, which has led to a generation who have acquired a software skills base as a prerequisite for working in a digital media sector. The educational organisation of this skills base reflects the complex and differential nature of the digital media industries and education and training in digital media is clearly organised along specialist and media specific lines, which reflect the external organisation of industry. It is not difficult to see the general lines of organisation of education and training in digital media, matching the organisation and divisions of labour. Not surprisingly the organisation of education and training for the digital media industries corresponds to our analysis of the 'layers' of computer mediated communication.

SOFTWARE/HARDWARE: SYSTEM AND SUPPORT

The near total application of ICT systems in advanced manufacturing and service industries has, over a relatively short period of time, led to the emergence of a large IT technical support sector whose job it is to manage the networks, which create platforms of communication and production in different organisations. The traditional media industries not only run information networks, but also require the support of technical production services. The technicians and engineers in film, photography, television and music production, who work alongside the producers and directors, currently work between analogue and digital equipment, often working at complex interfaces that still exist in getting digital and analogue technologies to work together. While traditional media production has developed clear separations and demarcations between production roles, they are less clear in digital media production, where there is greater overlap in technical operations, for instance in software manipulation where technical, conceptual and design decisions are closely related.

SOFTWARE USERS

The production of media products, which involve digital processes in their production, video and photography for instance, require the labour of a variety of specialist practitioners who take on specific roles, such as producing, directing, designing and technical realisation. These roles can only meaningfully be thought of within the context of the whole production process, and media production has developed roles which fit with the stages of production. Digital media production groups will have some kind of clearly defined hierarchical structure in the co-ordination of roles and functions inherited from previous modes of production. This is demonstrated by looking at the ways in which digital media practices are entering into the production processes of established media.

SOFTWARE APPLICATION IN FILM

A good example of software in use can be seen in the way in which film and video production has been changed by the application of software. Film as film is, we should remember, an analogue medium consisting of celluloid coated with light sensitive chemicals exposed to light. Film is essentially the same mechanical technology it was at the beginning of the twentieth century, although there has been a continuous process of technical refinements. Mainstream film production still uses film although most post-production processes are organised digitally. At the time of writing, mainstream film production is shifting rapidly to producing films on digital formats, leading to a decline in the manufacture of film itself. Films are also now being screened on digital projectors. These changes mark a major and radical set of changes in the film industry. The growth area for work in film is currently in post-production effects, such as editing, compositing and animating. Commercial films contain as a matter of course computer generated titles and special effects sequences as well as being graded and colourised digitally. The computers used for producing special animated film effects use dedicated software and at present require a lot of computing power to calculate and render sequences. Computer engineers and software designers, work closely with the special effects directors and computer animators to attain the effects that are now an expected part of an audience's enjoyment of mainstream film. Traditional film editing was based upon running actual film sequences backwards and forwards on spools so that it passed through a projection screen, which could be paused at individual frames. Editors would mark the beginnings and ends of sequences to be cut, which were then physically assembled in the right order and literally glued together to produce a master' copy, from which other copies could be made. The development of analogue video meant that film footage could be transferred to a video format, with a calibrated a time-code and a 'video mock-up' of the final editing sequence could be produced on video. This made the editing process quicker and easier, moving backwards and forwards and inserting sequences. Digital editing moves that process further on making it possible to move the sequences around at will. Like all digital files, film sequences can be cloned, copied and pasted almost at will. The editing process in non-linear since neither the film stock, nor the videotape has to be physically moved along a sequence, but instead the computer algorithms render film sequences as layers and timelines. There are two main points to make about the practice of digital film editing here. First, and undoubtedly, there is a powerful continuity with the conceptual skills of editing, which derive from a knowledge base of film language or more specifically film continuity editing. Film editing as the language of organising events in time and space, could be taught on any of the technologies of film over the last 100 years. However, the second point is that the introduction of non-linear digital editing has changed the technical possibilities of editing and this is bringing about new conventions of editing and hence modifying the language of film. The same two points apply to film animation. The point for the training of animation practitioners is that like film, the 'language' of animation can still be derived from the historical stock of techniques, knowledge and practices of animated film. However, digital computer animation has produced spectacular, feature length products, whose language may stay resolutely within that of film and animation traditions, but whose computer modelled and rendering objects and effects now encompass a range of graphic styles, from the fully realised photographic to that of the virtual rendering of any previous historical graphic style. Developments in high-end compositing and rendering software over the past decade make it much more likely that most feature film and television drama will make more use of what previously might have been termed special effects, but which are now increasingly a standard part of post-production.

IMAGE AS SOFTWARE

The introduction of software in photography has now reached a spectacular level and has replaced most of the analogue and chemical process of image production. It might now be considered that apart from the principle of the latent image formed through the aperture and lens of a camera, photography has been replaced by synthetic imaging technologies in which software, both in the camera and on screen produced what we accept as a photograph. But as with film, the language of photography continues to organise how images are conceptualised, composed and read. Historically it was the gradual improvement in digital file sizes, storage and transmission, which lead to a mixed economy of processes, with photographers not willing to invest in high cost high end digital cameras until the digital image file had the same image resolution capabilities as chemical negatives. Today the analogue and digital photographic technologies are seamlessly interfaced so that a digital file can be transferred to high end chemical negative or print, and chemical film can be digitised in order that it can be manipulated and distributed in any digital format or outputted to one of a number of high-end laser inkjet processes. It is possible to say that the photographer remains the photographer, whether they have film in their camera, a digital back on a professional system camera, or a fully electronic digital capture device. By this we mean again, that the 'language' of photography, being able to control light through shutters and apertures, and being able to compose meaning images through framing, angle and depth of field, remain the same and can be taught and acquired through either chemical or digital means. But these principles of analogue photography are increasingly coded in software, as Instagram, for example, exposes. The introduction of editing and manipulation software in the post production process of film and photography is now working its way back to software in the camera, which sets out the parameters of image capture and code. In photography it is possible to identify the development and use the image manipulation software program, Photoshop, as having transformed how photographic images edited, manipulated and transmitted. Industrially, photography is still regarded as photography, even though digital technology has all but replaced film and chemicals, darkrooms, graphic layout and compositing tables of newspapers and magazines. The photograph is now produced and increasingly lives on screen.

DIGITAL VIDEO: HARDWARE AND SOFTWARE COMBINE

Video is also a medium that has been transformed by digital technologies, but where the practices are reproduced within traditional production structures. Min-DV and Digi-Beta are digital video formats used for a variety of professional and amateur cameras. In the hobbyist domestic market Mini-DV formats are the norm in the miniaturised compact cameras of today. Home movies are now edited with stripped down non-linear editing software on Home PCs exported to DVDs or iCloud. In the latest developments moving image is being shot on digital single reflex cameras (DSLR) in high definition. Cameras capable of producing broadcast standard full motion image, is within the financial reach of a film or media graduates. Such equipment was once only the province of television production companies, or even film production companies, now the camera and editing equipment of many University media departments is on a par with London Soho editing studios. Of course there are differences in formats and quality across the range of digital equipment, but the principles of the camera and editing remain the same. So, here again we are confronted by the same twin recognitions. At one level digital video production processes are embedded in the continuous experiences of technical production which support the use of video in documentary, news and outside broadcast, location or studio drama. At another level the use of digital video cameras and computer-based editing by individuals and small production companies is changing not only who can make programs, but also how they are made.

SOUND SOFTWARE

Digital sound architecture, or sonic media, is emerging as a distinct set of practices out of the historical forms of analogue sound engineering and sound recording, closely associated with digital video. Sound as an independent form is as yet one of the least explored digital properties of online and interactive media, primarily because of the music and voice reproductive function of the digital medium. Of course our general argument that new technologies are in part an extension of existing technologies equally applies to the production and reproduction of music and sound. Sound engineering has adapted to the introduction of digital recording and digital transmission in radio for instance. Music production has used analogue recording, mixing and editing and there is an established musical use of electronic instrumentation.

SOFTWARE AESTHETIC

The point we are making about practitioner skill-sets being both continuous with traditions of media production, what we are calling the language of the medium, as well as those languages being changed by the possibilities introduced by software, is generalisable. The use of computer software for visual realisation by graphics agencies and architectural practices, builds upon a set of visual conventions derived from autographic practice, often encoded and mimicked by software tools and menus. Computer graphic programs convert the graphical conventional elements of drawing, lines, curves, tones, into pre-programmed behaviours, which can be combined with the digital typography and digital photography to produce a hybrid digital pixel palette. In addition this electronically combined drawing board, type-setting block, easel and masking frame is also a reprographic process for the duplication, storage and transmission to other forms of realised work. Such hybrid graphical tools can be used in many conventional processes to exactly replicate graphical conventions previously executed using a combination of autograph skills and analogue reprographic process. Equally they can be used to produce graphical representations of three dimensional spaces and structures and to produce seamless photographic and graphical montages, which are both conceptually and technically dependent upon the properties of the digital tool. The argument for the emergence of a distinct digital aesthetic is most prominent in the hybrid use of graphics programs. Such a distinct aesthetic as there is has been created by the practitioners of computer generated graphics programs.

SOFTWARE AS TOOLS

A further way of looking at software as culture is to consider the ways in which practitioners use software. In 2003 Adobe rebranded its Photoshop colour-editing program as Adobe Photoshop Creative Studio, creating its thirteenth issue since 1989, which is available in over 20 languages. In 2008 Adobe released a free web-based image editing tool for blogs and social networking sites and in 2011 a version for Android mobiles. The near universality of Photoshop makes it the most popular pixel-based image editing software. The latest version of Photoshop CS6 contains a redesigned unified interface, which was developed form professional designer feedback in order that they can more easily manage documents and palettes. The latest version also contains a video editing suite and enable vector graphic editing through it numerous tools within one program.

Adobe Photoshop tool bars contain some highly generic tools such as, zoom, select and text, other tools generic to drawing software, such as brush, pen and erase and then medium specific tools, such as dodge, blur, crop derived from the chemical darkroom of photography, and then tools for which there was no existing media equivalent such as layering, magic wand, which selects similarly coloured pixels, history brush, which restores pixels from a designated state, the clone stamp and the slightly mystical, and most recent tool the healing brush which corrects flaws. Again the reason for such descriptive detail is to underline the point that even the title of the tools reflect the hybrid and even somewhat schizophrenic nature of the command options. A graphic interface, which has the icons and titles of the tools and conventions of drawing and painting, combined with the operations of chemical photography together with a set of new options based upon pre-set computer behaviours and pixel cloning and adjustment.

LAYERS AND COMPOSITING

In addition to what are considered the basic operations of the menu and tools, Photoshop 7 contains more advanced operations, which control colour management, compositing, selection, history and navigation, gradients, layers and masks. Compositing groups the operations of the cut and paste of elements and selections and the cloning, resizing, pattern stamping of selections, which can be precisely positioned and aligned with seamless edges or divisions between elements. Colour management and gradient control tone and hue in different layers, masks and selections. The very early versions of Photoshop only allowed for any two moves in selection before the new configuration became fixed. It was not possible to go back and undo previous moves. The introduction of layers in Photoshop represented a quantum leap in digital image manipulation. Layers can be compared to clear acetate sheets, which are opaque where there is imagery and transparent where there is not. Each layer can be assigned a different opacity and a mode to control how that layer blends with the layers below it. The layers can be stacked in any order and remain active, with the user being able to turn layers on and off and to work on one active layer at a time. Because Photoshop makes it possible to keep all changed states active, until a final version is required, a way of charting the changes is necessary, otherwise the user would easily lose the order of actions they have made. Photoshop has a history palette that allows users to selectively undo up to a thousand previous states and to navigate through the moves they have made.

CONVERGENT SOFTWARE: THE STILL, MOVING AND GRAPHIC

Adobe acquired the After Effects software program in 1994, one year after its first release. After Effects combines animation and compositing of graphic files in two and three dimensions as well as altering the parallax and observational position. After Effects achieves the fusion of elements through a layer system in which each individual media object imported occupies a separate track on a timeline. This track-oriented system is, like Photoshop, a popular program because of its clear organisation of material. The interface consists of several active panels, which control the import of many different file formats, which can be composed within the timeline.

More significantly Adobe now offer a subscription to their Creative Cloud product a means of renting their entire suite of tools and server based storage and online sharing of production files. In conjunction with Adobe After Effects, the Creative Cloud service amounts to an entire production facility, which is available to individual users and companies through the desktop. In terms of our discussion of the language of digital media, Adobe Creative Cloud represents an enormous convergence of the moving, still, graphic and sonic image and is an example of the coming together of all three definitions of the language of digital media we have discussed.

MOTION GRAPHICS

Image editing and manipulation software has recently been reconceptualised around animation and what historically had been methods of producing film-titling sequences. In film titling sequences the term motion graphics, a technique produced by a combination of analogue film shooting and editing, has been in use since the late 1950s, noticeable in early James Bond films. But it was with video editing software in television production from the 1980s to mid-1990s that proprietary graphic systems were produced by the British company Quantel, such as Paintbox, Mirage, Hal and Henry, which met broadcasting standards for graphic titling. With the development of desktop software, in particular Adobe After Effects, motion graphics became a more widespread feature of media object produced for online consumption. Motion graphic software brings together a number of software toolsets such as colour correction compositing and editing with special effects. With the incorporation of frame positioning movement and 3-D elements, Autodesk's Maya and 3D Studio Max are software programs used widely in animation. Avid's Motion Graphics is a further commercially available software for professional motion graphic production. 3-D special effects in film major production are still produced on high-end computers using proprietary software. Motion graphic software can be divided into two types, video manipulation software packages, such as After Effects in which elements can be imported into and exported out of video shots, and 3-D modelling software, such as Lightwave, or Maya, in which objects can be modelled, rendered and animated. Motion graphics is an integration, or collection of techniques of collage and traditional animation, such as stop-motion and Cell animation. Motion graphic therefore represents a powerful form of convergence in software.

POWERPOINT AS CULTURE

Today there are many presentational software programs that are widely available and used as standard wherever a presentation is required, for example, Adobe Presenter 8, iWork: Keynote, and Prezi. Microsoft Office PowerPoint remains one of the earliest and the paradigm example and will serve as an example of the idea of software as culture. By this we mean that the software encodes cultural assumptions about knowledge and communication as part of the toolset it offers. Microsoft PowerPoint is an interesting example of a software program that contains a restricted and hierarchical model of knowledge presentation, which would have to be actively resisted in order to break with the assumptions written into the software. Bob Gaskins and Dennis Austin worked together to create PowerPoint in a company called Forethought, which was purchased by Microsoft Corporation for $14 million in 1987. Microsoft released PowerPoint 1.0 in 1987 for the Apple Macintosh and a year later developed a Windows and DOS version. PowerPoint was subsequently incorporated into the Microsoft Office suite of applications.

PowerPoint is a software program, designed primarily as an audio/visual aide in the presentation of information, whether in a lecture, classroom, or corporate event. In this respect PowerPoint is the digital equivalent, or extension of the flip-chart, white-board, slide-projector or overhead projector, which provides for the flexible combination of different forms of information, video, photographs, graphics, text and sound. PowerPoint's interface uses the language of the photographic slide, in such a way that that information can be composed on individual slides using a stripped-down menu of textual and graphic tools and hyperlinks. Individual slides can be ordered into a slide-show using a further menu of timings and animated transitions for the slides and the elements within a slide. The resulting set of slides can then be put into projection mode for presentation purposes either onscreen or printed.

Upon opening a new file PowerPoint offers the user a choice between a blank presentation and a set of pre-designed formats, based upon business models of planning and marketing. The pre-designed presentations have a graphic style background for each slide, incorporating colours and shapes, with simple hyper-linked cards, to navigate forwards, backward and home. The pre-designed presentations contain various graphic backgrounds, into which information, text, charts, photographs, video clips can be imported. PowerPoint has been organised, and conceptualised, as a sequencer of information. The pre-designed sheets and the menu of tools, combine so that the user enters whatever they wish to present within the given structure of hierarchies and sequencing. We could say then that the structure of PowerPoint renders all information as the points, the point of course of its trademark title. Knowledge, discourse, pedagogy, communication and exchange in the PowerPoint world of presentation takes the form of points, bullet points even, a staccato rendition in which argument and analyse is broken down into a hierarchy of nested points. The widespread availability of PowerPoint within the Microsoft office, has led to its popular use in education and the workplace in North America and Europe. On the positive side PowerPoint is a useful, simple to use, organiser and aide in presentation and marks an improvement upon the whiteboard and overhead projector for a number of reasons. PowerPoint files can be incorporated into any digital electronic communication, such as email attachments or web-sites, and they share, with all other digital files the ability for simultaneous transmission to unlimited receivers. PowerPoint allows for the combination of different information in digital form, so that photographic and moving images, together with sound files, graphics and text can all be displayed. Finally, PowerPoint creates limited animation and navigation, which allows any given body of information and ideas to be conceptually controlled. On the negative side, PowerPoint can and often does structure material in a hierarchical and linear cognitive mode, the templates and tools create a 'built-in predisposition' towards any given information, which 'over-determines' the content of any use. The use of titles, captions, clipart inserts, bullet points, charts, logos, combined with the animations and transitions to lock any given content or subject into a pre-set mould of communication. At its simplest, the criticism is that the world of complex and creative thought is reduced to a set of bullet points. Critics of PowerPoint have pointed out that it functions to reassure the presenter, rather than enlighten an audience, that the outliner causes ideas to be arranged in a deep hierarchy, which in turn reinforces an audience's linear progression through that hierarchy. (Tufte 2003:18) sums up the typical use of PowerPoint thus:

> At a minimum, a presentation format should do no harm. Yet the PowerPoint style routinely disrupts, dominates, and trivialises content. Thus PowerPoint presentations too often resemble a school play – very loud, very slow, and very simple.

While Tufte is right that many of us have sat through crude and simplistic PowerPoint presentations, we have to take care not to see this as exclusively determined by the technology and software. PowerPoint is prefigured in the ways described above, but the quality of a presentation using PowerPoint is also dependant on the context in which it is used and upon the user's understanding of why and how they are using it. Don Norman, an MIT researcher, responded to Tufte's critique in precisely this way,

PowerPoint is not the problem. The problem is bad talks, and in part, this comes about because of so many pointless meetings, where people with – or without – a point to make – have to give pointless talks. The problem is that it is difficult work to give a good talk, and to do so, the presenter has to have learned how to give talks, has to have practiced, and has had to have good feedback about the quality of the talks – the better to improve them.

(www.sociablemedia.com/articles_norman.htm)

The general point is of course that any software program, Photoshop would be another example, can be used creatively or routinely. The built-in predispositions of the emergent properties and behaviours of software programs that are structured through the interface menus and tools, need to be critically and purposefully understood, rather than simply employed because they are there. The uncritical and routine operation of software does represent one side of a divide, just as the design of software can reinforce limiting epistemologies and paradigms of thought and action.

The user whose knowledge is bounded by and within 'levels' will be limited to their own sphere of operation. In fact we could usefully label such positions on our continuum as that of the operational. The sphere of the operational holds for all the positions on the continuum, for the scientist just as much as the net surfer. We are not saying that the scientist with the 'deep' code of the machine is in the privileged position of overview. The scientist, or engineer or programmer will not necessarily have access to the know-how of software applications, or that of the languages of hypermediated communication, nor indeed the reflexes and responses of a gamer twitching in front of the screen.

C@SE STUDY

ILLUSTRATED CASE STUDY 3: DATA TAGGING

Tales of things

In a recent creative project, people who donated clothing and objects to a chain of charity shops in Manchester, UK were invited to record their personal stories about them, which are then 'tagged' to the items using QR codes. Shoppers in the charity shops were then able to download an app and use scanners built into smart phones to discover the stories behind the vintage and second-hand items. These details would otherwise be lost when an item is given away, and yet can be an important part of its history and adds personal value for the person who acquires it. This information can be treated as existing locally, in a shop or neighbourhood, but it can also operate globally. Information on the objects is managed through data clouds and can therefore be extensive, recording not only the personal stories associated with an object but where it moves, what financial transactions occur and what conditions it undergoes. Data from one object can be associated with another to form linked associations. Objects and their stories can be tracked online.

This initiative is one of the activities of *Tales of Things and Electronic Memory.* This creative research project reflects on the way that increasingly objects, artefacts and pieces of equipment have a digital capacity built into them, from items of daily household use such as fridges and washing machines to highly complex pieces of equipment like automobiles, but that even non-technological items can still have a digital presence. It highlights the way that network communications make it possible for information to be exchanged between items which carry their data code or IP address.

Tales of Things focuses on the way that stories about an object, or social memories, can be recorded, geo-located and shared. The way that information is used in the charity shop project illustrates how data tagging can reverse the usual process in which bar codes on object carry commercial information. It stresses that social memory is an increasingly important concept in digital culture.

The *Tales of Things* project responds to the concept of 'The Internet of Things', which refers to 'a ubiquitous form of computing in which every device is "on", and every device is connected in some way to the Internet . . . because they will have been tagged and indexed by the manufacturer during production' (http://talesofthings.com/about/).

The project researchers argue that:

> the implications for the Internet of Things upon production and consumption are tremendous, and will transform the way in which people shop, store and share products . . . every object manufactured will be able to be tracked from cradle to grave, through manufacturer to distributor, to potentially every single person who comes into contact with it following its purchase . . . In a world that has relied upon a linear chain of supply and demand between manufacturer and consumer via high street shop, the Internet of Things has the potential to transform how we will treat objects, care about their origin and use them to find other objects.

> (http://talesofthings.com/about/)

A critical aspect of the *Tales of Things* research involved exploring the role of material artefacts as 'things' increasingly become complemented by an equal amount of immaterial data such as peoples' memories and

C@SE STUDY

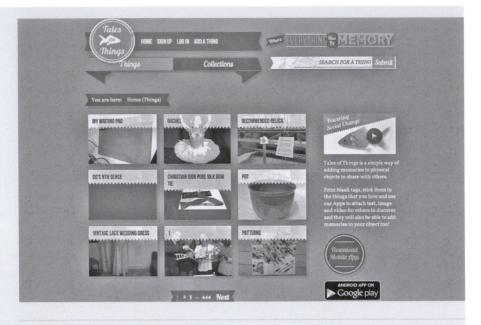

FIGURE 1

Tales of Things 'ghost object' at the National Museum Scotland with QR data stickers that enable museum visitors to upload their stories and tag them to objects

FIGURE 2

Shoppers in a charity shop in Manchester, UK, using the QR tags on second-hand objects

C@SE STUDY

C@SE STUDY

Figure 3
Shoppers in a charity shop in Manchester, UK, using the QR tags on second-hand objects

logistical data such as information, temperature and tracking data. The project also worked with the museums sector and this allowed the research team to explore the way that information is assigned to physical artefact in museums and how this can change as curators and visitors gain more technology to access the data clouds surrounding each exhibit. Another *Tales of Things* project was collaboration with the National Museum Scotland which involved the development of 'ghost objects' white-painted substitutes for more precious things that are kept behind glass. Visitors were able to handle the ghost objects, and tag them with their personal impressions. This form of user contribution shows how the management of data can have profound social uses in the cultural sector as well as in personal and social contexts.

Tales of Things and Electronic Memory (TOTeM) is a collaboration between Brunel University, Edinburgh College of Art, University College London, University of Dundee and the University of Salford, and is funded through a £1.39 million research grant from the Digital Economy Research Councils UK.

FIGURE 4
Shoppers in a charity shop in Manchester, UK, using the QR tags on second-hand objects

C@SE STUDY

C@SE STUDY

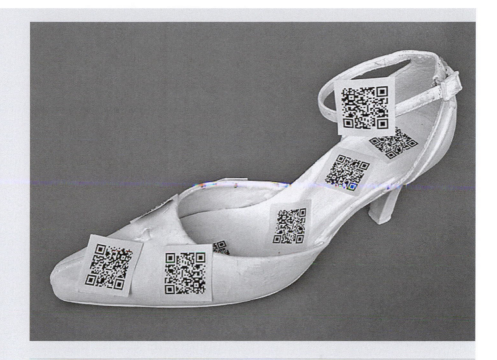

FIGURE 5
Tales of Things website enables people to track their objects online

CHAPTER 16

Digital code

At the centre of discussion about digital media language and the wider debate over the impact of new technologies on media, stand two key concepts or terms, 'code' and 'digital'. Understanding digital media crucially involves an understanding of what is entailed in the digital and its code. Such an understanding of the digital, as it relates to digital media, is best approached by a comparison with another term, the 'analogue'. This comparative approach has been adopted by a number of different writers when discussing the impact of digital technology upon specific mediums. Film and photography in particular have been analysed and discussed in terms of the historical shift from analogue to digital code.

The terms post-photography or digital photography are markers of a set of differences identified between the analogue medium of photography, based in chemistry, optics and mechanics and the new digital medium of photography based on optics, electricity and computing. Likewise, film has also been approached through a contrast of analogue and digital technologies in discussing the technical form of digitised video and the cultural form of film language (Manovitch 2001:50). To a lesser extent computer animation has also been explored through a comparison with previous forms of drawn and cell film animation (Darley 2000; Telotte 2008:59). In all three cases cited here digital media has been contrasted with a previous analogue form. In all three cases digital code is seen as the fundamental basis for considering changes in the nature and use of the specific mediums of photography, film and animation.

ANALOGUE MEDIA

All recording mediums prior to the advent of digital encoding can be defined as analogue. Photography, film, magnetic sound tape, vinyl recordings and videotape are all analogic in nature. Drawing, painting and sculpture are also analogical. All of these media contain material processes in which continuous physical inscriptions of some kind are made in or on surfaces. The brush marks on a canvas, ink rubbed into scored lines on an etching, the silver salts of the photographic print or the electronic magnetic signal on a piece of tape are all material equivalents. In all these examples one set of physical properties, light patterns, sound waves, etc., are being registered and ultimately inscribed into another physical medium. The sound waves of the human voice, spoken, or sung over the duration of time, are translated into patterns of signals on electro-magnetic tape. The light, cast across a rough wooden table top, becomes an analogous set of tonal differences registered by the light sensitive silver salt crystals held in suspension on the emulsion of the unexposed film in the camera. Both are transcriptions of one set of properties, light and sound, into another, chemicals and electromagnetic tape, which over time were developed as part of the technologies and mediums of sound recording and photography respectively. Another way of putting this is to say that the technological medium has reconstituted or transcribed the original voice or visual scene.

Analogue is a term used to define something as 'being like' or resembling something else. In the case of the photography the light and dark tones of the chemical grain of the negative is similar to the reflected light pattern of what was framed in the lens of the camera. In the case of television the light and sound of a scene is analogous to the audio-visual signals that are recorded continuously on electro-magnetic tape. An analogue sound recording on tape can be displayed on an oscilloscope as a visual representation of sound waves – the lines show all the different aspects of the signal. Simplistically, the lines represent amplitude (volume in audio – luminance [brightness] in video) – the distance from one peak (or trough) to the next represents frequency.

An easy, everyday example of an analogue recording would be a photocopy – the copy is analogous, but not identical, to the original, the image is always slightly degraded. If the photocopy is then copied and this copy is copied – the quality of the image gets progressively degraded. The same applies to analogue video and audio recordings. So analogic media record and store 'information' through some kind of material transcription, which transfers the configuration of one physical material into an analogous arrangement in another. The photographic negative is analogous to the light pattern, the videotape is analogous to sound and image recorded over time. One hour of unedited videotape equalling one hour of real time. The physically recorded material is culturally and technologically coded, so that the machines and their materials, together with our knowledge of seeing and listening, reconstitute the original through the analogy.

The continuous nature of analogue media marks a crucial difference from the digital. Electro-magnetic tape is a continuous surface upon which sounds are transcribed. The relationship between the sound and its recording is also continuous. The same is true for photography in the image forming properties of light sensitive film and papers. The photographic negative records the latent image of reflected light in a continuous relationship to the light as it strikes the surface of the film in different intensities. Putting this the other we can say that, neither magnetic tape, nor photographic film, record or transcribe the original signals by breaking them down systematically into units or bits. In analogue mediums there is no code as such, only the continuous medium of transcription.

Analogue media developed as part of the industrial revolution and the mass production of artefacts by a system of the division of labour and the replacement of human labour by machines. As such analogue media reflect the processes of standardisation in which production was divided into separate, simple, sequential activities, which could be endless repeatable such as the frames of a film or the dots of the half-tone process of newspaper photographs. However, analogue media were not interchangeable and each developed its own materials, properties and apparatuses. A camera could not be used for recording speech, just as the newspaper could not reproduce moment. Of course, film could reproduce a visual moment and sound but only by combining or synchronising the separate analogue media of film and magnetic tape.

Analogue media can now be defined retrospectively from the vantage point of the digital as continuous data or information in which the axis or dimension that is measured has no apparent indivisible unit from which it is composed. Conversely, we can understand that converting continuous data into a numerical representation is digitisation.

BINARY DIGITS

In contrast to the analogue the digital medium is not a transcription but a conversion of information. Digital media store information as formal mathematical relationships in abstract electronic forms. Digital is the generic term used for the processing and recording of information using binary code, the digits 1 and 0, which are represented in the registration of two different voltage levels in electronic circuits or in transit as electronic impulses. A digital file, whether it is a text, image or sound file is effectively a mathematical set of instructions, a long string of zeros and ones, written in computer code. The digital medium is defined precisely by the fact that it creates a systematic, intermediate code of discrete units. Digital code breaks everything down into uniform and exchangeable bits (or bytes). The full significance of this difference between analogue and digital takes time to appreciate, but it is this single fact of digital code, which accounts for most of the radical possibilities in the convergence of media and the creation of digital media.

The strings of binary digits are founded as mathematical formulas or algorithms, which constitute the digital code. It is this feature of digitisation which has meant that images can now be thought to exist as electronic data and not as the physical medium. Digital data is created by capturing and sampling at regular intervals.

DIGITAL CAPTURE

Capturing is achieved through interface devices with single or networked computers. The keyboard and mouse, for instance, are a means whereby a computer software program can capture the typing of this text. If I was in a drawing program right now I would be using the mouse and its screen avatar (an icon), to designate shape and colour which would be captured, or using a wackboard with a 'pen'. More easily grasped would be the example of image capture through a digital recording device. In the case of the light formed image of photography, a digital camera has a charge-coupled device (CCD) image sensor in the place of the older analogue film which captures an intensity and gives it a numerical, binary value. The analogue characteristic of chemical photography – the grain, tone and colour of an image – is simulated by assigning a value to a pixel in a digital image. With video it is the software that grabs frames, which can be streamed as video.

SAMPLING

The frequency of sampling determines the resolution of the data. Sampling turns continuous data into discrete data, which is quantified by being assigned a numerical value. Each sample intensity is converted to an integer number value.

STORAGE

It is the translation of the analogue image or sound into a numerical code that now enables them to be electronically stored and transmitted. What happens to any analogue media work once it has been digitally captured and electronically stored within the network of networked computers radically changes the ways in which we regard the work, how it can be used, who owns it and how it is controlled. Digital photographs circulating freely on websites and attached to emails are now regarded as 'information' along with everything else. Most obviously the digital image can be manipulated, combined and re-contextualised in any number of ways, as can textual and sound files.

CODE

It is the coded nature of digitised media that has resulted in a photographic or sound recording being understood as 'information'. A digitally produced, or reproduced media object becomes subject to algorithmic manipulation and it is the system of algorithmic coding, which allows us to now think of media as conforming to programmable rules. The importance of digital code is underlined by Manovitch (2001:27–48) who describes five principles of digital media as numerical representation, modularity, automation, variability, and transcoding. This is a useful taxonomy in which each term describes how digital coding treats a surface or a frequency as a set of separate elements that retain their separate identity while being able to be combined into more complex structures and functions. The above account of digital code functions well at a technical level. It is the account of the technical transcription or encryption of one form into another. Manovich's taxonomy goes some way to helping us see that digital media artefacts are products/outcomes of a specifically technical set of possibilities. Modularity creates the ability of digital media to clone any part of its code and make new combinations, for example, while variability creates the characteristics of mutability and change and so on. What a technical account of digital code doesn't do is help us understand how any digital media artefact means anything, other than at the very abstract level of saying all digital media is information. In order to understand how digital media artefacts mean anything we are thrown back into the cultural realm of language and it is here that we find the term code given precisely the role of explaining how meaning in language operates.

CULTURAL CODE

We have indicated how binary code is an essential technical characteristic of electronic digital media and computational systems, but code is also a central part of the analysis of cultural systems of communication. The concept of code is not new to thinking about digital technology. Code has been a broader way of thinking about communication throughout the twentieth century, both technically in analogue apparatuses and culturally in the analysis of meaning in language. The very idea of a media message involves the concept of code. Media messages are encoded by a sender and decoded by a receiver. In media and cultural studies code is generalised as, the rules or conventions by which communication takes place within a given medium. The coding and decoding of messages in newspapers, photographs, or Hollywood cinema are understood to have developed over time and subject to change because cultural rules can be broken and new rules learned. Code here is being used as a the collection of rules at any one time that govern the overall construction of film genres such as the western, thriller, comedy or those of a television soap-opera. In all of these cultural forms, codes and conventions organise the structuring of the story, plot, characters, acting, camera positions and lighting.

LINGUISTIC CODE

The specific analysis of linguistic code owes its origins to the foundational work of Ferdinand de Saussure (1857–1913) who developed the systematic study of signs. The study of sign systems was late taken up and applied to a wider range of ideas and objects, which could be said to be sign systems. Claude Levi Strauss (1958) applied a structuralist approach in anthropology to the study of totems and taboos. Roland Barthes (1975) applied a semiotic analysis to photography and cultural activities such as writing, fashion, exhibitions and film. The theoretical work of Jacques Lacan (1901–81) was an application of structural linguistics to Freudian psychoanalysis. But it was Ferdinand de Saussure who first developed the concept of language as a system of signs, in which the sign, composed of the signifier and signified, is the basic unit of meaning.

LANGUAGE AS A SYSTEM OF SIGNS

Conceptually the sign is the smallest unit of meaning in a system and is composed of the signifier and the signified in which the signifier is the material existence of the sign, while the signified is the mental concept to which the signifier refers. The relationship between the signifier and signified is arbitrary because there is no necessary relationship between the signified The relationship between the sign and its referent, the object or idea to which it refers is arbitrary within the system and is governed by cultural rules and conventions.

THE ARBITRARINESS OF THE SIGN

In the writing of Roland Barthes we can see the application of a semiotic analysis to the medium of photography. Barthes's analysis of the photograph returns us to the analogical nature of the medium of photography. On the surface the photograph does record, or sample and store, in digital terminology, visible reality into the discrete grain of the negative. On closer inspection, literally by physical enlargement the grain of the photograph cannot be meaningfully identified as units in a larger system, which could be defined as a code. This is why Barthes calls the photograph the perfect analogon and why he went famously to analyse the photograph as a message without a code. In 'The photographic message', Barthes develops a structural analysis of photographic meaning and in doing so identifies what he calls

Sign =		
signifier sign's image as perceived	+	signified the mental concept to which it refers

FIGURE 16.1
Diagram of Ferdinand de Saussure's analysis of the sign composed of two elements, which is central to semiological analysis

'the photographic paradox'. The photograph, unlike language, has no systematic structural code because the analogue medium of light sensitive chemicals on the celluloid negative, which forms the image cannot be broken down into discrete units. In the photograph there is the scene, which is a reduction but not a transformation of the literal reality. It is not necessary to divide the photographic message into units and signs, which are different from the object, as in language, there is no relay, no code, the photograph is an analogon. This is why Barthes says that the photograph is at this level message without a code, it is a continuous message. There are other messages (analogue mediums) without a code, yes, drawing, painting, cinema, TV, theatre, but they have an immediate and recognisable supplementary message which is the treatment and style. Barthes introduces a way to distinguish between the order of these messages:

- The analogon itself is the *denoted* message – the literal scene – the continuous message.
- The cultural message is the *connoted* message.

However, this duality of messages is not evident in the photograph. In the photograph the mechanical analogon, the light formed image fills its substance leaving no room for a second message, he calls this analogical plenitude, however this purely denotative status of the photograph is mythical – that is, its objectivity. The analogue photograph is not a transcription but a direct inscription of light, which makes it a message that is continuous with its referent. Barthes says that since meaning cannot proceed from this 'first order' of the photographic message, because the photograph has no code, then meaning has to develop through a 'second order', which is a cultural code of associative, or connoted meanings. The paradox is thus the co-existence of two messages the one without a code (the photographic analogue) the other with a code (writing, treatment, rhetoric of the image). This is a paradox not because of a collusion of the two messages, but that the connoted messages develops on the basis of a message without a code. The reason why it is important to understand the photographic paradox is because digital technology introduces a discrete technical code into the photographic image. As we have said the digital camera samples light values and converts them into a binary code, which are then given discrete values as pixels. The 'death' of analogue photography and the ushering in of the post-photographic era is based precisely upon the substitution of a digital code for the perfect analogon, which was the chemical photographic negative. Crary argues that we are in the midst of 'an image revolution in the formalisation and diffusion of computer generated imagery heralds the ubiquitous implantation of fabricated visual spaces radically different from the mimetic capacities of film, photography and television' (Crary 1999:1). Much of the general argument that the photographic image could no longer be trusted, ignored the fact that the photograph has always been a selective and constructed document, which gains meaning in its passage through technical mediation and cultural context. The fact that the digital image does have a technical

Table 16.1 Diagram distinguishing the technical differences between analogue and digital media

Analogue	Digital
transcription: the transfer of one set of physical properties into another, analogous, set	**conversion**: physical properties symbolised by an arbitrary numerical code
continuous: representation occurs through variations in a continuous field of tone, sound, etc.	**unitised:** qualities divided into discrete, measurable and exactly reproducible elements
material inscription: signs inseparable from the surface that carries them	**abstract signals:** numbers or electronic pulses detachable from material source
medium specific: each analogue media medium, bounded by its materials and its specific techniques	**generic:** one binary code for all enabling convergence and conversion between them

code has led to changes in photographic practice and a culture's reception of digital images. The digital code of the photographic image destabilises the relatively fixed analogue image and adjusts us to the mutability of code. This adjustment is still taking place in the emergent practices of digital image production, which make the intentional processes of image creation more apparent and compels us ot be more knowing about how images are created.

Digitisation is also the effective precondition for the entry of photographic images into the flow of information that circulates within the contemporary global communications network. It is the translation of the photographic image into a numerical code that now enables it to be electronically transmitted and effectively become electronic data.

CHAPTER 17

Case study
Curating the networked image

Interview with Katrina Sluis

Can a still image be still any more, or is it always changing when it is on a network? Photography has produced some of the most important imagery of the last century but digital processes through hardware and software have changed what a photograph can be and how it can operate. This conversation addresses how networked images can be produced by multiple people, or agents, and can operate in multiple ways for different purposes. It also considers what it means to exhibit digital images in a gallery and how digital literacy is replacing visual literacy as an important way of understanding the world around us.

KATRINA SLUIS: I am the Curator of the Digital Programme at The Photographers' Gallery, London. I am responsible for researching and producing projects, commissions and exhibitions, both online and offline. Working in the programming team, my specific focus is on recent social and technological shifts in the way photographs are created and disseminated in culture.

CURATING DIGITAL MEDIA

PETER: What is your background and how did you become involved with photography and digital media?

KATRINA SLUIS: I have a background in Fine Art. I originally studied painting and defected to the photomedia department in my final year. I was funding my studies by working on the helpdesk of the CompuServe, one of the world's first Internet service providers.

I was in the darkroom, making photographs but then also on the Internet and messing around with that. I initially saw these activities as of two separate sides of my life. But then cameraphones appeared, and photographic images became 'networked' though social platforms, and I became fascinated with the way that the web and photography were converging.

PETER: How do you define your position as a Digital Curator? What's the remit of the job?

KATRINA SLUIS: The job is mainly focused on creating projects that explore photography's life online and onscreen. This involves working with artists and photographers, writers, online communities and members of the general public. I also work closely with my colleagues in education and marketing who are also challenged by the way in which the digital is transforming all levels of the organisation. At the moment, the primary platform for the projects I curate is the media wall on the ground floor of the Gallery.

My role cuts across a number of different areas of knowledge, from contemporary art to media and cultural studies, computing and interactive media. Unusually for a curator, it requires a good practical understanding of software and other tools – one day I could be troubleshooting a video compression issue, the next day I could be giving a talk on search engine optimisation and photography.

PETER: Is your role also to introduce issues around digital culture into a relatively traditional organisation that works primarily with analogue culture?

KATRINA SLUIS: Definitely. The Gallery developed the role as it recognised that the medium was changing at tremendous speed and they needed to develop a digital strategy and a way of reflecting it through their programme. The way we interact with images online and through mobile platforms are changing older ideas around visual literacy, authorship, audience, creativity and the role of the gallery or museum. How does network culture challenge older curatorial models of selection, authority and value? How can the image world of the Internet and the gallery meet? These are questions we are grappling with.

PETER: What approach do you take to exploring the visual image in digital culture? All images are data and a great number of images are produced as visualisations of data and are not even necessarily intended to be seen with human subjectivity. However, do you think there is an increasing cultural need to examine material which is specifically designed to be used and read and exchanged as images?

THE IMAGE BEYOND THE PHOTOGRAPH

KATRINA SLUIS: The problem with the image is knowing where it begins and ends online. Is the notion of a discrete image a valid concept when you are dealing with the boundlessness of the Internet? Is the computer's interface an image? And which version of an image do you attend to? What is really interesting

FIGURE 17.1

The Digital Wall at The Photographers' Gallery, London. The Wall sits on the ground floor of the Gallery and is visible to passers-by on the street as well as Gallery visitors. The 2.7 × 3m video wall consists of 2 × 4 rows of 60 in Sharp PN-V602 LED Screens in portrait format mounted flush with the wall. The image detail shows a screen capture of an amateur home page from the free web hosting service Geocities, presented by artists Olia Lialina and Dragan Espenschied as part of their exhibition One Terabyte Of Kilobyte Age (2013)

Credit: photo Peter Ride

about the networked image is that an image can potentially be everywhere at once and be accessed simultaneously. Photographs now come to us in rapid volleys, presented on luscious displays, as slideshows or 'photostreams' yet at the same time it can be even more abstracted and diffused through computing and the conditions of its production. So I would say that what is really important about the image today is its ability to operate simultaneously as a photograph but also as data.

PETER: If the image still has an important place in our culture the role of photography must be more contested – or what a photograph is. On one hand we could say that, because the data can be output in any different form, a photograph is only a photograph if our frame of reference expects it to be that. But on the other hand we could also say that there are some qualities about the photographic image and the way photography has a role in our social life and culture that make photography remain a powerful force. As someone who started off working with photography, are you still intrigued by the photographic image or has your interest moved towards different forms of images?

KATRINA SLUIS: I'm definitely fascinated by the social and cultural life of images but I'm very interested in networked images as opposed to singular printed photographs. I'm particularly interested in working with photography that emerges from the contemporary image environment: from the proliferation of cat photographs online, citizen journalism, satellite and military imagery, the creation of 'photographs' by gamers to document their adventures in virtual worlds, for example.

There is a very interesting shift going on which is about the way in which the photograph has been part of the Cartesian representational scheme, in which its veracity and rationality has been part of its relationship to the 'real'. Now I

FIGURE 17.2

'Born in 1987: The Animated GIF', an exhibition of GIFs on the media Wall at The Photographers' Gallery 2012. This exhibition addressed a unique form of image which is best experienced via a screen: the animated gif. The GIF is an image file format created in 1987 by CompuServe as a portable, low bandwidth image file easily rendered by a web browser. Restricted to only 256 colours, and able to store multiple frames in a single image, the GIF brought animated movement to the static webpages of the 1990s in an era before YouTube and Flash (http://thephotographersgallery. org.uk/the-wall-2)

Installation photo © Kate Elliott, courtesy The Photographers' Gallery think the image is a two faced thing. On the one hand it points to objects that are real in the world: an image of a cat is still an image of a cat and we still recognise it as such. But at the same time, the way a single photograph can be simultaneously part of multiple sets, streams and interfaces, creates a kind of temporality that's related to dissemination and the way in which time operates over a computer network. Photography has been traditionally conceived as a frozen slice of time, a 'death mask', an indexical trace – but the networked image shows us something very different, it becomes much more relational and about multiple positions.

TECHNOLOGICAL INNOVATION AND ACCELERATION

PETER: Rapid technological innovation has affected all the media forms that dominated the twentieth century and if there were presumed certainties, or at least accepted ways of conceptualising media, many of them have been disrupted. Do you feel that it is possible for you to address the way that digital innovation is changing the way that photography is understood to operate?

KATRINA SLUIS: Digital technology is accelerating so quickly that I think it's very hard to keep abreast of how things are shifting. For example, the development of facial recognition technology and other kinds of computational processing are having a massive change on the way photographs are exchanged and potentially used. The new field of computational photography has emerged in which 'software is the new optics' and the camera is becoming increasingly software-ised. It calls for a much more transdisciplinary approach to the image. For scholars not familiar with the technology it is easier to stay at the surface of the image and continue to account for it using older methods. From this perspective it can seem that although there are increasingly multiple forms of images and practices, the photograph still operates in the same way. And as a result, even within new media studies having a straight trajectory or discourse about it is very difficult.

This is of course also a problem for the Gallery. It is therefore very important that the digital programme foregrounds the expertise of different online communities and diverse practitioners and find ways of collaborating across multiple fields and constituencies.

PETER: The cultural institution, as you have discussed, is very much based around the idea of the authorship of the image and the significance of its contribution towards visual culture. Do you think these concepts are still viable in understanding the digital and networked image?

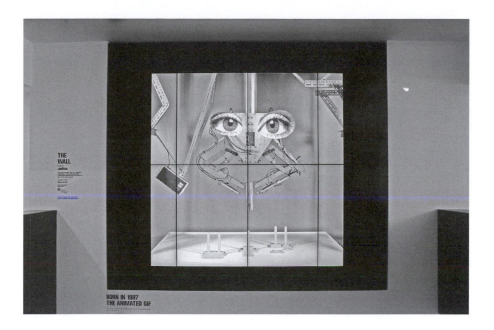

FIGURE 17.3
GIF by Wendy McMurdo exhibited as part of 'Born in 1987: The Animated GIF', an exhibition of GIFs on the media wall at The Photographers' Gallery 2012

Installation photo © Kate Elliott, courtesy The Photographers' Gallery

THE CHALLENGES TO AUTHORSHIP AND AUTHENTICITY

KATRINA SLUIS: Authorship is a very interesting issue in photography. Historically – writers have debated whether it is the camera or the artist that makes the image. Questions of authenticity and ownership become even more contested in networked image culture, where images can be appropriated, reproduced, remixed and remade in a few clicks. When someone looks at an image online it potentially modifies its context and potential future circulation. I am very interested in the politics of tagging, search algorithms, the role of metadata in relation to authorship, attribution and visibility of images online. The computer network challenges fixed notions of there being an authentic image or fixed viewing position. So it offers up a very different relationship between artist/author and audience to that of the museum.

PETER: These concepts can have huge impact on the role of exhibition and distribution of images. It creates major changes in the way that photography is seen as a highly popular and public medium. Many of these issues must present conundrums to a gallery. As a curator, what do you find are the challenges to grapple with in working in an art institution?

KATRINA SLUIS: Working in a contemporary digital image culture is extremely challenging because institutional frameworks aren't really set up to deal with the digital with all it means in relation to the ubiquity of images. On the one hand, photography institutions like to play off the fact that photography is a democratic and much more accessible form of art. But they also are steeped in the allure of the real and 'authentic' artefact. At the same time they have to ask how do you incorporate the public within the museum and how do you enable participation in an intelligent way. Of course the Gallery is very aware of this contradiction and a role like mine is needed so that the institution can explore these fundamental questions through practice and through research.

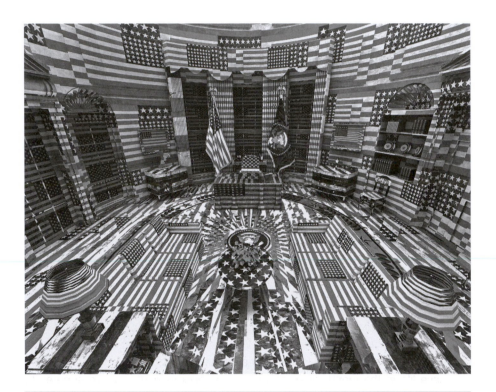

FIGURE 17.4
Jon Rafman *Jasper Johns Oval Office*, 2010. Jon Rafman *BRAND NEW BRAND NEW PAINT JOB*, exhibited on The Wall at The Photographers' Gallery 2013. Originally disseminated in blogform, Jon Rafman's *Brand New Paint Job* is a project where famous paintings are used to wallpaper amateur 3-D models collected from Google 3-D Warehouse. The project moves through a succession of hyper–real, lobbies, office spaces, cars and lounge rooms using a virtual camera. The resulting images reference the world of interior design magazines, 3-D gaming, social media mashups and synthetic photography

As a result there are huge challenges in terms of people getting to grips with questions of how an organisation can change culturally and how to bring in new ideas to the organisation. Another challenge is dealing with the idea that digital is cheap because it's seen as 'immaterial' and the presumption that there's not a lot of labour required. But of course it's never that easy, and while there are certain things that you are concerned about with a physical exhibition you don't have to worry about for the digital exhibition, there are other details that need to be considered.

THE NETWORK AND SOCIAL EXCHANGE OF IMAGES

PETER: You've spoken particularly about the importance of the network. What especially interests you about the way in which images can be exchanged and what this might mean as a form of social activity? How can you explore this within your programme?

KATRINA SLUIS: I think one of the most fascinating areas to consider is the social exchange of images. How is global image exchange undoing or calling into question, older forms of knowledge production and artistic production including notions of aesthetic potential? My strategy is to see the digital programme as developing a number of research questions and collaborating with others in order to start unpicking some of the questions about network creativity. I think a multi disciplinary approach is necessary because I don't think we can necessarily have the answers from one cultural perspective but these are questions that the institution is in a good position to grapple with and it can lead on.

PETER: In other words an important part of your programme is being developed through creating dialogues and creating conversations around the issues?

KATRINA SLUIS: Yes, absolutely, both with our audience and with various kinds of practitioners, whether they be scientists, bloggers, photographers, contemporary artists.

PETER: Without doubt there is much for a gallery to explore in the way that images have life in the world today and how they operate in the public sphere. To concentrate on the way images are exchanged and distributed, what aspect of the network image would you examine?

KATRINA SLUIS: I think we need to address the global image economy and the way in which images travel and migrate and consider how public institutions are part of that. Or to put it another way, what is the place of a photography institution in a culture where the average teenager is in contact with thousands of images every day?

When photography became digital there was an intellectual crisis in which the debate was primarily about what this meant for photographic 'truth'. However, commentators ultimately realised that even though the photograph had been transformed into pixels, we still perceived and understood photographs as we always had. We see that, for example, in the way blurred camera phone images are used in journalism – they continue to have authenticity. In a sense this concern is still part of the dominant idiom but that is not what was truly significant about the digital. Rather, I think digital photography's 'networkedness' is what is of continuing importance. This is transforming how we think about the photographic archive, visibility, time and space, private and public images. How do new platforms for image sharing relate to contemporary collectivity and cultural memory? This is a really important question.

PETER: And this is because we are now in a situation when the database is not only just a presiding metaphor for digital media but it is the actuality for much of the media that we encounter on digital platforms is driven by the database.

KATRINA SLUIS: It leads to questions of how we remember and represent the world, and the role of software in facilitating this. What forms of sociality and collectivity are possible on social media platforms?

FIGURE 17.5
Shironeko, aka 'Basket Cat' (courtesy http://photozou.jp/user/top/167308 CC BY–NC). *For the LOL of Cats: felines, photography and the web*, was an exhibition on The Wall at The Photographers' Gallery, 2012, which traced the persistence and popularity of the cat in and across photography and Internet culture

Installation photo © Kate Elliott, courtesy The Photographers' Gallery

NETWORKED COMMUNITIES AND IMAGE PRODUCTION

PETER: Communities operate in many way of course and while there are communities of interest that gather through social media, there are also communities of practitioners who collectively make work through open source or crowd sourcing. And are there ways in which exploration of this can take place through a visual medium in the gallery?

KATRINA SLUIS: All these different kinds of practices are valuable in helping us to unpack the way images are used, exchanged and valorised. I recently curated an exhibition that looked at cat photography and meme culture – from ASCII cats to 'cat shaming' and other practices. The web already does a great job of curating itself, so my approach was to work with those who were recognised collectors and curators of cat photography online. Cat photography ranges from the creative and subversive, to the banal and affective – does the exchange of such images create new social bonds? Or are image sharing platforms capturing and dominating our attention as part of what Jodi Deans calls 'communicative capitalism'? Of course the challenge is to tease out these issues in developing these projects.

PETER: In a sense you're operating within a very traditional notion of the cultural institution being part of the public sphere and yet bring into this the networked space, which is a very different public space and you are finding an overlap between the two.

KATRINA SLUIS: That's right. The Photographers' Gallery is not 'outside' the global image economy and representing it, but is actively part of it. We need to be more self-reflexive about the way images migrate across different boundaries and constituencies, and how our audiences use and make meaning from photography.

DIGITAL LITERACY AND UBIQUITOUS COMPUTING

PETER: Do you think gallery audiences need to be computer literate in the way that it is easy to expect art audiences to be visually literate?

KATRINA SLUIS: I think computer literacy is an important problem for all of us. In the forthcoming world of ubiquitous computing, understanding the culture of the computer will be increasingly important. As software and computing gets more and more complex it becomes black boxed. We can see this in the shift to a database driven web where we are not creating our own websites we are all putting our information on Facebook and social media has made publishing online as easy as writing an email. However, more of what goes on with the back end of these interactive image systems or social image systems is concealed. That's not to say that the cultural practices and what happens on screen isn't important. But what will be important is to make visible the means through which images come to our screens and the techno-social systems that support them.

PETER: What trends do you think your audience needs to think about in the next five years. What do you think they should consider as something which is going shift the way that we understand an image?

KATRINA SLUIS: I would say that photography's relationship to ubiquitous computing will be increasingly evident. From a cultural level, the automated collection and management images by machines will become more prevalent, in response to the deluge of video and images. Storing data isn't the problem anymore, it's negotiating it and creating meaning. YouTube has stated that it just can't begin to cope with how much video it's got, and what this means in terms of accessibility, so it's now rethinking its organisational premise. Looking towards the future the key will be in helping people find content and how to make sense of the deluge, the ubiquity of photography.

CHAPTER 18

Information

DATA

As more and more knowledge, in its representational forms, is converted into digital bytes it is transformed into a digital archive, a vast collection a global store of data. We would not commonly think of a piece of music, the complete works of Shakespeare, the facts contained in an encyclopaedia, a photograph or a poem as data, other than as the way in which they become stored in a computer or transmitted through the network of computers. We ordinarily distinguish data from knowledge as the prior, raw or untreated state of information. Data is a product of various procedural systems, as in a quantitative collection of material, the results of a survey for example, which is also understood as a body of information when it is applied in some context or situation. A computer operating system processes data, of a different kind, the algorithmically stored electrically impulses, coded as sequences of 0's and 1's. Data resides in the materiality of microchips of the CPU, in the switching between two states of electrical impulses, which create the combinations of coded instructions. A computer database stores information through the additional procedural programming and code of software which carries the instructions and choices for accessing data in a readable form. The distinction we are making may be regarded as quibbling since 'data' and 'information' are often used synonymously. However, the distinction is important when we relate our understandings of data, information and knowledge to the question of computer language and the preoccupation digital media practice has with databases, networks and software. We need to go further with this line of thought.

DATABASE

The shift from analogue to digital encoding, recording and transmission renders all manner of knowledge, facts, records, files, archives, text, numerical tables, images, sounds, films, all previously held in different material forms, Negroponte's 'atoms', into a common digital code, sequences of bits, 0's and I's, stored in the electrical stasis of computer microprocessing 'chips.' Such material, now encrypted as digital code, is collected, stored and retrieved through files and databases, which structure data according to institutional or individual categorisations of subject, type or procedure – that is, financial, medical, historical, legal, etc. The organisation of binary code in a database is subject to the classification of data by the different needs of access and retrieval, so in one sense we cannot abstract a primary 'data' from its specific structural organisation, which is also a binary code. Database programming has been developmental in computer science over the last 25 years and database models have shifted from simple 'flat file' databases which had only one record structure, rather like a spreadsheet and with no links between separate records, to contemporary 'relational' and 'object-orientated' databases, which separate the rules of access from those of the structure of data. Object orientated databases allow for the retrieval of combinations of data that were not anticipated in the design of the database itself. The general point to reflect upon is that databases are designed using mathematical and logical rules according to the perceived needs of the users to store and retrieve data. The general development of database design has been away from fixed structures and towards ever more fluid relationships between all data sequences. The reason why database design continues to develop ever more fluid characteristics can be glimpsed in the uses to which data is put. The idea of 'data mining' in which any given body of 'raw' data can be trawled through in different ways to reveal or uncover new and potentially useful or profitable information depending upon what you are looking for, is a prime example. Collecting and analysing user data is the basis of the latest dot.com development, in which Google and Facebook, to name only the largest, regularly collect and analyse personal data to personalise web browser interfaces and to push customised product information. Other services, such as Netflix, for example, sell user behaviour information to third parties. Amazon is also an example of how user behaviour is a source of information to be analysed and used for customised advertising purposes.

DATA CENTRES AND SERVER FARMS

The exponential increase in the volume of data held by the network of network computers has led Eric Schmidt, Google's CEO to claim recently that every two days now we create as much information as we did from the dawn of civilisation up until 2003. Schmidt added that, 'I spend most of my time assuming the world is not ready for the technology revolution that will be happening to them soon' (http://techcrunch.com/2010/08/04/schmidt-data/).

Historically large amounts of data was stored on mainframe computers, but with the growth of the WWW since the 1990s the Internet is being organised around large data centres and server farms in which thousands of connected computers perform the function of data storage and processing. Server farms use large amounts of electricity used not only in the running of the computers, but in maintaining them at even temperatures through cooling systems. Server farms are the libraries and museums of today, giant repositories of data, which is processed and accessed through interface indexes.

'Cloud computing' represents the latest development in commercial network services in which storage and processing is organised as a commercial service over a network. User data and software is no longer stored on the hard drive of a personal computer, but stored in remote server farms, metaphorically speaking 'in the clouds'. Cloud computing makes it possible for end users to access and manipulate data from browsers and applications contained on mobile and lightweight devices, making it possible to access information universally. Cloud computing also offers the resources of software applications on a shared basis to companies, who rent configurations of software applications and data storage rather than having to invest in the infrastructure of hard and software configurations.

DATABASES AS A PLATFORM FOR DIGITAL MEDIA

Databases constitute one of the fundamental platforms upon which digital media practice takes place, because accessible databases are used in digital media to construct interfaces to and multiple pathways through searchable data. The digital media object is, in this sense, to be thought of more as a conceptual map, made manifest through a designed set of instructions, for navigating a database, than it is a traditional finite work. But here we must be clear, once again, that in the cultural practice of digital media, the definition of technical databases used in computer science, to model and programme hierarchical, relational and object orientated structures of data retrieval is being extended and given a metaphoric if not symbolic extension of meaning. This is most clearly explained in relationship to the signifi-cance accorded to databases within the discussion of digital art. (Lovejoy 2004:165) states that 'the database itself and the three dimensional virtual space it exists in can be thought of as "true" cultural forms'. This is a reference to the World Wide Web and the Internet, seen, metaphorically, as a new form for structuring of cultural experience. Seeing the WWW and Internet as 'the database', amounts to a theoretical leap in which the specificity of different technical databases, scientific, financial, institutional, each with their own codes of access, are collectivised as a unified cultural form. Clearly the WWW is a major new cultural medium whose forms are, as we write, being worked out through the convergence and remediation of existing mediums, writing, photography, filmmaking, games, economic transactions, etc. The remediation argument (Bolter and Gruisin 1999), stresses the continuities between as well as the transformation of the digital extensions of analogue technologies and their corresponding outcomes in media forms. Lovejoy's desire to caste the database and its navigability as a 'true' cultural form, builds upon (Manovich 2001:219) who argues that the abstract paradigm of a database stands as a new model for the organisation of thought, hence as a new symbolic form of the computer age, The unfolding of this argument is important to grasp because it helps us understand much of the preoccupation in digital media with databases. The reasoning is based, as we have seen, in the discussion of code and on explaining the structurally linked hierarchy of computer levels. Digital code is the basis of computer data and how computers operate (CPU, ROM and RAM), and is therefore the foundational, or underlying level upon which the communicable level of human readable files is built. The total collection of items digitally encoded on computers and made available through Internet browsers and Search Engines (the non-proprietary software of HTML as well as the proprietary software of AOL, Windows, Netscape, etc.) share the logic of binary code. It is the abstract total of all computer stored data and its networked organisation that is being called the cultural form of the database and it is the binary logic, its code, that is being understood as the paradigm through which meaning is organised. The 'true' nature of this new paradigm of communication is to be found in the characteristics of the organisation of computer procedures. Digital code consists of non-continuous, separable and distinct sequences, which can be cloned and combined in any order. The relationship between the sequences is technically arbitrary, since there is no necessary relation-ship between elements of the system. A database is collection, or. a list, in which each item possesses the same significance as any other. Such a system can be characterised therefore as non-hierarchical and non-linear and it is these two char-acteristics, above all, which are defining of the new paradigm. (Manovich 2001:218), Lovejoy, Paul and Rush make the argument that the digital database is a new symbolic form for a new age, by opposing the digital data network to the fixed, linear and hierarchical mould of the older analogue forms, which, it is argued, tended towards the cultural paradigm of narrative.

NARRATIVE

Narrative symbolic form is the underlying structure of, linear perspective in painting, naturalist and realist representation in the novel, theatre, photography and film. The essence of narrative form is that it establishes a set of fixed relationships between people, objects and events in time and space, which are organised into linear or pictorial structures, which are then read or seen as corresponding to reality. In visual narrative forms, objects obey the rule of consistent perspectival diminishment towards a vanishing point on the horizon as they do in optical vision. In narrative film the spatial world or the viewer is 'mirrored' in the spatial editing of film sequences so that the events portrayed operate coherently in front of the camera. In the narrative novel characters relate to one another and events unfold in consistent time frames. The frame of the painting, the frame of the cinema screen, the proscenium arch of the theatre are all devices through which a reality is represented. The narrative structure of the painting, novel, film or drama allows us to view the dynamic unfolding of events and relationships within the reality framing device. In creating the representational window on to constructed realities, narrative form also establishes the position of the viewer/reader in their own separate contingent reality outside of the narrative frame. Narrative form thus formalises two realities, one of the body in time and space and the other of the mind that is engaged or occupied in the representation. The representational reality of narrative form is often described as 'illusional' since it is not contingent in time and space with the body. Although an audience or reader is rarely, if ever, confused about the difference between the contingent reality of their immediate senses and the constructed reality of the narrative they 'enter' when watching a film or reading a fiction. However, it is precisely the fixing of the two 'realities' and the 'suspension of disbelief' necessary to enter the narrative, that has been seen by the European Avant-garde in art and literature as a rejection of the immediate reality and its replacement by illusion. This argument becomes more than a matter of pointing out technical differences in styles of art or genres of media when it is framed by the wider debate about the relationship between representation and reality. The new paradigm of the database as the new cultural form, brought about by the development of networked computers, is one powerful position in this debate, which holds that representation can no longer give us any meaningful truths about or encapsulate current reality. Margot Lovejoy makes this explicit, 'The computer shattered the existing paradigm of visual representation by converting visual information about reality into digital information about its structure' (Lovejoy 2004:222–3). There are, as we have noted, Jenkins, Bolter and Gruisin, Lister *et al.*, those who counter this argument by pointing out that the predominant cultural languages of digital media built upon the database have been continuously adapted from the narrative forms of analogue media. It is also important to recognise that narrative forms are not monolithic and have been subject to continual development, manipulation and stylistic variation over time, through the invention of stylistic and rhetorical devices within the language of whatever medium. Thus for instance, many contemporary TV dramas break with nineteenth-century naturalism by including dead characters naturalistically within the action. But, as Manovich, argues, while a database can support narrative, there is nothing in the logic of the medium itself that would foster its generation. Once again we are returned to the question of whether there is a digital cultural language to be found in the paradigm of the database. However, the question of a new formal language is formulated, not for the first time, through a stark binary choice in which the narrative paradigm is cast as an older and ultimately historical ordering of experience, while the digital database paradigm is grasped as the new, current and forward looking order. Why is this argument so compelling and far reaching? The analytical purchase of the argument is the powerful degree to which it unifies a whole set of observations of the technological and cultural characteristics of digital technology, with a much wider set of systemic changes at the social and economic level. We

**Table 18.1 The contrasting media specific differences between analogue and
digital technologies**

Binary opposites used to characterise difference

Narrative	Database
representation	information
linear	non-linear
fiction	reality
illusion	control
fixed	relational
object	process
author	user
old media	**new media**

will return to the argument that narrative is a barrier to reality in the next section
on digital aesthetics, but first we need to complete the wider argument for the
ascendancy of the digital paradigm in the computer age.

INFORMATION

The argument that the computer database represents a new symbolic and cultural
form contains two related but different strands. The first part of the argument states
that because the database is the primary structure and mode of the computer it
is conceptually as well as technically its essential form. It is then argued that the
Internet and the WWW are the social embodiment of a global database, which
functions as a network containing a limitless amount of information in digitally coded
(database) form.

The digital encryption of potentially anything and everything, whether that be the
digital scanning of historical archives, telematic remote surveillance in real time, the
constant additions and revisions of texts, sounds and images on hyperlinked
websites, or the updating of stock market indexes now constitute a common
currency as digital information. The difficulty with the argument, as ever, lies in what
status or meaning is given to this recognition, what significance can be given to
computer data, understood culturally as information.

KNOWLEDGE IN THE INFORMATION AGE

One of the bases for the 'information age' lies in the economic investment in and
practical expansion of computer and telecommunication systems by both public
institutions and private companies over the past 25 years. It is now widely accepted

that networked computers and mobile telecommunication devices are central to many economic, industrial and social functions of the globalised world. The growth and centrality of the computer in the economic sector has been linked to the decline of manufacturing industry and the growth of the service sector in North America and Western Europe during the post-war period. For Castells (2001:64) the 'information revolution' represents a new kind of economic organisation in which information processing has superseded manufacturing as the dominant mode of production. In this new economic organisation, information becomes a commodity and a form of 'leading edge' economic power. Castells's view of an information economy, builds upon the wider analysis of a shift from production-led capitalism in the Western democracies to commodity-led capitalism in which communication technologies are centrally entailed. Both Jameson and Harvey elaborate upon the decline of a manufacturing economy and the rise of a commodity economy with a larger service sector as central elements in defining 'the condition of post-modernity'. Commodity-led capitalism is also the economic basis for the term hyper-capitalism, upon which Jean Baudrillard established his analysis of the new 'era of simulation' (Baudrillard 1983:4). While there are significant differences in the detailed arguments and the conclusions drawn by these theorists, there is a general consensus that a profound set of social, economic and cultural changes in the organisation of production and exchange have taken place since the 1980s whose effects are still being felt. Such theorists, including Jean Francois Lyotard, conclude that the mass increase in the use of computer technology and the application of increased scientific knowledge has also been central to the ways in which we think about knowledge, science and learning. That information is now regarded as the universal commodity of the computer age is now taken as a fact. But it is this very fact of regarding information as a universal common currency, a new commodity, which can be stored, processed, transmitted and received through computer databases and networks, that raises the issue with which we began this discussion by asking, what are the differences between data, information and knowledge. Lyotard (1979:5) argues that the 'computerisation of society' has changed the nature and function of knowledge such that it can only survive if learning is translated into quantities of information. Toffler (2006:5) says something similar when he points out that in a computerised society knowledge now encompasses data, information, images, symbols, culture, ideology, and values, to become not only intellectual capital but also a commodity.

TACTICAL MEDIA

Such perspectives are important for digital media practice, because they alert us a whole set problems related to the access, control and meaning of digital information. Hackers have already decided upon a strategy of resistance and activism in what they see as the global dominance of information. Here the global networked database is pictured as a new repository of (total) information and cyberspace is seen as the new territory in which gophers, crawlers, search engines contain the all-important algorithms of network 'intelligence'. The tactical media movement started in the USA in the 1990s. Gregg Bordowitz theorist/practitioner was one of the groups founding members. Geert Lovink has also developed tactical media perspectives and is a member of Adilkno, the Foundation for the Advancement of Illegal Knowledge, which is a free association of media-related intellectuals. Tactical media distinguishes itself from radical 'alternative' media of the 1960s and 1970s, on the basis that it is no longer possible to adhere to strict ideological positions or even to support the analysis of ideology, moving instead to what Lovink defines as 'pluriform'. Tactical media are engaged in an informational power struggle through gaining control over the informational bases of instrumental, structural, and symbolic forms of power. The Free Software Foundation (FSF), established in 1985, campaigns against the corporate proprietary ownership of access to digital information and believe instead in the computer users' rights to use, study, copy, modify and redistribute computer programs. Those academic and researchers who support the perspective that technology is 'socially shaped' argue that the 'black box' or technology contains social and economic values which have become invisible and naturalised and can only be revealed by analysis (Williams and Edge 1996). The notion of information as some kind of raw material and the database as its repository misses the point that data has already been 'worked upon', 'shaped' and hence given value in the process of becoming data. Such value is, as has been suggested above, ultimately its exchange value, knowledge as commodity, in which there are new procedures for tracking and auditing its acquisition. This, as Lyotard and others have subsequently elaborated, has profound effects upon the educational establishment in which the functions of knowledge, as research and as acquisition are located. Digital media practice which does not recognised the transformation represented by data processing, misses the structuring power of information and the emerging character of cyberspace.

ILLUSTRATED CASE STUDY 4: VISUALISING DATA

Maurice Benayoun, *Mechanics of Emotions*

Maurice Benayoun's *Mechanics of Emotions* series of art projects, considers people's emotional view of the world by analysing data on the Internet. Spatial mapping and temporal, real time, representation can provide data sets that are available for interpretation. However, his work shows that data is often presented as if it has no human or emotional connections. Instead, his work fuses these data sets with information that relates to social or political situations and to suggest that we also need to represent our personal subjectivities and responsibilities.

Maurice Benayoun says:

> With the communication networks, the world is now equipped with an extensive nervous system. From any point on the planet, we can feel in real time what's happening on any other spot as soon as it is connected to the net and English speaking. Internet is the first self-organised worldwide language-and-socially filtered observation system. It is now easy, thanks to any existing search engine running on the web, to build a semantic map of any concept. Not even trying to understand what is behind a single use of one word, we know now how many times a word is used in correlation with another.

> The information conveyed by the search engines, brings us daily a system of responses, which is supposed to reflect a sociologic, geographic, scientific reality. But, this system is affected by a linguistic (English language predominance) and technologic (geographic predominance of industrialised areas) filtering. Which representation of the world can we obtain through the network?
>
> (www.moben.net/e-mechanics/projet.php?id=28)

In *World Emotional Mapping* Benayoun tracks the usage of words on the Internet in correlation with locations. According to the number of occurrences, the original keyword is located on the map with the appropriate size.

Still Moving

Still Moving (2008) is an interactive piece of artwork, made of a dynamic sculpture of 3.5m diameter and 0.9m high, sounds and video projection. When it is touched, *Still Moving* produces music made of infrasound

C@SE STUDY

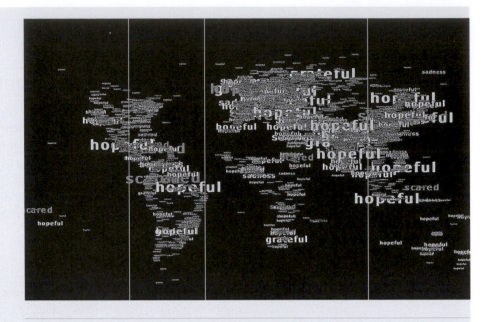

FIGURE 1
Maurice Benayoun, *World Emotional Mapping* (2005)

World Emotional Mapping (e-maps) (2005)

C@SE STUDY

FIGURE 2
Maurice Benayoun, *Still Moving* (2008)

FIGURE 3
Maurice Benayoun, *Still Moving* (2008)

C@SE STUDY

FIGURE 4
Maurice Benayoun, *Still Moving* (2008)

FIGURE 5
Maurice Benayoun, *Still Moving* (2008)

(5 to 20 Hz, that audience can only perceive with their bodies). The sculpture is built out of data extracted from a web analysis of the relation between 3,200 cities around the world and a lexical corpus related to the emotions.

Still Moving is a snapshot of the map of world emotions, sculpted from Internet data. *Still Moving* is a partly deflated globe but one where the relief is not related to geology but to emotional intensities that are registered on the Internet. The infrasonic music is triggered by the geographic areas being touched by the visitor. The data and graphic representations are projected simultaneously on the sculpture, making the interrelationships between the world, the digital data and the visitor's movements intelligible.

Emotion Forecast continuous to explore Benayoun's notion of Internet as the nervous system of the world. It takes data from the Internet that measures 48 emotions on websites related to current events in more than 3,200 cities worldwide, researches proximity of emotions and locations, and forecasts the tendencies for the next two days. It relies on a free software program to accumulate data from the web using algorithm searches for 64 emotions from 3,213 cities. For example, it counts how many times people in a certain geographic area use words like 'happy' or 'fear' on Facebook. Every day at the same time the software analyses a snapshot of the collected data and calculates predictions about how the world will feel over the following two days.

The *Mechanics of Emotions* series of work is part of what Benayoun calls 'critical fusion', the introduction of subjective fictions to data sets to critique it. The Emotion Forecast present a quantification of the human feelings in the way the financial stock market is usually represented.

The installation has been shown as a real time work on large urban screens in international city spaces, including Paris (Show Off, Fiac), New York (Streaming Museum), San Jose (Zero1, Biennial), Berlin and Melbourne.

C@SE STUDY

FIGURE 6
Maurice Benayoun, *Emotion Forecast* (2010–11)

C@SE STUDY

FIGURE 7
Maurice Benayoun, *Emotion Forecast* (2010–11)

Emotion Forecast (2010–11)

CHAPTER 19

Interface

The human computer interface can be thought of as three layers, which refer to the ways in which meaning is controlled in the relationship between user and machine. In this section we will look at each of these layers in turn, as well as discuss the relationship between them, but first, they can be summarised as:

1   The physical apparatus by which the user is able to operate the machine (and its operating system, the OS).

2   The software programs that organise the users' access and navigation of a database.

3   The cultural codes and conventions through which the user understands what data is and how they access and navigate it.

It is important to remember that the user encounters these three layers of the interface as one thing and that at the level of practice it is unnecessary to make, what are, after all, analytical distinctions. Such distinctions become important in reflecting upon practice. It is here, often in theoretically informed writing, that we understanding that the human computer interface is not simply an outcome of a technology, but a complex outcome of technological development and cultural modes of communication. This leads us to say that there is no necessary relationship between computer technology and the design and function of interfaces and that the relationship between them is a matter of convention and preference. Digital media practitioners do not always use a software application for the purposes it was designed for and graphical user interfaces can also 'get in the way' of the user's needs.

It is also possible in theory to envisage the HCI as consisting of only two layers, the computer layer and the cultural layer. Computer technology is young enough for more than one generation to be able to remember various stages of the progression of the three aspects of the human computer interface. In the short history of the PC, there are users who can easily recall the screen interface as exclusively based on text and in which navigation required memorising and typing long strings of commands in order to change applications or files, to copy or format a disk. The graphical user interface (GUI) of the 1980s, that is, the Apple Desktop and later Windows, changed all of that, but the recognition of the visible and invisible layers of command between the machine and the user's desired goal remains.

THE DREAM MACHINE

In most of the historical accounts of the emerging subject of digital media, reference is made to how humans have envisioned the creative potential of machines. In such accounts we recognise the central fact that humans have dreamt of making machines that are extensions of the human mind and body, in advance of an available technology to realise such dreams. Such discussion raises the issue of what we mean by the word human, in the human–computer interface (HCI), because it is a cultural and historical concept of human capabilities that guides machine 'intelligence'. The current collective concept of computer interface is the result of diverse human enquiry, intention and desire, it is the product of human knowledge and skill. Obvious as this is, it is an important addition to Molloy's point above that the human computer interface is not the result of one unified design concept and realisation, but rather the temporary outcome of many strands of human interest and intention. Ted Nelson, whose seminal publication of 1974, *Computer Liberation/ Dream Machines*, constituted a 'revolution' in thinking about the possibilities of interface, was very explicit about putting the 'human' at the centre of HCI:

> The exhilaration and excitement of the coming time is hard to convey on paper. Our screen displays will be alive with animation in their separate segments of activity, and will respond to our actions as if alive physically too. The question is, then: HOW WILL WE USE THEM? The design of screen performances and environments, and of transactions and transmission systems, is of the highest priority.[1]

Nelson, more than many others, recognised that the computer industry of the 1970s, dominated as it was by industry specialists and the academic computer programming laboratories, represented an orthodoxy, which controlled access to the increasing amount of information held on computer databases. His vision and his project were directed towards making computers more responsive to human needs. In 'Dream Machines' Nelson's view was that 'responsive computer display systems can, should and will restructure and light up the mental life of mankind'.

This was visionary thinking, coming as it did, ten years before Apple Macintosh launched its first version of the Desktop in 1984.

A key phrase in Nelson's view of future HCI, reveals his conception of the screen interface needing to be responsive to our actions, 'as if alive physically too'. Here we see the dream of the machine that is ultimately interactive, in which the layer upon layer of control functions have been erased so that, 'when the real media of the future arrives, the smallest child will know it right away'.[2] Nelson was not alone in wanting machines, which 'augment', 'extend' or 'facilitate' human thought and action. Nelson's vision owes a lot to Vannevar Bush who, earlier, working for the American government as the Director of Scientific Research and Development wrote 'As We May Think', which was published in Atlantic Monthly in 1945. In this article he sketches the possibility of a machine, the 'Memex', which, using supermicrofilm, would be able to bring files and materials on any subject rapidly up on screens mounted in an office desk. Both Bush and Nelson saw the development of such machines as dedicated to a great human goal. 'Presumably man's spirits should be elevated if he can better review his shady past and analyse more completely and objectively his present problems.'[3]

We can see in this history a dualism, written deeply into HCI development of creating interfaces. On the one hand there is a keen desire to minimalise, or erase completely, the layers of mediating technology and operating code, in order to maximise the immediate, intuitive and sensuous relationship with the content and data, and, on the other hand, there is an equally strong impulse to maximise the access to the control and manipulation of data through making the mediating layers of code visible to the user. This tension lies at the heart of interface design and development and is an important aspect of the cultural analysis of the use of computer interfaces. Bolter and Gruisin's concept of remediation precisely expresses the tension between the immediacy of the transparent interface and the hypermediacy of multiple access.[4]

PHYSICAL INTERFACE

At the level of physical interface design and development the issues of immediacy and hypermediacy, are embodied in the design and realisation of the material devices and technical apparatuses by and through which human communication with data takes place.

Touch, click, speak

The screen, the keyboard and the mouse still comprise the main physical interface for the desktop workplace, however, the touch screen and voice interface of tablets and smartphones increasingly become familiar modes of interface with more and more Internet transaction takes place through mobile technologies. The swipe, flick, tap of the touch screen has been the biggest single change to replicate the mouse and keyboard on screen.

Screens

The computer monitor developed with the first personal computers in the 1970s as an adaptation of the television monitor using cathode ray vacuum tube to transmit electrical triode scanlines. The first personal computer monitors only transmitted text and numerals to the screen and all commands were by text keyboard. The development of the graphical user interfaces (GUI) from the mid-1980s meant that the monitor could be used to represent a series of windows with graphic icons. The subsequent development of GUI has moved ever more to the animation of the screen in photographic, filmic and stereoscopic image and sound. The graphical screen is also a multi-windowed screen in which it is possible to run a number of programs simultaneously. However, the computer screen belies its origins in the television monitor and still provides cultural location of looking at screens. Of course we don't normally watch television sat at a desk, which as we have said before gives rise to the distinction that the PC is lean forward technology, while television is lean back. Little stays still in the converging world of digital media and the new generation of plasma television screens are being marketed as home cinema, just as the flat screens of the PC are promoted as the new place to watch TV. The development of liquid crystal (plasma) display and greater resolution and miniaturised data projectors all point to a greater 'flexibility' and detachment of the screen from the computers that drive them. Screens are now portable and scaleable, and linked with recent development in wireless technology screens are now even more fluid and flexible interfaces. Screens are now part of the general material fabric of everyday life, in architecture, town planning, clothing and fashion accessories and in domestic appliances.

Mouse, online presence and point and click

The mouse was developed at Stanford Research Laboratory (now SRI) in 1965 to be a cheap replacement for light pens, which had been used at least since 1954. The mouse was made famous as a practical input device by Xerox PARC in the 1970's. It first appeared commercially as part of the Xerox Star (1981) and Apple Macintosh (1984). The mouse is a peripheral control device of the HCI, which creates the 'point and click' culture of the graphical user interface. The advent of the mouse heightened the sense of the user's screen presence, which previously had been embodied in the blinking cursor. The graphical interface introduced an additional spatial dimension to the screen and the mouse provided the location and command tool in the form of the now universal pointing arrow or finger, or customised as another graphical avatar.

Avatar

The pointing arrow is the user's screen presence, which, within digital media is also referred to as an avatar. An avatar is, therefore, a control interface between the user and the program. Historically the word avatar refers to the incarnation (bodily manifestation) of an Immortal Being, or of the Ultimate Being. It derives from the Sanskrit word 'Avatara' which means 'descent' and usually implies a deliberate descent into mortal realms for special purposes. Among people working on virtual reality and cyberspace interfaces, an avatar is an icon or representation of a user in a shared virtual reality. In multi-user domains (MUDS) and multi user-object orientated environments (MOOS), players perform text-based characters, which explore environments and encounter other characters, which are also defined as avatars. The most highly developed graphical avatars reside in computer games, where an animated figure is controlled by the user to navigate graphically represented spaces and engage in contact with other graphically represented objects. Avatars focus attention upon the virtual dimension of computer mediated communication (CMC). At its most minimal level the pointing arrow, is the user's virtual presence in the computer's hard drive – that is, systems and applications. The graphic icon is the user's virtual presence within the network of networked computers and specifically within the online portals, browsers and domains, collectively known as cyberspace. In moving to describe the interface control established by avatars as, the user's virtual presence in cyberspace, or, more fully, remote human presence in virtual reality, a much wider and more philosophical set of ideas becomes entailed. This subject is discussed more fully in Chapter 25, but here it is worth looking briefly at how the avatar is thought about in the current range of GUIs. As we will see, the advent of the GUI brought with it the graphical spatialisation of the computer screen. This became the defining metaphor for thinking about communication through and with computers. Prior to GUIs computer systems and operations were interfaced numerical, textual, and sequential, after GUIs the interface presented the computer as a shallow spatial domain. With layers, compartments windows, files, menus and tools. This metaphorical spatialisation of data, as an office or desktop, controlled by pointing and clicking, more than invited the corresponding metaphor, of the user in the space. But what is meant by the user being 'in' the space? Canny and Paulos[5] take up the argument when they say that, 'when entering cyberspace it is the mind that enters, while the body remains outside as the mere transducer, moving text or audio data in through keyboard or microphone, and catching data from monitor and speakers.' (Goldberg 2003:269). The division of body and mind is established here as a problem or limit, rather than recognition that CMC is primarily an intellectual engagement with a medium whose interface is currently visual and auditory. The desire for greater embodiment in and of the interface is part of the cybernetic discourse in which the human-machine relationship is constructed around machine as an extension of the mind-body. Such interests lead, inevitably to a frustration with the current limit of the screen interface because it contains the relationship between the whole human, mind-body-environment experience and the online world in a restricted channel of reception. The desire for greater embodiment and presence in virtual worlds leads Canny and Paulos to ask, 'If we build avatars that "look" realistic enough, shouldn't the virtual experience be equivalent, or possibly better than the real?' (Goldberg, 2003: 277). In practice it leads them and many other cybernetic scientists and researchers to develop physical interfaces and computer programming that can 'match', 'imitate' or in their terms embody the richer sensorium of human to human communication. For the present, though, the online presence of the user remains firmly in the realms of the screen and the mind, while we do need to think about the slumped body.

Graphical user interface (GUI)

For digital media the development of the GUI represented a dramatic step forward for all computer users. Prior to the development of graphical user interfaces form the late 1980s, the means of controlling a computer was by means of lengthy commands and text-based operations.

A detailed history of computer interfaces development would show us a complex set of separate developments and interests, which were eventually drawn together. This is not unlike the history of other media technologies. For instance neither photography, film nor television can be understood as being 'discovered' or 'invented' in a single uniform process. The actual histories reveal that people were working on separate ideas, problems and approaches, which only, over time and in relationship to complex purposes and outcomes, came together to form what we now recognise as a fully formed medium. The same is true of computer-mediated communication and the specific development of the graphical user interface. However, a shorter summary of key events in that development would include, the invention of the basics of the point-and-click interface, the mouse, windows and menus in the 1970s by researchers at Xerox's Palo Alto Research Centre. It would also include the landmark product of the Apple Macintosh graphical desktop in 1984. The subsequent development, some ten years later, of Microsoft Windows 95 was seen as a copy of the Macintosh and new systems like Windows XP, Mac OS X, and KDE or Gnome on Linux are more or less variations on the original Mac interface.

With the introduction of full-screen graphical interfaces, from the mid 1980s the space of interface design was enlarged from one to two dimensions. This meant that it was possible for the user to directly manipulate graphical objects, including grabbing objects, moving them, cutting and pasting, changing size, and using constraints. Many of the interaction techniques popular in direct manipulation interfaces, such as how objects and text are selected, opened, and manipulated, were researched at Xerox PARC in the 1970s. In addition to graphical menus, full-screen interfaces often apply the function keys on the keyboard as a primary means of interaction. The two main advantages of function keys are that they serve as interaction accelerators and that there are so few of them that users often are able to learn them by heart. The introduction of the graphical user interface and direct manipulation was responsible for a massive expansion in the number of users since it made manipulation of data more immediate and straight forward and removing the need for learning complex keyboard commands. It also speed-up and simplified moving from one application to another, since they could be graphically represented as windows with their corresponding menu bars. For many of the earlier digital media practitioners, in particular photographers, typographers, layout and graphic artists, the graphical interface represented the user-friendly toolkit, which allowed for the immediate display and direct manipulation of visual elements.

BEYOND THE SCREEN

The physical interface of screen, keyboard and mouse have been seen by many as a limit upon the human computer interface in which the machine technology restricts the potential forms of interaction. Physical interfaces have been envisioned which are responsive a more complete human spatial/temporal sensorium, involving movement, sound and light. There are two strands of interface development and application involving more immersive interface environments. The first of these is represented by the development of virtual environments, in which the use of headsets and bodysuits renders it possible for the user to perceptually 'enter' simulated spatial environments, and augmented realities, in which a graphical interface is part of the body and environment relationship. Current research is on the use of interface glasses, which relay graphical information as part of visual sighting. Intelligent Architecture represented a dimension of augment reality interface insofar as spatial structures can include remote sensors linked to programming in order to offer the building user control of the physical environment.

If the screen has been seen to mark one limit of the physical interface then the keyboard and mouse mark another. The development of whiteboards, touch screens, light pens, sketchpads and voice activated software offer limited alternatives to the current control of the users on-screen presence by the keyboard and mouse. In the same way in touch the computer monitor is an adaptation of the television monitor, so the keyboard is an adaptation of the typewriter. It is an odd image to think of the computer as a combination of a television and a typewriter. First generation PCs were, of course, not much more than typewriters, calculating machines and textual and numerical databases. Today's PCs incorporate the function of television, radio and telephone. In looking through current research at MIT[6] it appears that future of user interfaces is in the direction of larger, information-abundant displays, which will utilise to a much greater the extended human perceptual skills in rich information spaces. A broader survey of interface development shows two trends, one towards a greater differentiation of users according to culture, age and occupation, with a strong emphasis upon learning communities, the second trend is towards interfaces that are more spatial, immersive, responsive and intuitive. Researchers are exploring systems, which have the ability to perceive, communicate and interact with the user using speech and vision. There is an interest in the development of highly interactive and information-rich virtual environments, which would have multi-modal input (visual, tactile, auditory and olfactory) to increase the user's sense of presence. Such research reinforces our view that the drive is for greater verisimilitude, greater immediacy if not spontaneity, in short, to build machines which behave more like us. How such developments will eventuate in applications across the work–leisure use of CMC is hard to predict, beyond the obvious interest in more immersive games environments and more layered screen-based interfaces. The development of physical interfaces based upon the human voice, facial or other body languages remains a frontier inhabited by those researching the development of deep immersive virtual environments.

CULTURAL INTERFACE

The cultural interface is the means by which we make sense of graphical user interfaces and computer operating systems. The cultural interface is the cultural language of computer mediated communication. The cultural interface consists of the codes and conventions derived from cultural interaction and communication. Another way of saying this is that the cultural interface is the physical interface, the computer operating system and the programming languages as they have been conceived at the practical cultural level. The graphical user interface of Microsoft Windows would be meaningless to anyone who is not already culturally familiar communication, which relies upon arranging and framing objects and icons within the spatial layout of frames. Indeed, if there are still human cultures where people have had no contact with desktops, books, texts and files, or screens with graphic, photographic and moving image representation, then a computer screen would make little sense at all. This is an extreme way of making the case for the cultural dependency of knowledge and understanding. But it is also the beginning of accounting for the cultural layer of the HCI as a hybrid of previous media forms and interfaces. Not that we were accustomed, prior to computing, to thinking of a painting or a book as an interface, although we have discussed how we imagina-tively interface with books and paintings. In recognising the cultural dependency of the computer interface on previous media we can also say that, like other media, the cultural interface is itself a code that carries cultural messages in a variety media.

NOTES

1   Nelson, T. (1974) *Computer Lib/Dream Machines*. Cited in Wardip-Fruin and Montfort (2003).
2   Nelson 1974:317.
3   Nelson 1974:47
4   'Tele-Embodiment and shattered presence: reconstructing the body for online interaction'. A fuller discussion of remediation is given in section two. In Bolter and Grusin (2000) *Remediation*.
5   'Tele-embodiment and shattered presence: reconstructing the body for online interaction'. Goldberg, K. (2003) *The Robot in the Garden*. Cambridge, MA: MIT.
6   MIT website and Negroponte's 2003 annual report.

CHAPTER 20

Interactivity

HOW ARE WE TO UNDERSTAND THE TERM INTERACTIVITY?

Interactivity is now a familiar and overused word in the everyday language of digital media, which for some theorists renders it vague and unhelpful (Manovich 2001:55), while others (Grau 2003:343) recognise interactivity as a defining feature of how artists have used technology. It is hard to ignore, let alone dismiss a discussion of interactivity, because there is not as yet another term, or even concept to describe how the user is 'positioned' in the human–computer interface (HCI), and because interactivity focuses attention on the engagement of the user of computer mediated communication. Interactivity is also a central concept in the further development and design of all graphical user interfaces (GUI), and is therefore central to computer architecture and computer design. In addition interactivity is an important concept because of the comparison it provokes with previous media communication, encouraging new thinking about old media. Because interactivity has become one of the naturalised everyday terms of digital media it has currency across a wide range of practices and productions. Interactivity is common to any discussion of the computer user experience and hence the design and development of both the physical and metaphorical interface with the computer and the data it allows us to access.

Interactivity we argue remains a key concept in digital media. It is a concept which marks out a set of defining and characteristic differences between analogue and digital media. Interactivity has been hailed as both the founding principle of a new medium as well as its defining myth. Interactivity is the bedrock of the claim for the radical newness of digital media in two important senses. First, the idea that new ways of accessing and manipulating data through HCI and GUI extend the human mind and create new ways of thinking. Second, that interactivity creates a new set of communication tools, which change the relationship between author and audience and hence offer new freedoms of expression. While there is substance in both of these claims, the major criticism is that digital media's transformative and emancipatory nature has not been borne out by the experience of most users of interactive computer products. On this critical view, computer interactivity is characterised as displaying limited choice and navigation within fixed and bounded programs.

PROGRAMMING

A concrete way of approaching interactivity in computer mediated communication is to focus upon the programming language that establishes the baseline possibilities of interactivity in the first place. The first principle of computer interactivity is that the user can interrupt a sequence of programmed information, whether in the form of image, sound or text and then choose to make a link to another part of the same sequence or jump to a new and different sequence. The user is able to move through the data-set in a branching structure, depending on the (hyper) links which have been programmed. The branching structure presents itself culturally as a mental structure of choices in which the user has to ask her/himself which path in the fork do I wish to take. The interactive designer has to build-in to the data-set a structure of forking paths according to some concept or logic, even if the logic is randomness. The multiple linking of messages or parts of a message was made technically possible by the creation of a system of labeling and addressing electronic information within discrete packages which could them be stored and accessed within a network of computers.

HYPERTEXT

Computer interactivity is based upon programming languages which get computers to 'talk to each other' in a common way so that pages of text, graphics and images stored on computers can be accessed and displayed across the network of computers. The basis for this language is the hyperlink, which is an element in an electronic document that links to another place in the same document or to an entirely different document. HTML is the universal language for publishing hypertext on the World Wide Web. It is a non-proprietary format and can be created and processed by a wide range of tools. The original concept of hypertext was developed by Ted Nelson in the 1960s who also acknowledged the earlier work of Vannevar Bush writing in 1945, in applying a concept of how the human mind works through the linking ideas and thoughts by association, to the computer. Nelson coined the term Hypertext to refer to a form of electronic text based upon non-sequential writing that branches and allows choices to the reader. For Nelson, Hypertext 'had no canonical order' and he considered that 'every path defines an equally convincing reading' (Nelson cited in Wardrip-Fruin and Montfort 2003:314) A (hyper)text now seen as network of possible texts cannot be taken as univocal since it is a multiplicity and it is in this fact that Nelson argued that hypertext changed the reader's relationship to the text and the relationship between author and reader since it gave the reader the ability to write back into the text. Later exponents of the radical potential of Hypertext argue that hypertext frees the reader from the hierarchical and fixed thought inscribed in the linear text (Landow 1992:6). Hypertext allows the reader to make lateral connections by mental association and deliberation through the branching structure. This, it is argued, encourages the reader to make novel connections and promotes a creative, more active and independent problem solving approach. On the other side of the argument it is evident that hyperlinking and hypertexts create problems of coherence and definition for the 'reader' within a text or sustained train of thought as well as broader problems of the lineage and authenticity of the intellectual sources of texts.

HYPERMEDIA

While the arguments about Hypertext as a radically new form of writing and consciousness continues to be explored, there is more general agreement that the interactive nature of hyper-linking can and does augment intellectual capacity and give greater and more immediate access to bodies of knowledge and media tools. The graphical computer interface presents a hypermediated environment that extends the notion of the text in hypertext to include visual, sound, animation and graphic content and these hypermedia texts are extended beyond the written or linguistic text.

It is the underlying numerical coding of digital media and the modular structure of the media object, which allows an infinite number of different interfaces to be generated from the same data. Digital media objects are not hardwired together as in analogue media which have closed elements within a fixed structure, digital media objects have an open and fluid state, as so many bits, and it is this which shifts the emphasis in communication towards the procedures of programming. The customising of data in user interfaces represents a major arena of such programming development since the elements remain separable and are only brought together by the programming of hyperlinks.

HYPERTEXT MARKUP LANGUAGE (HTML)

Hypertext markup language is a universal and networked application of hyperlinking. HTML is now the simplest way of adding human-readable data onto the Web, which was developed to allow unidirectional links to be made between documents.

Tim Berners-Lee wrote the first HTML language and defined the URL and HTTP specifications, which established the World Wide Web. His first program was later developed into Mosaic at the National Centre for Supercomputing Applications, NCSA and subsequently, Marc Andreessen, who had developed Mosaic, left NCSA to found the Netscape Corporation, which in turn set the stage for Microsoft. While Tim Berners-Lee, working at CERN, had developed HTML as a non-proprietary piece of software that could be used and developed freely, Netscape and Microsoft were established as commercial corporations looking to maximise investment, turn-over and profit. The division between these two institutional forms of software have given rise to the politics of the free software movement, and computer hackers who regard the Internet as a universal language beyond ownership. Conversely the interests of Microsoft and other large corporations are in code encryption and policing their legal rights to sell licenses to their software.

In terms of our discussion here on the practice of interactivity, it is the access, understanding and manipulation of the code upon which the software is written which is seen to guarantee greater control of the medium.

> I liked the idea that a piece of information is really defined only by what it's related to, and how it is related. There really is little else to meaning. The structure is everything . . . The brain has no knowledge until connections are made between neurons. All that we know, all that we are, comes from the way our neurons are connected.
>
> (Tim Berners-Lee 1999)

LINEAR vs NON-LINEAR

The problem with the arguments about the limits or possibilities of interactivity in digital media is the tendency in some writing and thinking has been to set-up binary oppositions in which, the interactive features of new (digital) media are all too easily set against the apparent non-interactive nature of previous (analogue) media forms. On this view, watching television, or film, becomes an essentially non-interactive experience, whereas clicking around the Internet, playing a computer game or using a CD ROM is, because it requires user participation to make links between the discrete parts. The extension of the same argument is that computer programs enable new structures in which the user can move through the (data) content at will, old media, film for instance, is a pre-set program, which cannot be altered by the viewer.

Another way in which this binary conceptualisation of interactivity has been employed is to say that digital media is non-linear, whereas old-media, film and television are essentially linear. The film will run its 90-minute course whether you stay and watch it or not. You can't intervene in the cinema performance or a broadcast television programme, all you can do is walk out of the cinema or turn the TV off, whereas the computer program allows the user to interrupt and branch. This difference is increasingly being eroded by digital television and DVD, which does allow for a greater degree of manipulation of pre-recorded material, and, of course, freeze-framing, fast-forwarding and rewinding is a long established part of the experience of analogue video watching. We will look at what is entailed by the idea of non-linearity in more depth, but the point about interactivity being made here relates to technology. Computer interactivity is, first and foremost, the ability of the user to interrupt a 'data set' and to be able to 'jump' from or 'link' any one discrete point to another. As we have established, video, like all analogue media, is a continuous recording of information, rather than made up from the discrete unit of digital code, so moving around a videotape requires the mechanical time to move the tape across the playback/recording cylinder. Digital information is constantly being reassembled in the much faster electronic time.

An extension of the claim for the liberating qualities of non-linear and interactive media is that the audience is put in a radically new position of active engagement, in contrast to old (linear) media, in which reception is essentially passive. This is one basis for the vogue definition of digital media as 'lean forward media' as opposed to old media as 'lean back media'.

Most critics of the claim for the new freedoms of digital media have gone to great lengths to demonstrate the actual continuities between old and digital media forms in order to show that much of what was being claimed for digital media was present in old media. A very obvious example is the printed book where, while the conventional organisation of text is from left to right and front to back, in the sequential order set out by the author, it is perfectly possible to physically and intellectually move around the text by turning pages and holding in the mind what you have read. Most comparisons of old and digital media establish that all media, from the printing press to television, borrow and reframe many aspects of previous and parallel media. On examination, the current stage of the development of digital media has been shown to contain obvious continuities with the forms and conventions of analogue media, while at the same time, re-ordering, re-composing their meaning and significance.

BINARY OPPOSITES

As we have alluded to above, one of the recurrent ways of expressing the defining qualities of digital media is to say what they are not. This has been done, as we have discussed elsewhere, by contrasting the operational qualities and possibilities of digital media with those of so-called old, or established media. In this way, for instance, it has been possible to contrast the digital photographic image, with the chemical photographic image, or the previous editing methods of film and video with those of digital editing. Through such comparisons it has been possible to discuss the similarities and the differences in the cultural codes and conventions,

Table 20.1 Binary contrasts of medium specifity between old and new media

Analogue	Digital
transparency	opacity
realism	montage/collage
linear	non-linear
non-interactive	interactive
passive	active
window on the world	windowed worlds
perspective	surface
proscenium	permeable space
old media	**digital media**

or what we have previously summarised as the languages of analogue and digital media. At the point of extreme difference a set of binary opposites can be posited which, if nothing else, demonstrates how, at an earlier stage in the development of digital media, the argument and the promise of a radical departure from old media was formulated.

One of the useful things about this exercise in defining binary differences is that it produces a group of related terms that operate at the descriptive level of computer mediated communication. The list of words in the left-hand column do resonate with what we have come to expect of film or photography. In their mainstream development film and photography have asserted media transparency and been commonly understood as windows on the world precisely in order to bring us realistic depictions of the outside world. In contrast words in the right-hand column of the above diagram have to be more speculative of the characteristics of a digital media, now defined in opposition to that which is old. But at a descriptive level we can have no quarrel with the fact that computer programs with screen and keyboard interfaces, have established conventions in which the screen is subdivided into a number of frames/windows, any one of which can be active at any one time. And we can go on to say that the screen interface is a surface, and although digital code can simulate spatial perspective, so that any one window can be arranged in a Cartesian spatial perspective, it remains a surface to be replaced at will by another surface. In this sense the surface is opaque and the collection of windows is a collage. It is also true that, while there is always a hierarchy of program com-mands, we can move within and between windows in a non-linear way insofar as we can 'jump' or move from point to point within an almost infinite network of points. But the point of the binary exercise is not to characterise old media as in some way limited and historical redundant against a forward looking and dynamic new set of achieved media possibilities. We have acknowledged that so-called old media has many of the qualities of digital media, our discussion of interactivity for instance, and that digital media has yet to demonstrate that it delivers the new qualities in all of those ways indicated by the list. In contrast to the tendency to use the binary exercise to uncritically reject old media as limited and applaud digital media as unlimited is its use in exploring the dynamic tension between each of the formal oppositional elements. In effect applying such formal oppositions becomes a fruitful way of examining old media from the vantage point of digital media and visa-versa. As has been pointed out all old media was new once and it is possible to reconstruct the historical formation of any medium where many more possibilities of use were present, than those that subsequently became settled. If we can see in those older formations of media the undeveloped, unsettled and unformed uses, then we can apply such an understanding to the current moment of digital media. On the basis of such historical insights we can conclude that current interests of fashions in digital media will give way to others and that some interests will predominate over others.

TECHNOLOGICAL INTERFACE

Interactivity in computer mediated communication (CMC) is currently governed by the manufacturing limits of the human–computer interface (HCI), which in its current and dominant form is that of the screen, keyboard and mouse of the PC. There are, of course, other material interfaces or peripheral devices, which when combined with software create interfaces using the human voice, or, with whiteboards and pens, using handwriting and drawing. More experimentally HCI can be through the whole body, using data-gloves and vision helmets, or, with remote sensors, but generally, interactivity is, for most people, limited to the interface of the screen and the devices (keyboard and mouse) for screen command.

The current limits of interface hardware and software is reflected in the idea of the impatient user in front of the screen, constantly clicking, waiting for screens to refresh, images to be rendered, files to be saved. Or, the frustrated user, who typically experiences the system crash or failed link. The experience of slowness, or error, in digital media are measured, not against the time taken in older media, but against an expectation of a technology which promises fluid an flexible connections in a near timeless (virtual) time. In any comparison of the time taken to perform similar functions in analogue media, searching a card index or the library shelves, writing a letter or developing and printing chemical film, it would be pointed out that digital media is super-fast.

In industrialised cultures the time spent in front of screens continues to expand, both at work and in leisure. The amount of information that is received onscreen publicly and privately corresponding increases. The time spent in front of screens, whether in the lean forward or lean back mode, presents us with a range of physical, social and intellectual issues related to the replacement of human to human communication with human-to-machine communication. 'Life on the screen', as Sherry Turkle has put it produces effects both upon the human body, now considered redundant or useless and social identity or the self, which in cyberspace is no longer considered unitary.

INTERFACE ANALOGIES

The analogies with other human activities, which have sprung up around the use of the Internet and WWW, reflect some of the different dimensions of the interactive experience. We will examine the cultural meaning of such analogies in the specific discussion of interface metaphors when we discuss navigation, but here analogies operate simply as the attempt to define the interactive experience. The experience of waiting for the next thing to happen is reflected in the intervals between the next big wave in the 'surfing' metaphor. An openness to mental changes of direction, interest and occupation is reflected in bookshop or library 'browsing' metaphor. The low level, partially distracted character of Internet browsing is often down-graded in the analogy of 'grazing'. The games player, whose rapid thumb pressing of the games handset, acts as an interface to her screen presence, is also an 'impatient user', ultimately frustrated by the physical limits of the interface. All of these modes of attention and engagement with computers suggest that there is a general striving for greater instantaneity, spontaneity, fluidity and intuition in the HCI relationship. This suppressed desire for greater freedom in the HCI is reflected in ongoing research and development, whether in the telematics of space robots, or ever more responsive games. It is also part of the discourse of the deep, immersive dream of virtual reality, which contains the desire for a limitless knowledge machine or simulated realities. Developments in artificial intelligence, robotics and nano-technology also push at the frontiers of the human-machine interface. All of these discourses contain, in different registers, the belief that current communicative tools could be extended by forms of increased end-user interactivity, characterised by the idea of greater freedoms or capacities of thought and communication.

INTERACTIVITY AND THE NON-HIERARCHICAL

The value of non-linearity in data access, retrieval and composition is further advanced by the recognition that digital programs, systems and networks are potentially non-hierarchical. In the place of traditional hierarchies of knowledge or information, reflected in the library, museum, archive and academy, the knowledge embedded in cyberspace is no longer seen as territorialised or governed. Know-ledge in cyberspace is imagined as horizontal rather than vertical and connections between objects and information are pictured as random until they are given meaning by the user, who 'authors' their own set, route or collection. The user is placed in the position of making novel connections between bits of data and the informa-tion and ideas they contain and hence can operate outside of the ways in which

Open order:

Fluid

Flexible

Non-hierarchical

Play

Choose

Control

knowledge and understanding hierarchically organisation is governed. Such modes of interactivity are seen to credit greater human agency to the user within these changing forms of communication. Making new and novel connections. Having greater agency, in a space which is conceptualised as horizontal is closely associated with established notions of human creativity and play.

The counter arguments are, once again, not against the principle or potential of CMC and CHI, for greater freedom of thought or communication for the artist, scientist or the population at large, but against the claim that it is an established fact. Early pioneers of cyberspace have long pointed to the increasingly prescribed organisation of Internet portals and the dominance of large corporations. Those scientists, programmers and artists who have advocated the development free-software, have developed incisive critiques of the new hierarchies and ideologies of software. More broadly studies of the cultural and social uses of Cyberspace/ CMC/HCI demonstrate that the qualities of greater human agency, freedom and play, are counterposed by greater human surveillance exploitation and cultural exclusion and narrow forms of end-user consumption.

CONTROL, AUTOMATION, VARIABILITY AND INTERACTIVITY

At the operational level of the HCI, interactivity can simply be equated with control of a technology and the short history of the development of HCIs can be understood as one of increasing and improving human access to and control of data storage, retrieval and manipulation. However, the discussion of and interest in interactivity stretches beyond the technical organisation of HCIs into culturally embedded applications and uses in which programmed interactivity is increasingly discussed in relationship to thought, knowledge, imagination and representation. These are, after all, the terms in which we approach the discussion of analogue media, precisely because the material and technical apparatuses have been subsumed within patterns of settled use. In film, for instance, the medium of light sensitive chemicals exposed on continuous strips of celluloid is no longer the point of interest, but rather what can be said or expressed through shooting film. The recent revival of interest in analogue film apparatus and its relationship to meaning has been re-invoked precisely because of the potential developments of digital, interactive moving image technologies. This is another aspect of saying that one of the un-looked for cultural outcomes of the development of digital media, is that it has provoked interest in re-examining the settled relationship we have to old media.

THE INTERACTIVITY OF OLD MEDIA

The differences between old and digital media, set in binary opposition, become much more problematic as a view of analogue media, because they define analogue media as historically closed. It is not possible to caste old media simply as non-interactive or linear, just because the user does not physically, literally, navigate the order in which data is presented. A painting on the gallery wall is a static object, a flat framed surface, which is viewed at once, and yet there is a physical interaction as the viewer scrutinises the surface at different distances. In reading the painted image the viewer's eye travels across the surface and her/his mind is actively seeking to interpret the given information. The mind will fill in elements where the visual information is incomplete in order to make sense of a figure-ground relationship or an implied spatial-scale relationship. Put this another way, for as long as the viewer is held looking at the painting the mind is deciphering elements of visual information in an interactive way in order to building up a set of meanings for the whole. The same model of the interactive viewer having to complete the image, can be said about photography and film. The recognition that old media also contain a physical and mental interactivity, should lead us to delineate carefully in descriptive accounts of digital media as exclusively interactivity, and question accounts of old media that suggests the viewer is passive or inactive.

It is important, therefore, to insist that interactivity, as such, is not new, it is just new to electronic media. We interact physically and psychologically with our environment and with each other as a defining aspect of our humanity and culture. At its most general the term interactivity applies to a multitude of human activities, encompassing such things as sex, reading a book, watching a play, conversation or playing games. At root, interactivity defines a certain kind of relationship between humans and/or objects within an environment. Interactivity is a relationship in which the actions and behaviours of people and/or objects are co-determinate. A working definition of interactivity might be, 'that which promotes or influences reciprocal action, or that quality which involves or encourages response'. Further, interactivity has been summed-up as, 'the mutual and simultaneous activity on the part of both participants, usually working towards some goal, but not necessarily' (Brand 1988:46). Both of these attempts to define interactivity involve the basic idea that an action on the part of one person or thing creates a reaction in or upon another, and so on. Conversation is a social interaction as the utterances of the participants are reciprocal. Culturally, interactivity has been applied to contexts in which individuals are actively participating and immersed in a constructed relationship to an environment. Education is a very good example of where interactivity has been deployed in argument. Traditional educational pedagogy, derived historically in different ways from scriptural iteration, can be seen as placing the learner in a passive position in which the student receives and copies that which the teacher transmits. Against this traditional pedagogic account, modern activity-based learning stresses that learning is enhanced by an interaction between the learner and the objects of learning. While Victorian pedagogy conjures up the image of the mute pupil rote learning by copying, the twentieth-century enlightened teacher encouraged pupils to question and discuss. Today there are still arguments among educationalists about how we learn and the best ways of learning. Liberal and progressive pedagogy underlines how increased pupil involvement and interaction encourages greater depth of understanding, while traditional pedagogy stresses the importance of teacher authority in defining the right orders of knowledge. It is no accident that computers have been increasing deployed in education, not only because ICT is recognised as central to the knowledge economy and information society in general, but also because interactive computer programming has been seen to provide interactive or programmed learning experiences.

It should be clear by now that interactivity is a general human quality and that technologies are not inherently or automatically interactive, quite the reverse in fact. In any history of machines, we would have to note that automation, not interaction was the goal of development. This is demonstrable in the historical trajectory of the industrial revolution, in which tools and operations were first mechanised and driven by steam power, and later in the more complex stages of mechanisation, powered by electricity. In each successive stage of industrial advancement, machines were produced which reduced the mental and manual labour of the machine operative. Today, aircraft are piloted automatically by machines and the role of the pilot is to watch the instruments that show the progress of the machine flying the aircraft. Workers in automated industrialised plants watch machines, periodically inspecting dials, levels, meters and carrying out certain manual operations thought uneconomic to program machines to do.

Automation brings about a relationship between human and machine not only of replacing human labour but also of putting human labour into the position of watching and waiting. It has long been pointed out that automation represents a deskilling of human labour in such machine/computer automated operations, rather than the development of a higher order skills involving creativity and thought. However, the discourse, which posits either the eventual dominance of machines over humans (the dystopian future) or humans over machines (the utopian future), is not the issue here, because humanity is not faced with a deterministic either-or-situation. Computer/machine complexes have been developed, which undertake a range of routine and repetitive tasks previously requiring the mental and manual labour of countless thousands of people. Equally, countless thousands of people now routinely interact with computer/machine complexes in the labour of creating, tracking and, crucially, consuming data.

While such macro observations of the characteristic organisation of labour in the Information Age, are sanguine reminders of the routine and repetitive nature of our interaction with computers, they should not detract us from looking, in some detail, at HCI interactivity in both its achieved and potential forms. It is important here to remember that we interact with computers in both wage labour and leisure time and therefore our relationship to the computer is typically one of both production and consumption. For most people this relationship might be experienced as one in which routine and repetition is the primary experience of computers in wage labour, while novelty, entertainment and choice is the experience of the use of computers in leisure. Certainly the marketing of computer-based domestic and personal digital media stresses again and again the increased choice and freedom afforded by computers, digital television, mobile phones and broadband access to the Internet. The numerically smaller number of people who use computers as professional producers, designers, architects, artists, photographers, filmmakers, musicians and programmers predominantly experience interactivity in terms of the use of the computer as a tool. But clearly interactivity increasingly and seamlessly crosses and re-crosses the boundary of production and consumption, work and leisure, in ways which bring into question previous divisions of producer and consumer, author and reader or storyteller and listener.

The promise of a radical shift of the relationship between producer and consumer because of computer interactivity is, as we have noted before, typically couched in terms of an as yet unrealised future potential, rather than any actual achieved modes. Commentators point to the relatively limited forms of programmed interactivity, rather than to any major area where the interactive potential autonomous programmable links between data points has transformed art, communication or modes of thinking. The Internet does represent the first truly digital media of the twenty-first century, which has been taken up and applied on a global scale and in a short space of time that has to be recognised as nothing short of astonishing. And yet at the same time as we can marvel at the scale of and speed with which this vast network has been established, the ways in which it has become embedded in everyday life are mundane. There is, however, something sterile in the rehearsal of the intellectual 'stand-off' between techno-sceptics and techno-utopians over the issue of current achievement and future potential. The arguments are not reducible to either, an ideology of a technological (determined) future, as the techno-sceptics have it, or simply a matter of the next technological (Romantic) leap forward as the techno-utopians typically frame it. Interactivity is in the here and now as all of the following, as ideology (discourse), as instrumentality (control), and as cultural products (objects). All three aspects are bound-up with understanding, use and production.

We can ground these arguments about interactivity by seeing how they are entailed in cultural projects involving the human-machine relationship. The term project is used here to signal how social and cultural applications of technological development, and intellectual reflection of such uses are grouped and related in practice – that is, how ideology, control and product are interrelated. There is a case for saying that what we are signalling as cultural projects of technology are the material-social manifestations of specific discourse or ideology. Developing the science and technology of putting a human on the moon can easily be seen as an example of a project of ideology as much as technology. The larger project of space travel is not simply a practical application of science and technology, but also a discourse about the future of humanity. The same will be true of the projects of human-computer communication, which form the discursive and practical framework of digital media.

In Part V we illustrate how the larger cultural framework of digital media operates by identifying two persistent technological discourses, which many digital media productions fit within. The first discourse is about relationship between the human mind and memory and the machinic extension of consciousness. The second discourse we identify as the relationship between human perception, representation and language and how machines can extend our perceptual and communicative world. Our distinction in discourse is comparable to Peter Lunenfield's characterisation of systems and operations for accessing the database as 'extractive' and interfaces, which invite us to navigate the database in graphic representational worlds as 'immersive'.

Summary of interactivity

- **Interactivity** is a naturalised everyday term in digital media.

- **Interactivity** has been hailed as both the founding principle of a new medium as well as its defining myth.

- **Interactivity** focuses attention on the engagement of the user of computer mediated communication.

- **Interactivity** is a central concept in the design of graphical user interface (GUI).

- **Interactivity** is an important concept because of the comparison it provokes with previous media communication, encouraging new thinking about old media.

- **Interactivity** marks out a set of defining and characteristic differences between analogue and digital media.

- **Interactivity** changes the relationship between author and audience.

- **Interactivity** is characterised as displaying limited choice and navigation within fixed and bounded programs.

- The **interactive** features of new (digital) media, are all too easily set against the apparent non-interactive nature of previous (analogue) media forms in *binary opposition*.

- **Interactivity** for most people is limited to the **interface** of the screen and the devices (keyboard and mouse) for screen command.

- Technological **interfaces** promise fluid and flexible connections to and between *data* in a near timeless (virtual) time.

- **Interactivity** is not new – it is just new to electronic media.

- **Interactivity** applies to a multitude of human activities,

- **Interactivity** is a relationship in which the actions and behaviours of people and/or objects are co-determinate.

- **Interactivity** promotes or influences reciprocal action, or that quality which involves or encourages response.

- **Interactivity** is the mutual and simultaneous activity on the part of two or more participants.

- **Interactivity** is a general human quality and that technologies are not inherently or automatically interactive.

CHAPTER 21

Case study
Image as data

Interview with Rainer Usselmann

How are complex datasets used to create still or moving images? In this conversation the director of a leading creative production and post-production agency explains how images are produced for corporate clients and how the industry has evolved over the last decade changing the role of photography, video and animation in the media sector. This study also reflects on the way digital technologies and networks are generating an image-saturated culture where software often defines appearance. It also addresses the ethical contradictions and complications of working in a culture driven by massive technology corporations.

Rainer Usselmann is co-founder and Director at Happy Finish, a world leading company specialising in retouching, CGI, animation and app-development. Happy Finish represents creative digital talent. Their artists work with international brands and agencies and produce augmented reality products and apps as well as retouching single images.

Rainer rained as an advertising photographer in Germany, and studied Photography at Bournemouth, UK, before taking an MA in History of Art. He has since collaborated with students, photographers, art directors and advertising agencies worldwide on award-winning fine-art, editorial and commercial projects.

TAKING CONTENT FROM CONCEPT TO PRODUCTION

PETER: How would you describe the focus of the work your company does and how you operate?

RAINER USSELMANN: Happy Finish represents artists who are visual content producers in the broadest sense. They create 3-D animations, grading for motion
pictures, produce TV commercials and are involved with app-development, but
it's all based on visual content. That's the focus.

PETER: When a client comes to you, what do they come for and what do they
bring? Do they come with images, a storyboard or a proposal?

RAINER USSELMANN: They come with a commercial concept. Usually clients are
working towards a marketing campaign like a launch of some sort and what
they need is to populate the various media channels that exist. The channels
may be print, online, iPhone apps, screens on the underground, social media,
or large scale animations for a trade fair. And all these different channels need
to be filled with visual content – and they turn to our digital artists to produce
content.

PETER: What defines your role? Is your job to strategise with them what content
works best for each of these places? Or have the clients already determined
that and so they mainly require you to produce the assets?

RAINER USSELMANN: It varies. Recently we have been discovering that the division
of labour between concept and production is blurring. In the past there was
usually a clear boundary between the people who came up with the concepts
and the people who produced the work but now there tends to be an overlap.
Producers are asked to conceptualise, more often than not, which leads to
fluid or hybrid structures. And this leads to having art directors particularly
suited for one particular thing working on a project because it requires their
particular skills.

GENERATING IMAGES FROM DATA FILES

PETER: To what degree are you working with images for the outset of a project?
Can you tell me about a specific project that is typical of your work?

RAINER USSELMANN: Recently, one of our teams of represented artists worked on
a project for one of the leading companies in the worldwide motor industry for
a new line of vans. They were asked to produce visual content more or less
from scratch in other words there was no traditional photography involved.
Instead they received from their client CAD data, which formed the basis of
their production workflow. It is important to stress that most manufacturing
processes, unless you're talking about some arcane niche, now use computer
aided design (CAD). Engineers design hugely complex products and goods
using 3-D CAD software before the first tools are milled or sintered and before
the first piece of metal is actually bashed.

As a result the workflow has changed dramatically from what it had been
20 years ago when a company, such as the one we are talking about,
would have had to make available actual pre-production models of their car
to do their marketing. They would have these prototypes insured at a huge

cost and managed major logistical problems to ensure secrecy and prevent damage because although the marketing materials had to be produced in advance the car would not have actually been launched. They would probably have had to ship not one but several cars in different trim levels to somewhere exotic where the weather was predictable in order to film and photograph it and bring a traditional post-production company onboard to oversee the final aspects of image production. This would have had to be done in absolute secrecy and the cars would have to be shielded from prying eyes – all in all a considerable logistical undertaking.

Now as engineering and design are firmly established in the digital economy the relationships and processes are completely different. Our artists work together with the engineers and asset managers of the company who send their CAD files directly to us. These files can be incredibly complex because they contain all the manufacturing and engineering detail of the car which needs to be stripped down because image production does not require the detail of the working operation behind the panels, just the information about the surfaces. Once the files have been simplified our artists produce a photorealistic representation of the vehicle, or whatever the object might be in 3-D. They then place the 3-D model in a HDRI (high dynamic range imagery) sphere.

In the whole process of image making, this is the only part in which photography in the traditional sense is involved. It requires a photographer to work in a specific location using a camera on a nodal tripod head that rotates along the optical axis of the camera. He or she then takes bracketed bursts of shots, in increments of angle depending on the lens they are using they then stitch together using five or six different exposures for each capture in order to achieve as broad a dynamic range as possible (up to 64Bit). Software subsequently melds all constituent shots with perfect overlaps to create a convincing sphere. In this manner the photographer creates the background and lighting reference for the entire CG scene.

Our represented artists might also be making use of commercial HDRI libraries, as there are now specialist providers that operate in the same way as traditional photo libraries who used to provide stills. Consequently a marketing department no longer needs to send a photographer out to a distant and expensive location but can buy a number of appropriate backgrounds from an HDRI library which they can then send together with the CAD data to the team of creatives who put the whole thing together.

Once we have the data, we would then place the car or object inside the HDRI sphere and the sphere is then, in turn, used to light the car and to produce reflections and interactions between the location and the object. We can also animate it to make the car move within that environment or make it interactive, for example, creating a functionality for iPhone or iPad apps where the viewer can tap on the image of the car to introduce different trim levels.

CREATING MULTIPLE OUTPUTS FOR DIFFERENT PLATFORMS FROM SAME SOURCE MATERIAL

PETER: Ultimately then, the workload is geared towards versatility, producing content for all the different channels of use using this method. The output could be any sort of image: a still image intended for magazine print or a billboard ad or could just as easily be an online animation. This means that the key aspect of production is that the core content has to operate as something that can be output in different ways according to different needs.

RAINER USSELMANN: That is increasingly where cost savings are being made. It's worth remembering that productivity gains are often the result of new technology. So if productivity means how much value a given specialist can produce in a certain amount of time, technology allows us to multi-task more effectively, which results in more products or services being produced in the same amount of time that in turn leads to reduced costs. This has been demonstrated, not just in media and marketing, but in all of the industries that have developed on the back of the personal computer boom since the 1980s.

The reason why the scenario I have just described is becoming ever more pervasive is that cost-saving is a major concern in any marketing exercise. This new form of production is not just a creative and logistical improvement but it offers huge cost savings. In the past marketing companies needed to produce distinct packages for distinct channels or media, hired a photographer to do a still shoot, a movie crew to shoot a TV advertisement and a web design company to produce interactive content. Now they can have a master package that serves, with a little bit of tweaking, any number of different channels and that results in a massive saving.

ECONOMIES OF OPERATING IN IMAGE PRODUCTION

PETER: How does a company like yours fit into the pattern of similar content producers given that you're not a big company and you're not affiliated to any of the major multinationals that handle image distribution? Do you need to be a small company to be effective in this field? And are your competitors international companies working with lower costs?

RAINER USSELMANN: We are a specialist competitor in the field. In London there are probably half a dozen companies of comparable size operating in this sector. Happy Finish however is unique because we are set-up as an agency representing independent digital talent with a great diversity of skills. This gives clients the opportunity to hand-pick the best specialists for a given project based on their portfolio and track-record rather than being lumbered with whoever happens to be available. Our artists work with a client base that is broadly international, with around 60 per cent of business from overseas. We are not comparable to the huge repro houses of yesteryear that produced massive amounts of output cheaply.

Happy Finish is more of a hybrid because of the way we are set-up and the range of skills offered by our represented artists from creative and conceptual all the way to logistics and production. There is a trade-off between having a huge factory operation and being creative enough to be able to conceptualise as well as produce content as cheaply as possible. Operating as our artists do there are no real advantages to economies of scale where clients might outsource to low-wage economies and produce stuff extremely cheaply, as other technical industries do. What our represented artists do is tied in with concept development, visual literacy, brand awareness and with all manner of things that go beyond merely producing stuff cheaply and all of this requires cultural knowledge. So there is only so much you can achieve through economies of scale.

SKILLS OF IMAGE PRODUCTION TEAMS

PETER: What kind of skills do you look for in the people who work for you? Are they generalists? Or do you require people with highly refined and particular niche skills to put together the kind of product you are talking about?

RAINER USSELMANN: A typical live project team is definitely made up of specialists even though there are certain overriding generic continuities no matter which channel they are producing the offshoot of your main asset for. This is what ad people often call the 'look and feel'. So in other words you need to make sure that a vehicle looks like the same in print when it is online, or on an iPad app.

Therefore there are overlapping individual core skills needed with all the people who provide input on colourisation and grading, the general family of tones and colours that are used throughout the different outputs, so that the 'look and feel' of the launch campaign has consistency. But as far as making the assets suitable for different channels you most definitely need specialists. Let's not forget that it begins with a wire frame on the computer which has to be skinned with surfaces that have the right properties and this requires specialists who can give metal exactly the right reflection and refraction properties so that it looks like the metal of a car. We represent modellers creating the basic structure of the vehicle from the CAD structure then others who specialise in texturing and UV Mapping.

For an iPhone app we represent developers who write code and who can translate the main asset into an interactive asset and these are different from the skills required from someone who produces an animation, or for example the van moving or the door opening. Therefore the whole workflow is a combination of different specialists working together for the duration of the project.

PETER: You've just described a whole range highly specific skills. So when you are assembling a team so do you work with company employees or do you assemble each team from freelancers?

RAINER USSELMANN: We mostly work with represented artists – that is, freelancers. We represent a number of generalists and they are particularly important for the continuities that I was describing because it's very important not to forget the bigger picture while you are still supporting all the particular niche issues. But there is a large number of highly talented specialists that the client might like us to bring on board if a particular job requires them. For example, a whole other area in CGI (computer-generated imagery) is particles and fluid dynamics.

If you're doing something for the drinks industry and it calls for the inevitable 'hero shot' of the bottle being emptied into the glass you need to get the flow of fluid exactly right. It's a very particular skill that a generalist would not necessarily have and it needs someone who is particularly good with that exact software. At the moment most specialists would use to create that photo realist behaviour of fluids or particles with a software called RealFlow.

In a similar scenario our artists also worked on a campaign where a racing car was supposed to crash through a brick wall and generate lots of flying debris – flying in a realistic way. So the client needed someone who could deal with particles, and write scripts that defined what particles can do, and a generalist would not be able to do that. So there is a wide range of different compartmentalised skills like that, that clients are interested in bringing together to deliver multichannel content.

MANAGING WORKFLOWS AND PROJECTS

PETER: Continuity and oversight must be crucial in the success a project of this scale. The specialists working in one particular area must find it difficult to know exactly what people in other areas are doing, no matter what generic understandings and skills people have. As a result the supervision of all these talents must be a very complicated thing to manage.

RAINER USSELMANN: It depends what the project is. We have dedicated CG producers to keep an eye on the whole operation to spot if there are any particular issues coming up or whether we have a bottleneck in the production. And if and when this is the case they would recommend the client to bring in new specialists with skills to help alleviate the bottleneck. So there has to be constant feedback between the producers and the client to ensure that everything is working.

PETER: What is your role with this? As a producer do you operate as the accounts manager and liaise with the client or do you take the role of the art director so that you are overall responsible for the creative production?

RAINER USSELMANN: It varies from project to project. I can be the first client contact in that I might go out to sell the idea of what skills our represented digital artists can bring to the table for a given client and a given project. But it can also be a case of providing art direction or being asked by clients to contribute a specialist skill.

PHOTOGRAPHY SOFTWARE, AND THE STILL IMAGE

PETER: What about the still image? You come from a background having trained as a photographer and you are known as an expert at post production work and photo re-touching. I know that the image re-touchers your company represents have done a large amount of business producing Photoshop work in the past . . .

RAINER USSELMANN: And we still do!

PETER: . . . so you have a commercial involvement in the photographic image. You have described the still image as an output of a digital asset. But do you think photography is as important now as it used to be?

RAINER USSELMANN: It's probably worth remembering Mark Twain when he said 'reports of my death are greatly exaggerated' and I think it will be foolish to predict the demise of the still image. For example in Asia print production is still on the rise. It may have reached saturation in the West but there are certain sections of the market where the overall volume may not be increasing but there is strong fragmentation going on. For example in the last ten years we've seen a huge increase in the number of fashion magazines so print isn't dead yet and the still image isn't dead. But we could say that the print image by itself is becoming less and less relevant. The print image that is part of a multichannel proposition is most certainly not dead.

PETER: What do you think is the most interesting potential for the still image as you come across it? We see examples of still images being dropped into Google Street view with ever greater complexity. Crowd sourcing results in images being gathered from the public, as well as professional sectors, which are stitched together so it is hard to see what are single elements although they are still in themselves single images. So while Facebook and Flickr continue to give us a single photographic images presented in the conventional form of the album we are also encountering them in all sorts of different ways embedded into virtual space. Is this a way that the still image is gaining a new role?

RAINER USSELMANN: This is not easy to address because we have to ask what is a still image? Is a web banner a still image? A banner is never one image it is a number of images that refresh according to who logs on. And this is not just for an interesting technological effect, but because it is more effective to target advertising to individual viewers and IP addresses then to create a massive billboard image that broadly targets everyone who drives past it on the motorway. So the problem is that the still image is not 'still' anyway. Ultimately you could say that the still image is a printed image that has been produced by pigment or ink on paper or substrate.

But commercially the photographic image has also been reasserting some of its most traditional forms. Recently there has been a resurgence of interest in nineteenth-century printing techniques. There are companies specialising in gum bichromates, platinum prints, salt prints even reproducing images in the style of daguerreotypes. You can't help thinking that maybe one way that the printed photograph will survive is in little niches along the long tail of cultural production where it links us to a sense of tradition and a sense of history and a sense of where the medium has come from. But that's not the mainstream and I think as far as that is concerned the still image by itself will become rarer and rarer. It will become much more integrated and embedded in media of all sorts whether it's sharing online, through interactivity or integrated into other media environments.

PETER: As an image producer, what interests you, still moves you and fascinates you about photographic images? Are you interested in images that are taken in a traditional way and link the maker to a real-world experience, or are you interested in images that have none of that indexicality and are mash ups, synthetic creations or data visualisations?

RAINER USSELMANN: That's a difficult question to answer because we're dealing with tons of images every day and to decide what it is you like about images or image making in the face of this avalanche we are part of is not easy. I don't like the fetishisation that has been going on with imagery for quite a while now. Fetishisation in the sense that images need to be heroic, images need to be eye-catching, images need to be extraordinary.

PHOTOSHOP AS INDUSTRY STANDARD

PETER: Do you mean in the commercial sector or more generally?

RAINER USSELMANN: More generally. It's hard to have images that are not manipulated or contrived or changed. When you look at landscape photography, or what passes for landscape photography, the photographers who produce images that are non-heroic appear to get overlooked in favour of those whose images are heroic. For example the tonal spectrum in much current landscape work is often out-of-this-world amazing, the skies are dramatically rendered, the colour spectrum is broad with great richness and things seem perfectly well tuned. But it's a phoney image all the same. We've introduced so much theatre into the visual image – and we can see that with applications like Instagram that can create a fake Polaroid or a Super8 feel.

This sense of theatre is so pervasive now because it is easy to inject. There are fashion photographers now who shoot directly on Instagram because it makes it so easy to create a look. So I'm more curious about photography that is nontheatrical and 'non-heroic' – perhaps in the Greenbergian sense. I'm not espousing a Luddite take on technology because I think this is not about technology. It is simply about the direction photography and image-making has been taking but technology accelerates it. I've never been as interested in the dramatic skies of Ansel Adams or the perfect moments of Cartier Bresson, I much prefer the imperfect, the quiet moment.

PETER: I'm interested in the fact that you are a Photoshop expert and a lot of your professional life has been spent making images more perfect for clients – or whatever they consider perfect to be. Do you think that the prevelance of Photoshop as an industry standard has resulted in expectations that images have to be 'better than perfect' or heroic, awesome and in some ways appear 'more real' than this world?

RAINER USSELMANN: Yes, absolutely. While you may be able to connect today's Photoshop heroics with Victorian Pictorialists and their painterly, allegorical use of photography, we are of course operating on a totally different scale of magnitude in terms of the production, proliferation and consumption of imagery. And in order to stand out and rise above the deluge of image making you have to be even more awesome and heroic than your competitor. At least that's what many a marketing manager would think. It would be counter intuitive to assume that this doesn't lead to dislocation of 'traditional' photographic aesthetics.

PETER: You've described how on some of your projects for clients generate still images as an output from complex data assets that will result in visual content of many forms. But what kind of clients are bringing you more traditional still images to work on and what kind of outputs are usually required?

RAINER USSELMANN: Many of our represented retouchers' clients still are, nonetheless, photographers who are, it has to be said, trying hard to evolve their own practice in the face of digital. Having said that there are still plenty of prints run out and proofs run.

IMAGE PROLIFERATION AND THE PHOTO AS STATUS UPDATE

PETER: One of the things that is obviously having a huge effect upon image culture is the huge proliferation of images largely because cameras are now on phones. People are using images to perform status updates online and images have taken over from some forms of written expression as instant communication, for example through Twitter. So sometimes it seems that basic information is being rendered now photographically as much as it is being rendered through text. From your point of view is this is a new form of a vernacular where images which are relatively inconsequential become extremely prominent?

RAINER USSELMANN: I think that is a very interesting development and I wonder when we actually started with stopping to privilege text; possibly a while ago not least with the advent of television culture. And it does seem that the photographic status update that is devoid of much meaning is now at least partially responsible for 'Big Data', the over- loading of corporate server farms around the globe. But, let's not forget, images also appear to be freer of the cultural- or class connotations and/or bias that often play their part when a piece of text is produced and disseminated.

PETER: Do you think this represents a new aspect of the democratisation of the means of digital production, which is something that was often historically linked to photography?

RAINER USSELMANN: In a sense, democratising the means of creative production has been fantastic as we no longer rely on privilege, money or access to be able to use certain types of technology. It's all quite democratic and nomadic in that I can buy software like Logic to make music. And if I'm talented enough, with a few hundred quid's worth of investment I can create music that is potentially just as sophisticated and relevant as what Kraftwerk did in the 1970s, 1980s and 1990s with their tens – if not hundreds of thousands of pounds worth of investment in studio equipment. So talent remains the only hurdle. This increase of access or lowering of the barriers of entry is a very important thing, not only because of the socio-economic implications, but also because of what it enables in terms of creativity and creative expression.

IMPACT OF COMMERCIAL INTERESTS AND THE UTILITY MODEL

PETER: There can be no doubt that the opportunities offered by digital technologies has created a range of opportunities for people by enabling access to resources that previously they could not have engaged with, and not only hardware and software but skills. This could be individually or could be collectively, for example through crowd sourcing or open source.

RAINER USSELMANN: I'm all in favour of a grassroots approach and empowering people but unfortunately – and there is a big but – the very commercial forces that have made this possible are now turning this democratisation process into a top-down utility model not unlike corporate gas, electricity or oil companies. The whole hippie IT culture that came out of California in the 1960s has run its course. And yet we're still camping outside Apple stores to get the new iPhone. And I think that is the true scandal.

Commercial interests are tying us ever more tightly to the utility model, or to use a prevalent euphemism, to proprietary ecosystems and I think that's very dangerous. We are now reliant on multi-billion corporate companies like Google,

Facebook and Apple to administer our social identity and sense of self. The contradiction is that in a physical world where we are becoming increasingly interested in localism and recognise that if we value local communities we need to support them locally we're doing the exact opposite in the virtual world, the non-bricks and mortar world. We are becoming more and more hooked to a non-local, centralised and unaccountable utility model that doesn't allow a great deal of inter-operability and that, I think, can't be good. So the democratisation of the means of production is perhaps only a great ruse in the context of the real economic interest being played out.

PETER: Then to return to what your company does, do you think that a company working in the digital sector can have a 'grassroots ethos? Do you have to be tied into a consumer, corporate-led ideology because of the software and hardware you use and your clients' expectations? Can you find a way to operate that is in keeping with your ethics and interests?

RAINER USSELMANN: Yes you can – a business is a living breathing thing and you can engender a culture of individual creative freedom. This was the main reason we set-up the way we did: as an agency representing independent creative talent, and not as a faceless, corporate, digital sausage factory.

C@SE STUDY

ILLUSTRATED CASE STUDY 5:
3-D MODELLING AS PORTRAITURE

Susan Sloan, *Studies in Stillness: Motion Capture Portraits*

3-D modelling and animation software combined with data derived from motion capture can allow artists to create images that reference real subjects but that also create fictions. Artist and researcher Susan Sloan achieves this in a series of 3-D human heads which raises questions about the possibilities of digital portraiture and about the creative exploration of data object relations.

An exhibition of the work of Susan Sloan, *Studies in Stillness: Motion Capture Portraits* was presented as part of The Photographers' Gallery's Digital Programme 2012 (see Chapter 17).

Sloan explores Motion Capture and 3-D animation techniques widely used in entertainment, medicine and the military as part of a programme of practice-led research begun in 2007, explains Katrina Sluis, Curator of the Digital Programme at The Photographers' Gallery.[1] Harnessing the gaze of ten cameras, Sloan records her subjects and maps their movements via reflective markers fixed to their body at key pivot and rotation points.

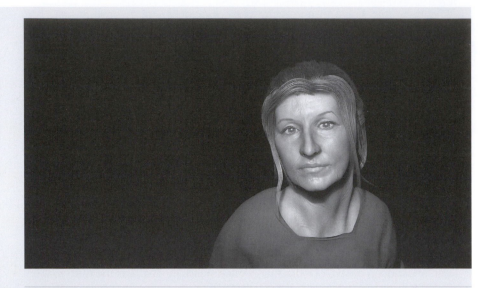

FIGURE 1

Susan Sloan, *Annie: Motion Capture Study*, 2011

Credit: Susan Sloan

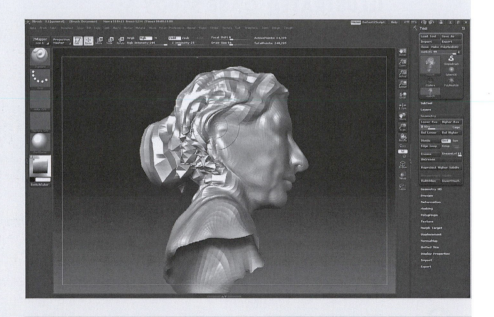

FIGURE 2

Susan Sloan, *Susan: Motion Capture Study*, 2011

Credit: Susan Sloan

C@SE STUDY

This tracking data is then fed back to a software system to create a virtual skeleton of her sitter. Using 3-D visualisation software, Sloan then sculpts this data into a visual representation of her subject, painting in facial details and animating their movement. When presented on the screen, these animated portraits fall somewhere between the hyperrealism of digital cinema and the synthetic world of the computer game character.

Sloan focuses on the simple gestures and movements of her subjects, positioning them in an empty space which serves to enhance even the subtlest of gestures. Framed as a single shot and composed around the head and torso of the sitter, her work refers to the traditions and conventions of portraiture, and raises questions concerning the convergence of painting, animation and photography.

SUSAN SLOAN: Working with people I know or meet by chance, I am attempting to capture a sense of stillness and perhaps the ordinary. There is no performance as such and no narrative unfolds in these works but rather, I am fond of the idea that time slows down as the viewer spends time watching the sitter 'sitting'. The portraits are not just an interpretation of the external visible characteristics of the sitter but

C@SE STUDY

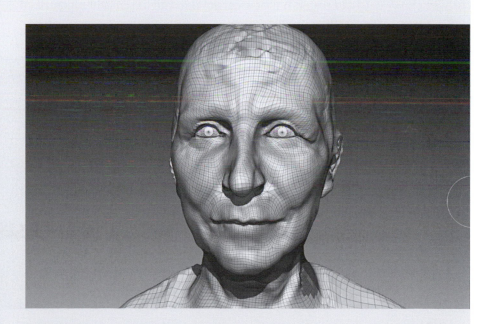

FIGURE 3
Susan Sloan, *Mary: Motion Capture Study*, 2011

Credit: Susan Sloan

also a document of their spatial co-ordinates, their motion and very often their emotions. Motion Capture is a document of existence in the same way that a photograph or a piece of video footage is. It is not one moment or an event captured in time but a document of an individual's movement and identity removed from a specific time and place.[2]

Susan Sloan's Motion Capture portraits are informed by two areas of motion study: Performance Capture and Gait Analysis. Performance Capture is often practised in the games and film industries where a performer drives a virtual skeleton, which in turn animates a 3-D character model. In these industries it is common for unwanted ticks and glitches to be 'cleaned up' from the motion capture data in favour of a more generic pose that can be stored and reused in multiple contexts. The removal of these individual characteristics also results in the removal of the performer's personality. Gait Analysis is the study of animal and human locomotion first pioneered by De Motu Animalium in the early 1600s and then later developed by Edward Muybridge and Étienne-Jules Marey in the early 1900s. By introducing Gait Analysis methods into the creative process Sloan preserves the performer's idiosyncrasies and by extension their personality. Sloan's work therefore presents an interpretation of the subject created out of a careful documentation and a sustained investigation of their movements.

C@SE STUDY

FIGURE 4
Susan Sloan, *Mary: Motion Capture Study*, 2011

Credit: Susan Sloan

NOTES

1   http://thephotographersgallery.org.uk/press-release-i-susan-sloan-i-studies-in-stillness-motion-capture-portraits-i-13-july-14-august
2   http://thephotographersgallery.org.uk/press-release-i-susan-sloan-i-studies-in-stillness-motion-capture-portraits-i-13-july-14-august

Part V

Media histories and theories

CHAPTER 22

Digital media histories

STARTING POINTS

A history of digital media will have to include a number of different strands of the historical development of art and media, their technologies, institutions and cultural forms. Initially such a history will involve something of the development of computing, electronics, robotics, optics, telecommunications, broadcasting, theatre, art, photography, film, literature, music and popular cultural pastimes. Such a list is daunting since it threatens to involve a history of every cultural means of expression and communication. The overriding reason why digital media needs such a multi-layered history is because of the hybrid nature of both the technologies and cultural practices gathered under the umbrella title. There is, as yet, no single, unified medium of digital media, in which technologies and cultural forms have been integrated, although computing is now the common factor. The current state of the practices of digital media are such that technically they still use a combination of digital and analogue means within a number of continuous cultural forms, which have converged in computing. Equally there is no single, or unified cultural idea of what digital media is; what knowledge and experience it deals with or the contexts in which it is applied. At present any history of digital media will need to account for the diverse developments that are constituted as digital media. A digital media history is better understood as a provisional and relational process of enquiry, because, while a unified and linear history can provide compelling stories of technological advancement or cultural continuity, they reduce and narrow our conceptual understanding of the current possibilities and purposes of what might turn out to be one new medium, or several forms within media. On one compelling current technological account, digital media is condensed into the image of the network, seen as the inevitable outcome of continuous technical advancement. In the culturalist account, digital media is seen as an extension of existing media in which a new set of technological tools are being used. Linear histories typically construct a chronological sequence of selectively significant events in order to argue that present outcomes and configurations, of either technology, or culture, are the logical and essential outcome of that history. An important cautionary point to remember is that any history, including this outline, is authored by individuals and groups working out of subjects, institutions, theories and perspectives, which will organise and promote what is thought to be valuable to include, or stress. Histories of any kind are essentially partial and partisan, they always come with a point of view. However, one should have the expectation that a digital media history will lay claim to its own authority based upon acknowledged and specific scholarship and research. We noted in the introduction how accounts of digital media are cast and shaped within other disciplines and practices, which is only to be expected and should not be dismissed, since there is no absolute position of objectivity in operation here. Any digital media history will, by definition, be an initial one given the relatively recent emergence of digital media practice, but it will also have roots in other disciplines, fields and subjects. For example, an understanding of calculating machines as a precursor of the many screen based mobile devices of today would be in all likelihood an essential component of a history of computing, while on the other hand, a history of typography and newspapers would be an equally important understanding for at history the graphical user interface. Digital media history is, then, better thought of in the plural as histories.

There are three broad strands of a potential digital media history, which are touched upon here; histories of material technologies; histories of telecommunication systems and histories of cultural and media practices. Put more generally, a digital media history requires an overview of the development of technological apparatuses, the ways in which they have been socially organised for communication purposes, and the cultural forms of communication they have been used for. In addition to historical accounts of machines, systems and products we also need to consider the social and cultural contexts in which such developments takes place and the intellectual models within which histories are constructed. But how is such a history to be constructed? We can formulate the dimensions of digital media histories as needing to take account of:

1   How reproductive and communication technologies have developed.

2   How the meanings of specific art and media artefacts relate to the technical possibilities of the medium and the cultural context in which they take place.

3   How media production embodies/reflects the larger economic organisation.

4   How the funding of scientific and technological research shapes the agendas and interests of its outcomes.

5   How prevailing theories of human perception and knowledge provide frameworks for thinking about the purposes and effects of media.

PROBLEMS OF HISTORICAL METHODOLOGY

Having cautioned against attempts to provide reduced, linear versions of a history of digital media, and stressing instead the need for more complex accounts, we are still faced with the need for historical selectivity. There are two main reasons for this. We cannot ignore the fact that there is something *new* about digital media, which is not accountable for in terms of existing continuous histories of media. It is important therefore for us to ask how the newness of the current digital media came about and to think about the distinct and different elements, which have combined to produce such a powerful form of communication and reproduction. Second, understanding the newness of digital media will not be achieved by treating the established history of media as an historical list of technological inventions. Digital media cannot be accounted for simply as the latest in a line of inventions, because, from the standpoint of how we use such inventions digital media is continuous with previous technologies as well as containing and reviving older media interests.

It is worth noting that the specific difficulty of historical method we are discussing here has been encountered in existing accounts of digital media. Let us go back to the idea, as (Lister *et al.* 2003:45) puts it that there can be 'no single, linear history, which will account for all that digital media embraces'. Lister outlines three broad paradigms within which histories of digital media have been constructed, the teleological, the genealogical and modernist aesthetics. These are useful categories with which to think about the problems of understanding the development of digital media technologies and practices.

THE LOGIC OF (TECHNOLOGICAL) PROGRESS

Linear histories of digital media, such as those of Howard Rheingold and Peter Weibel (Lister 2003:47) broadly fall into the category of historical accounts that create a narrative of (technological) progress. In such histories, progress is driven either, by some grand design of history itself, or in a subset of the same argument, by human genius and invention. An account of digital media in these terms would, therefore argue that our current media technologies and practices are the culmination of the historical progress, sometimes involving false starts and dead-ends, of all previous media, which contained the 'seeds' of, or prefigured, the present. In this way of seeing history the past is a preparation for the present and, by implication, the further unfolding of events into the future and towards some final goal. Such historical constructs are labelled by Lister as teleological. Teleology is a theoretical term in philosophy, which attempts to explain a series of events in terms of ends, goals, or purposes. Aristotle argued that all nature reflects the purposes of an immanent final cause.

An example of a teleological history of media would be one in which each historically ascending medium, television following radio for instance, emerged deliberately and inevitably in a process of continuous discovery and progress. A wider version of the same argument is one in which history is highly telescoped to suggest that the development of implements for hunting and cultivation contained the drive for space travel because tools, whether a stone axe or a rocket, are extensions of the human body in time and space. Such arguments are powerful and a persuasive view of human progress in which we come to see all of the subsequent historical refinements in tool-making as a preparation for our current ability to traverse outer space (this was alluded to in the opening sequence of Stanley Kubrick's film *2001*). Another example of the same argument applied retrospectively from the vantage point of digital media would be one which argued that the 35,000-year-old cave paintings of flora and fauna in Southern Europe and Australia, were made as immersive and virtual environments. In this example the enclosure of the cave and the light from the fire illuminating the painted representations on the walls, create a simulation of the external world. Our ancestors, looking at the flickering images of hunter and hunted could be likened to the contemporary game player in front of the computer screen. In this way of thinking the painted image on the cave wall and the computer screen are assumed by us to be connected by the continuous human drive to augment reality. At a larger level the same argument can be advanced to say that the European history of art and representation, which links fresco painting, oil painting, lithography, engraving, photography, telegraphy, film and television are the inevitable intermediate steps between the cave and the immanent next step towards a totally immersive virtual reality.

Such grand historical narratives are, as Lister points out again, arguments rather than necessary or absolute histories. As such, they are of interest and attention precisely because of their selective view (what they leave out of the account) and for their narrative content (the story they tell). In the case of digital technology it is the larger drives towards convergence, miniaturisation and automation of information that linear progressive histories have pointed up. These tendencies of technological development are, in the thinking of Baudrillard (1988), for instance, stages towards the visibility and at the same time the dematerialisation of everything, in his terms, the 'satellitisation of the real'.

MODERNISM, ART AND THE AVANT-GARDE

An emerging historical account of digital media can be found in mainstream art historical and museum contexts as well as in accounts of alternative radical media practices. This section considers both the *formalist* and *political* embrace of digital media within an art context, drawing out their differences as well as what unites them. The basic premise for considering digital media within a history of art is that over the twentieth century, artists have used technological mediums (photography, video, electronics and computers) to make works of art, which have been exhibited and collected, bought and sold by museums and private collectors. As such this collection of works can be thought of as a category of art, initially as electronic or digital art and more recently as digital media art as well as the political expression of *tactical media*. As a category digital media is being included within the history and criticism of art and in parallel 'digital media art' can be included as another strand of the wider category of a history of media. (Rush 1999:168) advances an orthodox art historical view of digital media in proposing that artists working with technologies represent a final avant-garde of the twentieth century. Following this argument through in outline is instructive, because, while it shares the same argument as teleological histories of technologies, it also suggests that the artist is someone who can explore and subvert the received wisdom and potential of technological advances.

The orthodox European history of art encourages us to see the development of visual representation from the Stone Age to the Industrial Age as a history of continuous technical improvements in the artist's ability to render likenesses, or apprehend external reality, more accurately through the technical mastery of the medium. Such a history is usually said to culminate in the development of photography, which could render likenesses perfectly through a mechanical means. Walter Benjamin pointed out that mechanical reproduction (the photograph) freed the hand of the most important artistic functions of pictorial reproduction. We will come back to consider Benjamin's fuller analysis of the impact of mechanical reproduction further on, since it has been highly influential in thinking about digital media. In the conventional history of art the advent of photography is seen as loosening the artist's dependency on the need for hand produced likenesses and hence hasten the end of the neo-classical academy of painters, and usher in modernism. During the period from the 1840s until the turn of the century, when Niepce, Fox Talbot, and Daguerre were perfecting the photographic medium, painting and sculpture continued to be dominated by the Academies of Art. The annual Academy exhibitions in London and Paris exercised a form of control over what was considered to be the correct subjects for art and how they should be executed. Rush starts his account of digital media in twentieth-century art by pointing out that twentieth-century art has had a persistent tendency to question painting as the privileged medium of representation. He points to the many renowned artists and art movements of the twentieth century whose work included everyday objects and materials other than paint and canvas. The use of 'new' mediums with which to make art is characterised as being driven by the experimental nature of modernist art. It is not hard to see how this argument is developed to account for contemporary digital media art. On this argument, Picasso's and Braque's incorporation of everyday materials in their paintings is essentially the same 'experimental' approach to the medium as that of contemporary artists who use analogue and digital media technologies and their contents in making art.

In putting together an account of the development of digital art (Paul 2003:8) makes the distinction between art that uses digital technologies as a tool for the creation of traditional art objects and art that employs technologies as its very own medium. While Paul is mindful that the distinction between technology as a tool and technology as a medium is a preliminary categorisation it does become the organising principle of her material and reproduces the distinction between tradition and the new. Both Rush and Paul conclude that new technologies will become more pervasive in art and everyday life. Scientific research in the areas of artificial life and intelligent interfaces, in digital and biological engineering and nanotechnologies is predicted to lead, inexorably, to some kind of final frontier of the human-machine interface in which brain-to-machine and brain-to-brain interactions are envisaged as an enfolding of the human body and the machine. In the visual arts ideas such as these have been actively developed by individual and groups of artists whose interests have focused upon cybernetic and electronic arts.

While a digital media art history, constructed along the axis of the advancement of experimental mediums, is a meaningful narrative, it is also a reduction of the fuller meanings, contexts and relations of art, because, once again it ties the motor of artistic development to technological progress as well as continuing to accept the category of art as uneffected by what surrounds it. A history of the avant-garde written as the singular preoccupation with the formal properties of the mediums of art will always be in danger of becoming another version of technological determinism in the guise of defining an artistic canon.

Margot Lovejoy attempts to avoid the co-option of digital media as simply a medium for artistic use by invoking Benjanin's analysis of 1939, that the function of art changes with technical revolutions. Lovejoy recognises that digital media presents a major challenge to contemporary art, not only as a new medium of communication, which challenges the function of representation, but one that changes the role of the artist. She rehearses a line of thinking about the historic role of artist as prophet, dissident and public intellectual, which is essentially in the tradition of avant-garde and modernist thinking and builds upon that tradition in outlining the role of the artist in a digital culture as being a 'citizen of the future', a cultural worker, involved in public art projects and striving to bring about a transformation in making art relevant and urgent to the needs of the present (Lovejoy 2004:282). Such a view of the progressive role of the artist is discussed programmatically by Lovejoy as thinking about the artist as a partner in innovation and the need for art schools to educate about digital media.

TACTICAL MEDIA

A variation on the artist as a social interventionist, or indeed 'citizen of the future' is expressed in the more dissident and anti-capitalist perspectives of **Tactical Media**, which emerged in the second half of the 1990s as a form of media activism expressly linked to the growing importance of the web and Internet. Strongly associated with the writing, teaching and projects of Gert Lovink, Tactial Media expresses the idea that artists and intellectuals associated with digital media can form tactical alliances with journalists, hackers and activists to confront as well as circumvent new forms of dominant control of media. Such temporary alliances can create new resources and open up new ways for audiences to participate in joint actions. Tactical Media can be seen as offering a redefinition of the role of the artist in a digital age, which is consistent with Lovejoy's account although different in context. Tactical Media differs to the degree to which it suggests that adapting mainstream art institutions or creating new or alternative digital media institutions would be politically limited since it does not take account of either the forces of dominant interests, nor the speed of change. For Tactical Media it is the Internet that provides the new environment within which a critical media art can flourish. *The Critical Art Ensemble* is an example of tactical media in action, in which a collective of practitioners with differing backgrounds and skills engage in projects which challenge what they see as undemocratic or unaccountable forms of cultural authority. There are a number of 'new media' organisations that operate in the shadow of mainstream contemporary art institutions with interests in art journalism, art criticism and 'net art' practices. In Britain, *Mongrel* and *Furtherfield* are notable as artist collectives who were early adoptors of digital media, while *MUTE* has over the same period provided a platform for critical perspectives upon art practice. In New York, *Eflux and iBeam*, similarly developed the practical and critical resources for new forms of media art practice, which are framed within continued notions of art but with web outcomes. Such organisations argue that digital media and its social and economic organisations demand new ways of thinking about art and the artist. They do this through independent projects, actions and alliances, while maintaining a dialogue with art insitutions and in insisting upon the productive category of art. We will return to the relationship between digital media practices and their cultural contexts later on in this section, but here it is important to note that tactical media and its associative groupings does now form part of the history we are outlining.

DIGITAL MEDIA AND THE 'NEAR FUTURE'

Many of the accounts of the relationship of art and technology we have come across are a specific version and reworking of the wider formulation of the relationship of society and technology. Hence the general and common argument is that art is being propelled by technology into a future role, function and form that is unlike anything that has gone before. The argument runs on that confronted by this overwhelming fact of the power of technology existing notions and practices of art are no longer relevant and that a profound and radical break with the past is being provoked by technology. In detail the reality and significance of a radically new technologically-based art is sustained by the claim that in the present a small number of farsighted artists and scientists are prefiguring a future where more advanced possibilities will be present. In the conventional twentieth-century art historical account, it has always been a small and selective avant-garde who have paved the way for digital media art. Charlie Gere attempts a history of new technologies in art in the British and American post-war context. This consists of a discussion of artistic ideas and practices that we can take to prefigure the current digital media art agenda. This is articulated as a set of practices marked out by their experimental interest in combining different media, using available media technologies and in performances or events that include interactions with audiences. The underlying interests of such practice are identified by Gere as a concern for exploring the boundary between art and everything else, music and noise in the work of John Cage, and the role of the audience in defining a work of art. Gere concludes that a post-war avant-garde, through their experiments with mixed or multi-media, set and agenda, or at least represent an art historical backstop, to contemporary digital media computer art (Gere 2002:82). One of the artists cited by Gere as influental in the post-war avant-garde is British artist, Roy Ascott, whose writing more than his art, operates as a manifesto for the future of art and technology. In his early writings he was explicit about the influence of the founding work of Norbert Wiener in cybernetics upon his thinking and develops the idea that only computer based art can establish a two-way exchange between the artwork and its audience (Ascott 2003:109). In subsequent writing, Ascot promotes a view of art and technology as a new social process in which 'the convergence of computers, communications, and biotechnologies, is leading to the reinvention of the self, the transformation of the body, and the noetic extension of mind. In the process, art has shifted its concern from the behaviour of forms to forms of behaviour'. And, in the reverse of this same process, 'Just as intelligence is spreading everywhere, leaking out of our brains and spilling into our homes, our tools, our vehicles, so too is connectivity. We are about to see the environment as a whole come online-a global networking of places, products, ideas, with the Internet as a kind of hypercortex' (Ascott 2003:356). The appeal of Ascott's ideas, influenced as they are by McLuhan's notion of expanded and globalised media, is that they promise a transformation of existing relationships between art and the individual. The argument is that technology can liberate human consciousness from existing set patterns and fixed modes of thought. Ascott argues that a 'technoetics', which means an embrace of technology and aesthetics, will be able to connect individual consciousnesses in a new kind of expanded collectivist or, in McLuhans global village, a tribal consciousness, which will supersede the traditional divisions between art and science, and between the human and the machinic.

THE WORK OF ART IN THE AGE OF DIGITAL REPRODUCTION

The notion that the function of art is challenged by changes in technology was principly expounded by Walter Benjamin and his work would have been known to both McLuhan and Ascott working in their different contexts. As (Lovejoy 2004:2) points out Walter Benjamin's writings from the 1930s were hugely influential to a generation of post-war cultural critics and several of his essays, including, *The Work of Art in the Age of Mechanical Reproduction* are benchmarks for a contemporary generation of students. Benjamin was himself influenced by the historical and dialectical materialism of Marx, with its stress upon analysing the economic and political forces that determine social structures and organise the functions of human exchange. Benjamin saw art and media as deeply tied to the social functions they perform and he explains historical changes in the character of art and media as a direct result of social, political, economic and technological change. Here Benjamin shares with the Marxist tradition the general concept of historical development propelled by the forces of human production. Late nineteenth-century European society was being shaped by an ever advancing industrialisation based upon the private ownership of the means of production and an increasing division of labour brought about by the increasing introduction of mechanical machines into all aspects of production, and of course reproduction. The social structure of a class society and the rise in the power of the organised working class and more generally for Benjamin, the emergence of the urban masses, were bound up with the crisis in art and culture provoked by reproduction.

Benjamin's view of the history of art and culture also reflected his acceptance of the concept of the historical development of productive forces and the means of production. He schematised the history of European art into periods in which art served different social functions tied to the reproductive forces and technologies of those periods. His view of art historical change was therefore based upon identifying the complex nexus of forces which propelled changes in the use value of art. This is why Benjamin's sweep of history starts with art serving the function of magic, later ritual and concludes, with mechanical reproduction, which changes the function of art from ritual to exhibition value, or art produced for reproduction. We can schematise this structural history of art's relationship to function and mediums in the following way.

Table 22.1 Diagram relating primary material technologies to socal and economic systems and their corresponding relationship to Walter Benjamin's historical scheme of artistic development (our emphasis upon art as information)

Technologies	Social/Economic System	Function of Art
Stone Age	tribal	art as magic
Bronze Age	hunter/gatherers	art as magic
Iron Age	feudalism	art as ritual
Print	merchantilism	art as cult of beauty
Machine	capitalism	art as art
Electronic	hyper-capitalism	art as information

For Walter Benjamin the advent of photo-mechanical reproduction profoundly changed the function and value of the work of art as well as creating new mediums for a new age. The photo-mechanical reproduction of the work of art, changed the perception and meaning of the work of art because it detached it from its location and context, 'the domain of tradition' and substituted the copy for its previous unique existence, or 'aura'. Benjamin goes on to say that reproduction in general led to a shattering of tradition and he linked that to the contemporary crisis of art hastened by modernism itself. He saw film as the new medium of the twentieth century and of a mass society and culture. He linked the ability of film to reproduce anything and everything and bring things closer spatially to that of the masses' sense of the universal equality of all things. He argued that this had the consequence of the further obliteration of the uniqueness of objects and establishment of transitoriness over permanence.

This short schematisation of Benjamin's view of art points up the modernist character of his thought, bound-up as it was with linking the new mediums of film and photography to radical social change. It is this link between new mediums and social and economic progress, which is being revisited in the digital moment. It is not hard to see the extension of his argument about the function of art changing again from the mechanical age to an electronic age in which digital reproduction changes the use value of art from art to that of information.

It is the potential insights afforded by the extension of Benjamin's argument in considering art (and media) in the age of electronic reproduction that interests us here, which bears upon our attempts to think about the historical emergence of digital media. The most radical insight afforded by the extension of his argument is not, it seems to us, that art is being led by a new avant-garde into a technologically driven future, but that the boundaries of art and all other media are blurring. We might argue with Benjamin that what has hitherto been regarded as the separate spheres of art and media are only maintained institutionally, since their purposes as information are now largely the same.

MICHEL FOUCAULT – HISTORICAL ARCHAEOLOGIES AND GENEALOGIES

If we are to be sceptical of the insights afforded by a technologically driven narrative of digital media histories and their projections into the future, what method of historical insight should we replace it with? Michel Foucault (1925–84), who held a chair in the history of systems of thought at the College de France, remains very influential in providing alternative models of history. Foucault was highly critical of the idea of history as a single, measured unfolding of events. He recognised that such a historical method had no critical means of reflecting upon its own participation in justifying those events (Foucault cited colonialism as the prime example in European written historical accounts from the nineteenth century). Foucault started from the proposition that history was written from the point of view of the present and that since the present is of necessity always being transformed, then history is always an account of the past from the interests, ideas and material arrangements of the present. Having recognised this he wanted to develop historical approaches that avoided, either, projecting meaning into history, or finding first causes (teleologies).

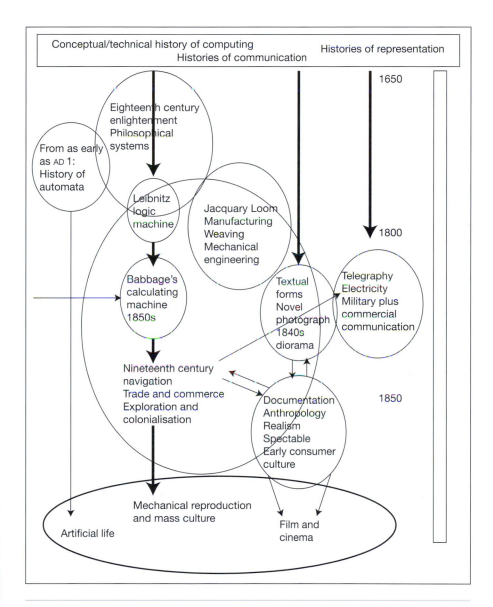

FIGURE 22.1

A simple model of the complex of histories 'through' and 'against' which digital media emerge

Lister 2003:52

His answer to these problems was to develop both an 'archaeology' and 'genealogy' of historical knowledge. Archaeology refers to the process of working through historical archives as a means of discovering the organising principles that produced the field of knowledge, science, art, medicine, etc. Genealogy is the process of analysing the historical relationships between truth, knowledge and power. Both genealogical and archealogical approaches involve a process of tracing out and uncovering the multiple beginnings and the complex and chaotic progression over time of knowledge and practices, which as often as not, involve gaps, leaps discontinuity and disjunctures.

Genealogies and archaeologies have found a fertile place in studies of digital media precisely because they avoid constructing technologically deterministic accounts of the kind we have just rehearsed. Historical affiliations, and resonances rather than origins are more typically what are looked for in accounting for the characteristic development of emerging digital media practices. A number of writers of digital media acknowledge their debt to Foucault in their studies of the formation of digital media. Bolter and Grusin acknowledge Foucault in terms of looking for affiliations between different media and systems of thought in their development of the concept of 'remediation' (Bolter and Grusin 2000:21). Andy Darley explicitly embraces a genealogical approach in looking at mechanised spectacle and popular entertainment as sources for thinking about digital animation (Darely 2000:37). John Tagg in his seminal work on the history of photography, seeks an explaniation of photography's 'identity' or nature, in the emerging social and political institutions of social regula-tion in the rapidly expanding industrial cities of the mid nineteenth century (Tagg 1993). Geoffrey Batchen, who explores links between the emergent technologies of photography, mechanical weaving, computing and photo-mechanical printing around the 1800s, also adopts a genealogical approach (Batchin 1999:12).

WHAT DOES AN ARCHAEOLOGICAL APPROACH TO DIGITAL MEDIA REVEAL?

Architecture

One of the illuminating aspects of applying Foucault's understanding of historical method is the recognition that history is written from the point of view of the present and that it is the present that organises our view of history. The present preoccupation with technologies should therefore tell us something about how the past is scanned through the prism (discourse) of technology. In this way previous analogue organisations of knowledge can be seen as technological practices. One example might be to describe buildings or cities as machines for living, which was indeed one of modernist architecture's dictums. We might now go further and ask what kind of machine certain modernist buildings, public housing for example, were meant to be and how such spatial enclosures embodied an organisation and externalisation of thinking. From the perspective of computing and digital media architecture can be seem as a specific technological medium and building forms can be undestood as technological 'machines'. An historical example of mapping the past in terms of the present, would be to see the Christian medieval cathedral, with its great enclosure of vertical space, stained glass windows, incense, organ pipes, choirs and the performance of communion as a hypermediated interface between humans and God. Bolter and Gruisin put this example the other way around and see the computer interface as remediating the medieval cathedral. In the same way eighteenth- and nineteenth-century museum and gallery buildings designed for the express purpose of storing and displaying collections of objects, might also be understood as a certain kind of precursor to the World Wide Web.

Circus and theatre

Interestingly, such approaches to a history of digital media take us away from the histories of art and the more obvious history of the computer, robotics, software or the Internet. Instead they tend to suggest that there are older and longer strands of interest, which resurface and are reawakened in new ways in digital media. In discussing the origins of digital animation and computer games (Darley 2000:37) points to the concentration of popular entertainments on fixed sites in London and Paris from the late eighteenth and nineteenth centuries. The circus and theatres, based around live performances of burlesque, pantomine, fairy plays, melodramas, farce and magic shows. Acrobats, conjuring, illusionism, high-wire acts, escape acts, puppetry and ventriloquisim provided an intense and visual pleasure. Elaborate props, mechanical and optical based special effects created sensational and spectacular effects that brought the crowds in. Darley points out that such popular entertainments contained a variety of programmes including illusion and trickery, which was designed to astonish and astound, stimulate and capture the eye and the gut, rather than the head, qualities and interests that he sees in special effects in contemporary cinema and computer animation. The point of such archaeological revisiting of early popular entertainments, is that they are done from the perspective of a new set of current interest in the present. The comparison between the emergence of popular entertainment in the rapidly expanding industrialised capital cities of Europe in the 1870s and that of the popular forms of digital media in computer games, special effects and computer animation now is a reminder that cultural forms do not develop along set lines. While the circus is just about still with us, live theatrical and dramatic performance has both declined and changed with the advent of other media, notably television. One of the underlying reasons for historically jumping to other periods in which new forms of entertainment and media emerged is to break-up and shed new light on the arguments for the linear progression of media and its meanings. By pointing up the continuities between the two distinct periods and their forms of popular entertainments it is possible to both identify common interests in the practices and skills of visual display and illusion, but also to put us in the position of distinguishing the new from the old. One of the most important tasks that Darley set himself in his work on visual digital culture, was to examine the new forms and techniques of digital technologies in the aesthetic context of early twenty-first-century culture.

Early cinema and photography

Of course, the aesthetic interest in spectacle and illusion represented by the circus and theatre was itself reshaped by the overlapping and emerging new form of film at the beginning of the twentieth century. This is why there is a similar argument for seeing the relevance to digital media of the early experiments in the light projection of images, first in photography and later in the moving image. The current fascination with interactivity, animation, collage and montage in digital media has strong affinities with early experiments with the stereoscopic, projected and moving photographic image. Yet in the conventional history of photography and film these early stages were seen as the relatively unformed experiments, discarded along the way to the fully developed forms of photographic realism and of classical narrative cinema. In both photography and film the general historical development is largely seen as the triumph of realism/naturalism, as it was previously in the history of European painting. But digital technology and digital media practices cast a new light on the interests, fascinations and experiences of the mid to late nineteenth century. From the perspective of digital media we are able to reconsider the moment when old media were themselves new. Here the interest in a range of technologies of vision, including the stereoscope, magic lantern, panorama and diorama, were not so many steps towards the inevitability of the codes of narrative cinema, but rather had their own particular visual and dramatic fascinations. The early histories of both film and photography identify parallel interests in realism and verisimilitude on the one hand and montage and fantasy on the other. We can put this another way and say that both mediums contained multiple possibilities for meaning and use with no immediately settled or dominant view. At the same time it is possible to see, as John Tagg does, that within these multiple possibilities of meaning and use, photography is given definition and identity by its constitution within a set of institutional and social relations. A set of relations that set the photogaph on the road to being regarded as a certain kind of evidence or truth (Tagg cited in Evans and Hall 1999:246).

Mechanical technologies

Chemical photography was a mechanical technology of the Industrial age, which developed from the 1840s onwards. The camera shutter was operated by levers and springs and later roll film was wound on by a simple spindle. The source of energy for forming the captured light image was natural sunlight. The main form for the viewing of photographs was the still print, which required no technology and even the light projection of the photographic image, in the magic lantern, was at first powered by an oil or gas lamp. In contrast to photography film needed electricity in order to have an audience. Film, which developed from the 1880s used electricity for motorised film recording and the electric light for film projection. In this last respect the emergence of cinema was as much the result of the electric light bulb and a source of regulated electricity as is was of the principle of film motion. Early applications of electricity and the moving image came together most obviously in the scientific and commercial enterprises of Thomas Edison. It was Edison who put the resources into creating an efficient incandescent light bulb, which he exhibited in New York in 1879 and it was Edison, who 17 years later exhibited the Kinetosope, regarded as the first public demonstration of the moving image. The Kinetoscope passed a strip of film rapidly between a lens and an electric light bulb creating the appearance of movement, which the viewer saw through a peephole at the top., The film was created by a motorised film camera, the Kinetograph, which was also developed in Edison's laboratories, by William Dickinson. There were of course parallel experiments in recording and projecting moving images in France with the Lumière Brothers and in London, Acres and Paul developed a successful machine to project films. By the turn of the century purpose-built cinemas were attracting paying audiences to watch a variety of short silent films, which in their subject matter emphasised above all the spectacle of movement. By 1898, the Lumière's company had produced a catalogue of over 1,000 short films for screening.

Telegraphy

Film had needed electricity in order to bring large groups of people together in one internal space to watch projected images of the external moving world, telegraphy had also needed electricity to send single text messages rapidly across large expanses of space. Telegraphy was developed in parallel with photography, from the 1830s onwards. The principle that the electromagnet could be used for long distance communication was demonstrated in the 1830s by sending an electronic current over one mile of wire to activate an electromagnet that caused a bell to strike. Samuel Morse later showed that signals could be transmitted by wire. He used electrical pulses to deflect an electromagnet, which activated a marker to produced written codes on a strip of paper, subsequently modified as embossed dots and dashes. This became known as Morse Code. The telegraph developed in close connection with the advancement of the railways, the telegraph being used to despatch trains and telegraph wires were built along railway rights of way. Until the development of the telephone from 1877 telegraphy dominated long distance communication. The general line of historical development in the advancing industrialising countries of Europe and North America from the 1880s onwards, was towards a unified, systematic and centralising system of communications, serving the interests of industry and commerce. This pattern of development, with its emphasis upon accurate and reliable information, transmitted at ever faster speeds across greater distances in a spreading network, continued throughout the twentieth century and today's global communications can be seen to continue many elements of the same demand.

Electricity

The development of a readily available and widely distributed and portable source of electrical energy was an inseparable part of the early development of cinema, telegraphy and telephony. Our current Information Age is precisely distinguished from its historical predecessor, the Industrial Age, on the basis of the unification of the source of machine power in electrical energy and the replacement of more and more mechanical machines by electronic ones. Digital media is therefore founded upon the scientific discoveries of electricity and the subsequent progress towards establishing a regulated system for the generation, storage and distribution of electricity. Obvious as it may sound, countries or communities without stable and sustainable sources of electricity can not, by definition, participate in digital media. The significance of electricity to digital media is not only that it is its obvious source of power, but that it is also deeply shaping of the form and content of the medium itself. The obvious parallel here is between the alternating current of a national electricuty grid and the network of networked computers through which electrically charged messages travel. The need for an ever increasing supply of electricity to power the expansion of the global network of networked computers, is bringing the debate about the effects of global communications and that of sustainable sources of energy into alignment with each other.

Marshall McLuhan was one of the first media theorists to recognise that electricity was the defining feature of television as a medium in 1968, just as Walter Benjamin in 1937 had pointed out that photography and film were above all mechanical modes of visual reproduction that had replaced hand production. The instantaneuous nature of electrical energy and the ability to control its voltage and current, is reflected in the central architecture of the computer. The networking of computers is parallel to that of an electrical grid system. Today in the USA, which has the largest use of high technology, approximately 40 per cent of annual energy consumption goes into the production of electricity. The speed of the application of electric light in the 1880s has striking parallels with the way in which the Internet took-off 100 years later. For example, Thomas Edison established the Electric Illuminating Company, which built a commercial generator in Manhattan in 1882, capable of producing power for 800 electric light bulbs. Within 14 months, it had 508 subscribers producing power for 12,732 light bulbs. Early power stations had to be close to the users of electrical power because the system used a direct current (DC) which diminished over distance. It was the development of the alternating current (AC), which could be boosted over distances, that provided the basis for a general system of distribution. The implementation of a widespread system of electric power for public and domestic lighting, heating and the powering of utilities took place over time and differentially across Europe and North America. The early companies were inefficient, when demand was small or irregular. Britain, which had a more developed system of coal gas lighting, was slower than the USA to adopt electricity. As the practical uses for electricity grew and multiplied, so did the demand for its production. Growth in distribution led to high voltage transmission and the interconnection of the modern power grid, with power plants able to be located at a distance from consumers. The development of a reliable source of electrical power and the development of utility applications went hand-in-hand. For media the availability of electrical power decisively altered the direction, scope and applications of the mechanical origins of image and sound recording. Newspapers and publishing, based upon mechanical technologies dominated nineteenth-century media. The electric motor was subsequently used as a source of powering newspaper presses and electricity was used to transmit telegraphic and telephonic messages, but in the twentieth century, television was the first pure electronic medium. The computer and computer networks are an application of electrical energy as well as representing the convergence of previous electrical applications.

Typewriting and the PC

The development of the typewriter and its transformation into the personal computer (PC) is another example of how different technological, communication and commercial interests paralleled each other over a long period before coming together in the computer screen and keyboard. The current networked PC is a digital technological recombination of the previous analogue technologies of the mechanical/electric typewriter, electronic calculator, television receiver, tape-recorder/player, photographic print room and telephone. The main way in which we interact with the networked PC, our interface with electronic information, relies upon a technical combination of the television cathode ray tube and the typewriter keyboard. The arrangement of the computer keyboard, in particular the configuration of the three rows of letters, remains the same as the Qwerty keyboard developed by Thales in 1867 and used in the typewriter he developed with an armament manufacturing company Remington. The keyboard was termed Qwerty because of the first six letters from the left on the top row.

There is a long pre-history to the development of the typewriter to be found in the development of moveable type and mechanical devices, but for our purposes we can start at the point at which the mechanical portable typewriter was commercially marketed in 1895 with The Underwood No. 1, designed by Franz Xavier Wagner. This was considered to be the first modern typewriter, because, unlike earlier models, the type was fully visible as it was being typed. In the space of three years the Underwood Company was producing 200 typewriters per week and by 1901, was producing the No. 5 model, which sold in millions over the next 30 years. The mass production and consumption of typewriters used in all forms of administrative communication, increased the speed and circulation of written texts. In this respect the mechanical typewriter had the same general effect upon hand production as other mechanical reproduction of the time, photography for instance. The basic components of the Underwood No. 1, the arrangement of the letters of the keyboard; the roller carriage; the ink ribbon cartridge and the mechanical levers have remained fairly consistent in all subsequent typewriter manufacture and were adapted in the electric typewriter. Just as Edison's 'speaking machine', the phonograph started off as a mechanical apparatus, without the use of electricity, so to did the 'writing machine' of Thale's typewriter and the 'seeing machine' of Fox Talbot's early camera. As we have already noted, although film cameras could be operated by a mechanical motor, film projection coincided with the electric light bulb. The development of a consolidated system of electricity supply hastened the combinations of previously separate modes of reproduction and representation. The contemporary technical convergence of analogue mediums in the digital is in this sense an outcome of the systematic application of electricity to mechanically based media apparatuses.

The electric typewriter was still being refined and produced for mass use in industry and commerce well into the 1970s, when electronic typewriters, which could 'memorise' what was typed became available and a decade after the first commercial computers were being produced by IBM. Typewriting was a widespread, available and established activity, while word-processing, had yet to be understood. In 1973 the magazine *Radio Electronics* contained an article outlining a TV typewriter, designed by Don Lancaster, which provided the first display of alphanumeric information on an ordinary television set. But also in the 1970s, the personal computer (PC) was being developed, which would use 'floppy' discs to store files and software. The immediate precursor of the floppy disc for electronic storage was the use of magnetic tape, which allowed typed material to be stored, corrected and edited prior to being printed. Magnetic tape was developed for sound recording purposes for military as well as commercial reasons by the Germans and Americans during the 1930s and 1940s. The fact that magnetic tape was used from the 1950s for storing computer data, also in research projects sponsored by defence funding in the USA, points us towards the increasing convergence of technical means within the framework of electronic technologies. The first commercial computer to feature a magnetic tape storage system, was the 1951 UNIVAC that had eight tape drives, separated from the central processing unit, CPU and the control console. Each tape drive was 6 feet high and 3 feet wide, used ½-inch metal tape of nickel-plated bronze 1,200 feet long. The whole computer filled a large room.

The term word-processing made an appearance in the marketing of an IBM magnetic tape computer in the late 1960s and had no widespread meaning until the development by IBM of the floppy disc for data storage in the early 1970s. The floppy disc opened-up the use of computers for word-processing to a much wider group because it was portable and compressed storage capacity. The floppy disc also separated software from hardware, because programs could be stored on discs, rather than being inseparable from the equipment. Word-processing allowed screen type to be understood as the creation of an open-ended document that could be continuously edited. The world of cut and paste had arrived and writing would never be the same again. Word-processing conjures up a lot more than typewriting. It involves not only the mechanical production of writing or speech into typography, but the larger process of composing, editing and even the laying out of text. Thus word-processing incorporates processes, skills, practices, previously associated with the work of the writer and the publisher. While typewriters were used in the production of writing by some writers, the dominant use of the typewriter was as a means of reproducing handwriting or speech in dictation or recorded speech as a typography. Word processing, made possible by the recording and display of type electrically extended the entire process of editing and correction, prior to printing. In the present, what we now call text as opposed to type, can be seamlessly transmitted, downloaded, stored and reassembled on the networked PC, laptop palmtop and mobile phone. The impact of these technological changes upon the meaning of writing and the status of texts is still being assessed, but it is likely that the production of on-screen text, using word processing software is changing the ways in which we write. The discussion of mobile phone 'texting', or email text protocols are but two simple examples where there has been considerable debate about the changing use of the written word. The concern for the exponential rise of plagiarism within the academic community, or the status of the author in hypertextual forms are more complex examples of the impact upon writing of word-processing in a networked communication system.

Early sound amplification, transmission and recording

Making historical connections between current digital media forms and practices and those of photography, film and subsequently television, brings to our attention the increasing primacy of vision in the historical account of media. This emphasis in thinking about digital media could be said to privilege the dimension of the visual over that of the textural or auditory. The increasing focus of intellectual interest around the power and influence of visuality in culture, is itself a counter to the previous dominance of literature in accounts of significant culture. Without displacing the importance of visual culture for digital media, and not wishing to engage in a hierarchy of the human senses and their corresponding cultural forms of transmission and reception, we do need to think about how auditory culture relate to digital media. Music is a major cultural and commercial force in the development and marketing of digital products and online services. Sound is very much a part of digital media and therefore we should at the very least recognise that the history of sound technologies and their cultural uses are important. Our sense of hearing and the cultural traditions of musical and oral communications are being attuned to a digital medium in which the auditory is as algorithmically and electronically captured as the visual and textual.

As with all of the media technologies we are considering, sound recording is best understood as developing over time and in relationship to interests and needs that continually change as new possibilities are grasped as well as initial ideas discarded. The principle of the light projected image had been developed in the Camera Obscura over at least 400 years prior to a means of fixing or recording of the image emerged with chemistry in the 1840s. The exact method of producing photographs from the early experiments using paper and glass positives, to the eventual settle method of the celluloid negative took place over the later part of the nineteenth century,

Kodak produced the first negative roll film camera in 1884. A similar historical pattern was followed with the development of sound recording methods.

Sound amplification also has a long history in the development of technological machines for the amplification of sound, but sound needed electricity and physics before it could be transmitted across distances beyond that of the range of the human ear. Alexander Graham Bell working in the United States had developed the microphone in relationship to his interest in human deafness and in 1876, developed an 'electrical speech machine,' which was to become the first telephone system. Here was an instrument that transmitted voices across space at the time and speed of speech. In the later part of the nineteenth century, telephony was used for communication between individuals and between fixed sites, as well as a popular form of public address related to live theatre and musical performances. By 1878, Bell had set up the first telephone exchange and by 1884, long distance connections were being made. The early stages of the development of Bell's electrical speech machines demonstrate yet again that technology and its cultural uses do not evolve in a linear fashion. The fact the telephony was conceived as a multiple public address system, rather than its eventual form of person-to person communication is a reflection of the nineteenth-century context of social space and cultural communication. Private conversation was still conceived of as something that took place face to face and private correspondence was fixed within the form of the letter. It is also interesting to note that it is theatre and public performance that again provided the possible cultural content for remote auditory transmission, the telephone as we know it only subsequently developed its own content as an extension of conversation.

In parallel with Bell, Thomas Edison developed his 'speaking phonograph' or, 'talking machine', which, as (Gitelman 2003:157) points out, he saw initially as revolutionising print, rather than as it later became a major technology for music reproduction. Edison's phonograph consisted of a cylinder covered with tin foil rotated by means of a hand turned screw, a voice cone, a diaphram and stylus. The soundwaves were converted into pressures through the diaphram, which in turn transmitted this to a stylus that made indentations across the surface of the tin foil. It was a crude mechanical device and shared little materially with Bell's speaking machine, which was understood initially to link aural experience and inscribed evidence between talk and some new form of text. What excited nineteenth-century listeners was the idea that the inscribed tin foil cylinders were literally speaking pages in which the exact words and intonation of the author could be reproduced. Like early photographs, each recording was itself a unique object, because it was not possible to reproduce multiple copies. In photography it was the development of the celluloid negative that created multiple copies and in sound it was the 78 rpm disc which extended a popular form of recorded musical sound.

The above accounts of early sound and vision technologies, serve to underline a number of important general points that should be borne in mind when considering the current moment of digital media. If we regard digital media as a new historical moment, then, we can equally regard old technologies as having been new once. Even our cursory glance at the early moments of image and sound recording demonstrates that the social context in which they first developed shaped a set of purposes and interests, which were not those that eventually came to dominate the twentieth century. Also it is clear that as new technologies of their time, they were very much indebted to existing media and cultural forms, in the ways they were used, popular theatre and newspapers being the most obvious examples. It should also be recognised that there was a strong emphasis on novelty and amusement in the demonstration and exhibition of what were considered in their time technological marvels.

Television

By the middle of the twentieth century much of the early experimentation with sound recording and transmission had settled into the patterns we now recognise as the telephone, radio and the record player. All of which were based upon different material, analogue technologies, each with their own commercial, industrial and institutional organisation. Now we face a new moment in which the recording and transmission of image and sound is converged in a common digital code of transmission and storage. While the technical code of image and sound is common in the digital, the cultural codes remain distinct, which is why, the institutions of radio, photography and music recording remain separate. However, it is also important to recognise that radio, music and photography all have an online presence and image and sound are major constituent elements of online and interactive media.

By the time of the first regular television broadcasts in Britain in the 1950s, listening to the radio, reading newspapers and watching films at a local cinema were regular features of everyday life for millions of people. The technology, which made the broadcasting of live pictures and sound possible, had evolved in a number of separate developments over the previous 50 years.

Television technology was based upon the development of the cathode ray tube (CRT), which still forms the picture tube of the analogue domestic television set. A cathode ray tube is a glass vacuum tube in which images are produced when an electron beam strikes a phosphorescent surface. The first cathode ray tube scanning device was the outcome of experimental scientist Karl Ferdinand Braun in 1897. Over the next five decades inventors and technicians worked in different countries, often in isolation or in competition with each other, on a range of technical apparatuses with no overall shared concept of what was to become broadcast television. In 1923 in Russia, Zworkin introduced the electronic television camera tube. In the UK, Baird and Jenkins worked upon systems using mechanical scanning devices. In the USA Farnsworth invented the image dissector and Allen Du Mont, patented high-speed manufacturing and testing equipment that resulted in dramatic increases in receiving tube production. In 1932, De Mont developed a cathode ray tube, which he called his 'magic eye'. Such developments were typical of a manufacturing mindset that initially saw the elements of was only later to become television as prospective technical apparatuses. The early technical experiments in transmitting and receiving images and sound as coded/decoded signals was socially understood as an operational communication system of interest to industrial, governmental or military purposes, rather than as a system of popular entertainment or national broadcast. By the late 1930s test transmissions of broadcast and received television image and sound were being made, but the transition from an organised system of radio broadcasting to that of television was not established until after the 1939–45 war in Europe. In Britain, the BBC had received its Charter as the national organisation for radio broadcasting in 1926. It was the BBC that produced the first national TV transmissions in 1951, British television could be thought of, for sometime after its inception as 'radio with pictures'. As Raymond Williams points out the development of broadcast television represents a technology of transmission developed before its content was thought of, or, put another way television was a developed technology looking for social and cultural purposes. Williams also points out, that parts of the content of early television transmission were and have remained by-products of the technology and that while radio transmission was a highly efficient means of broadcasting sound, television was an inferior means of transmitting images (Williams 1974:32).

The early developments of modern media point again and again to the fact that the material technologies were developed for local and partial manufacturing and commercial reasons of their time and that only over a longer period of time was an organised and systematic set of social communication purposes grasped. Modern media emerged over time through a combination of technological invention, commercial incentive, institutional development and creative content. This recognition is instructive when we come to consider how new technologies are being used in our own period. The video phone is a good example of Williams's point that products can be developed in advance of any social or cultural purpose or content. The low resolution digital video clips of the latest mobile phones are a by-product of technology. What applications will be found for real-time wireless digital video recording and transmission over the next decade is currently a matter of further speculation and market forces.

The historical development of television is also instructive when considering the rapidly and highly compressed development of the Internet and the World Wide Web. Technically the Internet originated through the selective and particular interests of scientific groups and military related government initiatives in the early 1960s in the USA, as we detail below. As Manuel Castells points out by the mid 1990s the WWW had exploded onto the world stage with about 16 million users, but even more phenomenal is the fact that in 2001 there were 400 million users, with predictions of 1 billion users, approximately a sixth of the world's population, by 2005 (Castells 2001). The extraordinary rapid growth of a global system of one-to-one and many-to-many distributed communication system stands in marked contrast to the development of television as a one-to-many, centralised system on communication. Moreover, the Internet and television share a technical history of the televisual transmission screen (CRT), now being overtaken by the application of liquid crystal screens (LCD) and plasma screens, which present the conditions for unprecedented convergence of distribution and reception systems. The question put by Bolter and Gruisin is whether the computer and allied institutions will take over the function of television, or television broadcast companies take over the function of the Internet (Bolter and Gruisin 2000:269).

The actual relationships between technologies and their social uses is, as the example of television suggests, extremely complex. A full understanding of the development of television, needs to take account of an historical period of social reconstruction and change after a continental war as Williams outlined. Post-war social and economic change created a new consumer society centred upon the domestic home. As the term, consumer durables, was coined to define a new set of mass produced products, such as radios cameras and television sets, which were in effect technologies of communication. The important social fact about the use of these post-war communication technologies was that they were consumed privately in the home, by a family unit that was more insular and less extended than previous family organisation. Television thus represented a highly centralised form of communication directed towards the isolated consumer, whereas theatre and cinema in the pre-war period had been popular social entertainments. The larger point here is that television developed in response to a new social organisation of which it performed a shaping role. The habits and patterns of consumption and use established by television are now being worked through the shaping of the popular consumption of digital media.

A note about videotape

Early television broadcasting consisted of live material, transmitted as it was produced in the studio or on location. This was because at the time there was no means of recording the televised signal. Live broadcasting put a limit on the amount of material that could be transmitted and early television contained intermissions between programmes and a limit to the numbers of hours of television per day. Early television scheduling and programming was therefore shaped by a system of what, in a post video age, we now call real-time transmission. Presenters and assembled casts of actors had to perform at the cue of the studio manager, much as actors did in the theatre. As we noted above analogue sound recording using magnetic tape reels had been developed in the 1930s ands 1940s, but no method had been found to record the image and synchronised sound of the televised recording. A method was found in 1951, when the first video tape recorder (VTR) captured live images from television cameras by converting the image and sound into electrical impulses and saving the information onto magnetic tape. The further development of the VTR and its take-up by television companies, radically changed the possibilities for television broadcasting since programmes could now be pre-recorded and edited prior to transmission. The advent of videotape recording did more than give television a means of pre-recording and storing televised material, it became a major means for the domestic consumption of feature films, an extension and eventual replacement for Super 8mm home movie making and an artistic medium in its own right. It is the video image and aesthetic, rather than that of film that has been incorporated into digital capture and used in digital media production. Videotape was also necessary to a generation of videogames that used television technology.

Computer games

In seeking to make links between the histories of theatre, photography and film and digital media we could be said to be privileging both vision and visual representation in media, to the exclusion of the other human senses, their corresponding knowledge and representations and recordings. A rejoinder to this is that the visual (photographic) image has rarely been reproduced without other kinds of textual commentaries, including oral ones in domestic photography, and that film and television are just as much organised by sound as by image. It can also be argued that our participation in and responses to photography, film and television are not exclusively organised by an overriding and singular mode of attention to either linear narratives or the realist discourse of representation. The embedded and lived modes of attention, to television for instance, include the experience of television within a larger social and perceptual field. Specifically we can include the experience of television as 'background', for instance, as well as modes of attention such as channel flipping which suggests that television can be enjoyed through fragmented, montaged and parallel modes of attention. So although analogue, terrestrial television is still accessed through a single screen in real time, it can be experienced as hypermedia in a combination with other domestic media, for example, watching TV with the sound off while listening to the radio, and by sequencing different channels. Digital television is already offering greater hyper-mediated experiences, for example on iBBC where programme text information and programme flows can be viewed concurrently on one screen.

The domestic reception of television provides the most recent historical context for the consumption of screen based, computer games. Essentially the video and computer game is interaction between 'reading' screen based audio/graphical representations and making programmed responses to the 'rules' or 'conventions' of a game by means of a physical interface (games console, keyboard, etc). We would expect, therefore, that a history of computer and video games would take into account these two elements, graphical representations on screens and the rules and conventions of games. The former we have already touched upon in discussing the antecedents of film and photography in the visual illusions and tricks of the circus, fairground and arcade. Such amusements, contained the fascination with naturalistic projections through which the real could, apparently, be captured and replayed and that the same apparatuses, techniques and technologies, could convincingly conjure-up the world of fantasy. These opposing fascinations with the recording of reality and the convincing representation of the obviously unreal, are contained in the history of photography and film, especially in animation and genres of film which rely on special effects. We would also have to add here the long history of narrative illustration, most obviously and recently manifest in comic strips. Digital media introduces techniques through which the visual conventions of recording the optically real can be seemlessly blended with the graphical representation of the optically impossible. Screen-based computer games make use of graphical conventions to do one of two things. In games such as Tomb Raider, or Company of Heroes, for example, it is important that the graphical representations conjure up a convincing and immersive three dimensional world into which the game player 'enters' through their optical positioning in front of the screen, or through a screen based avatar. The graphical conventions of this type of game strive towards filmic realism. On the other hand, games such as Sim City and Pokemon, still represent, or, better, model spatial worlds, and are less concerned with creating verisimilitude, than with offering the player a range of views and strategic reconnaissance of the world and the events in play.

Gaming and human play

Computer games are now an integral component of personal and domestic screen based media. Computer games represent a global industry with an economic turnover rivalling that of Hollywood film production. Computer games are an established part of popular culture, with dedicated websites, international competitions, High Street retail outlets, magazines and related product and merchandising in the toy industry. According to the forecasting firm of DFC Intelligence the worldwide market for video games and interactive entertainment is predicted to grow from $23.2 billion in 2003 to $33.4 billion in 2008.

Because of the scale of the games industry, the study of computer and video games is rapidly becoming an academic subject in its own right, with individuals and groups adopting a variety of points of interest and theoretical perspectives. At present there appear to be three distinct intellectual projects attempting to account for the current ways in which computer games are valued and understood as part of digital media. These projects roughly fall into:

- the sociological and cultural interest in studying how children and young people use computers and how this may or may not relate to the wider project of education and play;

- the analysis of games as narrative cultural texts, similar to films, books or television programmes;

- the analysis of games as meeting a deep human interest in mathematical puzzles.

Given the above we would expect a history of computer games to be informed by the wider history of pre-computer games, such as board or card games as well as an even wider history of cultural forms of play. Such a history would also recognise the complex cultural interrelationship between games and play based on mathematical puzzles and those based upon riddles, rhymes and other narratives. Analogue video-games replicated in a different medium, older cultural forms of physical games and sports that involved hand–eye co-ordination. The electronic relays of videogames, the games consoles were also reconfigurations of older mechanical interfaces of amusements in the penny arcades. The visual screen interfaces as well as the physical interface of the console of early videogames prefigured the graphical user interface (GUI) of the contemporary hypermedia computer. The first version of 'Spacewar' in which two players, used a trackball console to 'control' the simple graphic representations of two spaceships, which 'fire' at each other, was developed at the Massachusetts Institute of Technology in the 1960s. The videogame of 'Pong', was developed as an interesting diversion by programmers working for IBM. As Lister *et al.* (2003:333) notes computer games emerged from programmers wanting to know what more could a computer do than crunch numbers. Pong had a very basic screen graphic that used nothing more than a black screen with two white bars on either side, representing bats and a white dot as a ball. The (algorithmic) relationship between the bat, ball and blank screen created 'a game of tennis' in which the speed and angle of ball return was variably programmed to test the 'skill' of the players in predicting the position of the bat. It was introduced in 1972 and was a popular addition to the arcades and could also be plugged into the domestic television set by means of a programmed black box. In 1978, a Japanese company Taito, introduced Space Invaders, which proved to be exceptionally popular in Japan and North America. By the standards of contemporary photo-realistic graphics, Space Invaders used a very simple, schematic form of representation of aliens and humans and used a gravitational metaphor in which the top of the screen represented space and the bottom earth. The small, 'alien' shapes would descend in rows from the top and would 'fire' on the human shapes below, who could 'hide' under four 'shields', graphic dashes, or come out from their 'shields' and 'shoot' back at the 'alien's. The movement and firing positions of the humans were controlled by a keypad. Pong and Space Invaders involved using the screen as a spatial metaphor and the player–computer interaction simulated rapid anticipation and reaction times through hand–eye co-ordination of schematic onscreen avatars. The replacement of video by digital storage platforms, allowed games to use larger memory hungry graphic files and hence produce today's photo-realistic spatial worlds in which adventure games and shoot-em-ups can be set.

Automation of manual and intellectual labour

The interests of military organisations in advanced command and control systems, and the application of advanced technology to warfare are evident influences in the shaping of modern computer functions and applications. But to say that the personal PC and the Internet are simply spin-offs from military development is only partially true. There has been a much longer civil and commercial set of interests at work in the creation of machines that could repeat human actions, functions and tasks, which have also contributed to our conception of the computer. The most recent historical context for such machines was the European Industrial Revolution. From the late eighteenth century onwards in farming, cottage industries and then in industrial mills, there was an increasing application of machines to activities that had previously been carried out by hand. The textile industry introduced mechanical looms and weaving machines, which allowed cloth to be produced cheaper and in greater quantities than that of hand production. The Jacquard loom is an early example of the introduction of the automation of weaving whereby sophisticated patterns could be produced by 'programming' the loom using a string of cards with punched holes.

A hundred and fifty years after the Jacquard loom, analogue computers used linear punch-cards to create programs for processing data. In analogue computers, punched-tape was later replaced by magnetic tape. There is an even longer history of the use of calculating/counting 'machines', devised in order to simplify the complex processes of mental arithimetic, the abacus frame and the slide-rule being but two examples. The externalisation of the programmatic rules of algebraic and algorithmic tasks, previously carried out mentally by learned formulas, ran in parallel to the industrial conception of programming as the replacement of skilled human labour by the machine. This is demonstrated by the work of Charles Babbage (1791–1871), whose design for a mechanical 'Difference Engine', consisting of cogs, levers and springs, was a dedicated device intended for the calculation and production of mathematical tables for use in nautical navigation. From a contemporary position such mechanical analogue devices as we have briefly touched upon could all be called programmable machines for the production and manipulation of data. They are typically cited in technologically privileged accounts of the history of the computer as its precursors.

We have already noted that the development of electricity, as a readily available power source at the beginning of the twentieth century was a condition for the emergence of the technical apparatus of cinema, radio, telegraphy and telephony. The vacuum valve, provided the first means of converting an electric current into a system of signals that could have representational values in radio, television and analogue computers. By the 1950s valves, which were inherently unstable, were replaced by sold stated diode technology and magnetic tape was used to store programming information. Such a computer, which needed a large laboratory to be housed, was built by the American National Bureau of Standards and was known as the SEAC (Standards Eastern Automatic Computer) and was used for testing components and systems for setting computer standards. By the standard of todays miniaturised, micro-ship digital computers, the mainframe research computers of the 1970s were large complex and cumbersome amalgams of technical apparatuses and required long periods of development and were hence expensive to produce. *Computer development in this period was therefore governed by large-scale institutions that required functions related to complex information processing.* The ILLIAC IV mainframe computer, funded by the Department of Defense Advanced Research Projects Agency (DARPA) and developed by the University of Illinois, was used by the American National Aeuronautical Space Agency (NASA) and had a computation speed of 200 million instructions per second, enough, as it was refined, to command and control the Apollo manned flight.

The development of networked computers

From the standpoint of digital media we can now consider how the practices associated with the analogue technologies of recording sound, vision and movement and with two-way communications, converged in the networked digital computer. The social shaping of the development of the computer and computer networks centres upon a set of interlocking relationships between governmental military and defence departments, armament manufacturers and academic research. In practice the relationship between these three institutional sites, as we might call them, is most obviously expressed in the form of government funding for research and development projects and defence procurement contracts. This is why it has been said in many contexts that technological development in general is quickened, if not driven, by war, or in a more complex expression of the argument, by the permanent arms economy. The development of computers from the 1940s, clearly reflects such a grouping of interests and participation. In the USA and Britain some of the most influential scientists and mathematicians associated with key developments in computing were employed by or associated with government military research projects that had been established as a result of the Second World War in Europe. The now well rehearsed post-war history of the technological development and social shaping of the modern computer and the Internet makes the connection between scientific and military work very clear. The leading figures in the field of early computing, their institutional locations and the funding of their projects came together in a nexus of interests bounded by the Allied war effort against Nazi Germany and later in the US–Soviet axis of the Cold War. Vannevar Bush, whose seminal essay, 'As We May Think' (1945), outlined the concept of a multimedia computer, was Director of the US Office of Scientific Research and Development, responsible for the 6,000 scientists involved in the war effort. Norbert Weiner, who ideas on cybernetics have influenced thinking about the human-machine relationship, worked on a research project on improving anti-aircraft guns. In 1943 Alan Turing, a Cambridge mathematician was working on the British Colossus for military code decryption.

The development of a computer network, in which computers could 'talk to one another', first took place within the Advanced Research Projects Agency (ARPA), set up in 1957 within the US Department of Defense with the support of Vannevar

Bush in order to help the military use computers. In 1972 ARPA became DARPA, the Defence Advanced Research Project. (Slevin (2000:28) argues that the origins of the Internet are firmly rooted in the circumstances of the Cold War and the US fear that the Soviets could launch a long range nuclear attack with the rocket technology demonstrated by their Sputnik satellite in 1957. ARPANET was established in 1969 in order to develop a communication network for the exchange of research information between centres and to allow scientists and researchers to share information. The ARPANET linked the information carried on computers in different locations, which at the time, we should remember, were large, mainframe analogue computers in a distributed rather than central system.

One of the popular myths surrounding the development of the Internet was that it was purposely developed by US Intelligence during the Cold War as a non-centralised command system in the event of a Soviet first strike long-range nuclear missile attack. There is at least a grain of truth in this as (Slevin 2000:29) points out. The US Air Force commissioned research at the RAND Corporation to work on a project to see how the US Air Force could maintain control over its missiles and bombers in the aftermath of a nuclear attack. The answer they came up with was a network of computers, which would continue to function even if several of its distributed nodes were destroyed, as against a system with one centralised hub and radial connections, which if destroyed would stop all command and control between secondary centres. It was the concept of a distributed network in which all computers inter-linked that constitutes the current network of networked computers, which forms the basis of Internet and the World Wide Web.

The technical objective of the research agencies working for ARPA, was to develop computer codes for addressing electronic information in packets, which would allow networked computers to 'talk to one another', which became known as protocols. One of the original research aims, which supported the establishment of ARPANET, was for research centres to be able to share the use of on-line computer time at a point when mainframe computers were very expensive and needed large physical spaces to accommodate analogue memory. The system of technical networks, which emerged from ARPA's research became known as the Internet. The system of transmission protocols became known as the Transmission Control Protocol (TCP) and Internet Protocol (IP).

As Manuel Castells points out the Internet was not only shaped by government defence and scientific institutions but also the product of a grassroots tradition of computer networking. Here Castells recognises a constellation of interests combining libertarian scientists in university departments, networked PC users and the larger framework of defence initiated and supported projects. He formalises the culture of the Internet as being made up from four specific cultures, comprising the techno-meritocratic, the hacker, the virtual communitarian and the entrepreneurial. (Castells 2001:12) These are both accurate and evocative terms to describe the grouping of ideas and interest, or, to use one of our other more abstract terms, the discourses that manifested themselves in trends, approaches and beliefs in the Internet's purpose and possibilities. Understanding why we have the Internet as it is now configured, needs to take account of the close interrelationship between the cultural values of the individuals, communities and groups involved in computer science and programming, the institutional purposes for which computers were being built and the historical development of the technical apparatuses.

From telegraphy to the mobile

The historical development of telegraphy and telephony are interesting examples of how elements of technological discoveries were used in different social contexts and for different uses of comparatively long periods of time. Technologies for communicating messages over distances illustrate very clearly that the idea of technologies developing in logical steps for a single purpose is unsustainable. The principle of transmitting sound by means of mechanical vibration over an extended wire was recorded in 1667 by Robert Hooke, and while the idea of transmitting sound by means of electricity was mooted by a number of people in the intervening period and various experiments carried out, it was not until 1876 that Alexander Graham Bell files his patent application for the telephone. Early telepones could only be connected over relatively short distances and were single hardwired connections between two devices. The development of the telephone exchange during the 1870s allowed more telephone subscribers to be connected through a switchboard operated manually to connect lines. In contrast, telegraphy over the same period could send and receive text messages coded electrically over long distances and has been in use for business and official communication up until and still in parallel with the Internet. These early commercial applications of telephony stimulated new social demand among the growing middle and business classes, as much as they laid the foundations for greater and greater numbers of subscribers, such that by 1904 there were over 3 million telephones manually connected to switchboard exchanges in the USA in a population of approximately 82 million people. The mobile phone is a development of the second half of the twentieth century, dating once again from technology first proposed and developed at Bell Laboraties in 1947, but which required a combination of further micro electronics, omni-direction transmitter/receiving equipment and the allocation of radio frequences that did not come together with a commercial application in mind until the 1970s. Mobile phones are a cellular device capable of transmitting and receiving radio signals and requires a cellular network covering a wide geographic area. Prior to the development of the cellular network and the mobile device, mobile telephony was restricted to two-way radios fitted in police and taxi vehicles and trains. The first mobile phone prototypes were large and heavy, offering limited transmission time and whose batteries took long periods to recharge and early cellular networks were limited in range. The widespread us of mobile phones dated from the 1990s when the transmission and signalling technology became digital. By 2010 there was an estimated 6 billion mobile subscriberes world wide.

BACK TO THE FUTURE: NEW TECHNOLOGIES AND CONTINUOUS CULTURAL FORMS

In concluding our survey and discussion of the histories of digital media technologies and their evolving uses we return again to the provisional nature of current work in the area. A substantial history of digital media will have to disentangle the elements of digital media's technological and cultural hybridity. Such a history will be produced by continuous scholarship, research and theory. One such approach, which cautions against the tendency to construct a history of digital media as a singular new medium, is evident in *New Media 1740–1915* (Gitelman and Pingree 2003). Here the case is made that the study of digital media is not confined to today's digital media and that it is important to focus upon historical moments when old technologies were new. In excavating the new moment of old technologies it is possible to juxtapose older and contemporary media and examine continuities and discontinuities between them and take the view that digital media is, by definition, the uneven and never finally settled outcome of work upon material technologies in and through particularised social formations. Such a method works in both time directions. In the book, Erin C. Blakes contribution uses the contemporary concept of virtual reality, in order to show us how the Zograscope (a convex lens through which perspectival drawings could be viewed) was used by the middle classes in the 1740s to construct a simulacrum of polite metropolitan space. While Ellen Gruber Garvey, reminds us that domestic scrapbooks in the 1910s, employed conventions of bricolage and collage that are prescient of the graphic cut-and-paste repurposed content on today's websites. Such studies as these resist the temptation, which we have already discussed, to construct a teleological history where the early experiments with optical representations, remote communication or analogue sound recording, are configured as rehearsals in a seamless history resulting in the inevitable outcome of virtual and immerse media. Instead, by focusing upon media formations that failed to survive for very long, or what might now be deemed dead media, they suggest current digital media might also be looked at as in a state of flux and whose future is uncertain.

Typically the history of communication media is seen as dependant upon the history of scientific and technological invention that is most often written as the history of creative individuals who make scientific discoveries, which are subsequently given practical applications. While it is undeniably the case that we would not have the mediums we do without the dedicated and single-minded efforts of individual technological discovery, their efforts alone cannot account for why and how certain mediums became established. We discussed above Raymond Williams's seminal analysis of the development of television as being the outcome of a complex and changing set of social patterns, economic modes of production and political needs and values. He makes the startling, but also hard point to grasp, that there was nothing inevitable about the way in which television emerged as the domestic and privatised reception of centralised broadcasting. In other words we could have had a totally different kind of television, which would therefore have developed a different set of technological possibilities. Digital media, is renewing interests in one-to-one as well as many-to-many forms of interactive telematic communication which are currently being socially explored. The human interest in social communication and interactivity at a distance has a longer history and is not a product of a new technology. Television is an example of the social shaping of technology, which in Britain and Europe in the 1950s emphasised the interests of a strong and centralised system of national communication over and above that of a more distributed, local and two-way mode of interactivity. It follows for us that the same will be true about the social shaping of digital media. The networked computer and the Internet have been forged in some key respects in the same social and economic mould of centralised corporate interests as television was. The PC has been produced for and marketed as a domestic consumer durable for the family and home as was television and radio before that. Greater bandwidth, faster download times and larger file storage are primarily enlisted in the interests of gateway service providers wishing to capture the largest market share, witness the current battle between British Telecom (BT) and America Online (AOL), large corporate providers of 'content' for domestic consumption, in a development similar to the technical refinements of television in gaining greater picture and sound definition. Such developments overwhelmingly reproduce the one-to-many model of television in which the privatised domestic consumer is at a screen at one end and a few large international corporations who provide, and hence control, the 'content' at the other. This is one scenario that is forcibly illustrated in the digital convergence of television and the computer.

FURTHER READING

http://mediahistoryproject.org/
www.adobemuseum.com/

ILLUSTRATED CASE STUDY 6: CROWDSOURCING AND THE LONDON 2012 OLYMPIC GAMES

#Citizencurators was a social media project during the London 2012 Olympic Games designed to capture the experience of Londoners during the Olympic fortnight. The project was created for the Museum of London to enable it to collect tweets that could tell the story of everyday life in the capital as a way of collecting contemporary social history.

> We want your thoughts and opinions. What's it like for you, as a Londoner, during the two weeks of the Games? Use the hashtag #citizencurators to tweet your point of view. A moment, an observation, an annoyance, something that made you laugh, something that speaks of what its like to be in London while the Olympics are on.
>
> It doesn't matter if you live and work in Harlow, Croydon or Richmond – or the Olympic boroughs. Your life during the Games is relevant no matter where you are or what is happening. Sunshine or rain, people watching or at work, shopping or cycling, torch bearer or protester.
>
> If you tweet with the hashtag #citizencurators your tweet will become part of the public history of London, in the collection of the Museum of London. It's a world first (we think!) to crowd-sample an historical record this way, as it's happening. And by letting the citizens of the city be the curators.
>
> (Project Director: Peter Ride, University of Westminster)[1]

#Citizencurators was based on the principles of 'crowdsourcing' – the practice of obtaining contributions from the public, often in the form of expertise or knowledge. Using these principles, the project aimed to let the public – or citizens of London – select material for the Museum of London that was be representative of their lives. By using social networking the project planned to capture the minutae of everyday life and to get the flavour of the way that people used networks to exchange information and opinions. Crowdsourcing also enables access to unlimited numbers of people. Using it, the project could reach communities across London including a wide range of social groups with different cultural interests, of different ages, and provided a way to give space to otherwise marginalised voices. Twitter was chosen as the main platform for the project because it provided a commonly used and easy to manage stream of data, and in 2012 it was representative of social networking platforms.

C@SE STUDY

FIGURE 1
Twitpic of Olympic supporters in London submitted to #citizencurators

FIGURE 2
Twitpic of Olympic supporter in London submitted to #citizencurators

C@SE STUDY

FIGURE 3
Twitpic of bagels in the shape of Olympic rings in London submitted to #citizencurators

FIGURE 4
Twitpic of shirts in the shape of Olympic rings in a London shop window submitted to #citizencurators

C@SE STUDY

FIGURE 5
Tweet and pic of Olympic Games torch relay in London submitted to #citizencurators

FIGURE 6
Tweet submitted to #citizencurators

C@SE STUDY

C@SE STUDY

FIGURE 7
Twitpic of Olympic flags in London submitted to #citizencurators

A large body of Londoners use social networks to exchange information on what is going on in the capital especially via Twitter. The London 2012 Olympic Games was billed as the first social media Summer Games or the first 'Twitter Olympics'. It was expected that athletes, media and the public would tweet voraciously about the Games. Of particular interest to the project team was the way Twitter would be used instantaneously to communicate feelings and views around the Olympics.

The project was initiated by the Museum of London and the University of Westminster. Arts organisations and museums have often run social media projects, including Twitter projects, but it was rare, if not unique, for a museum to collect social media for a museum collection where it would

FIGURE 8
Tweet submitted to #citizencurators

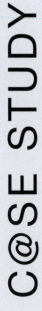

be kept in perpetuity as a record of social history. However, as explained by Hilary Young, Digital Curator at the Museum of London, 'my internal museum curator voice was asking "can we collect this?", "what do we do with it?" and "what is the object?"'[2]

The project used a unique hashtag #citizencurators which was publicised online and people were invited to use the hashtag through blog posts and by twitter advocates. A group of volunteers were also recruited who were committed to contributing tweets on a regular basis tagged with the project hashtag, but anyone who used Twitter was invited to use it to take part. By promoting a dedicated hashtag the Museum could make it clear all tweets that included it would be collected. This meant that it was unlikely that tweeters would use this unless they were intending their tweet to be part of the project.

The Museum considered many alternative approaches. One would have been to 'gather' tweets with daily trending hashtags. This would have generated a large amount of material but it would not have meant that people had willingly chosen to take part. Instead it was to keep the project to a small scale as this also meant that the content could be easily examined. The digital curators at the Museum also had to decide the best way to 'harvest' tweets. There were commercial software programmes available to do this but many of these programmes included clauses about third party rights in the content and future use thus limiting what the Museum could potentially do with the content in the future.

C@SE STUDY

FIGURE 9
Twitpic of Olympic Games tickets submitted to #citizencurators

Instead the Museum chose to use an opensource Twitter Archiving Google (TAGS) program, which used Google Spreadsheets for the data source and allows users to set up automatic collection of tweets that use the defined terms they set. The search criteria was then set around the project hashtag #citizencurators. It also harvested the following metadata: User ID number; From User; Text of tweet; Date stamp time and date; Geo coordinates; Language; To user; To User ID; Profile Image URL; Status URL.

Using this program the projects harvested approximately 7000 tweets that used the #citizencurators hashtag. It gathered tweets from approximately 600 unique Twitter user accounts, which covered a wide range of subjects like the following:

@ssswani: Olympics countdown: no hustle and bustle, it's such a lovely British summer day @ Deptford park #citizencurators

@realnickperry: There'a something both disconcerting and exciting about seeing landmark buildings taken over by entire nations for month #citizencurators

@deedeesvintage: Free park tickets are a belated gesture to the residents of @wickvillage. At first they wanted £16 and no one bought them. #citizencurators

Selections from the tweets collected were displayed at the Museum in a gallery display a year after the Games, in 2013.

As well as generating a collection of tweets for the Museum collection, the project also raised important questions about how social media can be managed. It raised concerns if it was practical to run a Twitter project along the lines of a participatory public event since a project of this form was potentially boundless. By its nature, a Twitter project is an open project in a public forum which has no walls, therefore there can be no control mechanism of an official or voluntary nature.

Reviewing #citizencurators at its conclusion, the Learning Officer at the Museum of London, Laura Lanin summarised the importance of a crowdsourcing project:

> The #citizencurators project highlights how communities can be brought together and experiences shared. From an outsiders perspective it appears that the project captured the spirit of London in August 2012 – in many of its guises and among many of its communities. Personally, I think the project was aptly named. After all,

C@SE STUDY

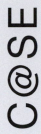

the #citizencurators itself provided a clear form of identity and community to belong to – even if it was only for a brief period in time.[3]

#Citizencurators was directed by Peter Ride and Hilary Young.

Notes

1   http://citizencurators.com/2012/07/26/so-whats-it-like-for-you/
2   http://citizencurators.com/2012/09/11/can-the-museum-collect-tweets/
3   http://citizencurators.com/2012/09/24/citizenship-and-citizencurators/

CHAPTER 23

Digital media theories

DIGITAL CULTURE AND GLOBAL ECONOMIES

The exponential expansion of computer networks and the increasing range of applications of digital technologies over the past two decades has important connections with the larger processes of globalisation. The networked society and the information revolution parallel and are entailed in the changes over a period of time from the older vertically organised economies of the first industrial nations, to the horizontally organised globally distributed production economies of today. The changes associated with globalised economics are closely associated with neoliberalism, which promotes a free market philosophy, privatisation and deregulation in opposition to social market economics that emphasise the role of government in planning and regulation. Economic globalisation can also be seen as the latest stage of multinational capitalism. Lev Manovich notes that twentieth-century media systems, such as Hollywood film and television followed the industrial logic of standardisation, while new media runs ahead of the mode of the new post-industrial economies through its logic of customisation (Manovich 2001:30). The wider concept of globalisation is also an emphasis upon the interconnectedness of people, countries, regions and economies on a world scale. The information superhighway is part of this globalisation process that has produced greater sharing and communication, but at the same time it maintains the divide between information rich and poor parts of the world. The Internet is both a continuation of a media and cultural imperialism in which a torrent of cultural traffic flows from powerful centres out to a periphery and a new form of many-to-many communication, which has created new social movements on a variety of scales.

New technologies and computer networks have quickened the possibilities for flexible systems of production, which in turn have created new transnational labour markets. The older, vertical organisation of production, recognised most clearly in the image of Henry Ford's motor company, in which cars were made in one place in a single ownership factory, has given way to a more spatially distributed (horizontal) system organised around out-sourcing, sub-contracting and just-in-time delivery systems and consumer led markets (Harvey 1989). Globalisation also describes how historically, industrial production, concentrated in the older industrial countries of Europe and North America, has declined and been redeveloped in the emergent industrial economies in South America, South-East Asia and China. Related to this shift in industrial production, new technologies have created the computer and information industries, which now employ increasing numbers of information workers on a global scale. It is these very same technologies and computer networks that transnational media corporations are using for instantaneous 24 hour global broadcasting, thus increasing the cycle of globalisation (Morley and Robins 1995).

POSTMODERNITY

Technology's connection with economic globalisation was explored through the arguments and ideas surrounding postmodernity and postmodernism and intellectual writers associated with the postmodern have led the discussion of the social impact of digital media. This is because many digital media objects display characteristics of the wider changes noted in the condition of postmodernity, such as ephemeral, 'cut and paste' and essentially 'bricolaged' nature of the digital aesthetic. The social and cultural dimension of globalised economic activity has been fruitfully defined as 'the condition of post-modernity' (Lyotard 1979, Jameson 1984 and Harvey 1990). The condition of post-modernity is another way of accounting for the relationship between technology and social and cultural development. Postmodernity is, as Fredric Jameson points out, a periodising concept, which connects the emergence of new aspects of culture with changes in social life and the new globalised, economic order. Postmodernism, as distinct from the condition of post-modernity, identifies trends, or distinct movements in theoretical thinking, art, architecture and cultural life. Postmodernism, in all its forms, argued that the changes in the world over since the Second World War have been of such a magnitude that we can no longer continue with the rationalist modernist paradigm of thought and action. Postmodernists argued that a radical reorganisation of philosophical thought and cultural activity was needed. Postmodernists typically pointed to such cataclysmic events as the Second World War in Europe, the Holocaust, the collapse of the Soviet Union, the AIDs pandemic and Chernobyl, which rationalist science and technological progress did nothing to stop.

David Harvey, gives a very concrete and still relevant image of the experience of the post-modern condition in his account of 'time-space compression'. He argues that the transition from Fordism (vertical organisation of production), to 'flexible accumulation', has brought with it two decades of time-space compression. Time-space compression has a disorientating and disruptive impact upon political and economic practice, class power and social and cultural life. Flexible accumulation has the characteristics of accelerated turnover time, a speeding up in labour process and an quickening of deskilling and reskilling. Interestingly enough these characteristics are now normal features of the informational workplace. In parallel with acceleration in production Harvey points to acceleration in exchange and consumption where commodities circulate faster with a corresponding shift from goods to services. This account of the condition of postmodernity, speculative in the 1980s has been a normal description of the culture of urban life at the beginning of the twenty-first century. What is more challenging is Harvey's analysis of the individual and social experience of the postmodern condition. Here he talks about a world, which has become volatile and in which everything is more ephemeral. A society in which the values of instantaneity, disposability, novelty and obsolescence have become naturalised. A throwaway society, where we have little attachment to anything, including idealism and people. This is a society in which permanence has been replaced by temporariness. The accumulative consequences of these features of time-space compression is a more fragmented or diversified society in which we experience sensory overload and in which we have less sense of future continuity. How individuals and whole cultures understand and cope with the effects of time-space compression is varied, according to Harvey and Jameson. More recent commentaries have emphasised an even greater speeding up of the experience of time with the idea of hypermodernity (Lipovetsky 2005).

A typical set of cultural responses to acceleration and information overload, has been to simply deny or block out the new experience and instead to revert to images of a lost past. Other 'negative' responses including excessive simplification and myopic specialism are set against the more positive response of being adaptable and fast moving. Such features were also noted by Simmel at turn of the century in Vienna and by Alvin Toffler in the 1970s (cited in Harvey 1989).

Jameson, Harvey and Castells have, in their different ways and at different times, all made a causal link between the rapid expansion, development, the application of digital technologies in communication media and marked changes in the character of individual social and cultural experience, which can be broadly characterised again as the condition of post-modernity. Jameson (1984) articulates what he calls 'a cultural logic of late capitalism' in which aesthetic populism dominates, history has been replaced with nostalgia and pastiche eclipses parody. Harvey identifies time and space compression as a feature of globalisation which brings with it an accentuation of the volatility and ephemerality of everything, the establishment of the values of instantaneity, disposability, novelty and obsolescence and the loss of a sense of future continuity (Harvey 1989). Castells places informational processing at the centre of social and economic production and suggests that the 'space of flows' of information is superseding that of the 'space of places'. All of these accounts point out that the postmodern condition is in part a consequence of the application of information technologies and that one of its key characteristics is the experience of excessive information, or information overload (Castells 1996).

Frank Webster takes issue with Baudrillard and the more general stance of the postmodernists who reject the idea that we can explain the postmodern as an extension of a modernist past founded upon historical progress and rational thought. For postmodernism the 'grand narratives' of scientific truth, technological progress, civilisation, capitalism and communism, which lay claim to the truth about progress and development, are no more than prescriptive and relative versions of the truth (Webster 1999:190). Postmodernism points to the limits of the modernist paradigm of rational, scientific thought on the grounds of the failure of historical progress in the twentieth century. Science and politics, the postmodernist argue, has so far failed to stop global warming, the destruction of the world's natural habitats, Chernobyl and Aids. In the postmodern persepctive rational political thought was also responsible for the rise of fascism and the failure of communism. Finally, the postmodernist argue that technology continues to produced super sophisticated military technologies and weapons of mass destruction (Virillo 2005). The cultural and intellectual strategies of postmodernism replaced the modernist search for absolute truth with relativism or 'versions of the truth'. Postmodernists replace singular prevailing discourses in science and philosophy, with a plurality of discourses especially those that celebrate differences of analysis, explanation and interpretation. The cultural strategies of postmodernism embraced the inauthentic, superficial, ephemeral and artificial arguing that without any means of attaining authenticity we are left with the inauthentic construction of the authentic.

Webster, as well as Jameson and Harvey, acknowledge these failures as contingent factors and can agree with the list of failures, but they also insist that they can explained by rational and scientific analysis rather than requiring a break with such methods.

HISTORICAL ANTECEDENTS: MARXISM

The writings of Karl Marx (1832–94) have had an enormous influence on intellectual thought and political movements over the nineteenth and twentieth centuries and still inform a great deal of intellectual work today. Briefly and broadly, Karl Marx, developed an analysis of how money and labour operate, which he published in 1885 as his major work, entitled *Capital*. Capitalism is the name associated with the economic system Marx analysed. In seeking to understand how the system of capitalism developed and what would happen to it in the future Marx established two related theories, historical and dialectical materialism, the first to explain the 'laws' of historical development and the second the 'laws' of the internal contradictions of the system of capital. Marx's work was hugely influential and was enlisted by revolutionary movements, communists and trade unionists across mainland Europe and became the founding theory of the Russian Revolution led by Vladimir Lenin (1870–1924). Although Marxism is primarily associated with a political critique of capitalism and with the revolutionary movements of communism, Marx's analysis of capital was also very influential in a much broader academic intellectual tradition of thinking about media and culture. Within this Marxist tradition attention was focused upon the question of how the economic base of society gave rise to the cultural superstructure, most specifically upon the ideological role of media in capitalist societies. The Frankfurt School in Germany, associated with the work of Walter Benjamin (1892–1940), Herbert Marcuse (1898–1979), Max Horkheimer (1895–1973), Theodor W. Adorno (1903–69) and later Jurgen Habermas (b. 1929), continued to develop and apply Mark's historical materialism to problems of the post-war division of Europe along capitalist and communist lines. This body of work, later known as 'critical theory' directly addressed the role of media and media technologies in cpaitalist mass societies and continues to be a reference point in the discussion of digital media. However, the hierarchical and fixed relationship between base and superstructure, in orthodox Marxist accounts, in which the economy determined and culture reflected, was increasingly challenged as failing to grasp the determining role of culture in producing and reproducing a dominant or ruling set of ideas or ideologies. The work of Michel Foucault (1926–84), who we have already discussed in relation to digital media histories, attempted a more sophisticated and complex analysis of the 'micro-physics of power' and his ideas of 'power-knowledge' and 'discourses', precisely addressed the process through which individuals come to occupy structured social and subjective positions. How culture in any one period or epoch operated to secure the dominance of ruling ideas, became a matter of intense analysis in the work of Luis Althusser 1918–90), Roland Barthes (1915–80) and Raymond Williams (1921–88).

The explanatory power of Marx's theories of historical and dialectical materialism reached a limit in European critical intellectual and academic circles during the 1980s, first in the face of the corruption of the Russian Revolution under Joseph Stalin, followed by the reunification of Germany in 1989 and finally in the dissolution of the Soviet State in 1991. Marx's basic theory of the economic base and the social and cultural superstructure, was seen to have failed to account for capitalism's continued creative force and spread and more importantly, while Marxism provided an explanation of class consciousness and class antagonism, it was felt by many academics, including feminists, to have an inadequate account of how individual subjectivity is produced. In European and North American universities, scholars developed more nuanced and complex accounts of the relationship between economic and cultural determinations. Such revisions to Marx's basic thesis were in part addressed to the problem of explaining the continued dominance of capitalism, against part of Marx's predictions that capitalism as a system would collapse under the weight of its own internal contradictions. The cultural turn was a reformulation of Marx in terms of a *cultural materialism*, associated with two schools of thought, post structuralism and the work of Michel Foucault, Jacques Derrida (1930–2004) and Pierre Bourdieu (1930–2002) and cultural studies, inaugurated by the work of Raymond Williams (1921–88) and Stuart Hall. (b. 1932) Cultural materialism was precisely concerned to understand how values and meanings were produced in practice and argued that the base/superstructre argument was an inadequate account of the economic and cultural process of production. It is not difficult to see the importance of such arguments for the idea of the creative, cultural and media industries, of which digital media is centrally a part. Cultural materialism continues to investigate the contradictions, inequalities and paradoxes of cultural practice under the economic conditions of global neo-liberal free market economics.

Post Structuralism emerged over the 1960s and 1970s and represents a profoundly sceptical view of the idea that human culture can be understood as a structuring system of languages, which mediated between our ideas and mental picture of the world and external concrete reality. The scepticism towards rationalist and scientific thinking was a response to problems those associated with post-structuralism perceived within the disciplines of linguistics, anthropology and semiology. Within structuralism these disciplines sought to discover and lay bare the underlying rules by which human culture was organised and through which meaning operated. The fundamental criticism made by post-structuralist authors was that thought could not escape the very structures it sought to detect as self sustaining systems and therefore could not be truly objective. Post-structuralism overlapped with postmodern thinking in developing a critique of the claim to scientific objectivity and in questioning the claim that human nature and humanity were given as essential terms, seeing instead that what it is to be human is historically relative.

Roland Barthes (1915–80) made a significant contribution to understanding the problems involved in the view that meaning originates with the author and lies in the text. Barthes was critical of the claim that language and its basic unit of meaning in the sign could hold constant and hence universal meaning and considered that a structuralist analysis of literary texts was a closed system of reference with little usefulness outside of itself. From this perspective Barthes was able to develop his view that there could be no ultimate meaning of a text and hence the very notion of authorial authority was called into question in the context of the proliferation of meaning in language. Barthes expressed this view in his book, *The Death of the Author* (1968) in which he crucially centred the meaning or unity of a text, not in its origins with the author, but in its destination with the reader. Barthes paved the way for considering how other signifying systems in culture as well as in photography relied upon being 'read' through connotation and myth. These were important developments in reading sign systems, which while relativised representational meaning, nevertheless held to the belief that representation was possible.

THE REAL AS SIMULATION – JEAN BAUDRILLARD

Jean Baudrillard argued that with globalisation and commodification European and North American societies have changed their system of representation from one in which there was a clear separation between object and subject, between the real and its' represented, to a new state of reality as **simulation**. Baudrillard was interested in developing an account of human activity in which the symbolic function of objects served the needs of unconscious structures of social relations. In the 'Ecstasy of Communication' (Baudrillard 1983), Baudrillard goes beyond his account of reality, defined by the symbolic exchange of objects, to claim that we have entered a new era of simulation or hyperreality in which the scene and the mirror are replaced by the screen and a network. To understand what he means by this radical replacement we first need to understand what he means by the 'scene' and the 'mirror'. For Baudrillard, mirror and scene are both symbolic qualities of 'the object'. The object is what is external to or produced by the subject, the self, which corresponds to our intimate universe, our imaginary and symbolic world. In this equation we are 'the subject'. Buadrillard argued that the opposition between object and subject and private and public used to define our relationship in and to reality. Hence we expressed our mental or psychological reality through making objects which opened up the imaginary depths, the deeper scene of our life. In the world before simulation, Baudrillard argued, art and communication comprised the realm of symbolic expression of our inner life and offered the possibility of reflexive transcendence, or enlightenment.

Baudrillard opposes this reality of depth with one of surface and excess. Today's reality of the screen offers a non-reflecting surface, an immanent smooth operational surface of communication. For Baudrillard it is technology, above all else, which has brought about the situation in which simulation is dominant. He identifies three scientific and technological tendencies, which he sees as irreversibly driving social change; (i) the functionalisation and abstraction of all operations in homegenous processes; (ii) the displacement of bodily movements and efforts into electronic commands and (iii) the miniaturisation in time and space of knowledge and memory. Baudrillard notes that outcome of these changes has been a dramatic 'emptying out' of the meaning of our active lives, rendering everything that used to fill the symbolic scenes of our life useless. In particular, he observes the effect of simulation upon our bodies, the landscape and public and private space. Baudrillard argues therefore that in place of a world of active signs and signifiers in which objects deliver messages, we are left only, as Marshal McLuhan argued before him, with the medium. In the collapse of private and public space everything becomes visible, or, as Baudrillard puts it: 'Today there is a whole pornography of information and communication, that is to say, of circuits and networks, a pornography of all function and objects in their readability, their fluidity, their availability, their regulation, in their forced signification, in their performativity, in their branching, in their polyvalence, in their free expression' (Baudrillard 1996:131). Such tendencies were observed by others post-structuralists and postmodernists, who drew parallel conclusions to Baudrillard in seeing how post industrial societies were changing as a consequence of a complex of global economic and technological processes, of which the increasing and extensive use of computing had given rise to the information economy.

Baudrillard poses many important questions in his polemical argument, which wants to insist that we must now understand reality as simulation. Perhaps the most important part of his argument for digital media is whether he is right to say that signs no longer bear any relationship to reality because in simulation there are no equivalents for the real, simulation does not reproduce the real but reduplicates and generates it. In 'The Ecstasy of Communication', Baudrillard was deeply pessimistic about postmodern capitalist society. He was, for example, called a 'Left Dystopian', while other academics and intellectuals have criticised Baudrillard as an eclectic and contradictory thinker, who is himself more a reflection of postmodern confusion than an analyst of the phenomena (Kellner 1995). Other contemporary academics continue to find his work important in exploring the effects of globalisation and the experience of cyberspace (Morley and Robins 1995).

We now acknowledge, as a matter of historical fact, that television was a significant element in reshaping the experience of the family from the 1950s onwards and now the computer and the Internet are an equally important feature of the domestic environment. As much as television is an entertainment commodity, to be bought and sold, it is also a medium of significant regulation and control. Its presence in the home, as Baudrillard says, positions the viewer at the centre of a control screen. Although TV is dominant and pervasive, it is also not total. People can and do switch television off and do other things. Of course, Baudrillard would go on to argue that the world of 'other things' is now defined in relationship to the TV and computer screen image. The rapid growth of the convergence of media in domestic online services gives substance to Baudrillard's argument of the increasing tendency towards the dominance of code and the abstract organisation of all operations. You can work, shop and play in the 'virtual' world of cyberspace without leaving the computer station. In the workplace, in scientific laboratories, more and more functions are organised and controlled by the operational systems of computers. However, life is still lived in the real world, which as Sherry Turkle points out, is still far more interesting than life on the screen (Turkle 1995:263). The Internet also opens up many more possibilities of users becoming producers of their own communication as well as consumers of information. One of the early arguments for the non-regulation of the Internet was that it was essentially a democratic medium, which would foster new forms of community and association. Against this claim for new forms of cyber-democracy, is the recognition that large sections of the world's population have no access to the Internet and that most of those that do have access are already being given a fixed and limited form of access. Baudrillard would have little sympathy with those who argue for the productive democracy of the Internet, instead insisting that those with access only enter the world of simulation faster to become transfixed in the face of excessive and total information.

The idea of the *Society of the Spectacle*, developed by Guy Debord (1931–94) is worthy of brief mention in the conext of the intellectual framing of digital media. Debord's Debord's work was broadly within the Marxist tradition and concerned with what he saw as the growing importance of systems of representation and their substitution for older, more 'authentic' forms of social life. He was not alone in seeing social life as being invaded by mass commodity production, Adorno and Baudrillard had developed different but essentially similar narratives. Debord traced the development of advanced capitalism and the mass media, which he defined as creating the society of the spectacle in which commodities substitute for social life or that social life had been commodified. Debord was highly critical of this development in which relations between commodities overtook relations between humans. The importance of Debord's analysis for digital media comes with his recognition that, 'The spectacle is not a collection of images, rather it is a social relationship between people that is mediated by images' (Debord 1993:12). The idea of the society of the spectacle remains an important one and in terms of the increasing use of screens both publicly and privately clearly relates to the increase in image use and circulation.

AESTHETIC OF THE SURFACE

Although Baudrillard announces the death of the spectacle with the arrival of simulation, Darley applies Debord's critique of the society of the spectacle when considering the digital aesthetic. He draws our attention to the ways in which the entry of the digital into film, animation and television emphasise and plays-up form, style, surface, artifice, spectacle and sensation. He points to players surfing the image in video and computer games through immersive graphics. Darley sees such decorative effects as a dilution of meaning and encouraging intellectual quiescence. Digital media's surface without depth, leads Darley to say that current fascinations lie in ephemeral, superfluity of the image, rather than with the image's representation of anything (Darely 2000:6). The aesthetic of the digital is then to be considered as an extension of the aesthetics of decoration and ornamentation, focused upon delight and sensation of the surface and spectacle. In emphasising the superfluidity of the digital image we are brought back, via another route, to the characteristic of excess within the postmodern experience

JEAN-FRANÇOIS LYOTARD (1924-98)

Lyotard's book, *The Postmodern Condition: A Report on Knowledge* (1979) is another influential post-structuralist analysis that takes to task the ideas of the Enlightenment and Marxism, for perpetuating unsustainable 'grand narratives' or 'metanarratives' upon which the very idea of modernity rests, such as the idea of linear historical progress and encyclopedic knowledge for example. Lyotard argued that grand narratives contained in science and Enlightenment rationalism no longer had the capacity to explain what was observable and happening in an increasingly technological age, which he characterised as a plurality of perspectives and the essential diversity of human ideas and beliefs. Lyotard observed that technological

Table 23.1 Diagram contrasting the cultural and artistic modes of modernism and postmodernism according to binary opposites

Modernism	Postmodernism
purpose	play
design	chance
hierarchy	anarchy
distance	participation
presence	absence
centring	dispersal
selection	combination
root	rhizome
depth	surface
orgin	difference
cause	trace
determinacy	indeterminacy
transendence	immanence
Analogue	**Digital**

developments in computing and media were leading to a post industrial knowledge economy, based upon linguistic and symbolic production. Knowledge was now produced as a commodity and for specific functionality within technological systems. The result of these tendencies, Lyotard argued, left knowledge without any over-arching structural or historical purpose and therefore knowledge has become relativised, or, as he put it, knowledge has to be understood as a series of language-games. Certainty had been replaced by a plurality of partial interpretations. Lyotard argued for attention to be paid to the relationship between micro-narratives within which truth regimes and ethics reside. Again it is not hard to see how, in outline at least, Lyotard's ideas have an analytical bearing upon contemporary debates about the production of data and its circulation in networks and it is relevant to consider how his account of language-games could be applied to the logic of software for example. Some 30 years later, 'The Condition of Postmodernity: A Report on Knowledge' remains important for the insights it affords into the ways in which the Internet is driving towards personalisation, which might well be understood within the terms of both the commodification of knowledge as well as being accounted for a establishing a plethora of micro-narratives.

RHIZOMATIC CULTURE

A rhizome is a plant, whose growth depends upon a rooting structure, which has no single stem and central root, but instead, has a branching system of roots that connect nodal points, from which other roots and nodes develop. Rhizomatic plants can be likened to any structure that spreads by reproducing versions of itself, such as a networked computer. Gilles Deleuze (1925–95) and Felix Guattari (1930–92) use the concept of the rhizome as an analytic metaphor for an alternative way of thinking about intellectual, social and spatial structures, orders and power relations. Like other post-structuralist and postmodernist thinkers we have touched upon, Deleuze and Guattari were seeking a theory of knowledge (an epistemology), to account for and critique the persistence of hierarchical forms of human thought and action and develop an alternative model that would liberate thought from hierarchical and binary dependencies. Deleuze and Guattari enumerate a number of principles of the rhizome, the foremost of which are connection, heterogeneity and multiplicity. These are the characteristics of a rhizome, which they define as essentially a non-hierarchical distributed, branching system in which all of the nodes, or points, are connected to each other. Deleuze and Guattari contrast the self-consistent heterogeneous aggregate of elements that are connected together in a rhizome, with that of stratified organisations, which are composed of layers of homogeneous elements. The importance of this contrast between two forms of organisation and thought is that the rhizome can be considered as fluid and plane-oriented, whereas stratification is linear and point-oriented. As a metaphor for spatial or social relationships, striated space closes off a surface, defines intervals and subordinates the trajectory to the point, whereas in the rhizome, or, as they put it, in 'smooth space', the self consistent aggregate, points are subordinated to the trajectory which can be considered as open and distributed. Deleuze and Guattari applied the metaphor of the rhizome to culture in order to counter prevailing and dominant linear, chronological and vertical models of knowledge development, focused upon causalty and orgin, characteristic of Enlightenment science and philosophy. In contrast the rhizome has no beginning and no end, it works by a ceaseless reproduction of connections between nodes with no centre or point of origin. Deleuze and Guattari characterised rhizomatic culture as nomadic, liquid, endlessly spreading as a body in a non-hierarchical manner into new spaces. They defined such cultural movement as 'smooth space' in order to emphasise that human thought, art and science was in a perpetual state of becoming. Deleuze's own philosophical thought and his intellectual output was prolific and focused upon philosophic questions of identity and difference. He argued that difference and repitition were key to an understanding of things in themselves and that experience of time and space is produced by diffential relations.

If is not difficult to see the relevance of the rhizomatic system to an account of cyberspace and the network of networked computers. The Internet is a non-hierarchical and dispersed structure and traversing cyberspace can be likened to journeys or trajectories without beginning or end. Such metaphorically open travels in cyberspace can also be contrasted to closed and fixed boundaries of identities and positions in the economically and socially contingent space of the 'real' world.

Deleuze and Guattari used the term rhizome to characterise their own method of research and theorising, making the point that philosophical thinking could have non-herarchical and trans-lateral forms of knowledge. Like other post-structuralists they rejected conceptions of knowledge based upon binary choices, or dualist categories, and wanted instead to explore a new epistemology based upon difference. Deleuze and Guattari's work, theoretically difficult as it is, has been taken up because it offers the digital media practitioner and user a new model of connected human agency, and a radical theoretical means of potentially realising the free autonomous subject whose desires and impulses can be cognitively mapped into networked space. A serious difficulty with Deleuze and Guattari's account for digital media practitioners is its very abstractedness and its metaphysical approach from which practical knowledge and action have to be metaphorically inferred rather than being able to be grasped in any programmatic way. Because of the dense and complicated character of their writing there is a danger in simplifying and generalising its meaning, which this short account runs the risk of doing.

PSYCHOANALYSIS

In thinking about media in general and digital media in particular it would be impossible to leave out of the intellectual account the importance of the work of Freud (1856–1939). This is because the notion of the self has been central to the content of media and artistic communication. How an individual represents herself and her reality has, until relatively recently, relied upon the established notion of a stable autonomous self, the individual, who is both a sender and receiver of communicable experience. In Enlightenment thinking, founded upon the physical sciences, reality is an external, knowable entity, which the autonomous individual has direct knowledge of and within which she projects herself. Up until the end of the nineteenth century, science and philosophy had conceived of the rational and conscious human mind, while religion and theology maintained the concept of the human soul. The relationship of the individual to reality establishes the difference between subject and object, which confirms both the external reality and the coherent separate self.

Freud's radical contribution to the understanding of the human mind is based upon his elaboration of the concept of the unconscious. Prior to Freud, philosophy had equated the human mind with consciousness founded upon reason. Freud argued that only a small part of mental activity was conscious and that the unconscious consisted of inadmissible and involuntary ideas, which also motivate behaviour. Reason was no longer to be regarded as the given order of the mind, but had to be struggled for in an otherwise ungovernable and irrational unconscious. Because the unconscious is by definition not open to direct inspection by the mind itself, its content and structure has to be inferred. Freud developed a theory of the unconscious based upon his treatment of neurosis and his analysis of the content of dreams. Freud argued that the unconscious is made up of impulses, desires or wishes, which get their energy from the primary physical instincts, of which sexuality was primary.

THE UNCONSCIOUS AND REPRESENTATION

Psychoanalytical concepts have been influential in the analysis of representation because they address the subject and the self. Psychoanalysis applied to art and cultural studies opened up the possibility that representation operated at the level of unconscious as well as consciousness both in its content and reception. Such a perspective led to an understanding that seeking satisfaction to unconscious pleasures could not be excluded from the account of representation. Freud's account of the unconscious is based upon his theory of polymorphous perverse infantile sexuality and the subsequent repression of unacceptable sexual wishes. Repression of unacceptable wishes leads to feelings of guilt, loss and anxiety, which become visible in clinical neurosis. Freud's sexual theory was also based upon the symbolic primacy of the male phallus, which structured sexual identity. The subordinated place of female sexuality in the symbolic order was criticised by feminist intellectuals but also used to analyse how patriarchy structured the sexual power of looking. This was famously applied in the analysis of Hollywood cinema by Laura Mulvey who used Freud's theory to demonstrate how men and women appear in cinema and how they are 'unconsciously' structured by 'the male gaze'.

Post-structuralist authors all present different critiques of structuralism, but common themes include the rejection of the self-sufficiency of the structures that structuralism posits and an interrogation of binary opposites that constitute those structures (Mulvey 1975). Writers whose work is often characterised as post-structuralist include Jacques Lacan (1901–81) Judith Butler (b. 1956) and Julia Kristeva (b. 1941)

The application of psychoanalytic ideas to digital media focuses upon three mains ideas. First, how the unconscious operates to position the fragmented subject/ user in cyberspace, second, on the fusion of human and machine in the creation of the cyborg and third, the projection of unconscious wishes into technology in the technological imaginary. These ideas continue to draw upon the psychoanalytic tradition in the projection of unconscious desires, arising from various forms of our misrecognition are projected into technology. The importance of the symbolic and the imaginary in psychoanalysis was developed by Jacques Lacan (1901–81) who applied a structural linguistic analysis to the elements and operations of the unconscious arguing that wishes, and desires form a symbolic signifying chain. Lacan's post-structuralist reworking of Freud included what he called a 'mirror phase' in which the infant child identifies itself with an image outside of itself and in the process, mis-recognises itself, creating the idea of 'the other'. Lacan calls the mirror stage the realm of the imaginary, which is a prelinguistic realm of images, whether conscious or unconscious, based in visual perception, or what Lacan calls specular imaging. Lacan's idea of the incomplete and fragmented self generated by the misrecognition that takes place through the image of 'the other' as self in the imaginary can also be applied to technology, in a way that gives technology the power of creating a realm of wholeness. Cyberspace and the Internet have been conceived as potentially spaces for the creation of new identities and freedoms (Blackman 1998, Turkle 1995). Technology is also thought capable of extending and changing the nature of consciousness and the body, as we explore further on.

THE PRACTICES OF EVERYDAY LIFE

Michel De Certeau (1925–86) built upon the work of Pierre Bourdieu (1930–2001) to define culture not as a collection of texts, artefacts and fixed structures, but as a set of practices. Culture as practice emphasised the process and operations that each of us perform on text like structures. de Certeau shifted our attention from representations in their own right to ways in which representations are used and consumed. Representation here is taken to mean anything from a newspaper to the street layout of the city. How we negotiate our encounter with representational space, media and institutional representations, all thought of in the structuralist and semiological sense as texts to be read, constitutes the practices of everyday life. The practices of everyday life are, according to de Certeau, not simply our conditioned responses to a given order of things, but acts of creative rebellion. Consumption is not a passive act, but a two-way process of resistance, through which the consumer can gain a temporary reversal of the flow of power. The idea that each one of us, in our everyday life, in work, in leisure, in consumption, practices a set of complex tactics through which we assert power can be applied to the new practices of online communication and the strategic power of representational space can be tactically disrupted by the user/consumer. The group Tactical Media make direct use of de Certeau's work in defining the tactical (digital media) practitioner, who they argue, can 'take us beyond the rigid dichotomies that have restricted thinking in this area for so long, dichotomies such as amateur vs professional, alternative vs mainstream, and even private vs public' (de Certeau 1988:53).

ACTOR NETWORK THEORY

Actor Network Theory has also been co-opted as a procedural way of understanding the relationship between humans, systems and machines in computer networked communications. Actor Network Theory (ANT) originated in the social sciences in studies of scientific and technological practices and networks and is most associated with the work of Bruno Latour. Latour argues that the notion of a fixed objectivity in social science is no longer tenable because it is part of the very things, 'technoscience' that it seeks to study. Instead he develops a relativist sociology in which the viewpoints of all the participants, including the scientist/observer at best form a metalanguage through which a viewpoint can be expressed. The impact of Latour's work upon digital media lies not only in its rejection of an 'objectivistic' science paradigm, but in the methodology he proposed to replace it. Latour defines both human and non-human elements and structures in the environment as actors who can makes other elements dependent upon themselves. Actors have interests that can come into alignment with other actors' interests to form an actor-network. Both humans and non-humans may be 'actants' in a network made up of social groups, entities, and artefacts who then become enlisted to reinforce a position within a network. ANT thus reverses our normal thinking about science and technology and nature and society, ANT argues that nature and society are consequences, not causes of human scientific and technical work. The inter-actions of people and machines should be understood as a continuous chain of 'translations' or 'recruitments' into their own languages and values and that in a successful chain technology becomes transparent and is taken for granted. The more a technological project progresses, the more the role of technology decreases, in relative terms (Latour 2007).

Marx and Freud created a theoretical legacy that has dominated post-war European thinking about individual experience and collective life, 'whole ways of life', and how they are structured by forms of economic and political power and the unconscious. The central endeavour of structuralism, semiology and post-structuralism, culminating in the various writings grouped around the idea of postmodernism, has been to give an adequate account of the structure, organisation and mechanisms by and through which individual consciousness and communication takes place within a given historical order. The effort within this intellectual project has been, overwhelmingly, to understand the unequal relationship(s) individuals and groups have to power and one of the central threads of this work has been the articulation of the structuring and organising power of difference in seeing 'the other'. The importance of these theoretical traditions to an understanding of digital media practice cannot be underestimated because we cannot detach the question of (differential) power relations, from how power, in all its forms, is communicated and mediated, and with what representational outcomes. Media and cultural symbolic forms and their technological apparatuses are deeply bound up with the articulation as well as disarticulation of power, media forms are in a sense the agents of power and hence an individual's relationship to media is also a relationship within the articulation of power relations.

In practice 'media power relations' means many things, from the direct question of who has material access to the production and reception of media, which is, as we know, highly differential in the digital divide, through to the more indirect ways in which power relations are embodied in any media form and with what representational outcomes in media artefacts. The question of whether digital media constitutes a new cultural form or paradigm, also contains the question of what power relations are structured in and by that form. We only have to look at the cultural politics of the Internet and its cultural forms of the WWW in such writers as Howard Rheingold, Manuel Castells, Gert Lovink, Jodi Dean and Tiziana Teranova and many others, to see that the Internet is a 'contested arena' and a 'site of struggle' in which individuals, groups and institutions engage unequally, not only in competition for specific voices, to get their message out there, but compete for the very definition and regulation of what cyberspace, more practically, online communication is and should be.

BRITISH CULTURAL STUDIES

Between the nineteenth-century tradition of thinking about culture and society as vertical hierarchies and recent contemporary thinking about culture and production as horizontal and networked, the concept of culture as 'a whole way of life' has had a significant impact and parallels the networked idea of culture as a collective. The concept of culture as a whole way of life is a complex one, because it now begs the question of whose culture, and the idea has been the subject of criticism in post-colonialist writings as potentially mono-cultural, nationalistic and eurocentric. Culture as 'a whole way of life' was also eclipsed by the postmodernist emphasis upon fragmentation and the rejection of any attempt to define a unified homogeneous culture and society. But the thinking of Raymond Williams, whose work does most to elaborate the idea of culture as a whole way of life, still contains several useful and pertinent concepts for the analysis of cultural change, and hence is relevant to the current moment of digital media, which we examine below.

The lineage of the idea of culture as a whole way of life is sketched by Stuart Hall following the seminal work of Raymond Williams in which Williams outlined the historical etymology of both culture and society. 'Culture', according to Hall is one of the most difficult concepts in the human and social sciences to define. In most cultural studies accounts of culture the modern point of departure is the definition of culture offered by Mathew Arnold as, 'the best that has been thought and said' in a society. Here the idea of culture is that of the summation of the greatest ideas represented in classic works of literature, painting, music and philosophy. Williams moved to define culture as 'a whole way of life', or as refined by Hall 'whatever is distinctive about a way of life' (1997:2). Academic work in the social and human sciences from the mid 1970s in Europe, North America and Australia, moved to what Hall called the 'cultural turn, in which the very idea and work of culture became more central in accounts of human social production and reproduction. Culture became not a debate about what should or shouldn't be included in the cultural list of hallowed objects, artefacts and works – that is, should we include Bob Dylan's songs as great works of an age, or 'Super Mario' for that matter, but rather culture was grasped as a process, a set of practices. Here culture becomes identified with the processes by and through which people produce and exchange meanings.

In Hall's account he goes on to say that culture is 'what distinguishes the 'human' element in social life from what is simply biologically driven'. Culture here underscores and includes the symbolic domain of social life. Culture is participation in the construction and reproduction of meaning in all its forms.

In helping students grasp a model of culture as the communication of meaning within a whole way of life, the Open University Popular Culture, Course Team, led by Stuart Hall, represented culture as a circuit (du Gay *et al.* 1997:1) This diagrammatic model was used to indicate the whole social process by which meaning is achieved. It was used in the practical analysis of the Sony Walkman (du Gay *et al.* 1997). In their different ways these practical and analytical accounts extend the thinking of Raymond Williams, who discussed the history of the idea of culture in terms of three definitions; the ideal, in which culture is the process of human perfection or universal values; the documentary, where culture is the body of intellectual and imaginative work; and, the social, in which culture is the description of a particular way of life. While Williams and his subsequent followers developed the later model, He also said that all three definitions of culture continued to operate and should not be considered mutually exclusive. In dealing with the problem of these three different ways of regarding culture Williams identified two operational levels of culture, the lived culture of time and place and the recorded culture as represented in language and artefacts. These two operational levels are actively connected by, (a) the operation of a selective tradition, which at any one time defined what was worked upon and included within the documentary level and, (b) a structure of feeling, in which the lived culture operated upon and was reflected by the documentary.

But to account for digital media within Williams's model of a lived culture and a structure of feeling presents theoretical as well as practical problems. Williams was writing significantly before the network of networked computers had started to develop. Williams was writing in and about a culture in which the organisation of media was highly centralised, something he analysed in detail in account of

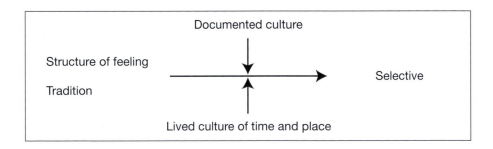

FIGURE 23.1
Schematic of Raymond Williams's distinction between received and lived culture, made in order to demonstrate how everyday life affects cultural change

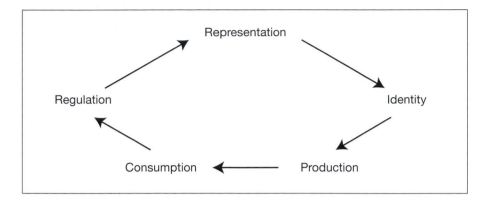

FIGURE 23.2
Schematic of Stuart Hall's 'circuit of culture', showing how representation is a complex social process

television (Williams 1974). Williams was also of a generation of intellectuals who were struggling to account for change within a class society based on an unequal distribution of power, while retaining the importance of the idea of a common and shared culture, deeply rooted in community and settled ways of life. This project of accounting for continuity as well as breaks in cultural and media communication still has agency in the discussion of digital media and remains the legacy of Williams in the British cultural studies tradition (Lister, 2003:85).

CREATIVITY AND DIGITAL MEDIA

Williams's tracing of the European tradition of thinking about art and creativity remains an important, yet overlooked, framework for considering digital media, precisely because digital media practices re-engage the central debates about the relationship between culture and nature, humans and machines and art and reality. The development of computers and networks has refocused attention upon whether we should understand our use of machines as an extension of the human body through new powers of sensory perception, remote operation and modes of thought. In itself this is not a new idea as we have seen, and in one general sense all tools can be considered as extensions of the body. The point of departure for digital media lies in the claim that computational power calls forth and demands a radically new kind of creative paradigm, one that requires us to break with the aesthetic aims and representational interests of previous media forms. Allied to the idea of a new creative paradigm for a digital media are a related set of positions, which posit that we have already reached a stage in our relationship with computers, their networks and interfaces in which the human mind and imagination can be liberated from the constraints placed upon it by the modes of previous expressive and communicative media (Minsky 1986). We need to be able to follow the argument for a paradigm shift in order to understand better what is actually being achieved across a range of digital media practices and how different practitioners formulate and understand their own aims.

William's account of the creative mind, starts by pointing out how our modern use of the terms creativity and imagination can be traced back to Renaissance thinking where there was a renewed interest in the work of Plato and Aristotle who both employed the idea of imitation (mimesis), although in different ways, to define the function of art. For Plato art (imitation or appearances) was a means to the expression of The Divine Idea, whereas for Aristotle, art (imitation) was a means of revealing what was universal.

Williams schematises four competing and overlapping models of art, which were operating from the Renaissance, and which continued partially into the modern period. These, he said were, art as the revelation of a hidden reality, art as the perpetual imitation and embodiment of the idea of beauty, art as the idealisation of nature and art as a form of human energy which vies with nature. It is the later definition, Williams argues, that became the basis of the Romantic view of art from late eighteenth century and which continued into the modern view of the artist argues that imaginative activity is uniquely human and not part of nature.

Williams was very good as providing synoptic overviews of highly abstract histories of ideas. In the following we have put his scheme in a diagrammatic form to show how he summarised the theoretical shift from classical to modernist conceptions of the relationship between art and reality. We have added the final section in order update and extend the debate, which we don't know whether he would have approved.

Williams refines his schema when considering the modern period. Here he says that art does one of three things, it is either a reflection of reality, a representation of a superior reality or an organisation and synthesis of reality. The realist discourse embraced art as a reflection, while the Romantic and idealists considered art as a superior reality. The idea of art as the organisation and synthesis of reality was distinctly modernist in tendency and, as Williams points out, was able to embrace the psychological models of Freud and Jung in seeing the artist as the emotional explorer in contrast to the scientist as the rational explorer. Like many other critics and commentators of the day Williams's accepts, although wants to move beyond, a classification of twentieth-century artistic activity in terms of nominalist categories. The conventional account of the modernist aesthetic establishes three categories, of human imaginative exploration; representational objectivity; emotional subjectivity and formal abstraction.

The major shift in Williams's own thinking about creativity in 'The Creative Mind' chapter (1961:19) comes with his attempt to move beyond the dualism, or binaries, inherent in the traditions of thinking about art, artists and creativity. He does this

Table 23.2 Section 1–3, shows Raymond Williams's (1965) schema elaborated in defining the role of artistic creativity in relationship to everyday life. Section 4 represents our addition

Platonist		
Man	natural seeing	appearances
Artist	exceptional seeing	reality
Romantic		
Man	natural seeing	reality
Artist	exceptional seeing	superior reality
Modernist		
Man	natural seeing	reality
Artist	exceptional seeing	art
Postmodernist [our addition]		
Man	constructed seeing	simulation/information
Artist	deconstructed seeing	art/knowledge

Source: Williams's scheme with our additions

by turning to the biological science of his day. He looked to the developing fields of the psychology of perception and the biology of the human brain for under-standings about how seeing, or more abstractly, perception, worked. Using the work of J. Z. Young and Russell Brain, Williams developed a model of creativity in which he was able to reject the human subject vs natural object, dichotomy by recognising that seeing, or sense perception, was an active process of interpretation in which each individual has to learn to see. For Williams, this was a fundamentally new starting point in thinking about art and reality as it allowed him to place creativity as an essential and necessary means by which every individual interprets the world, arguing that 'there is no reality experienced by humans into which our own observation and interpretations do not enter'. Experience and understanding of the external world has to be grasped as a continual process of learning and relearning in 'a whole process of social learning'. Williams seeks a unity of purpose between art and science, both, he argues are inextricably linked parts of a general human process of creative discovery and communication. In his model of the process, 'consciousness is part of the reality and the reality is part of the consciousness'. This is of course a highly abstract formulation of human creativity and Williams goes on to attempt to detail the process. For our purposes the most important part of the account considers how the creative process, in a period of rapid social change and disturbance requires us to construct new rules of communication, new languages or forms in order to grasp new experience.

Artists new language initial resistance eventual acceptance

Artists new language initial acceptance continued acceptance

Artists new language initial acceptance eventual rejection

Artists new language initial resistance eventual rejection

Art is an intense form of general communication and can quite literally lead to an enlargement of vision and an extension of our ways of seeing the world. But art not only serves the frontiers of knowledge but also encompasses that which is known and familiar. Williams sums up this profoundly social definition of the creative process in the following way. 'To succeed in art is to convey an experience to others in such a form that the experience is actively re-created, not contemplated not examined not passively received, but by response to the means, actually lived through, by those to whom it is offered' (Williams 1971:51).

DIGITAL MEDIA'S CULTURAL LOCATION

Given the short history of digital media practices we would reasonably expect its account to be at the level of 'the lived culture of time and place', with much less emphasis placed upon a documented culture. However, there is evidence of an increasing interest in the documentation and archiving of digital media artefacts, objects and products and there is a growing body of academic literature involved in defining histories, genealogies, and a canon. In Williams's model we would characterise attempts to define a digital media canon as the shaping of a future 'selective tradition'. As yet the archiving and evaluation of digital media is relative uncharted, although it is clear that some major art institutions, the Whitney and Tate Modern are beginning to assemble a selective canon, and the histories of digital media emanating from the Massachusetts Institute Press are also a construction of a selective tradition. In our terms a more important task in 'the lived culture' involves engaging with and looking at what people are actually doing with and in relationship to digital media. Digital media as art, as part of wage labour and as entertainment is not even the life span of one generation and there is little that we know in detail of its effects and affects upon perception, lifestyle and communication. This heterogeneity of experience does need to be described if we are to begin to have a substantial account of the lived culture of digital media. There is an argument here for case studies, descriptions and phenomenological accounts to be carried out in order to build a larger picture of what the practice of digital media amounts to. This is in effect is the argument for organising this book around case studies.

THE POLITICAL DEVELOPMENT OF THE IDEA
OF CULTURAL INDUSTRIES IN THE UK

The emergence of the 'cultural industries' since the 1990s can also be understood as a reflection of an economy based upon consumption and information. The cultural industries include many cultural activities and social occupations that would not previously have been thought of together. At the conceptual level the cultural industries now encompass everything from opera to online shopping, even though at the practical level they are still reproduced through different institutions. The key linguistic attribute of this new definition of a cultural industry, or more accurately, a collection of industries, revolves around a recent formation of ideas about 'creativity' and 'culture'. In the United Kingdom during the 1980s, the Greater London Council (GLC) developed cultural policies, which connected creative and economic activity in a new way. The GLC argument was distinct from the discourse that arose within industrial capitalism, and is still residually present, that economic activity guaranteed work and prosperity while culture was non-profitable and relied upon the support of the industrial and economic wealth makers. A society that regarded industry as the necessary economic base and culture as the contingent super-structure can now be seen clearly as belonging to an earlier period of capitalist organisation. In the wealthy countries of the globalised economy it is consumption that leads production and in a market of over-abundance there is no longer a hierarchy of needs, which in turn erodes distinctions between fashion, art and all other needs. GLC cultural policy reflected the erosion of structural difference between elite and popular culture at an institutional and political level by funding a wider range of contemporary and community activity previously considered to be outside of the remit of serious culture. The current concept of the cultural industries does contain two competing ideas of creativity, on the one hand creativity is a necessary condition of a culture of consumption, in which creativity has become a feature of commodification, and on the other hand creativity is seen as central to a culture based upon the free reign of human agency. The extension of these arguments can be recognised in a variety of ways within digital media practice, either as a continued challenge to settled, linear notions of nation, community and identity and to established notions of the institutional location of culture, or as opening up and driving new cultures of diverse production and consumption.

CHAPTER 24

A framework for digital media

A FRAMEWORK FOR CONSIDERING DIGITAL MEDIA IN CONTEMPORARY CULTURE

How in detail do these discussions regarding the cultural contexts and politics of digital media relate to practice? In what follows we discuss three ways in which we think digital media practices engage with as well as contribute to our current understanding of wider contemporary cultures. First, we discuss digital media as an extension of existing media forms and institutions in which we account for digital media as the result of the application of digital technologies to existing media practices. Here digital media is, as might be expected, thought of as a continuous extension of, rather than a radical break with, the current landscape of media culture. Second, we discuss digital media as it has been taken up and framed by the institutions of contemporary artistic cultures as a medium. This we assert, has become largely a matter of the way in which digital media is argued as the latest extension of the European modernist avant-garde in which the formal properties of a medium are prioritised over its conventional uses. Third, and much more speculatively, we discuss some of the ways in which digital media, now in its widest sense as the world of information and data, has been seen as challenging fundamental notions of thought and human nature. We have defined these three areas of discussion as follows and will look at each one in turn:

A   Digital media as a continuous extension of existing media culture in which the rules of representation are maintained.

B   Digital media as an avant-garde looking towards art institutions in which the rules of representation are playfully broken.

C   Digital media thought of as provoking a crisis in culture in which the rules of representation are abandoned in favour of the logic of the system.

A. DIGITAL MEDIA AS A CONTINUOUS EXTENSION OF EXISTING MEDIA CULTURE AND THE RULES OF REPRESENTATION

> The reassuring smell and touch of book pages, the anticipatory crackle of opening a new music CD, the cosy comfort of surrendering oneself to broadcast television's scheduling, the magical darkness of an audience watching a cinema, the warm community feeling of listening to radio – these aesthetics of media might now be forgotten. And the politics that accompanies them – the liberal, autonomous individual of print and film, the pacified consumer of broadcast media – might also now gradually dissipate with the advent of digital media, with their different aesthetics and politics.
>
> (Poster 2006).

Within this redolent image of our familiar media one can already detect a compression of different cultural periods. The warm community feeling of listening to the radio is perhaps a nostalgic reference to the use of radio during the Second World War, when it so successfully bonded people and state against the threat of the Third Reich and later during the reconstruction of the 1950s, before television was established. The experience of surrendering to scheduled TV from the limited number of broadcast channels is already an older experience that has been mixed with video, satellite and cable channels for at least two decades. Both of these cultural forms have been seen, in their turn, to dissipate, or change a previous set of cultural habits and responses. The book was thought defunct with the advent of mass television and video was championed as the end of cinema. In 2002 Poster gently posited the question of whether we were on the brink of witnessing a wholesale disappearance of the familiar landscape of media. In doing so he reflects upon the character of individual aesthetic response, at a particular historical moment of change, to the material and cultural mediums which make up the media-sphere. The 'magic' of cinema is still to be found in its unique combination of technical and cultural development. First, the aesthetic of cinema lies in the technical apparatus for projecting light through the exposed frames of film, to create the illusion of depth and movement on a flat screen. Second, the aesthetic of cinema lies in the development of narrative film story-telling through editing techniques. Finally, the aesthetic of cinema lies in the social organisation of entertainment in which large groups of people, who previously may have attended dance halls, music halls, or theatres, sit together in the dark, entranced by the silver screen. The aesthetic experience of cinema has taken over 100 years to develop to its present day form of the widescreen, 3-D, Dolby surround sound multiplex entertainment complex and film projection in major cinema chains is now giving way to digital projection. The same is true of television broadcasting, which started with the limited scheduling of live programmes, received with dubious picture quality on the original 9-inch black and white domestic receiver, but which is now increasingly viewed as a download on a computer. Technically the mediums of film and television have continued to develop along the cultural lines of greater verisimilitude or visual and auditory plenitude to the point where our domestic living rooms can be turned into a home cinema or concert hall, with large HD flat screens.

It is upon this contemporary landscape, in which the cultural forms of television and film continue, that we can clearly see how digital technology is continuous with those forms, although changing the ways in which they are produced and received. Digital technologies have been entailed in newspaper, film, television, radio and music production for at least 25 years and we can already experience some of their characteristic effects. At one level the engagement of digital technologies with existing media remains, 'behind the scene' as it were. The broadcasting of *The Archers* or any other longstanding radio drama on a digital signal will not alter the familiar cast of characters or the storylines, but technically, digital radio will allow a listener who missed the beginning of a programme to 'replay' that section and 'catch-up' again during the broadcast and of course that is only the beginning of the possibilities for digital reception and storage. But the point being made here is that at the level of the technical transmission, relay and reception of media, digital technologies enmesh with analogue counterparts to deliver the same content. But, as with our example of digital radio, this is only true up to a point, because it is, as we have previously discussed, the common technical code of the digital that allows for new ways of receiving, storing and copying material, which have as yet, to develop new patterns and cultural habits. Do we care that photographs in newspapers have been digitally manipulated before their conversion back to the analogue ink on the half-tone printers plates, or that books have been word-processed and laid-out on a computer screen, or that a favourite piece of music has been digitally remastered.

Such examples demonstrate that digital technologies and computing have been introduced into existing media forms in a process which is continuous with other historical developments. Of course people do care when it occasionally comes to light that digital code has been responsible for an unacknowledged alteration to some aspect of an analogue original, which they can't themselves detect. But such examples as there have been of digital skulduggery noticably in the press, have remained a marginal social concern and it is largely assumed that it is business as usual in media production houses, with editors exercising judgement and control.

In other areas of existing media, particularly in advertising, television, film animation and music production the digital has had obvious and dramatic effects upon the style and conventions of content. It is precisely in advertising that digital manipulation is most aesthetically visible in style though paradoxically achieved through the manipulation of invisible pixels. If digital manipulation has been disapproved of in one category of photographic imagery considered factual or documentary, it has been applauded for creating the seemingly 'impossible' illusions in photographic and film imagery, which are classified as fictional, fanciful or fantastic. The invisibility of the digital in one cultural register of 'information', in press and news coverage for example, is as culturally conventional as the visibility of the invisible in another, in advertising, in art or domestic photography. This acceptance of the digital simulating different photographic types, or genres, is nevertheless an extension of an existing cultural dualism, which has differentiated the genres of analogue photography over the past 150 years.

As with digital photography audiences have come to recognise and appreciate a particular digital aesthetic in film production, achieved 'behind the scenes' through the operations of technical compositing, rendering and editing. However, today's extraordinary special effects, widely applauded in mainstream cinema, build directly upon the traditions of analogue post-production techniques stretching back to the earliest film animation experiments of George Melies (1864–1903). Since the widespread use of three-dimensional mapping and rendering software in post production audiences have quickly come to expect film to be able to create credible and 'realistic' scenes of anything humanly imaginable, however fantastic. Our pleasure and delight in 'slight-of-hand' and convincing illusion also has a prehistory in painting, architecture, fairgrounds and the circus.

Much has been made of the radical change represented by the digital simulation of the photographic and film image. (Shaviro 2010, Barker 2013). The digital image was discussed in terms of whether it fundamentally changed the relationship the photographic image has to its referent in the real world. The digital replaces the material, continuous link between the light reflected from objects and the latent image formed by the camera and fixed by chemical action with electronic sampling registered by binary code. Much of the early discussion of the radicalness of the digital image was couched in terms of undermining photographic truth, but, as we have noted above and elsewhere, analogue photography also relied upon a constructed cultural rhetoric to establish veracity and meaning (Lister 1995, Mitchell 1998). Recent attention has been paid to the convergence of the graphic and photographic in the digital image, recognising that digital code processes the sampling of light through the lens of a camera in the same way as it does the sampling of any other visual source and hence essentially gives the same values to both. (Betancourt 2013). The merging of photography with graphics and film with animation, where the same principle applies, is a fruitful way of identifying the visual aspect of a digital aesthetic. However, when we marvel at the combination of epic scale fantasy with photo-realistic effects in many recent films, *The Hobbit: An Unexpected Journey* (Jackson 2002) or the *The Life of Pi* (Lee 2012) for example we are experiencing the established pleasure of narrative cinema of which the digital effects are part.

Because the digital simulates its analogue source it is not possible to easily distinguish, or separate, the aesthetic of digital compositing from the analogue effects of light and shadow and consequentially the experience of viewing is more one of recognising what the digital makes possible within the conventions of analogue media, ie, the special as opposed to normal, or ordinary effect. Audiences recognise and measure the scale of difference of the effect made possible by the digital, from those they have come to expect, or register as previously analogue. The measure of such changes in effect, will be tempered by the different ages of the audiences and their familiarity with film and with digital technology. But the ability of the audience to be 'taken-in' by a digital rendering of a photo-realistic effect while recognising it as an effect is a contradiction in the filmic experience, or a binary characteristic of digital media, which is extensively discussed by Bolter and Gruisin in their account of remediation (Bolter and Gruisin 1999). Bolter and Gruisin argue, as we discussed elsewhere, that remediation represents the competing interests in our attention to both immediacy – that is, to be immersed in the digital film effect and not notice how it is achieved, as well as what they call hypermediacy, which is the opposite fascination in precisely noticing how an effect is achieved and sustained. In our sustained interest in immediacy and hypermediacy in media, we often switch between the two modes within media experiences, which could be said to be two kinds of attention to detail. In media where the visibility of the means, would detract from our immediate pleasure of suspended disbelief, in which we are immersed in the moment by moment detail of the world/reality/story, we have to diminish, but cannot completely eradicate, our attention to the details of construction. At moments of obvious (special) effects, or, alternatively where the illusion fails to hold us 'in suspension', then our attention to the detail of construction comes to the fore.

It could, therefore, be said that the mode of attention to all media is one of an 'oscillation' between the detailed effect of transparency and that of technical mediation. It is in the detail of these two alternating modes that we can begin to distinguish a specifically digital set of effects and it is a collection of such digital effects that have been generalised as a digital aesthetic. What has been most often noticed in cultural forms, which have adapted to or are based upon digital technologies, photography, music, film, games and the Internet, are a number of common and characteristic responses to the way digital code changes, or simulates a previous analogue register. Our attention in such moments is, interestingly enough, upon noticing differences in technical effects while looking for bigger patterns and structures to form the linguistic syntax of the overall mediation. The digital image, sound and/or text, on a computer, television or projected screen is sill experienced as an analogue flow that is digitally simulated. This flow can be algorithmically programmed to be at the speed of speech and the persistence of vision, or, static, or anywhere either side of those two states. At many points the digital is a straightforward simulation of the effects of analogue recording, but at other points it is noticeably different from them and is therefore a registered digital effect. Such digital effects have been defined, often in opposition to the analogue, as the replacement of the analogue unilinear and continuous surface by one that is modular and variable. The digital aesthetic is most often defined against the analogue, while in existing cultural forms it is continuously entailed within them.

Television has been changed by the application of digital technologies, which have had powerful effects upon production, programming, scheduling, transmission and domestic reception. The introduction of graphic and animation software has changed the design of what we see on screen. The computer has interposed itself between the screen of the television camera and the screen of the television receiver so that we can no longer think of the two in a directly connected way in time, space, or place. Of course, the introduction of video recording in television changed any original historical notion of real-time correspondence in television broadcasting, so that 'live' coverage has become a convention. However, the control of onscreen material by a computer is, in part, an extension of the previous analogue practice of inserting pre-recorded video sequences into real time studio broadcast. But the digital computer, as the compositing and editorial control centre of televisual sequences, has made the space of the television screen closer to the multilayer, simulated screen of the computer screen itself. The effects operating within the rectangular frame of the domestic television screen already incorporate computer generated 3-D studio sets for news and current affairs programmes, studio sets that include teleconferencing and multiscreen displays, the mixing of live and recorded animation sequences and the inclusion of subtitling and running text.

In these ways the television screen is partially mirroring the windowed multi-application screen of the computer. What the broadcast, cable and satellite television screen can only do in a limited way at present is to allow the viewer to act back, or interact with the material. Currently the digital signal allows those who can receive it to have a number of limited options within programmes. But the speed of the convergence of the television and computer is, as we have discussed previously, a matter of resolving competing commercial interests in media ownership as much as it is of technical application at this point in time. The convergence of the networked PC and domestic television reception is a complex example of remediation in which, at one level, the content of television, largely news and entertainment, remains culturally continuous, but delivered and received through digital technologies, while at another, the content of television, both discrete programmes and flows, is being reconfigured by the computer.

Television is characteristically a 'lean-back' media while the computer and Internet is a 'lean-forward' media. As a way of characterising the typical difference between the viewer of television and the user of the computer lean-back and lean-forward is a highly successful contrast and conveys the dominant way in which the viewer or user is 'positioned' or, structured, by particular media. Lean-back carries that sense of passivity involved in a common cultural habit of watching television, while lean-forward accurately indicates a work ethic associated with using a computer. We have discussed elsewhere the suggestion that television is distant and passive, while the networked PC is close and (inter)active and recognised that this is a much overused simplification for the types of response to both media. But what the contrast between lean-back and lean-forward media does is to remind us, not only of what is significantly different between television and computing, but what they have in common. While our bodily posture may be typically different, we can also recognise television's undoubted ability to sustain attention and involvement – that is, we are clearly interacting mentally, as well as recognising the distracted state of being in front of a computer. Both are screen media that deliver overlapping content but in different ways. Indeed many of the uses of the Internet are highly conventional, such as shopping, corresponding, and a general repurposing of much of existing media content. This is what has led some commentators to say that the Internet is continuous with previous cultural forms as well noticing the persistent force of 'old media' (Curran *et al.* 2012). As we have said the Internet is closely bound up with existing media because existing broadcast and print media have developed closely associated ancillary websites and realised the value of marketing within social media. In this respect the Internet is rapidly reflecting the dominance of major media producers and distributors, The most visited website in the UK is the BBC Online for example.

The earlier arguments of Sherry Turkle and Howard Rheingold and others, writing in the 1990s about the radical, subversive or liberationist possibilities of cyberspace, stand in stark contrast to the Internet and WWW today, which is structured along highly commercial and conventional lines of commodity consumption and private communication. In her recent book, *Alone Together* (Turkle 2013) revises her earlier view of a complementary relationship between life on and off screen and now argues that increasing time spent online is socially regressive. This is a very good example of how existing media forms, news and feature journalism, advertising, broadcasting and the retail and service industries, have 'acted-back' upon, or 'colonised' the potential of a digital medium to create new cultural forms and shaped cyberspace along familiar lines of the one–to-many forms of communication. The recognition that the WWW has recently developed along dominant corporate and commercial lines should not blind us to the many ways in which, as a medium, it has extended and built upon private and personal forms of communication and exchange. There are new kinds of exposure between the use of the open and non-hierarchical network and mainstream media, such as journalists pick-up on personal Webloggs, the 'Bagdad Blogger', for example, as a source of information and as the network is used for social campaigning. Such examples, while framed within the conventional structure of news journalism or democratic politics, are examples of the Internet's potential for greater access to a much wider range of people to produce media on the web. In this description of the Internet and cyberspace, digital media is clearly developing in a close and continuous relationship to existing cultural forms of communication in which the media languages are modified and extended, rather than radical transposed. Against this description of converged media as familiar and continuous we need to bear in mind that the common practice characteristic of social media are increasingly shaped and controlled by a few large corporations, with it is argued a limiting of the possibilities for independent public thought and action (Dean 2010, Lovink 2012).

The rules of representation

Looked at as a continuation of existing media forms, digital media has been analysed through established traditions of thinking and analysis in terms of ownership and control of the means of communication and what values get reproduced. Up until the present moment studies of media have focused upon how things in the world become represented. Attention has been paid to the forms in which media (technology plus cultural language) mediates between an external reality, society, nature, culture, and the position and interests of individuals and groups within and towards that reality who either make or receive media messages. This way of thinking is concerned with what view of reality is contained in media representations and how any given representation constructs views of reality. While it has long been argued that media has a problematic relationship to the real and that we should recognise the arbitrary nature of the rules, codes and conventions through which the real is constructed in media, the basic analytical model continues to distinguish between the representations of reality constructed by media and an external reality. This model can be defined as the representational paradigm and can focus upon either the rules of media construction by which reality is mediated, or upon the subsequent effects or outcomes of media representations in the social world. The representational paradigm applied to digital media objects and practices would therefore account for particular meanings, effects and outcomes within the established rules of representation, as they are practised and articulated at various levels in the cycle of culture (Hall 1997). While recognising that there are problems for the representational paradigm applied to the network, it has to be acknowledged that representational paradigm remains strongly embedded in media studies and used to look at digital media objects.

B. DIGITAL MEDIA, THE AVANT-GARDE AND BREAKING RULES

If digital media in mainstream media has been understood by us primarily as extending and building upon the rules and codes of established representational forms, digital media in the contemporary arts is, as we go on to describe, typically characterised as defining a set of practices that break with the realist representational paradigm. Earlier in this section we surveyed the institutional and cultural contexts in which the contemporary fine arts have engaged with digital media as both a technology used by artists, in which it is considered as no more than a new set of tools for a continuous set of artistic purposes, and as a radical medium of expression in its own right, a 'truly' new cultural form, which breaks with previous practices of art and requires new definitions. The difference between these two views revolves very precisely around whether 'tool' is understood as, either, a neutral carrier of the content crafted by the producer, or as having a charged content built-into it, whether recognised by the producer or not. The conceptualisation of digital technologies as part of a continuous set of cultural forms and purposes, tends not to see digital tools as carriers of new content, or shaping new purposes. Artists working with digital technologies as 'neutral' tools tend to work within existing art forms and institutions, for example, artists using digital photography for print display in galleries. Where digital technologies are thought to constitute a new medium of symbolic expression then the idea of the digital tool is invested with a content particular to itself and extended to the point where the tool is defined as a new medium through which new perceptions, thoughts and experiences can be grasped, in some Net Art practices for example. It is the later definition of digital technology, as a new (artistic) medium, that the radical potential of the form is seen to require a break with the continuous purposes and language of both representation and established art institutions.

Initially we can be clear about the fact that a wide range of artists are using the network as a means of information and dissemination about their work, which, as we discussed in mainstream media, is continuous with existing purposes. Here the Internet is a conventional marketing and publicity form for individual artists, art institutions and organisations. Artist websites on the WWW are little different from any website in that they are typically used as a means for users to access information contained on a database, mirroring modes of print information, such as posters and catalogues. Virtual galleries and museums with virtual tours have been constructed using databases of digital photographic reproductions of collections produced in other forms. Images and text show and describe the documented work of performance, painting and installation. The Google Art project is a highly resourced example of an immersive approach to virtual toura. Museums and galleries also use the Internet to publicise their programmes and collections, and their websites clearly function as a marketing, information and educational service, directed primarily at maintaining and increasing visitor attendance. The content of individual artists websites will vary between the design styles of personal websites and those of institutional and organisation sites. The navigation and links contained on artist websites will relate to how much material they carry and whether they function to disseminate information about the artist and their work, or whether the site itself is constituted by the artist as an artwork. There is, as to be expected, a very large variation in the status and quality of artist websites because the WWW is essentially a self-publishing form. Museums and galleries function as gatekeepers as well as legitimators of the status of art and the question of whether the WWW has widened access for a greater number of artists to existing or new audiences, buyers or collectors, would require substantial empirical research. In our view and experience it is more likely that the Internet reproduces reputations that are made through existing institutional arrangements. In its most inclusive grasp, Net Art, or, less prosaically, art on the web, has to be understood as both relatively uncharted territory as well as reflecting the existing social organisation of art practices and economies.

However, the Internet is also used by a range of younger artists and organisations dedicated to the production and development of digital media art projects. It is also the case that some national and international art institutions, the Tate and the ICA in London and the Whitney and Dia-Centre in New York, for example, have developed links to specific 'digital art' projects. We should also note here, as we have earlier, that there a small number of European based international organisations for the advancement of electronic arts that have been in existence for well over a decade, the standing conference on Electronic Arts, ISEA (International Society for Electronic Arts) and Arts Electronica as well as the Institute at Karlsruher and the journals, *Leonardo* and *Wired*. It is in this arena, jostling alongside everything and everyone else in cyberspace, that the more serious claim for digital media as a radically transforming art is to be found.

Screens and time

Digital media is still predominantly screen based in it reception, however much it gestures at other interactive interfaces. The computer screen is a televisual screen in origin and the flat plasma screens of today have merged with the screen of the television and computer. Most of the published accounts of digital media's emergence within contemporary art point out the historical importance of video as a medium and video as an art form in extending our notion of space and time within the work of art. In contemporary art, the video image, whether mounted on monitors or projected, extended the idea of representation beyond the still image and its frame. In contrast to the fixed, framed image of the photograph or painting, television cameras and screens allowed for real-time communication in local space or remotely, which brings the viewer closer to the contingency of the real, without the apparent mediation of representational illusion. The counter argument is, of course that television cameras and transmission still mediate what passes before them both technically and culturally. However, real-time video does create the dynamic of telepresence. The argument about screen media being in a dynamic rather than static relationship to the external object, or, referent, 'the real', is extended with the arrival of the digital and the network because now the screen's image can multiplied and reduplicated – that is, the networked image is a simulation, rather than a representation of 'the real'.

The photographic image in networked culture

How, in network culture, in the emerging economy of the image, in the new spaces of image circulation, is the historically defined idea of the photograph to be regarded? The visual images and animated graphics encountered on screens are no longer met in isolation, in print, books frames and albums. Indeed the torrent of digital images produced by computers will only exist as files, retrieved on screen through the intermediary of software. The screen image that appears on palmtop, laptop and desktop computers come through a graphic interface as an embedded file; the image will typically be surrounded by text and graphics, which set out the procedures by which the file can be manipulated, filed, tagged and transferred. Images can be viewed, resized, edited and deleted instantly at any stage in their screen life. The swipe, tap and pinch of the mobile and tablet touch screens allow images to be scrolled, enlarged and reduced. They can be arranged in countless albums, become searchable through the addition of tags, copied, displayed and published. In short, images are accessed, viewed, shared, altered and stored online within a seamless and interactive flow. Martin Hand usefully points out that digital imaging has shifted from a professional or specialised process to a routine and unavoidable aspect of everyday life. At the same time, he points out that what was once amateur or snapshot photography has become potentially global in scope. 'Where many once imagined a future of digital simulation and virtual reality we now, arguably have the opposite: the visual publicisation of ordinary life in a ubiquitous photoscape' (Hand 2012:1).

The photograph in computing has become mutable, fugitive, fleeting and restless. In its boundless quantities it is repetitive and replaceable. But what is still taken to be the photographic image on the computer screen has also become an emanation of light, an intensity. It is more of an 'image-potential' than a fixed image through variable scalability of all its visual parameters. The photographic image on high-resolution LED screens are filled with brilliance and brimming with detail. They are, as has been noted more abstractly elsewhere, the more real than real and the digital photograph might better be thought of as the **synthetic image** (Rubinstein and Sluis 2013).

Interactivity and the virtual replacing the image in art

A clear expression of the argument that digital media art marks an end to modernist art and aesthetics is to be found in Rush. For Michael Rush the new digital aesthetic is founded upon the principle characteristics of interactivity and virtuality, he points out that 'Interactivity is a new form of visual experience. In fact, it is a new form of experiencing art that extends beyond the visual to the tactile', and that, 'Current immersive environmental let alone whatever lies beyond such virtual realities is dictating a new discourse' (Rush 1999: 216). Rush's argument here is, reasonably, speculative and comes as the conclusion to his general argument that digital media is the culmination and possible closure of an avant-garde art movement that started with Marcel Duchamp. Rush sees Duchamp, along with the Dadists as replacing the received canon of artistic practice based upon an aesthetic of beauty, with an aesthetic of the everyday (object) derived from the machine age. With the new features of interactivity Rush sees the final end of the artist as arbiter of the art object and the end of invested meaning. With the realisation of the virtual Rush sees the end of the object itself and its replacement by simulation.

The argument that interactivity puts the viewer in a new position of choice and active participation in the face of a digital work of art, rests upon the assumption that previous forms of art experience involved a form of looking and seeing which was passive and non-participatory. As we have said previously this is a flawed argument and makes a false dichotomy between viewer (passive) and user (active). We can say, with Raymond Williams, that for any work of art to succeed even partially it must have an active sender and active receiver. The receiver as much as the sender of the message has to actively decode meaning through their cultural and experiential knowledge. It follows therefore, that communicative interactivity existed long before computer programs allowed for programmed choice. Looking and listening inevitably involve choice and selection. Bolter and Grusin cited the medieval cathedral as a hypermedia environment, because it contained several layers of simultaneous attention in the architecture, paintings, stained glass windows, music, sermons and incense. The passivity of the contemporary viewer of Leonardo Da Vinci's painting of *Mona Lisa* hung behind bullet proof glass in the Louvre is an example of the way in which the museum has produced a hierarchy of space and our access to it. We have come to see how art is pre-packaged almost commodified in the contemporary art experience in ways which limit the viewer's own creative agency. Rush's criticism of the passivity of packaged museum experience, is the flip side of the claim that the network represents a non-hierarchical space where human agency is given back to the user through the necessity to practically interact with the computer. We would say that human agency is always given limits by the circumstances in which we interact, whether in front of a computer screen, or the *Mona Lisa*. What we are meeting in this comparison between the painting and the computer screen is a new juxtaposition between the conventional art object and the virtual, networked communication, which (Rush 1999:216) identifies as spaceless, timeless, imageless experiences.

A pluralistic approach to digital media in art

The assertion that digital media represents another 'death of art', is less evident in (Paul 2003), who takes a more pluralistic view in which digital technologies are seen as the latest in a long line of historical interest in and relationship between art and technology. She does make the categorical distinction, which we have discussed above, between digital technologies as either 'tools for artistic use' or digital technologies as 'a new medium'. Like Rush, Paul identifies the aesthetic of digital media as arising from the characteristics of digital computer use, its capacity for being interactive, participatory, dynamic and customisable. In discussing these attributes of digital media Christiane Paul takes the approach, also adopted by (Lovejoy 2004), of classifying digital media arts projects around a number of themes. Some of the themes, such as teleprescence, telematics and telerobitics, databases, data visualisation and mapping indicate the preoccupation of digital media practitioners with the technical possibilities of the medium, for remote interaction in real time, for example, or with cultural forms of accessing, traversing or realising abstract digital data. Other themes, such as, text and narrative and interactive gaming suggest the ways in which digital media is remediating older cultural forms. The theme of the body and identity and tactical media activism more obviously register the cultural politics of digital media and the ways in which the computer and networked online communication has created new ways of thinking, presenting and communicating about ourselves. The concerns of digital media with the themes which Lovejoy identifies, echo a wider set of social concerns. These can be defined as (i) the greater dimension of surveillance in everyday life, (ii) the potential fragmenta-tion of any unified notion of the self in disembodied online forms of communication, and (iii) the undemocratic powers of corporations to dominate and control the organisation and access of the Internet. We should also note, as indeed Paul and Lovejoy do, that these concerns are not new to digital media and that politics has been a strong current throughout the modernist movements of the twentieth century. In this sense the themes of digital art identified by Christiane Paul can be seen as continuous with the modernist focus upon the autonomous individual, social identity and the democratisation of art. What is different in the debates about digital art is that there is a new (postmodernist) intellectual discourse, which is redefining the central relationships between art, reality, society and the individual.

These recent accounts of digital media and digital art have an uneasy relationship to wider theories of technology. Primarily digital media in art practice is accounted for by established modernist art history and theory. The argument here is the familiar avant-garde notion of the artist as a person who rejects established ideas and boundaries, who breaks the rules, in order to bring us new experience. But at the same time these accounts also argued that digital media brings forth the need for a completely new language and way of thinking. 'Interactivity, though still primitive and dependent on photo-based media, might generate art for which no vocabulary yet exists' (Rush 1998:217), or 'Current immersive environments let alone whatever lies beyond such virtual realities is dictating a new discourse' (Rush 217), or 'In all likelihood, digital technologies will become more and more pervasive and will not constitute a category in themselves but become an integral part of life and art in general' (Paul 2003:212). How far technology is moving the goals posts of what distinguishes art, from other forms of technological mediated communication, remains ambivalent in the above accounts. (Lovejoy 2004:278–280) argues that artists working with new technologies embrace technology both as medium and a tool and that they can occupy a space which 'reconfigures the negotiation of cultural meaning'. This, she argues, can take a number of forms, from critically examining contemporary media-dominated cultural conditions, to reflexively examining the process of representation itself. This is a useful, pluralistic account that describes new media art as exploring not only the technology itself as a medium, but also recent political cultural themes such as exposing dominant narratives of mass media (control and surveillance, for example) and redefining the geography of culture by challenging received notions of identity and place.

A parallel definition of new media practice can be found in (Graham and Cook 2010), in which they point out that there is a history of innovative cultural practices using digital media that extends beyond art to include commerce, education and social communication and that the use of the term media is often blurred between these fields. If for example, the practices of new media are not considered as fine art, but science and technology, then a whole set of activities, for example, kinetics and data visualisation could be included. In addition, the experimental categories of practice in which art and technology are present are also considered within an interdisciplinary field involving cybernetics, sociology, education, art and technology. Graham and Cook make a plea to redefine media as behaviour as one way of connecting the research interests of artists, scientists and technologists on the one hand and redefining how audiences become involved in technological artworks on the other and they cite Dietz definition of new media art practice as being involved in interactivity, connectivity and computability as an example of their approach to curating new media.

Breaking the rules

Digital media art practices are united in the description given here by a common set of strategies for challenging, breaking, inverting or subverting the rules and responses of existing art and media forms and languages. But why, we might ask, should we limit the idea of digital media practice as breaking the rules, to an avant-garde notion of art practice? It can be argued, in the same terms as Walter Benjamin did in 1939, that any truly new medium not only forces into history a new way of seeing and registering reality, but also irrevocably changes the existing function and meaning of art. Isn't the digital medium an extension of Benjamin's argument that photography and later film ushered in an art made for reproduction as well as reproducing by mechanical means all previous art? The digital is reconfiguring and hybridising existing media forms and isn't it, therefore, changing the function of art as well? This point is not lost on the accounts of digital media art we been considering. Graham, Lovejoy, Rush and Paul acknowledge that Benjamin's argument is highly relevant to any attempt to grasp how digital media is changing the ways in which art is made and understood. What all of them point to is the less than stable boundary between art and all other digital media. While most accounts of digital art and digital media recognise that the new medium changes the relationship of the artist and audience in ways which give the user more agency and control there is less recognition that digital media repositions the producer.

Mark Poster also explicitly acknowledges the importance of Benjamin's argument to the present moment of the work of art in the age of digital reproduction. Poster notes that with digital media 'the work of art is a collective creation combining information machines with engineers, artists and participants in a manner that reconfigures the role of each' [such that] 'Art is then not a delimited object but an underdetermined space in which subject and object, human and machine, body and mind, space and time all receive new cultural forms.' Poster also notes, with Rush that, from the position of digital media, modern art can now only reproduce itself as an object and a commodity, which reinforces the older mode of representation and distinction between subject and object, whereas 'the art of networked computing invites the participant to change the real' (Poster 2006:127).

What is becoming clearer in current debate about art and technologies, is that it is networked practices which now present the biggest challenge to existing

Table 24.1 **Walter Benjamin's historical scheme of art's relationship to economimc organisation**

Walter Benjamin's historical scheme	
Tribal cultures of hunters and gatherers	Art as magic
Agrarian cultures of unified religion	Art as ritual
Secular cultures and the rise of capitalism	Art as beauty
Industrial cultures of capitalism	Art as art
Post-industrial and post-modern culture	**Art as information** [our addition]

definitions of both established notions of art and media communications. Settled distinctions between art and media are now challenged both within the contemporary institutions of art and art education on the one hand, and within thinking about networked media commununcation. We can see how some of these arguments play out in the next section, entitled appropriatelt, 'the crisis of representation'.

CHAPTER 25

The network and the crisis of culture

The discussion here represents the third perspective in looking at the contempoary framework of digital media. It builds upon the summaries provided in intellectual histories as well as the discussion of the contexts of digital media practice. This section sets out an alternative path from thinking about digital media to the two perspectives already discussed; either, that digital media is continuous with existing media, or its avant-garde extension. What follows also takes up again questions of the status and impact of networks as a primary way of thinking about digital media. The ways in which the study of digital media is promoted and taught in education, what examples, thinking, ideas and subject disciplines it draws upon, is largely dependent upon how academics position themselves within or across the three perspectives outlined. The idea that digital media, or networked media is continuous with previous media organisations is the default position of sociologically-based media studies, while the idea that digital media represents a new artistic avant-garde has been taken up within art history and theory and some aspects of contemporary cultural studies. In effect each field of enquiry frames digital media as a different object, within different knowledge paradigms. Hence in sociology, digital media is framed by the overriding idea of social communication, art theory wants to look at digital media primarily as a new aesthetic medium, while in the third perspective, which overlaps with science and technology studies, digital media is overwritten as an information system. Writers associated with the third perspective, which argues that digital media should be understood as something different from old media and represents a radical break, more often demand that digital media requiries new forms of study, generating new knowledge and new methods of research. The argument for thinking that digital media requires new modes of thinking also carries with it an urgency and appeal for academia and education to catch up with a world changing before our eyes. Such a perspective is not initself new, but is rather an extension of those who originally argued that the Internet was a radical new alternative form of communication and thinking such as Marvin Minsky, Howard Rheingold and Arthur Kroker, and requires a new study of information systems, Freidrich Kittler, Lev Manovich and Mathew Fuller and Alexander Galloway.

> The time in which we had to make a case for 'the media' in general is well behind us. The term 'media' is well under way of becoming an empty signifier. In times of budget cuts, creative industries and intellectual poverty, we'll have to push aside wishy-washy convergence approaches and go for specialised in-depth studies of networks and digital culture. The larger picture no longer provides us with critical concepts. It is time for digital media to claim autonomy and resources in order to, finally, leave the institutional margins, and catch up with society.
>
> (Lovink 2012:74)

Taken to its logical extreme the argument that digital media is a radically different paradigm of communication which breaks with the system of representation that has been in place since the Renaissance, provokes a major crisis in prevailing conceptions of culture and communication. In what follows we outline what is meant by the system of representation and discuss the current debates about whether we should look for an alternative explanation of what is happening in the human/computer networked interface and why.

Narratives of a crisis in the human relationship with technology have been consistently imagined within the popular genre of science fiction since H. G. Wells (1866–1946) wrote *The War of the Worlds* in 1898. In science fiction there is a prevailing narrative of the near future in which further scientific and technological discovery leads to a condition in which machines are invested with autonomous power that ultimately escapes human control. There are of course many versions of this central theme, which stretch from the very near future in which science and technology are seen as largely beneficial to human life, to a world gone wrong in which humans become locked in mortal combat for control of the planet against the machines they have created; or, that we can no longer distinguish ourselves from the cyborgs we have created; or indeed, that humans are reduced to the source of energy for a simulated reality controlled by a database. Such are the plots rehearsed in such films as Ridley Scott's influential film *Bladerunner* (1982), or *The Matrix* (2001), Spielberg's *Minority Report* (2002) or more recently *Source Code* (2011) or, the novels of William Gibson. As Lister *et al.*, point out there is a history to the ways in which science and technology have been configured in the popular imagination. (Lister *et al.* 2003). Within such histories the idea of human replacement by machines in the form of automatons and the merging of human and machines in the form of cyborgs has been articulated with varying degrees of seriousness, but always reflecting current popular understandings about scientific and technological development in relation to human social organisation. It might be asked why there is such a developed fascination with the idea of the human versus machine opposition, when in reality mechanisation and automation have a long history and continue to be applied to more areas of social life for benefical reasons, although always organised within unequal social conditions. Science fiction expresses and possibly assuages current anxieties about the consequences of technology in the service of unelected, secretive and often despotic organisations, most often set against the Herculean resistance of a few individuals who break free and who embody the essential decent values of humanity. Current commentaries about technology in the factual world can and do often repeat this kind of essentialist duality between 'man and machine', reinforcing the separation between humans and technology which is unhelpful. Equally the events surrounding Wikileaks are cast in the mould of independent minded indidivuals having to battle against the combined forces of state and corporate interests.

Within the social sciences and cultural and media studies we have already rehearsed the arguments, from Benjamin, McLuhan and Williams that human perception and representation change in relationship to what are primarily technological develop-ments. In subsequent media theory, Jean Baudrillard, and Paul Virillio argued that technology has reached a stage where it has already produced a world of simulation in which representations can no longer guarantee the existence of the real. In a further set of developments the works of Catherine Hayles and Donna Haraway question whether our notions of what it is to be human, derived as they are from the Humanist and Enlightenment distinctions between man and nature can be sustained in the face of our relationship to technology (Hayles 1999, Harraway 2003).

IDENTITY

What is at issue in arguments about the relationship between humans and technology is how humaness is defined and how we distinguish this from everything constituted as the non-human world. We have already made reference to the profound unease with the idea of technological progress based upon scientific and rational certainty that emerged with post structuralist thought from the 1970s and postmodern thinkers in the 1980s. One of the contextual underpinnings of this period of intellectual uncertainty was precisely the 'real world' in which technology had been deployed with such disasterous effects by various industrial states in pursuit of what Lyotard termed 'grand narratives' of national interest. Part of the postmodern response to such unease and criticism of scientific and intellectual rationalism was to question the philosophical ideas upon which human certainty was established by the subject/ object dualism. This long standing concern in philosophy and the philosophy of science, came to the fore with post-structuralism's criticism of systems of knowing based upon essential difference(s) between objects and subjects and its own efforts to account for difference as a relative process. If there can be no essential difference between objects and subjects, then what produces difference other than the system (semiotic) of differences? If difference is only produced as a product of a sign, then how is human identity to be differentiated from everything that it is not? The unsettling of what were previously considered known and fixed relationships between people objects and things has become a focus for concern in understanding how humanness or identity is produced, or modified by our participation in computer networks.

POSTHUMAN

In responding to the essentialist problem of Humanism, various theoretical positions of the 'antihuman' or 'posthuman', have been developed in which humaness is understood as historical and relative. In such perspectives the human cannot be defined in opposition to technology, but in an embrace with it, or that the human relationship to technology has already changed the neurological patterns and functions of our brains (Hayles 1999). The position of the post-human include ideas that we are already cyborgs because of our relationship to technology, or that technology can be grafted on/into the body. The anti-human remains an intellectual position from which to rethink the subject/object relationship and problems associated with how and what we know about the external world. The post-human questioning of the system of knowing and representing what we know follows the route we have outlined from structuralism, post-structuralism, postmodernism to our present dillemas.

Whether at a metaphorical or actual level the post-human is conceived as the merging of human and machine. In hard science, in artificail intelligence (A1), in neural-networks and nanotechnology, the machine is being conceptualised as organic, self-modifying, and intelligent. In medical science we are already incorporating technology into the body in routine ways such as pacemakers, artificial joints and contact lenses. More radically biotechnology is drawing upon the discoveries of DNA, the Human Genome Project and Stem Cell research to provide bioengineering, including cloning of the human body. The convergence of nanotechnology, bio-engineering, information sciences and cognitive research does centre on projects which extend or merge the human and machine in real ways and for particular purposes. But it remains a large leap from current scientific research to what is still the science fiction of robots, cyborgs or replicants. (Fukuyama 2003) sees bio-technology creating a future in which the issue will not be about how changes in our external environment may harm us, but about changes to what being human is. (Pepperell 1995), sees the challenge posed by biotechnology and the recombinant DNA possibilities of the human genome project as an alteration on the level of the human soul, and that complex machines are an emergent life form.

The idea of the posthuman is also employed to account for the reconfiguration of human subjectivities in cyberspace. Here the post-human is being employed, not to envisage individual humans as technologically reconfigured bodies, but to account for how notions of identity are changed through our interactions with machines. (Harraway 1990) extends the discussion of the posthuman to include our cultural and psychological response to a world in which information and its systems dominate, arguing that we have the anxiety of becoming posthuman, or not knowing if we are human, because of a paradigm shift in which a networked cybernetic system is installed as the medium of communication and knowledge.

COMPUTERS, MIND AND CONSCIOUSNESS

One of the common elements of thought to arise from the post-structuralist and postmodernist strands of thinking, is that with the application of computers to more and more human functions, the strict separation of human and machine can no longer be maintained. In the technoscientific domain, actor network theory argues that 'actants' can be both human and non-human. In Baudrillard's era of simulation the human is faced with a new ecstasy of communication, likened to the position of the schizophrenic who can no longer separate him/herself from the totality electronic impulse. In cybernetic theory human behaviour is analysed as a functioning machine system. In Deleuze and Guattari's operation of the distributed self the human is conceived as a 'desiring machine'. In all of these accounts nature and reality are no longer opposed to human history and activity but, rather, seen as extensions, or products of human activity. It follows therefore that if humans produce nature then humans produce themselves and hence any absolute division between what is and is not human can no longer be maintained. Technology from this perspective is not to be considered an antithesis to nature, or the body, but as their extensions. Conversely, we can no longer define what is human in opposition to the machines and technologies that humans have built and adapted themselves to. Just as computer architecture structures the organisation, access and navigation of electronic databases, so to the human mind can, by analogy be seen as a database consisting of all that an individual has learned and experienced. Neurology and psychology have long been preoccupied with how human memory and thought is structured, how the mind accesses its own database.

The anthropomorphism of the computer is not so much a reflection of the inexorable development of the computer towards independent consciousness, but more a reflection, like that of the car, of its familiar repetitive functions in everyday life. However, computer networks are also thought of as neural networks and the world network of computers is, metaphorically, likened to the human brain, just as the brain has been described as functioning like a computer. Outside of the AI computer science laboratory, the promise of an autonomous thinking machine is much more located in a cultural discussion, as the long established genre of science fiction writing demonstrates. This is also what we earlier referred to as the technological imaginary. Digital media artists, continue to explore the idea of machine intelligence or consciousness, Harold Cohen's *Aaron* project being just one celebrated historic example, but in general the main drive of computational power, whether for military or civil application, has been to assist and extend human operations in thought and action. Computers are centrally entailed in a greater and greater range of both routine and extraordinary operational systems and until relatively recently this fact when recognised, was somehow shocking. The fear of computers taking over the world stands in marked contrast to the fact that it is getting harder to think of human activities that aren't assisted by computers.

Interactivity and its relationship to human thought is part of the larger technological cognitive mapping project in which, over a long history, machines have been conceived and built that either mimic or aid human thought. This can be reformulated as an intellectual and practical project that has a sustained interest in machines that 'think' independently of human thought, and machines that aid our thinking. Independent thinking machines are the province of the discipline of artificial intelligence (AI), while the broader application of machines to think with is the application of computational power to specific tasks previously carried out by mental processes. These two strands have a common route in the conceptualisation and writing of computational code. The computational power of the PC expands exponentially with an increase in the functions and operations of 'intelligent' software.

REPRESENTATION

The theoretical dillema of the subject/object relation between the human and computer has a counterpart in the digital media interface, which focuses upon how in computer mediated communication (CMC), the computer interposes itself between senders and receivers and between the source coding and software application. CMC as we have described elsewhere still operates on the basis of a cultural language, even though it relies upon and is coded by a 'non-human' language. Those who argue that digital media is a radically new cultural language emphasise the machinic and informatic side of communication, relegating the issue of representation to that of an older semiotic of media studies which it is argued is unable to encompass the non-representational system of digital data. The new position argues that while humans are responsible for creating a machine code, humans can't speak to one another in machinic code. The problem of the machine layer and the cultural layer remains a central problem in studying what is going on in the network and one of the reasons why research into the social and cultural effects of CMC are outstripped by the fast pace of technological application. However much the system of cultural representation belongs to the previous organisation of media, it cannot reach into computer systems and remains tied to remediated or simulated cultural forms.

For the time being we are stuck with representation even though machines have outstripped representation's human rules. Cultural representation is a specific form of human communication, such that, on the one side, language, texts, images stand in the place of the thing itself and, on the other hand, that the language text, image can be interpreted so that the thing represented is present to the receiver. Representation therefore, involves both the formal system of signs and the embedded traditions and mental pictures and cognitive maps by which signs are known and interpreted. From the period of the Enlightenment the secular representational systems of Western European societies were based upon the discourses of rationalism and realism, through which the human centred world was organised and described. It is the representational system which gives meaning to the ethical, political and philosophical dimensions of human life. Government is a prime example of a representational system of democracy, just as art and science investigate and record the world through representational systems of thought and communication. While the representational systems of art, philosophy and politics remain in place in the conduct and organisation of institutional knowledge and everyday life, the same systems of representation have been called into question philosophically and outstripped in computing. The crisis of representational can be understood as both (a) a gap between a developed body of critical thought and continued cultural practices, and, (b) that representational meaning is inadequate to grasp networked communication. Thus the representational system of thought and the representational systems of communication remain in a progressive crisis of representation (Cohn 2006). While still very abstract as a description the experience of a crisis of representation can be pointed to in many aspects of social life, indeed at its most encompassing whole societies could be said to be experiencing a crisis of representation.

POLITICAL REPRESENTATION

Social democracies rely upon a political system of representation, based upon constituencies and parties at local and national levels producing representational government. The democratic system of representation relies upon individuals voting and there has been a noticable trend in the UK, as elsewhere of a decline in the number of people voting. Social democratic politics depends upon a concensus of what government in the public interest is and in turn this relies upon the existence of a strong sense of the public realm and of individuals identifying themselves with citizenship. Social democratic government is founded upon a trust on the part of those represented that their political representatives will act in their interests and voters have to have sufficient belief that governments can govern and will carry out its election pledges. Many of these assumptions have been sorely tested in the recent period when national governments are seen not to be able to effect change in the system of global market forces and when politicians have been revealed as pursing self interest over the interests of constituents. More significantly the marketisation and commodification of many more aspects of social life can be seen to have eroded people's sense of belonging to a community, or having common interests. In a world run on the basis of the market and individual consumers, what is the place of representative democracy. It could therefore be reasonably said that the political system is experiencing a crisis of representation and one of the dimensions of the change to the system of how people represent themselves and feel part of communities or not is the spread of the Internet.

VISUAL REPRESENTATION

Visual representation can also be said to be experiencing a crisis. The impact of the digital upon photography was summed up by Mirzoeff (1999:88) in asserting 'that the photography is no longer an index of reality. It is virtual, like its fellow postmodern visual media, from the television to the computer'. More than this, Mirzoeff saw in the visualisation of things not in themselves visual and in the acceleration in the global circulation of images as an end in itself, a more general crisis of information expressed in visual culture because 'The extraordinary pro-liferation of images cannot cohere into one single picture for the contemplation of the intellectual' (Mirzoeff 1999:8). While visual cultural studies signalled a crisis in the system of representation, it nevertheless continued to treat the digital image as a representational system, at the same time as it continues to point out that the apparatus upon which such representations are made has changed the relationship of the image to what it represents. From a contemporary vantage point this now represents a stage in an unfinished argument that continues to run and inform current thinking. The first phase of theorizing digital culture announced the crisis of representation, while the current phase has to confront the problem of non-representation and its hybrids. A politics of network culture precisely addresses the processes of subjectification produced through the human computer interface and how this changes existing subject positions in public spaces, including that of the cultural space of the Internet.

THE DIGITAL AESTHETIC AND THE LOGIC OF THE SYSTEM

The globalised world, the networked society and the informational mode of develop-ment are all concepts based upon the centrality of the computer in production, exchange and consumption. The processing of data treats all knowledge as information. Attempts to define the primary aesthetic of the digital have focused upon the nature and essential characteristics, in theoretical terms the ontology, of the digital computer.

The aesthetics of analogue media, film for example, is seen to arise from its materiality, the way in which the film frame is an optically focused, light exposed image and that movement and duration are achieved through running twenty four film frames per second through a camera and projector. But the aesthetic of film is not reducible to its ontology, its material technology, because film form also includes narrative language derived from literature and storytelling. As we have noted, whereas analogue media continuously inscribes without breaking down the signal or source into discrete units, digital media convert the original source through capture and sampling into a code. This difference has led to defining code as the essence of digital media and most descriptions of a digital aesthetic start from the essential characteristic of numerical representation and procedural operations such as automation and modularity. It is the mutability of information in digital form that has been seized upon as a defining quality of a digital aesthetic. Digital data is continually open to change through endless recombination, and are collected, stored and transmitted through numerical representation. These technical qualities have, as we have seen, led to the descriptions of digital media as non-hierarchical and non-linear. But, as we noted with film, a full account of the aesthetics of film has to include its' developed languages and the same is true for a digital aesthetic, which cannot be fully discovered in its procedural functions, or reduced to its essential electronic binary form. The language of digital media, as we have gone to great lengths to demonstrate, still crucially depends upon the culturally developed sign systems of image, music, orality, script and text, which the digital is technically simulating. However, this dependency is not absolute because while digital code technically simulates, it also culturally repurposes. The hypermediated computer screen and online communication adds to and changes the quality of screen representations as well as the relay of the message.

AESTHETIC OF SYSTEMS

In the cultural practices of digital media, including their theoretical and educational discourses, we can detect arguments in which there is a strong insistence that a 'true' digital aesthetic will emerge from work focused upon code, the database and the mutability of data rather than work based upon the digital simulation of representational forms in immersive and hypermediated screen media. The argument against digital representational forms is that they reproduce all the previous analogue moments and the attendant cultural problems that post-structuralism and post-modernism identified with those representational forms. Realism, narrative and the authorial voice were exposed in theoretical analysis as closed systems that could not guarantee reality or truth. Systems of representation are, it is argued, based upon the myth of the unitary and coherent subject/self and its binary relationship to the external object and reality. If the representational forms of analogue media only give us a relative and oblique view of what is contingent and real then it follows that a new paradigm or guarantor of the real must be found. The new symbolic form of the networked database, founded upon code and the mutability of information, is perceived as a means to liberate knowledge, experience and sensation from the fixed and closed analogue forms and their hierarchical institutional regimes. However, in order to find this new means of communication and self recognition, further cultural and theoretical articulation of the ontology of the computer will have to be undertaken.

LINGUISTIC REPRESENTATION

The counter to the argument that the representational paradigm should be rejected because it reproduces an outmoded subject/object discourse is at one level very simple. As yet, no meaningful replacement to the developed systems of representation exists and therefore they continue to operate, for good and ill, as the dominant and shared mode through which the self and external realities are communicated. Saying this does not deny either the recognition of the problems of representation, nor, the desire and need to find more meaningful forms, which are closer to and engage with postmodern experience. The analysis of language(s) as a system of signs in which meaning is assigned to the subject and object within the signifying system and hence finally does not guarantee externality, demonstrated categorically the constructed nature of all representation. In revealing the nature of signifying systems, structuralism and post-structuralism both signalled a new crisis in representation and created the analytical means through which the constructed nature of given representational discourses was deconstructed. Deconstruction reveals the operational and mediating discourses at work within representational systems for critical producers and readers. Deconstruction of a signifying system thus constitutes a revision to rather than a transformation of the system itself. What is evident in both the argument for the overthrow of the notion of representabilty and the argument for it continued revision is that the digital represents a new set of possibilities, which engage with the acknowledged need and desire to go beyond the current limits of representation.

The central problem for developing a digital media language and a post-representational account based upon the networked database is that computer code is an abstract mathematical formula and data is written in a computational procedural programming language. The network of networked computers is understandable in its technological structures as are the procedures of online communication, but we don't 'read' lines of code, neither can we communicate directly through programming language. These organising levels of relay and command remain invisible. While the human computer interface relies upon the procedures of code and programming to create meaningful communication, it actually takes place through software tools, which convert code to knowable language – that is, text, image, sound, graphic, spreadsheet.

POLITICS OF THE NETWORK

According to (Lovink 2012) 'the Internet is over' as a result of the collapse of the libertarian concensus model of its origins in the face of its corporatisation. Lovink argues that Web 2.0, a term popularised by Tim O'Reilly, was in effect a commercial regrouping of Silicon Vallery companies in the aftermath of the dot.com crash. Venture capitalism saw a new opportunity for big returns on investment. The question of how to make money from the Internet, which was limited in Web 1.0

to subscription, advertising and lost leaders for other arms of corporate business, was solved in Web 2.0 by data mining and selling data to third parties. Control of distribution channels, through search algorithms and RSS feeds meant that online socialising and uploading and downloading of information could be monetised by Google, Apple, Amazon and Ebay.

(Curran *et al.* 2012) makes a parallel but different series of observations in assessing the claims that the world is being remade by the Internet. He identifies five claims which he argues, are more limited than previously imagined. The claim that the nternet has modified the nerve system of the economy in terms of the market configuration, the voume and velocity of data supply in the global financial transactions remains true, but is in effect much more contiuous with the previous lines of closed market systems of information management. The idea championed by politicans and business strategists, that the Internet would be a geyser of wealth cascading down on investors has also proved illusory in light of the Internet bubble crash of the late 1990s in which investors lost money and in light of the most recent financial crisis of 2008. Both of the above factors leads Curran to the view that the value of the interent economy has been oversold and has not produced a level playing field between large and small companies.

FREE LABOUR

To critics of the corporate 'take-over' of the Internet, social networking, which had been celebrated as a new and open form of sharing and community, has also become incorporated into business management strategies and that Flickr, Wikipedia, MySpace, Twitter, Facebook and YouTube become self-serving enclaves, with little progressive outcomes for social life. Social media is no longer understood as the dawn of a new era of participatory citizenship, but a new form of free labour. Tiziana Terranova was one of the first scholars to point out that 'working in the digital media industry is not as much fun as it is made out to be' She goes on to observe that;

> The 'Net Slaves' of the eponymous Webzine are becoming increasingly vociferous about the shamelessly exploitative nature of the job, its punishing work rhythms, and its ruthless casualisation. They talk about '24–7 electronic sweatshops' and complain about the 90-hour weeks and the 'moronic manage-ment of digital media companies.' In early 1999, seven of the fifteen thousand 'volunteers' of America Online (AOL) rocked the info-love boat by asking the Department of Labor to investigate whether AOL owes them back wages for the years of playing chat hosts for free [Lisa Margonelli, Inside AOL's 'Cyber-Sweatshop', *Wired*, October 1999:138]. They used to work long hours and love it; now they are starting to feel the pain of being burned by digital media.
>
> (Terranova 2013:33)

Terranova articulated the idea of free labour at the conference, 'The Internet as Playground and Factory' in 2009, which was held at Eugene Lang College in New York and supported by Yale and Parsons Universities in which she developed the idea of 'digital labour' in relationship to classical economics. She linked the expansion of social networking and the monetisation of data to the financial crisis of 2008, suggesting that cultural expression and social cooperation are in effect forms of economic exploitation of free labour, which challenge the social vision of free market economics and what is currently understood as labour. The argument here is that our social and personal investment in time spent on the Internet is being monetised and hence eroding the difference between paid and unpaid labour. On this view that capital can now extract exchange value from the intimate and personal forms of exchange which takes place outside of wage labour in social networking.

COMMUNICATIVE CAPITALISM

The current political critique of the corporatisation and industrialisation of the Internet points to the spread of networked computing, what people are doing in the network and how this is monetised as an illustration of a new phase of global capitalism. On this view the Internet is instrumentalising what was previously understood as our independent and free social life outside of wage labour. In this analysis the object of digital media, understood in the sense of CMC, is now considered to have extended its reach to our most intimate and personal lives, whether we are online or not. The widening horizon in which digital media is understood as economically, politically and socially systemic has be expressed in terms of communicative capitalism by Jodi Dean (Dean 2009). She illustrates her argument by pointing out that while the Invasion of Iraq by the US under the Bush Administration was met by a wave of social protest, much of it expressed online, the message was ignored, or as she puts it not received:

> So, despite the terabytes of commentary and information, there wasn't exactly a debate over the war. On the contrary, in the days and weeks prior to the US invasion of Iraq, the anti-war messages morphed into so much circulating content, just like all the other cultural effluvia wafting through cyberia.
>
> (2009:52) http://commonconf.files.wordpress. com/2010/09/proofs-of-tech-fetish.pdf

Why has this happened, Dean asks, when the Internet is such a powerful tool of democractic expression, why isn't democracy listening? Her answer is that communication has itself become commodified so that more and more aspects of social life have been 'reformatted' in terms of the market and spectacle. The effect of this is depolitising since views and opinions even strongly collective political views are treated as nothing more than another message contributing to the content circulating 'out there' in an 'echo chamber of like minded people' rather than a social action that demands a response. Communicative capitalism is for Dean a strange merger of liberal democracy and capitalism in which the values of democracy take material form in networked communication technologies, but instead of leading to more equitable sharing and participation, global communication undermines political opportunity:

> The only thing that is relevant is circulation, the addition to the pool. Any particular contribution remains secondary to the fact of circulation. The value of any particular contribution is likewise inversely proportionate to the openness, inclusivity or extent of a circulating data stream – the more opinions or comments that are out there, the less of an impact any one given one might make (and the more shock, spectacle or newness is necessary for a contribution to register or have an impact).
>
> (Dean 2010:55)

The idea of digital labour and communicative capitalism reverse engineer the idea of the Internet as a free space and a new form of the public sphere and creative commons. As critical perspectives on Internet practice they are central to the notion of a crisis within the democratic political system of representation as well as pointing to the fact that representational systems need responses as much as they need messages. The image of the Internet as a void in which messages circulate without response is chilling and leads to the view that the network of network computers is a self-serving technical beaurocracy. Under the microscope of critical theory, the logic of the Internet's own non representational system appears to sweep all before it, leaving the academic critique, along with everything else, sidelined in a commodified system of messaging. If this seems too bleak an outlook in accounting for what in others terms might be experienced as the positive side of social media and the creative practices of digital media, then it is.

ATTENTION ECONOMY

Critics of the growing corporatisation of the Interent, the monetisation of Internet traffic and the growing dependences upon online networked communication, have also pointed to the way in which the attention economy works. (Goldhaber 1983) developed the idea that there is a limit to how much information anyone can assimilate from the massive amounts of instantly available information on the Internet. How do we choose which pages of the web to look at and how long can they sustain our attention. In view of the recognised problem of the limits of attention in relation to the vastness of information a field of commercial expertise has arisen in order to help content producers and distributors manage the attention economy in terms of the flow of information and user interface design, aimed at ensuring that the user will receive relevant content first. While those wishing to manage the flow of data take the attention economy as a business proposition through increasing forms of personalisation, critics point out that the information overload creates its own problems of authenticating the provenance of the source and well as leading to attention deficit as users flick and click across pages. The idea that we sit in front of a computer screen distracted, addicted and deluded into thinking we are in control of information and communication, is expressed in *Alone Together* (Turkle 2013) in which she reverses her earlier perspectives that *Life on Screen* (Turkle 1997) represents a positive and beneficial extension of personal life, advocating the need for Americans to now turn-off their computers and re-evaluate what they are doing.

GOOGLE – THE FILTER BUBBLE

The tension between customisation and data mining is explored in Eli Pariser's book, *The Filter Bubble: What the Internet is Hiding From You* (Pariser 2012). Pariser's argument starts by the assertion that a momentous moment in Internet history went unnoticed when in 2009 Google announced its 'personalised search for everyone', in which the Google search engine would use 57 signals from where you log in, to what you search for, to make guesses about who you were and what kind of sites you'd like. The era of web personalisation had arrived. As Pariser says, most of us would assume that when we Google a term we all see the same results, which are the ones that the company's Page Rank algorithm suggests are the most authoritive based upon other page links. But since December 2009 this is no longer true and you get the results that Google's algorithm suggests is best for you. The change of the Internet to personalised searches could be said to be a response to the problem of the attention economy, in which the computer is programmed to deliver only things it knows, or rather guesses you will be interested in. However, personalisation also marks a fundamental change in the Internet from a medium where 'anyone could be anyone' to 'a tool for soliciting and analysing our personal data'. As Pariser says:

> According to one *Wall Street Journal* study, the top 50 Internet sites, from CNN to Yahoo to MSN, install an average of 64 data-laden cookies and personal tracking beacons each. Search for a word like 'depression' on Dictionary.com. and the site installs up to 223 tracking cookies and personal tracking beacons on your computer so that other Web sites can target you with antidepressants.
> (Pariser 2012:6)

While Google for now at least has promised to keep your personal data to itself, other web sites and apps don't and information supplied by users through their use of websites can be sold on to third-party data companies. But while this customisation of information makes money from advertising by pushing personalised products towards you, it has far greater implications on how you will receive all the information, from what media you watch, what news you get to how information is configured. There are three major problems with what Pariser calls the filter bubble. The first is that you're alone in it. In an age of shared information and the search for communality the personalisation of data isolates the user. Second, the filter itself is invisible to the user. The algorithms that are setting the parameters of the computer defining who you are and what it thinks you want are opaque. Google is making guesses about you but not telling you the criteria upon which it is making them. Third, you don't choose to be filtered and hence cannot make a judgement about how the filter is giving you a particular perspective or take on the information coming to you.

NON-REPRESENTATIONAL STRATEGIES

In attempting to move beyond the problematic of the representational paradigm, with its subject/object dichotomy, objectifying gaze and fixed order of time and space, some digital media practitioners and theorists have sought alternative models and strategies. Such strategies are present to some degree in all digital media work that make technological mediation present. In such work the technology is not simply assumed as a carrier of some message or content, but actively worked upon so that the user or participant becomes aware of the underlying orders and logic of the networked system and its code.

Digital media practice that sets itself the task of critically engaging with and moving beyond the forms of discursive power represented by online networked communication has been most recently influenced by post-structuralist and postmodernist theoretical perspectives developed from the 1980s, which cluster around a set of interests in non-hierarchical, participant, interactive and relativist modes of thought and action. But it is also the case that this agenda for change has much longer roots in two opposed intellectual traditions. The renewed focus upon the processes of computing and the social construction of networked communication can be found in the 'actor-network' theory of Bruno Latour and the 'tactical practices' suggested in Micheal de Certeau's *The Practice of Every Day Life* (1984). The emphasis upon processual knowledge and practice as a means of theorising the human–computer relationship brings with it a politics of intervention consistent with the materialist tradition. On the other hand the human–computer relationship is theorised in terms the concept of affect, those direct mind/body responses which come before and escape rationality and language. The complex set of ideas related to 'rhizomatic systems' in the work of Gilles Deleuze and Felix Guatarri are an example here (Deleuze and Guatarri 1987).

How might we find a way out of the current Internet dilema, what are the strategems and tactics available to us in the everyday uses of computer mediated communication. How can the analysis and critique of the corporatisation and monetisation of network traffic be usefully returned to questions of digital media practices. Against communicative capitalism's view of the Internet as a message without a response, Manuel Castells points out that in *networked social movements* humans do create meaning by interacting with their natural and social environment, by networking their neural networks with the network of nature and with social networks. He points to the ways in which a combination of the Internet and mobile technology played a positive part in the 'Arab Spring' and that without social networking campaigning groups such as Occupy would not exist (Castells 2012). Henry Jenkins talks about bottom-up, rather than top-down approaches and promotes the idea of *spreadable media* in which there has been a shift from distribution to participatory cultures. His view is that while the managers of the attention economy attempt to get traffic to be individualised, centralised, unified and prestructured in order to attract and hold attention – that is, to stick, the collectivist approach is in contrast, collaborative, open ended, grassroots socially dispersed, diverse and motivated. This is a positive message for the network, even though serious detractors would point out that Jenkins's strategum for spreadable media can easily be coopted by those wishing to hold our attention and does not in itself undermine the tracking and monetisation of personal data (Jenkins 2013).

GREY MEDIA – BACK TO MEDIATION

In the book *Evil Media* (Fuller and Goffey 2012) reformulate the importance of mediation for an understanding of computer mediated communication, concentrating not upon the semiotics of image and language, nor upon the obvious technology, but rather upon what they call the gray ontology of media. This is a way out of the logic of representation, which as we have rehearsed fails to account for the logic of the system, and a way out of the opposition between human and technology. Gray media amounts to 'an aesthetic that is indiscernible or inseparable from the technologies, techniques, practices, and devices that make up much of the abstract infrastructures of contemporary societies'. Gray media is about the unobtrusive processes that are working away in the background, giving shape to activities and events. It is a recognition of the complexity and sophistication of digital media. For Fuller and Goffey digital media needs to be understood not only in terms of its rhetoric and discursive conventions but also through its formal logics, technical protocols and social proprieties. Gray media is a kind of transcursivity across the deterritorial spaces of digital communication, an attempt to trace all those 'mid-process', which have affects as well as decision making outcomes. As they put it:

> By gray media, we mean things such as databases, group-work, software, project-planning methods, media forms, and technologies that are operative far from the more visible churn of messages about consumers, empowerment, or trhe questionable wisdom of the information economy.
>
> (2012:1)

METHODOLOGY

Throughout all of our discussions about how digital media is understood lies the recognition of its hybrid, pervasive and complex character in which the social and technical cannot be separated. The problem in analysis has been that the intellectual tools for understanding this new object of attention have not been as sophisticated as the object they are trying to illuminate. Digital media has been accounted for in the social or the technical register, but as yet no synthesis has been achieved. Digital media has been studied within the logic of representational and within the logic of systems. The attempt to build a method of study for computer mediated communication has so far called upon many knowledge frameworks that again reflect the complex and hybrid nature of the object. All of the digital media theorists we have looked at recognise the inadequacies of their own accounts and call for new kinds of research to grasp the complexity of the object under consideration. There is a general sense that the legacy of critical thinking about media and society which flowed from the post structuralists now stands at a distance from the contemporary moment of networked culture. While contemporary critical theory has much to say that is valuable about the current direction and control of the Internet and its impact upon social communication, it falls short of any practical alternative strategies of how to engage with the Internet differently. Curiously, the current character of critical debate about power and control of the Internet is itself continuous with the critical tradition in which media has always been viewed. Digital media is a product of the convergence of a number of socio-technical as well as medial systems, which produces a hybridity of practices, organised on large and small scales. All three of the perspectives offered for thinking about digital media lead out to real contexts and practices in which digital media is involved. This is why digital media will be discussed in different registers of concern, from the scientific, technical, social and aesthetic. However, there is a complex and increasing interrelationship between the context of practices and it is here that the need to construct a new platform for discussion is being tried.

CONCLUSION

How are we to leave these theoretical trends, cultural interventions and intellectual arguments and how do they relate to digital media practices and the practitioner? Of course there can be no final conclusions only a continual dialogue. The pace of change in digital media is such that, on the surface, there is a shifting set of preoccupations. What we can say and have said throughout this book is that precisely because of the instability of technologies in a period of rapid change, we all need some kind of map, however incomplete, as a guide. But, rather like the Deluezian notion of smooth space our journeys are not to be plotted between two fixed points but rather thought of as trajectories, which cross and re-cross each other. However, we are not saying that the map is a rhizomatic network, we are still committed to the idea that it is possible to gain an overview, that there are important historical perspectives and that the map attempts some kind of comprehensiveness of the field that is digital media. On the other hand perhaps it is also true to say that today the student of digital media can enter and exit the debate at any point. Theory has its own practice and at many points the practice of theory is only remotely connected to the contingencies of technical and social practices. Practice proceeds through practice and its rules are different from those of theory. But theory is also an abstraction of concrete practices, an attempt to grasp the complexity of practice in another form of knowledge. What the practitioner needs, what all of us need, is really useful knowledge, which can illuminate our efforts and struggles to both make sense of a complex world and to make communicable sense within it.

Much that is really useful in digital media arises within its own practice, but other things do not and theory, from a number of the sources we have identified can shed light upon and inform practice. Digital media practices are fundamentally communicative practices, which take place in definable social and cultural circumstance and between groups and individuals. The most exciting and creative cultural dimension of digital media is that it represents a challenge to established ways of thinking about the communicative process. It challenges the notion of the artefact and instead reminds us of the importance of process. Digital media confronts any settled notion of sender and receiver, artist and audiences, producer and consumer and instead invites us to articulate the space and method of interaction. Digital media invites us to explore what the medium itself is and how our thinking and ways of seeing are potentially changed and extended by it. Finally, digital media challenges some of our most cherished institutional categories of human activity and encourages us to revisit settled histories.

There is a tension between the highly commercial and profit driven practices of ecommerce, the dot.com economy and securitised systems on the one hand and the radical openness of the Internet on the other. The established institutions of education, media broadcasting, the press and the cultural institutions continue to reproduce themselves along familiar lines of power and purpose, co-opting new technologies and the new medium to familiar often uncritical purposes. However, the convergent tendency of all digital media threatens to break across establish boundaries and suggest new purposes, productions and points of entry to practitioners. Digital media practices actively seek new contexts, new audiences and collaborations, from an existing stock of historical cultural politics. Museums, galleries universities, schools, community centres, theatres, concert halls, dance venues, clubs, even regular workplaces are being challenged by the new communication media, whether that is recognised or not. They have been changed for the worst if technology has been introduced in ways, which are not critically reflected upon, because they will, as Jean Francios Lyotard pointed out be processing knowledge as units of information exchange, rather than as something really useful. They will be changing for the better wherever digital media is engaged in the process of making meaning which is critically and (inter)actively worked upon and (inter)actively received (Lyotard 1979).

Communication through online networked media is powerful, sophisticated and compelling, and yet so much of what circulates visibly remains superficial, while so much that is structuring remains concealed. Producing complex, deep and sustained communicative forms and making the deeper language of the Internet accessible is the real prize for future generations. The greatest challenge in the short term is to develop human computer interfaces that reveal, rather than conceal their own selective operating principles and which extend the openness that has carried the medium to its present point. The second major challenge is for computer users to be able to maximise its advantages while minimising its risks. There is a dialectic of opposites, which is part of the shaping of the future of digital media for all of us. On the one hand the networked computer has given us immediate access to a great diversity of material, which is only a couple of clicks of a mouse away. It has given us a machine that can perform a wide variety of functions at incredible computational speeds. It has given the world a new means of communication that connects the one to the many and the many to the many. All of these aspects are positive and being extended as we write. On the other hand, the new medium now presents us with a new set of problems of centralisation, covert control and the exploitation of users. We are currently struggling to find better tools and forms for navigating databases and being able to make discerning judgements about the quality and worth of what we find and there are few channels of evaluation and critical reflection within navigable modes. We are also struggling with crucial issues of public and private modes of access to information and modes of address. The third and final challenge of digital media is to ensure that it develops as an open and democratic medium and for that to happen, great efforts will have to be made by governments of the world and collectivities of users to put limits upon the most aggressive and monopolistic commercial practices in order to ensure that we continue to expand its great educational and creative potential.

Glossary

We do not aim to provide a comprehensive glossary of unfamiliar technical or theoretical terms used across the new media field. Instead we focus on a small number of key terms, which reflect the discussion of this book and which we consider to be core terms in new media practice. As we have discussed, technological as well as cultural discourses have their own languages, which are full of short-hand terms that label and code conceptual definitions and practical processes. Traditionally print encyclopaedias, dictionaries as well as manuals, provided indexed word definitions; however, today online communication supplements and augments printed sources in electronic form. One would expect therefore to find a book on new media pointing the reader in the direction of useful websites, hyperlinks and search engines.

USING GOOGLE (WWW.GOOGLE.CO.UK)

It is hard to think of an online search and find situation in which you wouldn't use Google, so much so that the word has become a verb. Web searches using Google are fine as long as you are aware of how searches are optimised and that therefore you don't assume that the top page of searches represents the most authoritative source of what you are looking for. Refining and cross referencing searches is very important in the context of study. Google is now the Internet's biggest search engine and in 2011, according to its own statistical data received over 4,717,000,000 each day. Google has recently been valued at $249.9 billion, by Bloomberg in October 2012 on the American stock market, which makes it the world's biggest media company by stock market value. The popularity of Google as an accessible and simple search engine is reflected in their grand mission statement to 'organise the world's information and make it universally accessible and useful' (source: http://en.wikipedia.org/wki/Google. Accessed 09/06/05).

USING WIKIPEDIA (WWW.WIKIPEDIA.ORG)

We suggest that you build upon our deliberately limited, keyword glossary, by using the web to search for a wider range of technical definitions and theoretical definitions, to build up your knowledge and understanding of the new media field. It is important to bear in mind in this process something we have insisted upon throughout this book, which is that linguistic definitions are dynamic and always part of a chain of developing and changing meaning. Wikipedia is a good tool for getting cross-checking facts or getting a first idea of what something is or is about. Wikipedia is a first rather than last destination and should always be used with other reference sources.

Analogue

An important term in understanding the significance of digital code. Prior to digital media all media were analogue in that they employed some form of continuous material signal such as light or sound, which was physically inscribed onto a recording medium, for example, magnetic tape or chemical negative. The resulting representation of image or sound or both, was analogous to the original source. In contrast digital code is a transcription of one source of signal into another form such that the source is segmented into a discrete code. The continuous nature of analogue encoding makes the resulting media, photography, film, sound recording, less open to manipulation and change.

Applied/abstract theory

The distinction made in this book between abstract and applied theory is an important way of drawing attention to the value of theory for practitioners by recognising differences in what theory does. Abstract theory refers to the analytical discussion of concepts and ideas derived in one way or another from the discipline of philosophy, which are believed by a community of interest to shed light upon the general condition of a set of practices, for example when discussing the general condition of human perception of reality. Applied theory is where general concepts are deployed or used to discuss particular problems or specific ideas in practice, which produces a body of writing about the practices of new media.

Code

Has a technical as well as a cultural meaning. Technically code is a component of a message system in numerical, linguistic or auditory form, which relays a set of instructions, information or meanings. Morse code is a clear example of the relay of a linguistic system into an electronic auditory system. Semaphore used a system of flag positions to send messages where the sender and receiver were in visual sight of each other. Digital code is the base system of binary numbers, zeros and ones which create computer data. Programming languages, such a Java, or HTML uses code to create instruction patterns for computer operations. Code has a wider cultural meaning related to communication media. Film lighting formats can be said to be codes, narrative story lines and characters have familiar and repeated patterns of action and resolution that can be said to be codes. There are behavioural and dress codes that vary from culture to culture.

Collaboration

In its positive general use the term collaboration simply means to work together upon a joint of common purpose or activity. Traditionally media production has involved the collaboration between people with specific roles and skill sets organised through a division of labour. Newer kinds of collaboration are emerging in online media in which people establish roles and contributions between themselves in an evolving process or joint intellectual effort.

Convergence

Refers technical to the drawing together of previously discrete analogue technologies in digital form such that functions and tasks previously carried out by different media technologies are now functions of one machine. This is true of both the production of media, in digital image compositing and editing for example, and the distribution of media, where online services can deliver radio, television and print media. Convergence also refers to the bringing together and overlapping of media practices, where knowledge, skills and understanding of different analogue media practice are brought together in digital hypermedia and multimedia.

Cyberspace

A literary term for the Internet and online communication. A term originally coined by science-fiction writer William Gibson to describe a fictional computer-generated virtual reality. A conceptual space where computer networking, hardware and users converge. The term has become generalised to describe any kind of digitally generated three-dimensional sense of space.

Digital

A form of information, which is encoded, stored and transmitted as a sequence of discrete electrical units. The units are based upon a mathematical binary code, zeros and ones, which are used by the computer to form a code or strings of information. Digital media is amenable to mathematical manipulation of its code and is hence thought to be more mutable or open than its analogue counterpart. It is the single fact of the discrete, segmented character of digital code upon which many of the claims for new media are made.

Digital media

While the term digital media, emphasised a technological definition of practice, it has come to be the generally accepted term to describe the technical environment of computer based communication. Digital media accounts for the fact that the majority of media is now produced using digital hard and software as well as providing the platforms for networked communication.

Discourse

A way of thinking about language and ideas as they are used and employed in specific historical periods and institutional settings, such that what is taken to be an objective body of knowledge is understood as the elaborated sum of arguments, theories, ideas and descriptions that surround and are embedded in a particular social organisation. The term discourse allows us to connect the abstract power of language to define meaning with institutional forms of power so that we can see that discourse and its specific language is capable of constructing it own objects of attention and importance. New media is still emerging as a set of practices, but already, as we have shown in this book, there are a number of discourses at work seeking to define the object of new media.

Hybridity

Hybridity refers to something of mixed origin or composition and became an important cultural concept, which challenged racial or national essentialism, suggesting instead that individuals and societies were the product of mixing. In art, hybridity de-emphasised the importance of singular or pure traditions, a counter to European Modernism for example. In digital media the concept of hybridity emphasises that new media objects are combinations of human and machines as well as recognising the 'cut and paste' or 'mash-up' character of digital processes.

Information

The main discussion of the term information in this book revolves around the idea of information as facts or data, or as knowledge derived from experience, study, instruction or derived from events and situations. In the first account, information is understood as the pre-processed or raw material to be worked upon, whereas in the second account, information is closer to knowledge that has been worked upon or is a result of what is known. It is important to distinguish between these two definitions and not reduce all accounts of information to data.

Interactive

Used in two importantly different and often conflated senses, interactivity refers to both, the ability of the computer user to technically interrupt a programmed sequence in real time and the process of psychological investment and engagement as a viewer, reader, audience or spectator with a media and communication form. In the first case technical interaction refers to the forms of making programmed choices in navigating databases. The ability of the user to interrupt a sequence and make further, branching choices within the program. In the second case, interaction refers to the complex processes of human sense perception and cognitive forms of interpretation of sensory information.

Interface

In general usage a form, physical, mental or social, which is interposed between two separate states or substances. Applied to new media an interface has a number of specific meanings. (i) The physical interface between the computer and the human user is constituted by the peripheral devices of the keyboard, mouse and screen, but a voice activated piece of software could also be the interface for command and control. (ii) The graphical user interface (GUI) consists of a software program, Windows operating system for example, which enables the user to navigate files and programs stored or accessed by the computer. (iii) Graphical user interfaces use cultural metaphors, such as the idea of a desktop and office filing formats to make command, control and navigation of digital data intelligible and is therefore a cultural interface.

Method

On one level, method hardly needs an entry in a glossary, however, it has an importance and singular use in art and digital media that should be noted. A method is a regular and systematic way of accomplishing something such as a routine, a formula, a recipe. When a new problem or possibility has been glimpsed, which hasn't been tried before, then its realisation calls for the invention of a new method. Equally in art practice the invention of a method is a way of producing a new object. For the student of digital media, understanding what is entailed in the development of method is a crucial step.

Navigation

Applied to new media navigation is a spatial metaphor derived from the physical plotting or steering of a course over land, sea or air, which has been applied to the actions of programmed choices in using a database or the WWW. Since progression through a database in non-linear, and made of a branching structure, the process of moving through data is considered to be an act of navigation.

New media

The term new media arose in the 1990s in order to emphasise and define a range of cultural and artistic uses of screen and computer based media, which were distinct from older analogue media forms, such as photography or film as well as to distinguish an emergent group of practitioners working across a range of artistic, media and social contexts. The term new media placed greater emphasis upon creative use than upon technology.

Networking

Currently a very widely used term to describe deliberate social interaction in pursuit of an individual goal or informal membership of a social group. While networking has become professionalised as a term referring to how individuals develop and maintain a career, it also refers to specific technical activities of online communication, such as producing a formal interactive network.

Paradigm

Is used as an alternative to the term discourse and describes the governing ideas of a particular time, or culture or subject. Scientific paradigms define the limits of meaningful questions and formulations about knowledge at any one time. Thomas Kuhn (1962) in his thesis on The Structure of Scientific Revolutions, identified a paradigm shift as occurring when the problems posed within an existing scientific knowledge frame outweigh the solutions as to provoke a crisis in the governing ideas, the paradigm. In new media the establishment of digital networked systems has been said to constitute a new paradigm of thinking and representation.

Remediation

Is an important concept in new media, first developed by Marshall McLuhan (1964) to describe how a new medium in its early stages relies upon, i.e. adapts, co-opts or incorporates elements of previous media. For McLuhan this was summed up in his idea that the content of any medium is always another medium. So, for example, early film staged narratives using theatrical conventions of scenes and acts, while television used theatrical conventions of the interlude and presenters. Bolter and Gruisin (2000), developed the idea with respect to digital media by pointing out that digital media used the content and form of all previous media. In explaining this they identified two moments of the remediation process. *Hypermediacy* describes the multiple applications that can be active on the desktop, creating a rich media environment in which the user places a high value on the mediating functions of different applications that allow multiple forms of attention. In contrast *immediacy* is a feature of media where there is little or no sense of mediating presence only a direct sense of the content of media. Immediacy is a feature of screen media that operate like a transparent window on the world, creating the sense of immediate and direct contact with the content. Whereas immediacy is associated with new media which attempts to create immersive environments, hypermediacy is associated with extractive database searching. According to Bolter and Gruisin, immediacy and hypermediacy and constantly vying with each other in the process of remediation.

Simulation

Is generally used to mean an imitation of something else and has many uses to describe representations, mock-ups, modelling. In computer science it refers to the technique of representing the real world with a computer program. In digital media simulation is an important conceptual term to describe a media object that has no equivalent in the real world, but is the product of a computer system that mimics representation of the real.

Synergy

Synergy in the context of media production, refers to the creative cooperation and interaction among groups that produces an enhanced effect, such that the combined outcome is greater than what would have been produced by only one component.

Synthetic image

This is an emerging term to describe the digital photograph and is intended to draw attention to the distinct differences between chemical photo-optics in which it could be said there was a natural process of light registering difference values on the negative film and the process of computer imaging in which the values registered are predefined by variable algorithms. The term is closely related to the idea of simulation to draw attention to an image which has been produced by machine processes.

KEY TECHNICAL TERMS YOU MIGHT NEED TO RESEARCH IN MORE DEPTH

Technical acronyms and terms

AI	artificial intelligence
AL	artificial life
APPS	software applications
Avatar	onscreen presence of the user in graphical form
Bandwidth	the amount of information, measured in kilobits per second, that can be transmitted through telephone system

Broadband	High bandwidth modems that increase the speed of information transfer/downloading
Bits	A single unit of binary code, used to denote transmission rates per second
Byte	A unit of eight bits, equal to storing 265 characters, or shades of an image, denoting data storage size, hence megabyte to denote 1 million bytes.
BLOBs	Binary large objects
Bluetooth	A short range wireless connection between computers and peripherals
COOKIE	An information reference saved on a web user's hard disk drive by a website
CACHE	An area of computer memory used to hold recently acquired data
CAD	Computer-aided design
CGI	Computer generated imagery
DVD	Digital video disc
CD	Compact disc (recordable)
CD-ROM	Compact disc (read-only memory)
CMC	Computer mediated communication
Domain	The location of a website or group of websites
Flash	Vector-based graphics and animation format with small file sizes
Flame	An abusive email
GUI	Graphical user interface
GIF	A graphic file compression
GPRS	Global positioning response system
HTML	Hypertext mark-up language
http	Hypertext transfer protocol
ICT	Information and communication technology
ISP	Internet service provider
LAN	Local area network
Java	Programming language
JPEG	A compressed graphic file used for photographic images
MUDs	Mutli-user domains
MOOS	Multi-user domain, object orientated

MODEM	A device that enables a computer to interface with a telephone line
OS	Operating system
PC	Personal computer
PDA	Personal digital assistants
Pixel	Individual unit of value in a raster grid which determine by their size and number the resolution of an image
Server	network of computers that control shared resources for workstations
Streaming	transmission and downloading of compressed data of video, animation of graphic files (MPEGs) at frame rates which operate at the persistence of vision.
TCP	Transmission control protocol
URI	Uniform resource identifier
URL	Universal resource locator
WiFi	Wireless frequency connection to Internet

Health and safety

How individuals cope with the immediate physical and psychological effects of spending large amounts of time in front of screens, using keyboards, clicking away at the mouse varies enormously. In the workplace there may be a positive health and safety culture that promotes good practice, while in others, and we suspect most, the policy is a bureaucratic paper document filed away somewhere while the culture is one of ignorance.

How we sit at a computer and in what kind of chair is very important to our bodily wellbeing. The height of the screen on the desktop in relationship to our eye level and how the screen is positioned will also have effects upon our posture and eyesight. The position and angle of the keyboard and mouse will affect our arms, wrists and hands. Repetitive strain injury (RSI) can be a long-term severe disability arising from prolonged use of the mouse and keyboard in unsupported arm and hand positions. The British Health and Safety Regulations (1992), relating to the use of Display Screen Equipment, lays out a code of practice, which employers must adhere to. It has been acknowledged that prolonged work with visual display units (VDUs) can create a range of health problems including, headaches, stress, eye strain, and bodily aches and pains. VDUs give out both visible light and other forms of electromagnetic radiation, which can be harmful above certain levels. However, levels of radiation from VDUs are considered to be well below safe levels as set out in internal regulations. Many people working in digital media will be self-employed and unaware of health and safety practices. Many more people are domestic and private users of computers and will be equally unaware of the health and safety executive directives of working with visual display equipment. Common sense should somehow indicate two key things about living and working with computers, first that we need to consider how we position our bodies in relationship to the workstation, and second, how long we spend at any one time in front of the screen. You should take regular breaks from working at a screen, allowing your body and mind to be temporarily diverted by other activities and tasks. But in reality we ignore common sense over and over again as we become absorbed or engrossed in onscreen communication, or as the pressure of increased workloads pushes us towards unreasonable deadlines. Only the conscious establishment of a positive and health culture of the office, study or personal space, can counteract the built-in tendency within human computer communication to forget the body, and this is always hard won.

Useful websites on health and safety

www.mda.org.uk/health.htm
www.hse.gov.uk
www.totaljobs.com/editorial/getadvice_worklife/going_freelance/going_freelance.
   shtm

Trade Unions

Trades Unions remain important organisations, even though digital media developed in a period of deregulation. Belonging to a union, where they represent employees, is important because they support individual members working conditions and they work with management to improve the overall conditions of work practices, often campaigning for improvements in working hours and working environments. Membership of trade unions and professional associations has declined in the UK over the past two decades as a consequence of changes in government legislation and deregulation of the public sector employment. This does not mean, however, that trades unions no longer play an important part in negotiations on work practices with employers and government departments. There are a number of national unions that relate to media workers, which if you are employed in a large company you should be aware of. The main media related unions are: BECTU, the Broadcasting, Entertainment, Cinematograph and Theatre Union; NUJ, The National Union of Journalists; ACTT, The Association of Cinematograph and Television Technicians. More generally NUT, The National Union of Teachers and NATFHE, The National Association of Teachers in Further and Higher Education cover the interests of teachers and lecturers in digital media. Of course, the National Union of Students is a good starting point for participation in a national organisation that campaigns for the interests of people in education.

Bibliography

Althusser, L. (1971) 'Ideology and Ideological State Apparatuses', in *Lenin and Philosophy and Other Essays*. London: New Left Books.

Aranda, J., Wood, B. K. and Vidokle, A. (2010) *E-Flux Journal: What is Contemporary Art?* Berlin: Sternberg Press.

Ascott, R. (1989) 'Is there Love in the Telematic Embrace?', *Art Journal 49* (3): 24–7.

Ascott, R. (2000) *Reframing Consciousness*. Bristol: Intellect Books.

Ascott, R. (2003) *Telematic Embrace: Visionary Theories of Art, Technology and Consciousness*. Berkeley, CA: University of California Press.

Athique, A. (2013) *Digital Media and Society: An Introduction*. London: Polity.

Bachelard, G. (1994) [1958] *The Poetics of Space*. Boston, MA: Beacon Press.

Barker, T. S. (2013) *Time and the Digital: Connecting Technology, Aesthetics, and a Process Philosophy of Time* (Interfaces: Studies in Visual Culture). New England, NE: Dartmouth College Press.

Barthes, R. (1975) *S/Z*, trans. Richard Miller. London: Cape.

Barthes, R. (1983*)* *Simulations*, trans. Foss, P. New York: Semiotexte.

Batchin, G. (1999) *Burning with Desire: The Conception of Photography*. Cambridge, MA. MIT.

Baudrillard, J. (1983) *Simulations*. New York: Semiotexte.

Baudrillard, J. (1988) *The Ecstasy of Communication*. New York: Semiotexte.

Baudrillard, J. (1993) 'Hyperreal America', *Economy and Society 22* (2): 243–52.

Baudrillard, J. (1996) [1968] *The System of Objects*, trans. J. Benedict. London: Verso.

Baym, N. (2010) *Personal Connections in the Digital Age*. Cambridge: Polity.

Bell, D. (1994) 'The Coming of the Post Industrial Society: A Venture in Social Forecasting' in J. Bender and T. Druckery (eds), *Culture on the Brink: Ideologies of Technology*. Seattle, WA: Bay Press.

Bell, D. and Kennedy, B. (2000) *The Cybercultures Reader*. London: Routledge.

Benayoun, M. (2010) 'The Nervous Breakdown of the Global Body: An Organic Model of the Connected World', published in *Proceedings of Futur en Seine 2009, The Digital Future of the Cityediteur*: Cap Digital. www.benayoun.com/projetwords.php?id=158 [accessed 30 March 2013].

Benjamin, W. (1974) 'The Work of Art in the Age of Mechanical Reproduction', in *Illuminations* (1969). New York: Schocken, Heinemann.

Berger, J. (1972) *Ways of Seeing*. London: BBC/Penguin Books.

Berry, D. M. (2011) *The Philosophy of Software: Code and Mediation in the Digital Age.* London: Palgrave.

Berners-Lee, T. (1999) *Weaving the Web: The Past, Present and Future of the World Wide Web by its Inventor*. London: Orion Business Books.

Betancourt, M. (2013) *The History of Motion Graphics*. Maryland, MA: Wildside Press.

Bishton, D. (1991) *Digital Dialogues: Photography in the Age of Cyberspace*. Photo Paperback, Vol. 2, No 2. Birmingham: Ten 8.

Blackman, L. (1998) 'Culture, Technology and Subjectivity', in J. Wood (ed.) *The Virtual Embodied: Presence/Practice/Technology.* London: Routledge.

Blake, E. C. (2003) 'Zograscopes, Virtual Reality and the Mapping of Polite Society', in L. Gitelman and G. Pingree (eds) *New Media 1740–1915*. Cambridge, MA: MIT Press.

Bolter, J. and Gruisin, R. (2000) *Remediation*. Cambridge, MA: MIT.

Boyd, F. and Dewdney, A. 'Technology and Cultural Form', in M. Lister (ed.) *The Photographic Image in Digital Culture* (1996). London: Routledge.

Brand. G. (1988) *The Media Lab: Inventing the Future at MIT*. London: Penguin.

Briggs. A. and Burke. P (2010) *Social History of the Media: From Gutenberg to the Internet*. London: Polity.

Brinkman. R. (2008) *The Art and Science of Digital Compositing: Techniques for Visual Effects, Animation and Motion Graphics*. Burlington, MA: Kaufmann.

Buck-Morss, S. (1995*) The Dialectics of Seeing: Walter Benjamin and the Arcades Project*. Cambridge, MA: MIT.

Bush, V. (1945) 'As We May Think' in Wardrip-Fruin, N. (2003) *The New Media Reader*. Cambridge, MA: MIT.

Castells, M. (1996) *The Rise of the Network Society*. Cambridge, MA/Oxford, UK: Blackwell.

Castells, M. (2001) *The Internet Galaxy: Reflections on the Internet, Business and Society*. Oxford: Oxford University Press.

Castells, M. (2012) *Networks of Outrage and Hope: Social Movements in the Internet Age*. Cambridge: Polity.

Chun, W. and Keenan, T. (2005) (eds.) *New Media, Old Media: A History and Theory Reader: Interrogating the Digital Revolution.* London: Routledge.

Cohn, J. S. (2006) *Anarchism and the Crisis of Representation: Hermeneutics, Aesthetics, Politics.* Cranbury, NJ: Rosemont.

Cook, S. (2008) 'Immateriality and its Discontents: An Overview of Main Models and Issues for Curating New Media', in C. Paul (ed.) *New Media in the White Cube and Beyond: Curatorial Modes for Digital Art*, pp. 26–48. Berkley, CA: University of California Press.

Crary, J. (1999) *Techniques of the Observer: On Vision and Modernity in the Nineteenth Century*. Cambridge, MA: MIT.

Critical Art Ensemble (1994) *The Electronic Disturbance*. Brooklyn, NY: Automedia.

Cubitt, S. (1998) *Digital Aesthetics*. London: Sage.

Curran, J., Fenton, N. and Freedman, D. (2012) *Misunderstanding the Internet (Communication and Society).* London: Routledge.

Darley, A. (2000) *Visual Digital Culture*. London: Routledge.

Dean, J. (2009) *Democracy and Other Neoliberal Fantasies: Communicative Capitalism and Left Politics*. Durham, NC: Duke University Press.

Dean, J. (2010) *Blog Theory: Feedback and Capture in the Circuits of Drive*. Cambridge, MA: Polity.

Debord, G. (1993) *Society of the Spectacle*. New York: Zone Books.

de Certeau, M. (1988) *The Practice of Everyday Life*. Berkeley, CA: University of California.

de Landa, M. (1991) *War in the Age of Intelligent Machines*. New York: Zone Books.

de Landa, M. (1993) 'Virtual Environments and The Rise of Synthetic Reason', in M. Dery (ed.) *Flame Wars*. Durham, NC: Duke University Press.

Deleuze, G. and Guattari, F. (1987) *A Thousand Plateaus: Capitalism and Schizophrenia*. Minneapolis, MA: University of Minnesota Press.

Department of Culture Media and Sport (DCMS) (2013) 'Making it Easier for the Media and Creative Industries to Grow, While Protecting the Interests of Citizens', at www.gov.uk/government/policies/making-it-easier-for-the-media-and-creative-industries-to-grow-while-protecting-the-interests-of-citizens [accessed 30 March 2013].

Department of Trade and Industry (DTI) (2012) 'Creative Industries', at www.ukti.gov.uk/export/sectors/creativemedia/item/280680.html [accessed 30 March 2013].

Department of Trade and Industry (DTI) (2012) 'Winning In Today's Market: Highlighting Key Trends in Sales, Marketing and Account Management', www.ditto.tv/docs/Winning_In_Today_s_Market.pdf [accessed 30 March 2013].

Dixon, S. (2007) *Digital Performance*. Cambridge, MA: MIT.

Dovey, J. (ed.) (1996) *Fractal Dreams: New Media in Social Context*. London: Lawrence & Wishart.

Druckery, T. (1996) (ed.) *Electronic Culture: Technology and Visual Representation*. New York: Aperture.

du Gay, P., Hall, S., Janes, L., Mackay, H. and Negus. K. (1997) *Doing Cultural Studies: The Story of the Sony Walkman*. London: Sage.

Ess, C. (2009) *Digital Media Ethics*. Cambridge: Polity.

Evans, J. and Hall, S. (1999) *Visual Culture: The Reader.* London: Sage.

Everett, A. and Caldwell, J. T. (eds) (2003) *New Media: Theories and Practices of Digitextuality.* London: Routledge.

Federal Networking Council (1995) 'FNC Resolution: Definition of "Internet"', at www.livinginternet.com/i/iw.htm [accessed 21 July 2013].

Ferster, B. (2013) *Interactive Visualization: Insight Through Inquiry*. Cambridge, MA: MIT.

Foster, H. (ed.) (1985) *Postmodern Culture.* London: Pluto Press.

Foster, H. (2001) *The Return of the Real.* Cambridge, MA: MIT.

Foucault, M. (1971) *The Order of Things: An Archaeology of the Human Sciences*. New York: Vintage.

Foucault, M. (1977) *Discipline and Punish: The Birth of the Prison*, trans. Alan Sheridan. New York: Vintage.

Friedl, M. (2002) *Online Game Interactivity Theory*. New York: Charles River Media Game, Delmar Publishing.

Fuller, M. and Goffey, A. (2012) *Evil Media*. Cambridge, MA: MIT.

Fukuyama, F. (2003) *Our Posthuman Future: Consequences of the Biotechnology Revolution*. London: Profile Books.

Gallagher, R. (2013) 'Software that Tracks People on Social Media Created by Defence Firm', *Guardian Online*, 10 February. www.guardian.co.uk/world/2013/feb/10/software-tracks-social-media-defence [accessed 21 July 2013].

Galloway, A. (2012) *The Interface Effect.* Cambridge: Polity.

Garcia, D. and Lovink, G. (2006) *Tactical Media*, www.waag.org/tmb/abc.html.

Garvey, E. G. (2003) 'Scissoring and Scrapebooks: Nineteenth-Century Reading, Remaking and Recirculation', in L. Gitelman and G. Pingee (eds) *New Media 1740–1915*. Cambridge, MA: MIT.

Gere, C. (2002) *Digital Culture*. London: Reaktion Books.

Gibson. W. (1984) *Neuromancer.* New York: Ace Books.

Gitelman, L. and Pingree, G. B. (2003) *New Media 1740–1915*. Cambridge, MA: MIT.

Goldberg, K. (2003) 'Tel-Embodiment and Shattered Presence: Reconstructing the Body for Online Interaction' in *The Robot in the Garden*. Cambridge, MA: MIT.

Goldhaber, M. (1983) *Reinventing Technology: Policies for Democratic Value.* London: Routledge.

Google Analytics. (n.d.) 'Analytics Intelligence', at www.google.com/analytics/features/intelligence.html [accessed 21 July 2013].

Graham, B. and Cook, S. (2010) *Rethinking Curating: Art after New Media.* Cambridge, MA: MIT.

Grau, O. (ed.) (2003) *Virtual Art: From Illusion to Immersion.* Cambridge, MA: MIT.

Grau, O. (2007*) Media Art Histories.* Cambridge, MA: MIT.

Hall, S. (1997) *Representation: Cultural Representation and Signifying Practices.* London: Sage.

Hand, M. (2012) *Ubiquitous Photography.* London: Polity.

Hansen, M. (2006) *New Philosphy for New Media.* Cambridge, MA: MIT.

Haraway, D. J. (1991) *Simians, Cyborgs and Women: The Reinvention of Nature*. London: Routledge.

Haraway, D. (2003) *The Haraway Reader*. London: Routledge.

Harries, D. (ed.) (2002) *The New Media Book*. London: BFI.

Harvey, D. (1989) *The Condition of Post Modernity*. Oxford. Blackwell.

Hayles, K. (1993) 'The Life Cycle of Cyborgs: Writing the Posthuman', in M. Benjamin (ed.) *A Question of Identity*. New Brunswick, NJ: Rutgers University Press.

Hayles, K. (1999) *How We Became Posthuman: Virtual Bodies in Cybernetics, Literature, and Informatics*. Chicago, IL: University of Chicago Press.

Hayles. K. (2012) *How We Think: Digital Media and Contemporary Technogenesis*. Chicago, IL: University of Chicago Press.

Jackson, P. (2002) Director, *Lord of the Rings*, Santa Monica, CA: Miramax.

Jameson, F. (1984) *Postmodernism, or the Cultural Logic of Late Capitalism*. London: Verso.

Jenkins. H. (2001) 'Convergence? I Diverge', Henry Jenkins, Digital Renaissance. http://web.mit.edu/cms/People/henry3/converge.pdf [accessed 21 July 2013].

Jencks, C. (1999) *The Postmodern Reader*. London: Academic Editions.

Jenkins, H., Ford, S. and Green, J. (2013) *Spreadable Media: Creating Value and Meaning in a Networked Culture*. New York: New York University Press.

Jones, S. (ed.) (1994). *Cybersociety*. London: Sage.

Kahler, M. (2009) *Networked Politics: Agency, Power, and Governance (Cornell Studies in Political Economy*. Ithaca, NJ: Cornell University Press.

Kellner, D. (1995) *Media and Culture*. London: Routledge.

Kenderdine, S. and Shaw, J. (2012) *Pure Land: Inside the Mogao Grottoes at Dunhuang*. Hong Kong: Run Run Shaw Creative Media Centre, City University of Hong Kong.

Kimbell, L. (ed.) (2004) *New Media Art: Practice and Context in the UK 1994–2004*. Manchester, UK: Cornerhouse.

Kitchin, R. and Dodge, M. (2011) *Code/Space: Software and Everyday Life*. Cambridge, MA: MIT.

Kittler, F. (1990) *Discourse Networks*. Stanford, CA: Stanford University Press.

Kroker, A. (2008) *Critical Digital Studies: A Reader*. Toronto, ON: Toronto University Press.

Kuhn, T. (1962/1970) (1070, 2nd edn, with postscript) *The Structure of Scientific Revolutions*. Chicago, IL: University of Chicago Press.

Lacy, M. (2013) *Security, War and Technology: Paul Virilio and the Global Politics of Disappearance*. London: Routledge.

Landow, G. (1992) *Hypertext 2.0: The Convergence of Contemporart Critical Theory and Technology*. Baltimore, MD: John Hopkins University Press.

Lash, S. (2002) *Critique of Information*. London: Sage.

Latour, B. (1992) 'Where Are the Missing Masses? The Sociology of a Few Mundane Artifacts.' in W. E. Bijker and J. Law (eds) *Shaping Technology/Building Society: Studies in Sociotechnical Change*. Cambridge, MA: MIT.

Latour, B. (1993) *We Have Never Been Modern*, trans. Catherine Porter. Cambridge, MA: Harvard University Press.

Latour, B. (2007) *Reassembling the Social.* Oxford: Oxford University Press.

Lee. A. (2012) Director, *The Life of Pi*, Los Angeles, CA: Fox Pictures.

Lipovetsky. G. (2005) *Hypermodern Times*. London: Polity.

Lister, M. (ed.) (1995) *The Photographic Image in Digital Culture*. London: Routledge.

Lister, M., Dovey, J., Giddings, S., Grant, I. and Kelly, K. (2003) *New Media: A Critical Introduction*. London: Routledge.

Lovejoy, M. (1992) *Postmodern Currents.* NJ: Prentice Hall.

Lovejoy, M. (2004) *Digital Currents: Art in the Electronic Age.* New York: Routledge.

Lovink, G. (2011) *Networks Without a Cause: A Critique of Social Media*. Cambridge: Polity.

Lovink, G. (2012) 'Media Studies: Diagnostics of a Failed Merger', *Limina 2*: 72–91.

Lunenfeld, P. (ed.) (1988). *The Digital Dialectic.* Cambridge, MA: MIT.

Lunenfeld, P. (2000) *Snap to Grid: A User's Guide to Digital Arts, Media, and Cultures.* Boston, MA: MIT.

Lynch, J. (2012) 'Olympus OM-D E-M5 Review', *Wired*, 25 June. www.wired.co.uk/reviews/cameras-and-camcorders/2012–06/olympus-om-d-e-m5 [accessed 5 March 2013].

Lyotard, J. (1979) *The Postmodern Condition: A Report on Knowledge*, trans. by G. Bennington and B. Massumi. Minneapolis, MN: University of Minnesota Press.

MacKinnon, R. (2012) *Consent of the Networked: The Worldwide Struggle for Internet Freedom.* New York: Basic Books.

Mackay, H. and O'Sullivan. T. (ed.) (1999) *The Media Reader*. London: Sage.

McLuhan, M. (1964) *Understanding Media: The Extensions of Man*. New York: McGraw-Hill.

Manovich, L. (1996) *What is Digital Cinema?* www.manovich.net/text/digital-cinema.html.

Manovich, L. (2001) *The Language of New Media.* Cambridge, MA: MIT.

Markoff, J. (2002) 'Technology's Toxic Trash is Sent to Poor Nations', *New York Times*, 25 February.

Meikle, G. and Young, S. (2011) *Media Convergence: Networked Digital Media in Everyday Life.* London: Palgrave.

Merleau-Ponty, M. (1962) *The Phenomenology of Perception*. London: Routledge & Kegan Paul.

Minksy, M. A. (1986) *Society of Mind.* New York: Simon & Schuster.

Mitchell, W. (1998) *The Reconfigured Eye: Visual Truth in the Post-Photographic Era.* Cambridge, MA: MIT Press.

Mirzoeff, N. (1999) *An Introduction to Visual Culture*. London: Routledge.

Morely, D. and Robins, K. (1995) *Spaces of Identity: Global Media, Electronic Landscape and Cultural Boundaries.* London: Routledge.

Morozov, E. (2012) *The Net Delusion: How Not to Liberate The World.* London: Penguin.

Mulvey, L. (1975) 'Visual Pleasure and Narrative Cinema', in S. Hall (ed.) (1999) *Visual Culture: The Reader*. London: Open University/Sage.

Murray, J. H. (1997) *Hamlet on the Holodeck: The Future of Narrative in Cyberspace.* New York: The Free Press.

Murthy, D. (2013) *Twitter: Social Communication in the Twitter Age*. Cambridge: Polity.

Negroponte, N. (1972) *Soft Architecture Machines.* Cambridge, MA: MIT.

Negroponte, N. (1995) *Being Digital*. London: Hodder & Stoughton.

Oatridge, N. (2003) 'The Wapping Dispute', at http://dspace.dial.pipex.com/town/square/ac567/Wapping4.htm.

Pariser. E. (2012) *The Filter Bubble: What The Internet Is Hiding From You*. London: Penguin.

Paul, C. (2003) *Digital Art*. London: Thames & Hudson.

Paul, C. (ed.) (2008) *New Media in the White Cube and Beyond: Curatorial Modes for Digital Art.* Berkeley, CA: University of California Press.

Parry, R. (2009*). Museums in a Digital Age*. London: Routledge.

Pavilik, J. and McIntosh, S. (2011) *Converging Media: A New Introduction to Mass Communication.* Oxford: University Press.

Penny, S. (ed.) (1995) *Critical Issues in Electronic Media.* Albany, NY: SUNY Press.

Popper, F. (2007) *From Technological to Virtual Art.* Cambridge, MA: MIT Press.

Pepperell, R. (1995) *The Post Human Condition*. Bristol, UK: Intellect.

Poster, M. (1990). *The Mode of Information.* Oxford: Polity.

Poster, M. (1995) *The Second Media Age*. Oxford: Polity.

Poster, M. (2006) *Information Please: Culture and Politics in the Age of Digital Machines*. New York: Duke University Press

Plant, S. (1997*) Zeros + Ones: Women, Cyberspace + the New Technoculture.* London: Fourth Estate.

Postman, N. (1993) *Technopoly: The Surrender of Culture to Technology.* New York: Vintage.

Richin, F. (1991) *In Our Own Image: The Coming Revolution in Photography*. London: Aperture.

Rheingold, H. (1991) *Virtual Reality*. New York: Simon & Schuster.

Rheingold, H. (1994) *The Virtual Community: Homesteading on the Electronic Frontier.* San Francisco, CA: Harper Perrenial.

Robins, K. (1996) *Into the Image*. London: Routledge.

Rubinstein. D. and Sluis. K. (2013) 'The Digital Image in Photographic Culture: The Algorithmic Image and the Crisis of Representation', in M. Lister (ed.) *The Photographic Image in Digital Culture*, 2nd edition. London: Routledge.

Rush, M. (1999) *New Media in Late 20th Century Art*. London: Thames & Hudson.

Ryan, M. L. (2003) *Narrative as Virtual Reality: Immersion and Interactivity in Literature and Electronic Media* (Parallax: Re-visions of Culture and Society). Balitmore: John Hopkins University Press.

Shanken, E. (2009) *Art and Electronic Media.* London: Phaidon.

Shaviro, S. (2010) *Post Cinematic Affect*. Ropley: Zero Books.

Slevin, J. (2000) *The Internet and Society*. Cambridge: Polity.

Sluis, K. (2012) 'Susan Sloan, Studies in Stillness: Motion Capture Portraits', The Photographers Gallery, London. http://thephotographersgallery.org.uk/press-release-i-susan-sloan-i-studies-in-stillness-motion-capture-portraits-i-13-july-14-august [accessed 30 March 2013].

Springer, C. (1991) 'The Pleasure of the Interface', in *Screen*, *32*, No. 3. Oxford: Oxford University Press.

Springer, C. (1998) 'Virtual Repression' in *Virtual Dimension*, John Beckman (ed.). New York: Princeton Architectural Press.

Spurgeon. C. (2008) *Advertising and New Media*. London: Routledge.

Stam, R. (2000) *Film Theory: An Introduction*. New York: Blackwell.

Stone, R. (1995) *The War Between Desire and Technology at the Close of the Mechanical Age*. Washington, DC: MIT.

Tagg. J. (1993) *The Burden of Representation: Essays on Photographies and Histories*. Minnesota, MN: University of Minnesota Press.

Telotte, J. (2008) *The Mouse Machine: Disney and Technology*. Urbana, IL: University of Illinois.

Terranova, T. (2004*) Network Culture: Politics for the Information Age*. London: Pluto Press.

Terranova. T. (2012) 'Attention, Economy and the Brain', in *Paying Attention, Culture Machine 13*. www.culturemachine.net/index.php/cm/issue/current [accessed 10 April 2013].

Terranova, T. (2013) 'Free Labor', in T. Scholz (ed.) *Digital Labor: The Internet as Playground and Factory*. Cambridge, MA: MIT.

Toffler, A. (1980) *The Third Wave*. New York: Pan.

Toffler, A. (2006) *Revolutionary Wealth*. New York: Random House.

Tribe, M. and Jana, R. (2007) *New Media Art*. Cologne: Taschen.

Tufte. E. R. (2003) *The Cognitive Style of PowerPoint: Pitching Out Corrupts Within*. Chesire, CT: Graphic Press.

Turkle, S. (1997) *Life on the Screen: Identity in the Age of the Internet.* New York: Simon & Schuster.

Turkle, S. (2013) *Alone Together*. Philadelphia, PA: Basic Books.

UNESCO Global Alliance Team (2006) *Understanding Creative Industries: Cultural Statistics for Public-Policy Making*. Paris: UNESCO.

Virilio, P. (1995) *The Art of the Motor* [*Art du moteur*] (English edn, trans. Julie Rose). Minneapolis, MN: University of Minnesota Press.

Virilio, P. (2000) *The Information Bomb*. New York: Verso.

Virilio, P. (2005) *Speed and Politics* (Semiotext(e) Foreign Agents series). Cambridge, MA: MIT.

Waldby, C. (2000) *The Visible Human Project: Informatic Bodies and Posthuman Medicine*. London: Routledge.

Wardrip-Fruin, N. and Montfort, N. (2003) *The New Media Reader*. Cambridge, MA: MIT.

Webster, F. (1999) *Theories of the Information Society*. London: Routledge.

Wessels, B. (2009) *Understanding the Internet: A Socio-Cultural Perspective*. London: Palgrave.

Wiener, N. (1954) *The Human Uses of Human Beings: Cybernetics and Society.* Michigan, MA: Houghton Mifflin.

Williams. R. (1961) *Culture and Society, 1780–1950*. London: Pelican Books.

Williams. R. (1965) *The Long Revolution*. London: Pelican Books.

Williams, R. (1974) *Television, Technology and Cultural Form*. London: Fontana.

Williams. R. and Edge. D. (1996) 'The Social Shaping of Technology', *Research Policy 25* (6): 856–99.

Winston, B. (1998) *Media, Technology and Society, A History from the Telegraph to the Internet*. London: Routledge.

Wombell, P. (ed.) (1987) *PhotoVideo.* London: River Oram Press/Boston, MA: Houghton-Mifflin.

Wood, J. (1998) *The Virtual Embodied*. London: Routledge.

Woolley, B. (1992) *Virtual Worlds*. London: Blackwell.

Index